Music in the Twentieth Century

GENERAL EDITOR: Arnold Whittall

Satie the composer

Frontispiece   Satie in 1917.

Satie the composer

ROBERT ORLEDGE

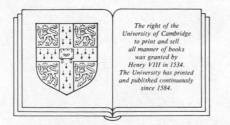

The right of the
University of Cambridge
to print and sell
all manner of books
was granted by
Henry VIII in 1534.
The University has printed
and published continuously
since 1584.

CAMBRIDGE UNIVERSITY PRESS

Cambridge

New York   Port Chester   Melbourne   Sydney

Published by the Press Syndicate of the University of Cambridge
The Pitt Building, Trumpington Street, Cambridge CB2 1RP
40 West 20th Street, New York, NY 10011, USA
10 Stamford Road, Oakleigh, Melbourne 3166, Australia

© Cambridge University Press 1990

First published 1990

Printed in Great Britain at the University Press, Cambridge

British Library cataloguing in publication data

Orledge, Robert
Satie the composer.
1. French music. Satie, Erik, 1866–1925
I. Title
780.92'4

Library of Congress cataloguing in publication data

Orledge, Robert.
Satie the composer / Robert Orledge.
    p.   cm.
Includes bibliographical references.
ISBN 0 521 35037 9
1. Satie, Erik, 1866–1925 – Criticism and interpretation.
I. Title.
ML 410. S196074 1990
780'.92 – dc 20   89–22309 CIP MN

ISBN 0 521 35037 9

ME

*To Ornella Volta and
the future of the Fondation Satie*

Contents

Illustrations

Preface

Writing a book about a composer as complex and secretive as Satie is a daunting prospect. He rarely allowed himself to be drawn into detailed discussion of his art, and whilst he spent many a lonely hour in the distant Parisian suburb of Arcueil devising logical systems of musical organization, the logic behind the compositions that emerged often defies rational explanation. This may well be the reason why all recent books on Satie – from Myers (1948) to Gillmor (1988) – have avoided what seem to me to be fundamental questions: How did Satie compose? And why did he write what he did? Roger Shattuck touches on the subject briefly in *The Banquet Years* (1968, 130-1, 155-6), but the only systematic study that enters into any technical detail is Patrick Gowers's pioneering paper on 'Satie's Rose-Croix music (1891–1895)' (1965-6, 1–25). Thus the evidence in some 200 composition books in the Bibliothèque Nationale, Paris and the Houghton Library at Harvard University has been waiting to be evaluated in full for many years, and so I make no apology for not offering yet another chronological study of Satie's life and works, or for omitting what some might regard as essential background information. There is no detailed account of the genesis of *Parade*, for instance, or any systematic appraisal of the literary merits of Péladan or Cocteau. Apart from an initial chronology, I have only included facts relevant to my argument at the time, and due to the way in which this book is organized there are occasional duplications between sections (notably in the Appendix) which I have chosen to leave in, rather than resort to elaborate cross-referencing. Anyone more interested in a chronological line of enquiry is directed to Alan Gillmor's excellent *Erik Satie* (1988) which deals with every aspect of Satie's career in comprehensive detail. For a quick summary, the article on Satie by Gowers and Wilkins in *The New Grove Dictionary of Music and Musicians* (1980, vol. XVI, 515–20) is strongly recommended. Nor do I make any apology for not discussing Satie's literary output, for this has been thoroughly explored in Ornella Volta's *Erik Satie: Ecrits* (rev. ed. 1981); a triumph of meticulous scholarship.

Instead, I have chosen to cover as many aspects of what made Satie 'tick' as a composer as I could, from his catalytic relationship with Debussy and the 1917 expression of his compositional aesthetic, through his attitudes to counterpoint and orchestration, to the cross-fertilization from painting, sculpture and the other arts that add new dimensions to his later theatrical works. Again I make no apologies for incorporating detailed case-histories of emergent compositions *en route*, for that is where my main interest lies. And if I have indulged in this rather than in an in-depth analysis of Satie's music *per se*, it is because I believe that the latter *can* prove counter-productive in Satie's case. The ideas behind the works can, in some instances, be more significant than the music they generated, and if we expect to find Satie's music functioning as an end in itself, or as more than the sum of its constituent parts, we are likely to be disappointed. For, more than any other composer of his time, Satie sought to break down the barriers between the arts and to look at music afresh as a vital part in the interaction between various levels of aesthetic experience; as a contribution towards a larger, and always thoroughly modern, whole. To be chic – to have style, elegance and artistic skill – was the ultimate accolade that Satie sought for himself, or bestowed on friends like Matisse and Radiguet in his later years. Given his insatiable desire to incorporate new concepts into his music, and to be an instigator of, or a participant in, the latest artistic developments, it is easy to see why artists like Matisse and Picasso admired him so much. As his friend Brancusi said, perhaps with Satie in mind: 'To see far is one thing, but to go there (or farther) is another.' Paradoxically, although he always looked to the future, Satie's later work was very much of the moment. It is only in the light of this observation that we can begin to understand why he found it so difficult to adapt the end of *Parade* for Diaghilev in 1919. As he then observed, 'the times have moved on since 1916': *Parade* was already past history.

But behind what may appear to be a frivolous mask and a career of anarchic iconoclasm, Satie remained a wholly serious and professional composer (despite his championship of the artistic amateur). Once he began writing, the composer soon replaced the calculating systematician, with an overriding brief of simplicity, brevity and clarity, and a continual desire for artistic renewal that found its fruition after the First World War in the *esprit nouveau*, of which he is the perfect embodiment and, some might say, the inventor. Despite the decadent circles in which he moved, his was an essentially moral art, and it was precisely because he so disapproved of the immorality of former friends like Auric, Poulenc and Cocteau that Satie refused Marcel Raval's offer to write a chronicle of his life for the journal *Les Feuilles libres* in 1924. 'It would be impossible to publish it', he told Raval in a letter. 'If you went ahead with it, you would have to break with friends' (Volta, 1989, 197). Satie was never one for compromise of any sort, and if he could not express himself freely, he preferred to remain silent. So too did his friend Henri Sauguet, who even found a title – *Erik Satie the Mysterious* – for the book he planned (Sauguet, 1983, 242). But when he tried to write it, 'it seemed to me that he whispered "shut up" in my ear. "You're not going to tell them all that, are you? I forbid you to do it."' Such is the power of Satie's posthumous presence that I know the feeling well! But it has not deterred *me* from writing *Satie the composer* and I hope that Satie would at least have approved of my lack of compromise within it. Doubtless many of its speculations will be undermined as new facts come to light, but if this book provokes as many questions as it tries to answer, my many years of research will have been worthwhile.

Robert Orledge
Liverpool

Acknowledgments

My largest vote of thanks in preparing this book must go to Ornella Volta, the indefatigable *animatrice* of the Fondation Satie, to whose headquarters at 56 rue des Tournelles, Paris 3 all Satie enthusiasts are directed. She kindly provided any material I required from her vast treasure-trove, and allowed me access to her invaluable collection of Satie letters, documents and photographs, from which I have drawn extensively in the present study. In short, I have tried to do for Satie the composer what Volta has done for Satie the writer in her annotated *Erik Satie: Ecrits*, which collates years of painstaking research into a definitive statement. In France too, I owe a substantial debt to Satie's heir, M. Joseph Lafosse-Satie, for permission to publish material for which he holds the copyright, and to the composer Robert Caby, who allowed me to publish material from his collection and passed on his personal reminiscences of Satie to me. The staff at the Bibliothèque Nationale (under François Lesure, and now Mme Catherine Massip) have proved as patient and helpful as ever in satisfying my insatiable appetite for Satie manuscripts, and I should like to thank Mme Massip in particular for helping me to obtain microfilms, and for allowing me permission to cite examples from Satie's notebooks there (in conjunction with Mme Ippolito of the Service Juridique). The remaining music examples come from published editions by Salabert and Eschig, which are available in England through United Music Publishers. In Paris, I should also like to express my gratitude, for various reasons, to Frédéric Caby, Thierry Bodin, Yves Koechlin, Mme Madeleine Li-Koechlin, Mme Madeleine Milhaud, the late Henri Sauguet, Laurent François, Gérald Hugon of Editions Eschig and to Dr Jeremy Drake of Editions Salabert, for allowing me access to the Satie manuscripts there and for helping me with my problems over *Relâche*. I am also indebted to the Fondation Satie and to Ornella Volta for allowing me to cite extracts from the complete edition of Satie's *Correspondance*, which she is currently editing in three volumes.

In America I should like to thank Carlton Lake, Cathy Henderson and the staff at the Harry Ransom Humanities Research Center at Austin, Texas; Mr Rodney G. Dennis and the staff at the Houghton Library at Harvard University; Linda Lott, the Garden Librarian at Dumbarton Oaks; and J. Rigbie Turner at The Pierpont Morgan Library, New York. All have allowed me access to their valuable manuscript collections and permitted me to cite extracts from them. Those in New York come from the Frederick R. Koch Foundation Collection, on deposit in The Pierpont Morgan Library, or from the Mary Flagler Cary Collection there. In New York I should also like to thank James J. Fuld for access to his collection, and Mrs Heidi Nitze for permission to publish extracts from the rare edition of Satie's *Sports et divertissements* in her collection, which contains Charles Martin's 1914 illustrations as well as those of 1922.

In England my thanks go to Dr Patrick Gowers, Dr Nigel Wilkins, Gavin Bryars, Joanna Talbot, Graham Hayter, Hugh Cobbe, Dr Oliver Neighbour and especially to Charles McFeeters. Within the University of Liverpool I should like to thank Dr Monica Nurnberg (for help with French translations), James Wishart, Dr Ian Williamson, Suzanne Yee and the University Photographic Service, the staff of the Sydney Jones Library and the late Dr Michael de Cossart for his unfailing help and encouragement. I owe a special debt to the Liverpool University Research Development Fund, and to Professor Michael Talbot for his continued support and belief in my research. Without his help in securing Sabbatical leave in 1988–9 *Satie the composer* would never have been completed. I should also like to thank Roger Nichols for helpful advice in planning this book, and the publisher Marion Boyars for allowing me to cite extracts from Ornella Volta's *Satie Seen Through His Letters* (in English translation by Michael Bullock). It was only through Mme Volta's kind co-operation that many of these letters appear in the present study. Lastly, my thanks go to my editor Penny Souster, who encouraged me to write this book in the first instance, and to my invaluable sub-editor Rachel Neaman.

Abbreviations

The system of abbreviations used is that found in *The New Grove Dictionary of Music and Musicians* (ed. Stanley Sadie, London, Macmillan, 1980). A few additions, differences and items which need reiterating are listed below:

General abbreviations

MS, MSS	manuscript, manuscripts
OS	orchestral score
red.	(piano) reduction
SIM	Société Internationale de Musique
SMI	Société Musicale Indépendante
SN	Société Nationale de Musique
VS	vocal score

Abbreviations for recurring sources and library sigla

BN   denotes a manuscript in the Département de la Musique in the Biliothèque Nationale, 2 rue de Louvois, Paris 2. Thus BN 9573 is Bibliothèque Nationale notebook MS 9573. As these notebooks are now in a fragile condition and are undergoing restoration, they can only be consulted by special permission from the director of the Music Department, Mme Catherine Massip

F-Pfs   Paris, Archives of the Fondation Satie (56 rue des Tournelles)

Ho   denotes a manuscript in the Houghton Library at Harvard University (MS Storage 159; Woods Bliss collection). Thus Ho 5 is Harvard notebook MS 5

US-AUS   Austin, Texas, Harry Ransom Humanities Research Center (document in the Carlton Lake coll.)

US-NYpm   New York, Pierpont Morgan Library (document on deposit from the Frederick R. Koch Foundation)

Vc   Erik Satie: *Correspondance (édition intégrale, réunie, établie et commentée par Ornella Volta)* (Paris, Editions du Placard, in preparation in 3 vols.)

Ve   Erik Satie: *Ecrits (réunis, établis et annotés par Ornella Volta)* (Paris, Editions
            Champ Libre, rev. ed. 1981)
Vl   Volta, Ornella: *Satie Seen Through His Letters* (London and New York,
            Marion Boyars, 1989). These extracts use the English translation by
            Michael Bullock
Vy   Volta, Ornella: *L'Ymagier d'Erik Satie* (Paris, Editions Van de Velde, 1979)
W   Wilkins, Nigel (ed. and trans.): *The Writings of Erik Satie* (London,
            Eulenburg, 1980)

Chronology

1865	19 July	Jules Alfred Satie (1842–1903) of Honfleur marries Jane Leslie Anton (born in London of Scottish parents) at St Mary's Church, Barnes, Surrey.
	Aug	During their honeymoon in Scotland, Eric is conceived.
1866	17 May	Eric-Alfred Leslie Satie born in Honfleur (88 rue Haute).
	Sept	Eric baptized in Protestant Church, Honfleur.
1868	17 June	Sister Louise-Olga-Jeannie born. Summer holiday spent in England (Brighton) in 1867 or 1868.
1869	21 Oct	Brother Conrad born.
1870		Satie family moves to 3 Cité Odiot, Paris 8.
1872	8 Oct	Jane Satie dies. Eric and Conrad sent to live with paternal grandparents, Jules and Eulalie, in Honfleur. Eric enters Collège d'Honfleur (Lycée Albert Sorel) where he excels
	4 Dec	only in history and Latin. Rebaptized into Catholic Church.
1874	—	Begins music lessons with M. Vinot, organist at Eglise St-Léonard and pupil of Niedermeyer. Studies include solfège and Gregorian chant. Influenced by eccentric uncle Adrien ('Sea-bird') who loves boats and horses.
1878	summer	Grandmother drowned. Eric rejoins father at 2 rue de Constantinople, Paris 8. End of formal schooling, but taken by father to lectures at Collège de France, and studies Greek and Latin with M. Mallet.
1879	21 Jan	Alfred Satie marries Eugénie Barnetche (1832–1916: a piano teacher, pupil of Guilmant and Mathias). Eric hostile to her.
	8 Nov	Enters preparatory piano class of Emile Descombes at Paris Conservatoire.
1880	Jan, June	Takes piano exams. Is described as 'gifted but indolent' after performance of Hiller's Piano Concerto (Op. 69) in Jan. Father establishes music publishing business (early 1880s), moving to 70 rue de Turbigo, Paris 2 (1881), 6 rue de Marseille, Paris 10 (1883) and finally to 66 boulevard

		Magenta, Paris 9 (1886). Publishes own salon compositions and those of his wife.
1881	June	Eric described as 'laziest student in the Conservatoire' by Descombes after performance of Mendelssohn's Piano Concerto in D minor (Op. 40). Descombes recommends 'two hours practice each day' in Satie's copy of Mendelssohn's Piano Works (Peters Edition), but Satie is already more interested in finding a distinctive form for his signature on the cover than in mastering the contents of the book (now in the James J. Fuld coll., New York).
1882	15 June	Plays Finale of Beethoven's A flat major Sonata (Op. 26). Fails to impress examiners and is dismissed from Conservatoire.
1883	4 Dec	Admitted as auditor in harmony class of Antoine Taudou.
1884	9 Sept	First composition, a brief Allegro for piano, written whilst on holiday in Honfleur. Eric now signs himself 'Erik' on all his compositions (though he used the Eric form on other documents as late as 1906).
1885	6 Nov	Performs a Chopin *Ballade* and is accepted into intermediate piano class of Georges Mathias. Writes *Valse-ballet* and *Fantaisie-valse* (salon pieces published by father in *La Musique des familles* on 17 March and 28 July 1887).
1886	—	Meets Spanish-born poet José-Maria Patricio Manuel Contamine (known as Contamine de Latour) and sets *Les Anges*, *Les Fleurs*, *Sylvie* and *Elégie*. Develops penchant for mysticism, studies Gothic art, becomes known as 'Monsieur le Pauvre'. Writes 4 *Ogives* for piano.
	June	Plays Mendelssohn's Prelude in D major (probably Op. 104 No. 3). Mathias's verdict is 'worthless. Three months just to learn the piece. Can't sight-read properly.'
	15 Nov	Volunteers for military service.
	end Nov	Leaves Conservatoire.
	9 Dec	Departs with 33rd Infantry Regiment for Arras (Pas-de-Calais). Deliberately contracts bronchitis to escape boredom of military life.
1887	Spring	Discovers Flaubert (*Salammbô*; *La Tentation de Saint-Antoine*) and novels of Péladan (during convalescence).
	18 May	Hears première of Chabrier's *Le Roi malgré lui* at Opéra-Comique. Presents Chabrier with a dedicated score. No acknowledgment received by Satie.
	—	Sets *Chanson* (Contamine de Latour).
	?1–18 Sept	*Trois Sarabandes*.
	Nov	Released from military service.

	?Dec	Leaves home for large room at 50 rue Condorcet, Montmartre with 1,600 francs from father. Frequents Chat Noir cabaret at 12 rue Laval (later rue Victor Massé) where he probably sees Henri Rivière's shadow theatre production of *La Tentation de Saint-Antoine* on 28 Dec. Is introduced to Rodolphe Salis as 'Erik Satie – gymnopédiste' and is later engaged as orchestral conductor (by 1890). Adopts Bohemian life-style and dandified appearance. Meets Dynam-Victor Fumet and humorist Alphonse Allais.
1888	Feb–2 Apr	*Trois Gymnopédies*.
	18 Aug	First *Gymnopédie* published by Alfred Satie in *La Musique des familles*.
	?Nov	Publishes third *Gymnopédie* privately, using his father's printer Dupré.
	1 Dec	Advertises third *Gymnopédie* in *La Lanterne Japonaise*, for which Satie begins to write under the pseudonym 'Virginie Lebeau' (Nov).
1889	–	Publishes 4 *Ogives* privately.
	8 July	Writes *Gnossienne* (known as 'No. 5') and sketches *Chanson Hongroise* after hearing Javanese and Romanian music at Exposition Universelle. Begins to frequent Edmond Bailly's Librairie de l'Art Indépendant, where he meets esoteric writers like Victor-Emile Michelet, Villiers de l'Isle-Adam, and probably Debussy.
	20 July	Announces courses of piano lessons at 50 rue Condorcet.
1890	?Spring	Moves to smaller room at 6 rue Cortot to escape creditors. *Gnossiennes* 'Nos. 2 and 3' (and probably No. 1) – introduces humorous texts into music and dispenses with bar lines. Meets Joséphin Péladan, self-appointed leader of the Ordre de la Rose-Croix Catholique, du Temple et du Graal and later becomes its official composer and chapelmaster (by May 1891).
	5 Dec	*Danse* for small orchestra (later incorporated into the *Trois Morceaux en forme de poire*).
	31 Dec	Meets Catalan painters Ramón Casas and Santiago Rusiñol at Ball at the Moulin de la Galette.
1891	20 Jan	First Rose-Croix music (published in 1968 as *Première pensée Rose + Croix*).
	21 Jan	*Gnossienne* known as 'No. 4'.
	–	Quarrels with Salis and leaves Chat Noir to become second pianist at Auberge du Clou (30 avenue Trudaine). Friendship with Debussy develops. Portraits of Satie begin to appear in Salons; he becomes more widely known. ?Auditor

		at Guiraud's composition classes at Conservatoire (arranged by Debussy)?
	28 Oct	Contributes *Leit-motiv* to Péladan's novel *Le Panthée* (in his cycle *La Décadence latine. Ethopée*).
	2 Nov	Sets hymn *Salut Drapeau!* from Péladan's play *Le Prince du Byzance*.
	?Dec	Writes incidental music for Péladan's 'Pastorale Kaldéenne' *Le Fils des étoiles* (scored for flutes and harps).
1892	10 March	*Trois Sonneries de la Rose + Croix* performed at inauguration of First Rosicrucian Salon at Galerie Durand-Ruel.
	19 March	3 Act-Preludes to *Le Fils des étoiles* performed at First Soirée Rose + Croix at same venue.
	May	Applies for election to the Académie des Beaux-Arts after death of Ernest Guiraud.
	June	Visits Comte Antoine de La Rochefoucauld in his chateau at Ménilles. Writes two preludes for *Le Nazaréen*, a chivalric play by Henri Mazel.
	22 July	Opera *Le Bâtard de Tristan* (libretto by Albert Tinchant) is announced in *Le Courrier de soir* for performance at the Grand Théâtre de Bordeaux: the first of many such hoaxes involving incomplete or unstarted projects (this one being a parody of Wagnerism with a fellow-pianist at the Auberge du Clou).
	14 Aug	Breaks with Péladan in archaic open letter published in *Gil Blas*; asserts his complete artistic independence.
	27 Oct	Debussy dedicates copy No. 45 of his *Cinq Poèmes de Baudelaire* to 'Erik Satie, a gentle medieval musician lost in this century'.
	17 Nov	First version of the mystical ballet *Uspud* completed with Contamine de Latour.
	16–17 Dec	Second version of *Uspud* copied overnight to present to Eugène Bertrand, Director of the Paris Opéra on 17 Dec. The meeting was only agreed after Satie challenged Bertrand to a duel. Satie's impractical conditions assist the rejection of this 'Christian ballet', but the event acquires great prestige in left-wing Montmartre society.
	?25 Dec	*Noël* performed at Miguel Utrillo's new shadow theatre in the basement of the Auberge du Clou. Text by Vincent Hyspa (lost, as is score).
1893	14 Jan	Start of affair with painter Suzanne Valadon ('Biqui') who moves into an adjoining room in the rue Cortot.
	21–3 March	9 *Danses Gothiques* composed to restore peace of mind during Satie's stormy (and only known) relationship.

2 April	Draws two portraits of Valadon, one accompanied by a musical dedication: *Bonjour Biqui, Bonjour!*
20 June	End of liaison with Suzanne Valadon.
—	Meets Ravel at Café de la Nouvelle Athènes. His first composition *La Ballade de la Reine morte d'aimer* shows Satie's influence. Satie writes *Vexations* in which a self-repeating fragment is itself repeated 840 times. Also writes *Eginhard. Prélude* (play lost).
Sept–Oct	3 *Gnossiennes* appear in *Le Figaro musical* (Nos. 1, 3) and in *Le Cœur* (No. 2, published as 'No. 6').
15 Oct	Publishes 'Epître de Erik Satie: Première aux Artistes Catholiques et à tous les Chrétiens' in *Le Cœur* to announce the foundation of his Eglise Métropolitaine d'Art de Jésus Conducteur, of which he names himself 'Parcier et Maître de Chapelle'. Begins *Messe des pauvres* (1893–5).
1894 March	Jules Bois's esoteric play *La Porte héroïque du ciel* published by Librairie de l'Art Indépendant, together with a prelude by Satie, dedicated to himself.
30 April	Second application for election to Académie des Beaux-Arts after death of Gounod.
17 May	Angry letter to Saint-Saëns published in *Le Ménestrel* after Satie's candidature is again rejected by Académie.
June	Alfred Jarry praises La Rochefoucauld's portrait of Satie, exhibited at the Salon des Indépendants.
1895 —	With a small inheritance Satie publishes extracts from his compositions, plus attacks on his enemies in the critical press and theatre. Becomes more paranoid and isolated.
24 Jan	*Commune qui mundi nefas* (extract from *Messe des pauvres* and attacks on Lugné-Poë, director of Théâtre de l'Œuvre).
8 March	*Intende votis supplicum* (*Dixit dominus* from *Messe des pauvres*, with attacks on Lugné-Poë and the editors Alfred Vallette, Alexandre Natanson and Léon Deschamps).
9 April	Small *Uspud* brochure. Extracts from ballet plus attack on Alexandre Natanson (of *La Revue blanche*). A large *Uspud* brochure had appeared in 1893, giving the text of the second version all printed in lower case.
14 May	*Cartulaire. No. 1–63* of the Eglise Métropolitaine (attacks on Henry Gauthier-Villars ('Willy'), Lugné-Poë, exhibits in the artistic Salons, and M. Ribot, President of the Cabinet).
18 June	*Cartulaire. No. 2–63* (attacks on Lugné-Poë, Laurent Tailhade, plus typical apocalyptic traits from the Eglise Métropolitaine).
June	Extracts from *Messe des pauvres* appear in *Le Cœur*, with

the first article on Satie's music by his brother Conrad. Satie purchases 7 identical maroon velvet suits at the Department store 'La Belle Jardinière' and his 'Velvet Gentleman' period begins (see Fig. 0.1), marking the end of the so-called 'Rose-Croix' period.

1896	30 April	Third unsuccessful application for election to Académie des Beaux-Arts after death of Ambroise Thomas.
	25 July	Inheritance exhausted by publishing activities and generosity to Bohemian friends. Moves into tiny 'placard' at 6 rue Cortot at 20 francs a quarter. End of Eglise Métropolitaine.
1897	Jan	*Gnossienne* 'No. 6'.
	20 Feb	Première of *Gymnopédies* Nos. 3, 1 (orch. by Debussy in 1896) at Salle Erard, conducted by Gustave Doret.
	March	*Pièces froides* (*Airs à faire fuir*; *Danses de travers*).
	—	First popular cabaret song, *Je te veux* (Pacory) probably dates from 1897.
1898	Oct	With Henry Pacory and the artist Augustin Grass-Mick, Satie visits the suburb of Arcueil-Cachan (10 kilometres from Paris) and rents a room at 22 (now 34) rue Cauchy in Arcueil. The room had belonged to the colourful tramp Bibi-la-Purée (André Salis, who was related to Rodolphe Salis of the Chat Noir cabaret). Satie is to remain here till his death and no-one is allowed to penetrate his isolated sanctuary. Over the winter of 1898–9 Satie gradually settles in and begins his daily routine of walking to and from Paris, drinking and composing in cafés *en route*. Often visits Debussy at 58 rue Cardinet, after he moves there in Sept 1898.
1899	March	To gain money, starts accompanying Vincent Hyspa in Montmartre cabarets like La Boîte à Fursy.
	Summer	Collaborations with Jules Dépaquit on ?shadow play *Geneviève de Brabant* and pantomime *Jack-in-the-Box*. Writes song *Un Dîner à l'Elysée* with Hyspa.
	19 Oct	Witness at Debussy's marriage to Rosalie (Lilly) Texier.
1900	—	Article on 'Les Musiciens de Montmartre' for *Guide de l'étranger à Montmartre*. Begins to settle in Arcueil; locals regard him as enigma. Period of cabaret songs (many of them arrangements), theatrical projects, and uncertainty as to future direction as serious composer.
	18 April	Prelude for *La Mort de Monsieur Mouche* (3-Act play with Contamine de Latour).
	5 Aug	*Verset laïque & somptueux*, last of the 'musique à genoux', written for collection of *Autographes de Musiciens Contemporaines* at time of Exposition Universelle (see Fig. 0.2).

0.1   Satie in the garden of a suburban tavern in his 'Velvet Gentleman' outfit, 1895.

0.2   Satie in 1900.

	9 Dec	Ravel presents Satie to pianist Ricardo Viñes at Concerts Chevillard.
1901	March	*The Dreamy Fish*, music for a story by Lord Cheminot (Contamine de Latour): some Debussyan influence. Another parallel enterprise *The Angora Ox* probably dates from 1901.
1902	March	Waltzes *Tendrement* (formerly *Illusion*) and *Poudre d'or* registered with Société des Auteurs. Paulette Darty ('Queen of the Slow Waltz') begins to sing his songs.
	27 June	Finds Debussy's *Pelléas et Mélisande* 'absolutely astounding'.
1903	April	Receives only 76 centimes in performing rights for year.
	Nov	Completes *Trois Morceaux en forme de poire* for piano duet, based on works from 1890–1 and more contemporary cabaret songs. Is pleased with result.
1904	10 April	Attacks critic Henry Gauthier-Villars ('Willy') at Chevillard concert. Is ejected by Municipal Guard.
	26 July	Première of 'intermezzo américaine' *La Diva de l'Empire* by Paulette Darty in revue *Dévidons la bobine*.
	Aug	Begins collaboration with Maurice de Féraudy and Jean Kolb on 1-Act operetta *Pousse l'amour* (lost).
	Sept	Dominique Bonnaud founds cabaret La Lune Rousse and Satie transfers allegiance to this (1904–?11). Many shadow plays produced here by Bonnaud.
	19 Oct	March *Le Piccadilly* registered with Société des Auteurs.
1905	—	Continues writing and arranging cabaret songs for performance with Hyspa, Darty etc., including *Chez le docteur*, *L'Omnibus automobile* (Hyspa); *Impérial-Oxford*, *Légende Californienne* (Latour); *Allons-y Chochotte* (D. Durante).
	Oct	Against Debussy's advice, enrols at Schola Cantorum. Begins counterpoint course with Roussel (1905–8) and attends parts of d'Indy's 7-year *Cours de composition musicale* between 1905 and 1911 (or 1912). Studies analysis, form, sonata construction, orchestration (1909–10) with d'Indy.
c. 1906	—	Replaces 'Velvet Gentleman' look with final appearance as bourgeois functionary, complete with bowler hat, wing collar and umbrella. Sets *Chanson médiévale* (Catulle Mendès) as Schola exercise. Many other undated pieces, like *Profondeur*, *Effronterie* (?1909) belong to Schola period, during which Satie writes numerous chorales, fugues and minuets as spin-offs from his academic studies. Labours to perfect 'modern fugue' and continues writing minuets till at least 1920. This represents one aspect of his lifelong fascination with dance music (1885–1924).

1906 July   *Passacaille.*

21 Oct   *Prélude en tapisserie*, notable for its fragmentary mosaic construction.

1907 Summer   Completes *Nouvelles 'Pièces froides'*, in which Satie tries out piano styles of Fauré and Debussy in Nos. 1–2.

22 Nov   *Pousse l'amour* produced at Comédie Royale.

1908 15 June   Obtains diploma in counterpoint from Schola Cantorum signed by Roussel and d'Indy, with the comment 'très bien'. Satie can now pass 'exclusively to the study of composition'.

Aug–Sept   Begins *Aperçus désagréables*, writing the *Choral* and *Fugue* as duets to play with Debussy (who tells Francisco de Lacerda on 5 Sept that in the fugue 'boredom disguises itself behind wicked harmonies' and the influence of the Schola can be recognized).

—   Attends Radical-Socialist meetings in Arcueil, and participates in charitable activities of its Patronage Laïque.

1909 4 July   Awarded Palmes Académiques for services to Arcueil community.

7 Aug   'Vin d'honneur' as tribute to Satie at 43 rue Emile Raspail, Arcueil.

17 Sept   *Le Dîner de Pierrot* (probably a collection of cabaret songs arranged as a fantasy by Dépaquit) performed in Arcueil.

Oct   Begins Schola orchestration course with d'Indy.

17 Oct   Contributes anonymous column 'Quinzaine des Sociétés' to *L'Avenir d'Arcueil-Cachan* (till 20 Nov 1910). Gives solfège lessons on Sunday mornings.

24 Oct   Matinée Artistique organized by Satie as 'Directeur du service intérieur du Patronage Laïque' with Darty, Hyspa and Dépaquit. Probably includes fantasy *La Chemise*, as rehearsal for performance by Darty at La Scala, Paris on 21 Nov.

1910 15 March   Resigns from Patronage Laïque after differences with committee, but still helps with youth work by raising funds to take party of 12 children on outing to Vaux de Cernay (8 Sept).

24 Oct   Annual Matinée Artistique poorly attended and Satie soon withdraws from all local involvement.

1911 16 Jan   Ravel plays second *Sarabande*, Act 1 Prelude to *Le Fils des étoiles* and third *Gymnopédie* at SMI concert. Satie tells Conrad (17 Jan) he is confused by enthusiastic reception for his early works amongst young anti-d'Indyites, who found his recent work dull. Now the 'fruits of [his] profound ignorance' (which led him to enrol at the Schola) were being acclaimed! Satie also denounces his cabaret work as 'more stupid and dirty than anything' (Vl, 27–8). He has clearly reached a turning-point (see Fig. 0.3), and begins helping the first of his young protégés, Roland-Manuel, whom he introduces to Roussel (27 July).

25 March	Debussy conducts his orchestrations of the *Gymnopédies* at Salle Gaveau (Cercle Musical). Satie is dismayed that Debussy should be jealous of his success (11 April).
June–Sept	*En Habit de cheval*, the culmination of '8 years work' to arrive at new 'modern fugue'. *Sarabandes, Trois Morceaux en forme de poire, En Habit de cheval* published by Rouart-Lerolle. Meets Stravinsky *chez* Debussy.
1912 Feb	Begins regular ironical journalism with article on Ambroise Thomas in Roland-Manuel's *L'Œil de veau*.
April	Begins association with *Revue musicale SIM* (1912–14) with 'Mémoires d'un amnésique'. Considers himself as phono-metrician rather than as musician.
17 June	Too poorly dressed to attend orchestral première of *En Habit de cheval* at SMI.
1 July	Chosen by young musicians as candidate for 'Prince of Musicians' title.
11–23 July	*Préludes flasques (pour un chien)*. Rejected by publisher Demets.
12–23 Aug	*Véritables Préludes flasques (pour un chien)*. Rejected by Durand, but now accepted by Demets, who asks for more such pieces. The pattern of the 'humoristic' piano pieces of 1912–15 is now established, many of which are first performed by Ricardo Viñes.
1913 Feb–March	*Le Piège de Méduse*, comedy in 1 Act by Satie (with 7 dances for Jonah the Monkey). Prefigures surrealism.
21–6 Apr	*Descriptions automatiques.*
2 June–25 Aug	*Croquis et agaceries d'un gros bonhomme en bois.*
30 June–4 July	*Embryons desséchés.*
23 Aug–5 Sept	*Chapitres tournés en tous sens.*
9–17 Sept	*Vieux sequins et vieilles cuirasses.*
early Oct	*Pièces enfantines* (published as *Trois Nouvelles Enfantines* in 1972).
10 Oct	*Menus propos enfantins (Enfantines I).*
22 Oct	*Enfantillages pittoresques (Enfantines II).*
26 Oct	*Peccadilles importunes (Enfantines III).*
16 Nov	*Les Pantins dansent.* 'Poème dansé' for Metachoric Festival of Valentine de Saint-Point (second version performed 18 Dec).
Dec	Meets Georges Auric after he writes perceptive article on Satie (at age of 13) in *La Revue musicale*.

0.3   Satie around 1911.

1914	—	Meets Valentine Gross (Valentine Hugo after her marriage to Jean Hugo on 7 August 1919) at private première of *Le Piège de Méduse* at the home of Roland-Manuel's parents (1 rue de Chazelles). First use of prepared piano.
	17–30 Jan	*Choses vues à droite et à gauche (sans lunettes)* for violin and piano.
	15 Feb	9 fake 'Commandements du Catéchisme du Conservatoire' appear in *Revue musicale SIM*. Satie angrily tells editor Ecorcheville he always signs what he writes for publication and that he must print an apology (8 March).
	14 Mar–20 May	*Sports et divertissements* written for Lucien Vogel, accompanied by drawings by Charles Martin. Texts by Satie. Work only published in 1923 (with second set of 1922 drawings by Martin, showing influence of Cubism).
	25 June–3 July	*Heures séculaires et instantanées*. Satie forbids texts to be read aloud during performance.
	21–3 July	*Les Trois Valses distinguées du précieux dégoûté*.
	1 Aug	Joins Socialist Party (after assassination of Jean Jaurès on 31 July).
	Aug	Meets Diaghilev *chez* Mimi Godebska. Acts as Corporal in Home Guard in Arcueil.
	30 Sept	Takes brother Conrad on tour of old Montmartre haunts. Conrad records his brother's views on a variety of subjects from Debussy to Vaughan Williams.
	20 Nov–2 Dec	*Trois Poèmes d'amour*. Poems by Satie (modern equivalents of 13th-century French troubadour poetry). Meticulous quest for perfection in simplicity.
1915	Aug	Appeals to Dukas for financial assistance from charitable institutions. Tells him: 'This War is a sort of end of the World that is more stupid than reality' (Vc).
	23 Aug–6 Oct	*Avant-dernières pensées*, dedicated to Debussy, Dukas and Roussel.
	18 Oct	Meets Cocteau and Gabriel Astruc *chez* Valentine Gross, to discuss plans for Cocteau's production of *A Midsummer Night's Dream* (in association with the Cubist painter Albert Gleizes). Satie composes *Cinq Grimaces*, but the production at the Cirque Médrano falls through.
1916	Jan	Teaches composition to wealthy chemist Albert Verley. Makes orchestration and piano duet reduction of *L'Aurore aux doigts de rose*, the second of Verley's *Pastels sonores*. Sends piece to Varèse in America.
	14 April	*Daphénéo* (Mimi Godebska) and *Le Chapelier* completed, the second song being an adaptation by René Chalupt from Lewis Carroll's *Alice in Wonderland*.

18 April	Lecture on Satie by Roland-Manuel at Société Lyre et Palette.
2 May	Receives Cocteau's initial plans for *Parade*.
26 May	*La Statue de bronze* (first setting of poetry of Léon-Paul Fargue).
30 May	Granados–Satie concert *chez* Mme Bongard 'for the benefit of artists affected by the War'. Satie plays *Avant-dernières pensées*. Programme illustrated by Matisse and Picasso.
July	Satie plans ballet for Diaghilev based on La Fontaine's fables.
24 Aug	Picasso joins *Parade* team. Satie begins composing ballet in earnest, inspired by his new ideas.
2 Nov	First lecture: 'Les Animaux dans la musique' at school of Professeur Lucien de Flagny (25 rue de la Tour).
19 Nov	Première of *Les Trois Valses distinguées* at Société Lyre et Palette (6 rue Huyghens) in conjunction with first exhibition of Negro sculpture in Paris, and a modern art exhibition (Matisse, Picasso, Modigliani, Kisling, Ortiz de Zarate).
1917 6 Jan	First signs of work on *Socrate* to a translation of Plato by Victor Cousin. Commission by Princesse Edmond de Polignac.
9 Jan	Finishes piano duet score of *Parade* (minus opening *Choral* and *Final* (Part 4)).
8 March	Breaks with Debussy over his derogatory opinions expressed about *Parade* during rehearsals.
8 May	Finishes orchestration of *Parade*. (*Choral* and *Final* added in April–May 1919.)
18 May	Première of *Parade* by Diaghilev's Ballets Russes at Théâtre du Châtelet. Scandal ensues; Satie accused of 'Bochisme'.
30 May	Sends insulting postcard to Jean Poueigh (Octave Séré) who had complimented Satie on *Parade* on 18 May, but then published a hostile review in *Les Carnets de la semaine* on 27 May (without mentioning the music itself)! Poueigh brings a libel case against Satie and wins. Satie is condemned to 8 days in prison plus a fine of 100 francs, with 1,000 francs damages, despite Cocteau's spirited defence (12 July). Satie appeals against the judgement (27 Nov), and after higher intervention the sentence is suspended and the Princesse de Polignac helps Satie pay his fine.
6 June	Auric, Durey and Honegger organize hommage to Satie in Salle Huyghens (Montparnasse). From this and subsequent 1917–18 concerts in the rue Huyghens at the Théâtre du Vieux-Colombier, Satie forms a group of Nouveaux Jeunes,

0.4   Satie around 1917.

to which the names of Tailleferre and Poulenc are added, plus Milhaud and Koechlin in 1918. Satie later resigns from the group, but from this loose affiliation of independent, radical composers Les Six emerge (being so named after the title of an article by Henri Collet in *Comoedia* (16 Jan 1920)).

July *Sonatine bureaucratique*, an early example of neo-classicism modelled on Clementi's Sonatina in C (Op. 36 No. 1).

Aug Restarts work on *Vie de Socrate*, but is distracted by problems of Poueigh case.

— Writes first 'musique d'ameublement' (*Tapisserie en fer forgé*; *Carrelage phonique*). Writes vital statement of compositional aesthetic ('Subject matter (Idea) and Craftsmanship (Construction)') on cover of BN 9611, during composition of *Mort de Socrate*.

1918 5 Feb Lecture: 'Eloge des critiques' given before first concert of Nouveaux Jeunes at Théâtre du Vieux-Colombier.

25 March Death of Debussy. Satie reconciles himself with him shortly before, and is glad he did so.

3 April First performance of parts of *Socrate* by Jane Bathori and Satie for dedicatee, the Princesse de Polignac. Extracts from *Mort de Socrate* (Part 3) are also performed *chez* Bathori on 24 June. Satie claims he owes his 'return to classical simplicity with a modern sensibility' to his Cubist painter friends (Vl, 152).

— Cocteau publishes *Le Coq et l'Arlequin* which deifies Satie as the leading musical spirit behind the post-war *esprit nouveau* (with its vital elements of surprise, simplicity, popular artistic roots and essential Frenchness).

23 Aug Reaches depths of despair in 'J'emmerde l'Art' letter to Valentine Gross. Satie lonely and in dire poverty as all his wealthy friends have left Paris for the summer. He asks Gross to find him paid work, however menial. Gross contacts M. Lebey who suggests that Satie creates a new teaching course. Satie eagerly proposes a title, the *Modern Musical Aesthetic*, but nothing comes of the plan.

Oct Satie revises orchestration of *Socrate*.

1 Nov Resigns from Nouveaux Jeunes to pursue independent course.

1 Dec Satie proposes to give a lecture and concert tour of America to his friend, the author Henri-Pierre Roché, now working in New York (letter in *US-AUS*). It is to include *Socrate*, his 'lucky star' in which he places his hopes for the future.

1919 21 March *Portrait de Socrate* (Part 1) performed at Adrienne Monnier's bookshop La Maison des Amis des Livres (7 rue de l'Odéon;

		where Satie is a frequent visitor) before a prestigious audience.
	late April–early May	Revises *Parade* for Diaghilev, adding 3 minutes of new music (the *Choral* and *Final*).
	7 Aug	Satie and Cocteau witness marriage of Valentine Gross to Jean Hugo.
	Aug–Nov	5 *Nocturnes* (Nos. 1–3 form group in D major). Return to systematic approach to composition, with increasing seriousness of purpose after *Socrate*.
	11 Oct	Returns to journalism (after break in 1915–18) with 'Notes sur la musique moderne' for *L'Humanité*.
	11 Nov	Declines to write article on Ravel for Georges Jean-Aubry. Relations with Ravel at low ebb and deteriorating.
	Nov–Dec	*Trois Petites Pièces montées* for orchestra.
	—	Contacts with Dada movement of Tristan Tzara begin. Meets pianist Jean Wiéner. Begins to move in more exalted social circles and delights in shocking high society with his Bolshevist sympathies. Increasing concern in final years to make music new, chic and Parisian.
1920	14 Feb	First public performance of *Socrate* with piano (SN).
	23 Feb	Première of *Trois Petites Pièces montées* at Comédie des Champs-Elysées.
	8 March	Première of *Musique d'ameublement* (*Chez un 'bistrot'*; *Un salon*) with Milhaud at Galerie Barbazanges (Faubourg St-Honoré), in conjunction with exhibition of children's drawings and comedy by Max Jacob (*Ruffian toujours, truand jamais*).
	May–Nov	Articles for *Le Coq [Parisien]*, together with contributions by Cocteau, Radiguet and members of Les Six.
	June	*Premier Menuet* (the only one of many such to be published during Satie's lifetime).
	7 June	Première of *Socrate* with orchestra during Festival Erik Satie (Salle Erard) by Marya Freund.
	July–Oct	Composes 3 dances and an intervening ritornello, *La Belle Excentrique* for dancer Caryathis (born Elisabeth Toulemon).
	Sept–Dec	*Quatre Petites Mélodies*, settings of Cocteau, Radiguet and an anguished *Elégie* by Lamartine, dedicated to the memory of Debussy and their 30-year friendship.
	22 Nov	Hears reading of *Paul & Virginie*, a libretto by Cocteau (with contributions from Radiguet). Work on this 3-Act *opéra-comique* occupies much of Satie's time between 1920 and the end of 1923, when he abandoned it. Little music, however, has survived from what was planned to be Satie's final masterpiece. The work was intended for production at

		Jacques Hébertot's Théâtre des Champs-Elysées, and a contract was signed on 26 Nov 1921. Diaghilev took over the project in 1922.
1921	April	'Cahiers d'un mammifère' appear in *L'Esprit nouveau*. Satie visits Brussels and Ghent to hear first Belgian performances of *Socrate*. Delivers lecture on Les Six in Brussels (11 April); meets E. L. T. Mesens.
	24 May	Public première of *Le Piège de Méduse* at Théâtre Michel. Satie tries to get performance stopped as he dislikes Pierre Bertin impersonating him as the Baron Medusa. He also objects to having the 7 dances performed on piano rather than in his new orchestral version (which is eventually conducted by Milhaud).
	June	Suggests to Louise Norton that they collaborate on a ballet based on Lewis Carroll's *Alice in Wonderland*. During summer, also collaborates on ballets with painter André Derain (*Supercinéma* for Ballets Suédois; *La Naissance de Vénus* for Diaghilev).
	14 June	Première of *La Belle Excentrique* (Théâtre du Colisée).
	July	2 aphorisms (written Jan) appear in Francis Picabia's Dada journal *Le Pilhaou-Thibaou* (special edition of *391*).
	Aug	'Eloge des critiques' published in *Action*.
	30 Aug	*Sonnerie pour réveiller le bon gros Roi des Singes* (appears in first issue of *Fanfare*, 1 Oct).
	Dec	Joins Communist Party (after Congrès de Tours).
	3 Dec	Helps Man Ray construct his first 'Ready-Made' sculpture (*Cadeau*). Meets Constantin Brancusi.
1922	–	No music survives from 1922, but Satie closely involved in Dada movement and literary activities (often to launch new ephemeral journals) in 1922–4 (see Fig. 0.5).
	17 Jan	Historical 'préambule' by Satie to introduce concert by Marcelle Meyer (with première of *Premier Menuet*).
	31 Jan	Public première of *Sports et divertissements* by Marcelle Meyer (Salle de La Ville d'Evêque).
	Feb	Article on Les Six published in *Les Feuilles libres*. Participates in abortive Congrès de Paris, convened by André Breton to challenge Tristan Tzara as leader of Dada movement and to define parameters of Dadaism.
	17 Feb	Satie presides at public trial and condemnation of poet André Breton at Closerie des Lilas.
	Mar–Nov	Contributes articles to *Catalogue* to publicize Pierre Trémois's bookshop (14 rue de l'Université).

0.5 Satie in his first smoking jacket, 1922, a present from M. Henriquet, proprietor of
the 'Old England' store in December 1921.

	April	'Office de la domesticité' and more 'Cahiers d'un mammifère' in *Le Cœur à barbe*.
	6 July	*Trois Morceaux en forme de poire* played during Tzara's chaotic 'Soirée du Cœur à barbe' at Théâtre Michel. Satie declines to attend second soirée planned for 7 July, but this is cancelled anyway! End of Dada as a movement.
	July–9 Aug	First article on Stravinsky (for Sybil Harris of *Vanity Fair*, published in Feb 1923 in USA).
	15–25 Aug	Article on Debussy for *Vanity Fair* (not published during Satie's lifetime).
	Oct–Nov	Second article on Stravinsky ('Propos à propos de Igor Strawinsky') published in *Les Feuilles libres*.
1923	Jan	Meets members of Ecole d'Arcueil (organized by Milhaud around Henri Sauguet). They include Henri Cliquet-Pleyel, Roger Désormière, Maxime Jacob and Baron Jacques Bénoist-Méchin. All except the last are pupils of Charles Koechlin, and Bénoist-Méchin soon leaves group.
	Mar–April	'Les "Périmes"', article in *Les Feuilles libres*.
	28 Mar	*Tenture de Cabinet préfectoral*. Furniture music for Mrs Eugène Meyer (Junior) of Washington D.C.
	May	5 *Ludions* (Fargue).
	30 May	*Divertissement (La Statue retrouvée)* performed at Masked Ball *chez* Comte Etienne de Beaumont (2 rue Duroc). Collaboration by *Parade* team (Picasso, Cocteau, Satie, Massine). Score now rediscovered (see Ex. 88). Fargue not credited as author at private première of *Ludions* at same Masked Ball. Breaks with Satie.
	July–Dec	Recitatives for Gounod's opera *Le Médecin malgré lui* (for Diaghilev).
	Sept–Oct	'Parlons à voix basse' in *Les Feuilles libres*.
	—	Plans ballets with Derain (*Concurrence*; *Couleurs*).
	Nov	First signs of *Relâche*, which grows from ballet *Après-dîner* by Blaise Cendrars. Satie acts as catalyst.
1924	3–7 Jan	Travels to Monte Carlo for première of *Le Médecin malgré lui* (5 Jan). Programme by Laloy makes no mention even of Satie's name. Breaks with Auric and Poulenc for their friendship with Laloy and Cocteau, who indulge in opium-smoking parties and other vices (much to the disgust of the hyper-moral Satie). Stands in corridor throughout train journey back to Paris, fuming.
	Jan–Feb	'Recoins de ma vie (Mémoires d'un amnésique)' in *Les Feuilles libres*.

Feb	'Extracts – de malt' in *Création*. Plans short operas (?) with Tzara and ballet *Quadrille* with Braque.
15 Feb	'Ballets Russes à Monte Carlo (Souvenirs de Voyage)' in *Paris-Journal*. Unflattering to Auric, Poulenc.
Feb–May	Ballet *Mercure* with Picasso, Massine for Comte Etienne de Beaumont's Soirées de Paris.
April	Important article 'L'Esprit musical' in *Sélection*. Given as lecture in Brussels (15 March) and Antwerp (21 March) during Satie's second visit to Belgium (with Milhaud).
June–July	'Cahiers d'un mammifère (Extraits)' in Picabia's journal *391* (Nos. 17, 18).
15 June	Première of *Mercure* ('Poses plastiques en 3 tableaux') at Théâtre de la Cigale, Montmartre.
June–20 Oct	Composes *Relâche* as 'Ballet instantanéiste' in 2 Acts with Picabia and Borlin for Rolf de Maré's Ballets Suédois. Is only product of Picabia's extension of Dadaism as Instantanéisme (living for the joy of the moment only).
21 Oct	Tells Marcel Raval that *Relâche* marks start of a new period, and prepares for battle with Breton and Cocteau.
26 Oct–10 Nov	Adds *Cinéma* to accompany Surrealist film shot by René Clair that June (as interval feature in *Relâche*).
Nov	'Nouvelle direction du vent' in *Le Mouvement accéléré*, No. 1. Renewed attacks on Auric, Poulenc.
27 Nov	Planned première of *Relâche* cancelled due to illness of Jean Borlin (choreographer, male lead).
4 Dec	Scandalous première of *Relâche* at Théâtre des Champs-Elysées. Satie drives onstage with Picabia at end in conductor Roger Désormière's 5CV car.
1925 Jan	*Le Pou qui grimpe*. Prospectus for exhibition of Normandy artists: La Belle Edition. Rapid decline in health due to cirrhosis of liver and pleurisy. Cared for at first by Milhaud, Braque and Derain. Jean Wiéner arranges room at Grand Hôtel, Place de l'Opéra, but Satie dislikes it and moves to Hôtel Istria, Montparnasse, then headquarters of avant-garde. Last letter, to Mme Guérin (7 Feb). When Satie's health declines further, Comte Etienne de Beaumont arranges private room in Hôpital Saint-Joseph, rue Pierre-Larousse (15 Feb). Satie remains cheerful and courageous to the end, and is tended by Robert Caby, a young composer he met in 1923. Refuses to see those with whom he had quarrelled.
1 July	Death of Satie (8 pm: see Fig. 0.6).

Erik Satie sur son lit de mourant   RCaby 1925

0.6   Satie on his deathbed, 1925. Bust by Robert Caby.

Some descriptions of Satie

From *Memoirs of an Amnesiac*: 'Odd Corners of My Life' in *Les Feuilles libres*, No. 35 (Jan–Feb 1924), 330:

'Hair and eyebrows dark brown; eyes grey (probably clouded); stormy brow; nose long; mouth medium; chin prominent; face oval. Height 5 feet 6 inches [1.67 metres].

The description on this document dates from 1887, the time when I did my military service in the 33rd Infantry Regiment at Arras (*Pas-de-Calais*). It would not fit me today.'

From Templier (1969), 55–7 (trans. by Elena and David French):

'He. . .was much like the satyr Marsyas: a short greying goatee; rather thick lips, twisted into a teasing smile which could at times be cruel; a sensual, greedy nose. The expression of his eyes, hidden behind a pince-nez, could change at a moment's notice from gentle to teasing to furious. . .His face, crowned by a strangely pointed skull, was quite beautiful, enigmatic and ever-changing. . .His dress was conventional: he often wore a dark grey jacket and a black coat with collar turned up. With his umbrella and bowler hat, he resembled a quiet school teacher. Although a Bohemian, he looked very dignified, almost ceremonious. A soft, deep voice, unhurriedly familiar and friendly, transformed his words into mysterious confidences. He was seized by unexpected bursts of laughter, which he would stifle with his hand. He walked slowly, taking small steps, his umbrella held tight under his arm. When talking he would stop, bend one knee a little, adjust his pince-nez and place his fist on his hip. Then he would take off once more, with small, deliberate steps. None of his friends could keep up with him on his long nightly walks. He hated the sun. . .His odd character, his fits of melancholy, drove him out of doors in the most terrible weather. . . His conversation was extremely entertaining. Very talkative, he would watch the person to whom he was speaking, through the corner of his eye, judging the effect of his jokes. In the company of a few close friends, he would be truly delightful. Smoking innumerable cigars, he would discourse at great length on any subject with extraordinary lucidity.'

From Valentine Hugo: *Notes for a portrait of Satie* (1958, 3–4; kindly communicated to me by Thierry Bodin):

xli

'There was an aspect of [Alfred] Jarry in Satie's character. He was less open, however, less jolly and superficial, but more dry, more cutting, and more prickly. His return fire was more offensive. . .Satie ate slowly. He kept a piece of bread back during dessert. After carefully removing the crust with his knife, he would carry it cautiously from the table in order to eat it with his coffee. [Although he loved good food and wine,] I never saw Satie become boorish or drunk. . .He never seemed to be of any particular age: he was neither old, nor young.'

From Madeleine Milhaud, during an interview with Roger Nichols (Exeter University, 4 June 1987):

'Satie led a sad life, rather lonely. He was attracted by young children. . .by youth and purity. He shared their joys and hopes. They made up for a deficiency in his own character. They took him as a sort of mascot and thought he brought them luck. Satie found this strange, as he had no luck himself. . .He was a most lovable person: unpredictable, with a certain charm. His way of speaking was very spontaneous – the complete opposite of his writing. . .Satie never told a dirty story; I never met anyone so polite. But he could be very violent. As Cocteau said: "Satie never blows up without a reason." Everything Satie did was logical, based on the fact that he was very sensitive and could be hurt by the slightest thing. It was logic carried to an extreme. Look at it coldly and it makes sense. He had no feeling for the mores of his time. . .He was extremely proud and he never showed his poverty to anyone. Satie wrote that: "Poverty entered my room one day like a miserable little girl with [large] green eyes" [in a letter to his brother Conrad on 17 Jan 1911].'

From a letter by Francis Picabia to the poet André Breton of 17 Feb 1922 (just after Breton's 'trial' at the Closerie des Lilas, at which Satie presided). Cited in Sanouillet (1965) 516:

'Satie's case is extraordinary. . .He's a mischievous and cunning old artist. At least, that's how he thinks of himself. Myself, I think the opposite! He's a very susceptible man, arrogant, a real sad child, but one who is sometimes made optimistic by alcohol. But he's a good friend, and I like him a lot.'

From Darius Milhaud's description of Satie in the Hôpital Saint-Joseph in 1925 (*Notes Without Music*, 1967, 148–9):

'He had never been ill before, and everything gave rise to dramas, from taking medicine to having his temperature read. . .Satie asked Madeleine to pack his suitcase. As she knew he was likely to fly into inexplicable rages if things were not placed exactly in the way that he wanted them, she asked Braque to stand between them so that Satie might not be able to watch how she packed his case. . .Satie's only toilet accessories were a scrubbing-brush and a piece of pumice-stone, with which no doubt he used to rub his skin.

Despite his intolerable sufferings, he still retained his own characteristic brand of wit. When [Jacques] Maritain brought a priest to see him, he described him to us next day as "looking like a Modigliani, black on a blue background". When Monsieur Lerolle came to see him about publishing *Relâche*, he insisted on being paid at once: "You never need money so much as when you're in hospital", he remarked slyly. Hardly had Lerolle paid over the money, than he hid the banknotes between the sheets of old newspapers piled up on his suitcase, together with all sorts of papers and bits of string. Satie refused to allow anything to be thrown out, and loved to accumulate all kinds of odds and ends. . .When at his request, Madeleine went to fetch a bundle of laundry from his concierge in Arcueil, she was dumbfounded to discover that it contained eighty-nine handkerchiefs.

As soon as Poulenc heard of his illness, he asked me to beg Satie to see him. Satie was touched by this, but refused, saying: "No, no, I would rather not see him; they said goodbye to me, and now that I am ill, I prefer to take them at their word. One must stick to one's guns to the last."'

1

Satie's career as a composer: some interpretations

Satie would have been delighted by the confusion caused by the many conflicting interpretations of his career, for it would appear that a credible overview can be devised to fit virtually any theory a writer happens to favour. At the same time, these conflicting opinions are themselves a testimonial to the diversity of Satie's œuvre and to the extent of its cross-fertilization with the other arts, and few of the interpretations given below are devoid of all merit. The overriding problem is that the line of consistent development one might expect to find in a composer who is universally acknowledged as a seminal influence on twentieth-century music is conspicuous by its absence. Thus the *Sarabandes* of 1887 are harmonically more sophisticated than his final ballet *Relâche*, which in turn demonstrates the same influences from cabaret and the popular song as the *Trois Morceaux en forme de poire* of 1903 (itself using material dating back to 1890). But in Satie's defence, Fauré's song *Nell* (1878) is outwardly similar to *La Mer est infinie* from his last song-cycle *L'Horizon chimérique* of 1921. Both Fauré and Satie shared a gift for constant renewal within an apparently limited textural range, and both refined their musical expression to its bare essentials in later life by giving it greater contrapuntal strength. But there the similarity ends, for the results are as different as chalk from cheese: chiefly because Satie insisted that his music should retain its melodic links with its popular roots, and because he entirely rejected the nineteenth-century concepts of Romantic expressiveness and thematic development. For Satie was, first and foremost, a man of ideas, a precursor of virtually everything from neo-classicism to minimalism (and even muzak). He was the first to reject Wagner's influence on French music; he by-passed Impressionism and the beguiling orchestral sonorities of Debussy and Ravel; and his art derived more from painters (especially the Cubists) than from any composer, alive or dead. But his attitude in pursuing his chosen path towards ultimate simplicity, brevity and clarity of expression should be seen both as essentially French and as a positive achievement, however much rejection it entailed *en route*. Furthermore, it was an isolated path which Satie knew would engender much hostility, and his moral courage and self-sacrifice in pursuing it should compel admiration rather than pity.

Satie's own autobiographical sketches are couched in his customary ironical vein. Their tangential construction and refusal to elaborate mean that they offer little help towards establishing a definitive interpretation of his complex career. Yet the aggressive stance, the 'take-it-or-leave-it' attitude, confirm the presence of a character with extraordinary self-awareness who viewed his precursive art in all seriousness beneath the exterior humour. In his earliest sketch, made for his publisher Demets in 1913 (Ve, 142–3; W, 79), Satie 'classifies himself amongst the "fantaisistes"', that is, amongst the group of young poets (including Francis Carco and Tristan Klingsor) established around 1911 who were admirers of the irony and scepticism of Toulet and Laforgue, and such an extra-musical perspective is by no means uncommon. Satie continues, without any undue modesty, as follows:

> Short-sighted by birth, I am long-sighted by nature. . .We should not forget that the master is considered, by a great number of 'young' composers, as the precursor and apostle of the musical revolution now taking place. Messrs Maurice Ravel, E[mile] Vuillermoz, Robert Brussel, M[ichel]-D[imitri] Calvocoressi, J[ules] Ecorcheville, Roland-Manuel etc., present him as such, and what they say is based on facts beyond all challenge.

Lastly, to suggest how carefully considered his music was, Satie observes of the 'beautiful and limpid *Aperçus désagréables*' that their 'subtle composer is justified in declaring: "Before I write a piece, I walk round it several times, accompanied by myself."' A truly sculptural approach.

In his last autobiographical essay: 'Recoins de ma vie' (Ve, 25–7; W, 63–4), it is clear that the anti-French criticisms of *Parade* in 1917 still rankled in 1924, and that Satie was aware of the effects of his volatile temperament on others. How much his self-imposed privations for the sake of his music cost him can be seen beneath the ironical surface of the following extract:

> I lost no time in developing an unpleasant (*original*) originality, irrelevant, anti-French, unnatural etc.
>
> At that time, life became so impossible for me that I resolved to retire to my estates and pass the remainder of my days in an ivory tower – or one of some other (*metallic*) metal.
>
> That is why I acquired a taste for misanthropy; why I cultivated hypochondria; why I became the most miserable (*leaden*) of men. It upset people to look at me – even through hall-marked gold eye-glasses. Yes.
>
> And all this happened to me because of Music. That art has done me more harm than good: it has made me quarrel with many people of quality, most honourable, more-than-distinguished, awfully genteel people.

Two months later, Satie expanded on the role of music in his life with even greater seriousness:

> Music requires a great deal from those who wish to serve her. . .A true musician must be subjugated to his Art;. . .he must put himself above human miseries;. . . he must draw his courage from within himself,. . .from within himself alone.[1]

But in the last months of his life Satie was, in contrast, gleefully anticipating the scandal that *Relâche* would provoke, and drawing up battle positions against his now entrenched enemies Cocteau and Auric, and the newly-founded Surrealists, led by André Breton. 'With *Relâche* we are entering into a new period', he told Marcel

Raval on 21 October 1924. 'I say this immodestly, but I say it. . .Picabia is cracking the egg, and we shall set out "forward", leaving the Cocteaus and other "blinkered" people behind us' (Vl, 197).

All of this suggests that Satie saw his career in terms of either a single unbroken line based on what he had tried to achieve in music, or as a series of new departures with intervening periods spent in an anguished search for the right way forward. All that can safely be said is that he never looked backwards, and it is important to try to interpret his career from within, rather than with the judgment of hindsight. The latter can suggest an orderly succession of conventional periods, and I shall try to demonstrate how contradictory and confusing this approach can become.

If we take the new departure approach, Satie's career can be divided into as many as eleven sections, as follows:

1 1884–5. Salon music, loosely in the style of his step-mother Eugénie Barnetche.

2 1886–90. Harmonic experimentation inspired by Gregorian chant (*Ogives*), the use of unresolved sevenths and ninths in Chabrier's opera *Le Roi malgré lui* (*Sarabandes*), and Romanian folk music heard at the 1889 Exposition Universelle (*Gnossiennes*).

3 1891–5. Systematization of chord progressions and the juxtaposition of harmonic cells in the so-called Rose-Croix music (*Fête donnée par des Chevaliers Normands*; *Danses Gothiques* etc.).

4 1897. Greater rhythmic and textural flexibility, developing repetition on a broader basis (*Pièces froides*). This new departure was cut short by the upheaval of moving to Arcueil in 1898.

5 1898–1904. Search for a new direction to avoid the influence of Debussy (experimented with in *The Dreamy Fish*). The cabaret influence becomes more pervasive (*Jack-in-the-Box*). In his uncertainty Satie resorts to self-borrowing (*Trois Morceaux en forme de poire*). Although he described this last work as a 'prestigious turning-point in the History of My life' (on the Paris Opera MS, Rés. 218, 30), it was rather a summary of his achievements to date, and its lead was not followed up.

6 1905–12. Years of study at the Schola Cantorum lead to an increasing linear strength in the *Aperçus désagréables*, and the creation of the 'modern fugue' in *En Habit de cheval* (1911).

7 1912–15. 'Humoristic' piano pieces (*Véritables Préludes flasques* onwards). The rediscovery of Satie by Ravel in 1911 had led to the publication of his earlier music and, in 1913, a demand for new compositions.

8 1915–17. The discovery of Satie by Cocteau propels him further into the limelight and a career in the theatre. Association with Picasso brings Satie into close contact with Cubism in *Parade*. First *musique d'ameuble-ment* (1917). Satie now works mostly to commission as he broadens his range of social contacts.

9 1918–20. Increasing seriousness of purpose (*Socrate*), and a return to systematic composition (*Nocturnes*). Return to cabaret style in *La Belle Excentrique*.

10   1921–3. Satie works mostly on articles and the opera *Paul & Virginie*. Ballet plans with Derain and close involvement with the Dada movement.

11   1924. Return to the stage with *Mercure* and *Relâche* (new period).

In contrast, most writers on Satie divide his career into two, three, four or five main periods. Patrick Gowers heads the list with five, 'conveniently' corresponding to

> the decades of his life. In his 20s [1886–96] he wrote first the early piano works then the Rose+Croix music, in his 30s mainly cabaret music, in his 40s – after his time at the Schola – the 'humorous' piano music and in his 50s [1916f.] a suddenly far more varied output including the three main ballets, *Socrate*, songs and piano music.   (Gowers, 1980, vol. XVI, 517)

This interpretation has the merits of being clear-cut and memorable, but the major turning-points of the move to Arcueil and the rediscovery by Ravel both fall in mid-period, and the final period includes compositions as radically different as *Socrate* and *Relâche*.

Those favouring four periods include Wilfrid Mellers and William Gray Sasser. Mellers (1942, 215) places his divisions at 1900, 1908 and 1916, though he does attempt to relate them to the concepts of isolation and irony in Satie's life (ibid., 222). However, 1908 has no claim for special consideration other than being the year when Satie passed his counterpoint exam at the Schola Cantorum and began the *Aperçus désagréables*, and very little is known about his activities in 1900. Sasser makes the more conventional divisions of 1885–95, 1897–1911, 1912–15 and 1916–24 (1949, 139–45; 1952, 112–17), stressing that these represent different facets of the same, very diverse mind, with development being replaced by the metamorphosis, selection and elimination of stylistic elements as Satie's career proceeded. The second period is transitional rather than self-contained, and melodic considerations are seen to predominate over rhythm and harmony (with some justification).

The tripartite approach is chosen by Alfred Cortot (1938, repr. 1985, 56), in a parallel to Beethoven's career that Satie would have loathed. Cortot divides Satie's piano works (only) into a period of mysticism and medieval influences (1886–95), a mystifying and 'Chat Noiresque' period (1897–1915), and a period of 'musique d'ameublement' (1916–25). However, all this is not as unlikely as it may seem, for the classification of the final works as 'furniture music' has support from Satie himself.[2] He planned *Socrate* as such, for instance (Templier, 1969, 46), and by an extension of this principle there is a functional/sonorous background element to most of his non-descriptive theatre music, from the 'static sound décors' of *Le Fils des étoiles* (1891) onwards.

Louis Durey, an arch-enemy of Satie, also supports a three-period solution. In complete contrast to Sasser, Durey (1930, 163–4) claims that the first period (up to 1895) is 'characterized by harmonic preoccupations' with 'melodic ideas being almost non-existent'. (Perhaps he had forgotten the *Gymnopédies* and *Gnossiennes*?) This period was 'followed by a long silence' (again untrue) in which Satie 'perfected his *métier* at the Schola Cantorum'. After this his writing 'becomes melodic' suddenly – and vivacious and eccentric. But after the success of *Parade* in 1917 (the end of Durey's second period), he claims that Satie again lost his way, by trying 'to venture into serious music' with *Socrate* and the *Nocturnes*. These 'disclosed a paucity of means which in vain was described as simplification', and Satie only 'returned. . .to his true nature' with his final period ballets *Mercure* and *Relâche*. Here he recaptured the eccentric charm and humour of the 1912–15 piano pieces, which Durey obviously considered the zenith of his career.

Several writers divide Satie's career into two. His first biographer, Pierre-Daniel Templier, and the devoted researcher into all things Satiean, Ornella Volta, both favour the move from Montmartre to Arcueil in 1898: whereas the philosopher Vladimir Jankélévitch and the composer Charles Koechlin both vote for Satie's entrance to the Schola Cantorum in 1905, with the emphasis shifting from early mysticism to later mystification (see Jankélévitch, 1957, 188; Koechlin, 1927, 9, 18–19). Koechlin (1924, 195) considers the works of his first period to be mainly harmonic in origin, with the emphasis shifting towards counterpoint afterwards. Both 1898 and 1905 have their merits as bisecting points, though if I had to pick one it would be 1898.

A slightly different approach to the bi-partite view is taken by Roger Shattuck in *The Banquet Years*. Here he says that Satie enjoyed two *careers* as a composer, one in the nineteenth and the other in the twentieth century (after 1910) – his 'second coming'.[3] The 'essential unity' for Shattuck 'is always in the melodic line' (1952, 53), a view which is supported by Satie's compositional aesthetic of 1917. His hypothesis is also borne out by the fact that Satie's greatest crisis seems to have come in 1911, at precisely the moment when his music was rediscovered by Ravel. As he explained to his brother Conrad on 17 January, the day after Ravel's concert at the SMI:

> In 1905 I put myself to work with d'Indy. I was tired of being reproached with an ignorance of which I thought I must be guilty, since competent people pointed it out in my works.
>
> After three years of hard work I obtained from the Schola Cantorum my diploma in counterpoint, signed by my most excellent master, who is certainly the most knowledgeable and the best man in this world.
>
> Here I am then, in 1908, holding a certificate that gives me the title of con-trapuntist. Proud of my knowledge, I set to work to compose. My first work of this kind is a *Choral & fugue* for four hands [the *Aperçus désagréables*]. I have often been insulted in my poor life, but never was I so despised. What on earth had I been doing with d'Indy? The things I wrote before had such charm! Such depth! And now? How boring and uninteresting!
>
> Whereupon the 'Jeunes' mounted a campaign against d'Indy and played the *Sarabandes* and *Le Fils des étoiles*, and so on, works that were once considered the fruits of a profound ignorance – wrongly, according to these 'Jeunes'.
>
> That's life, *mon vieux*!
>
> It's total nonsense. (VI, 28)

The single line view, with or without detours, also finds several advocates, though the prevailing catalyst varies. For the composer Maxime Jacob (1930, 128–9), the thread of 'Christian sobriety' pervades all Satie's works in a spirit of humility and renunciation: whereas for the Normandy historian, André Bruyère (1970), Satie's childhood experiences in Honfleur conditioned the remainder of his career. Thus the teaching of the local organist M. Vinot (1874–8) fostered his lifelong love of Gregorian chant, whilst the architecture of the church of Saint-Léonard inspired Satie's meticulous Gothic calligraphy and the thousands of strange drawings that became his later obsession. Then, at the concerts of the Honfleur Philharmonic Society in the Town Hall, Satie would have heard numerous waltzes, some of them by Vinot himself, hence his enduring interest in dance music. Even more remarkably, Bruyère traces links between Honfleur street names and Satie's bizarre titles – like the *Croquis et agaceries d'un gros bonhomme en bois* (1913) and the rue Homme-de-Bois (which was adjacent to the rue Haute where Satie was born). But it is certainly true that our childhood experiences condition many of our tastes and outlooks in later life, and that Satie was fascinated by the world of children, so this hypothesis may not be as fanciful as it sounds.

Another single-line view comes from Marc Bredel's thought-provoking psychological investigation of Satie (1982, 157), which sees the 1886 *Ogives* as a blueprint for Satie's later career (coupled with the 'static sound décor' principle of *Le Fils des étoiles*). Rather than periods, Brédel maintains that there are two 'aspects' to Satie's career (ibid., 162): 'the esoteric – works composed from interior necessity; and the exoteric – more popular works written to earn a living'.

The interpretation of the American scholar Steven Moore Whiting also demands serious consideration (1984, 127, 202–8). This is that Satie's involvement with cabaret music and the world of Parisian Musical Entertainment runs as a continuous thread throughout his career. By focusing on what others bypassed, and by questioning the whole function of music and its relationship with the other arts and with society, Satie managed to convert popular music into a serious art and break down the barriers between the two. One problem here lies with the esoteric early works, but if we consider Gustave Doret's account (1942, 98) of Satie performing his wierd ballet *Uspud* as a hilarious entertainment at the Auberge du Clou in the 1890s, or using his *Gnossiennes* to accompany shadow theatre spectacles at the Chat Noir, everything begins to make more sense. And we have seen how Satie's *Gymnopédies* came into being to justify his introduction to Rodolphe Salis as 'Erik Satie – gymnopédiste' when he sought employment at the Chat Noir in 1887. After the move to Arcueil in 1898, Satie still remained actively involved with the cabaret world (to earn a meagre living) until at least 1909, accompanying popular singers like Vincent Hyspa and Paulette Darty at venues such as La Boîte à Fursy and La Lune Rousse. Indeed, he was known to his friends in Arcueil as a writer of popular songs rather than as a serious composer, and the thread can be seen extending in various forms in his later career. Firstly, his 'humorous' piano pieces of 1912–15 make extensive use of thematic quotations from popular operettas, folksongs, and popular and military tunes. Secondly, he told the composer Robert Caby that he saw *Parade* as being set in a cabaret, or 'boîte', with the later addition of the opening Chorale as being like opening up that same 'box' to reveal the entertainment inside.[4] Thirdly, we find Satie using popular dance-forms like the waltz and cancan in *La Belle Excentrique* in 1920, and both his final ballets *Mercure* and *Relâche* employ a music-hall idiom, the latter quoting popular songs like 'The Turnip-Vendor' and 'Cadet Rousselle'.

The only possible flaw with this interpretation is that Satie apparently hated being forced to earn his living in the 1900s from cabaret work. He told Conrad[5] in the same letter of January 1911 quoted earlier that he had now 'renounced' this work. The *Café-concert* 'was no field for me to be working in. It is more stupid and dirty than anything' (Vl, 27). But this surely refers to the necessity Satie had had to face over some twenty years of working in a milieu that showed no regard for the serious art that was his main priority. Neither does it rule out his taking the accessibility of the *Café-concert* and elevating it to a higher artistic level. In addition, this particular letter shows Satie in a particularly despondent and confused state as to his future, and it should not be taken as the gospel truth with regard to his whole career in popular entertainment. He undoubtedly enjoyed the Bohemian life in and around the Montmartre cabarets, and it was there that his friendship with Debussy began. So we should not easily assume that cabaret work suddenly became (and continued to be) painful to him after the move to Arcueil, however much his seriousness of intent had increased in the interim. Perhaps the true thinking behind this 1911 letter lay in the inevitable recognition that he had wasted so much valuable time in the directionless years around the turn of the century, and reflects his frustration in knowing that his uncompromising and precursive art was always destined to be misunderstood.

Obviously, all these manifold interpretations of Satie's enigmatic career contain elements of truth, even if none of them represents the complete answer. Thus, to a certain degree, they are complementary and interdependent. There is certainly a cabaret thread running through a complex career that does broadly sub-divide at the move to Arcueil in 1898, even if Satie did not find his true direction again until the *Véritables Préludes flasques* of 1912. Whilst only the eleven-point 'new departure' approach given earlier takes every aspect into account, it is too complex to be my final choice. My own view is that Satie's career must be seen as a single span whose unconventional direction was determined by his continual rethinking of the whole aim and aesthetic of music as a reaction to nineteenth-century practice and excesses. A natural tendency towards simplification, succinctness and economy underlies all his work, rather than any desire to make a virtue of his technical limitations. With an enviable talent for self-publicity, Satie made a positive and quick response to the changing circumstances in which he found himself, always contriving to stay one step ahead of his potential rivals and remain the instigator of new ideas. He was extremely sensitive to prevailing social and artistic conditions, and, being intensely self-critical, he published only what he considered appropriate for a particular time. As he moved politically further and further to the left, so, paradoxically, his contacts and commissions with high society grew, much to his delight. As the self-appointed guardian of the avant-garde, the personification of the post-war *esprit nouveau*, Satie rejected all concepts of music as bourgeois entertainment, and in later life he set out deliberately to shock and scandalize his audiences in an uncompromising and aggressive manner that was far from being the result of an inferiority complex. As he explained in 1922 to Henry Prunières, the editor of *La Revue musicale*, he belonged to the generation of his music, and anyone who did not take him seriously was beneath contempt.

2

Why and where Satie composed

'Work is not always as unpleasant as books maintain', Satie told André Derain in September 1921 (Vc), in an effort to stimulate some action on their ballet *La Naissance de Vénus*. Since *Parade*, Satie had instigated numerous ballet projects with Diaghilev's Ballets Russes in mind, both because he was stimulated by the fusion of the arts in the theatre and because Diaghilev allowed him financial advances on projects in hand. We know this through a letter from Satie to Diaghilev in April 1924 asking him when he can draw on the account for the ballet *Quadrille* (planned with Georges Braque) and how much the 'advance' is likely to be. That few of his plans materialized was not Satie's fault, for he thrived on such projects and the artistic and social opportunities they provided. The fact that the majority of the letters concerning these projects come from the summer months shows that the annual exodus of his wealthier friends for the South of France left Satie lonely and depressed in dingy Arcueil. The demand for his music dried up and so did the loans he relied on to keep body and soul together. In such moments he often questioned why he composed at all and his anger at what music had done to him often bursts forth in his wartime summer letters. His morale reached its nadir on 23 August 1918 when he complained to Valentine Gross that 'I am suffering too much. It seems to me that I am cursed. I loathe this beggar's life. I am looking for and want to find a position, an employment, however menial. I *shit* on Art: it has "cut me up" too often. It's a mug's game – if I may say so. . . For the last month and more I haven't been able to write a note.'[1]

But if we compare this with Satie's frame of mind when he began *Socrate*, the picture on 18 January 1917 is altogether different, especially as the Princesse de Polignac had that day sent him an advance on her far-sighted commission. Again he writes to Valentine Gross: 'I'm working on the "Life of Socrates" [the original title]. I found a fine translation. Victor Cousin's. Plato is a perfect collaborator, very gentle and never troublesome. It's a dream!. . .I'm swimming in happiness. At last, I'm free, free as air, as water, as the wild sheep. Long live Plato! Long live Victor Cousin! I'm free! Very free! What happiness!' (Vl, 154).

These two letters should be taken as extremes of Satie's mercurial temperament. The intervening norm (if Satie could ever be described as normal) was one of constant hard work – drafting, honing down and polishing his music with meticulous care.

For Satie composed from an inner necessity, because he never seriously considered anything other than a life devoted to music. All he wished for was the freedom to compose what he wanted when he wanted, without material constraints, though the coincidence of all these ideal factors in *Socrate* was a rare event. If his financial irresponsibility only made matters worse, his precarious situation channelled his inventive mind into numerous projects as a result, for he was only truly happy when he was creative and there was a demand for his music. In short, when the way forward was clear to him.

It might also be said that Satie composed to attract attention to himself, for he thrived on notoriety and the maxim that 'there is no such thing as bad publicity'. However much he put on a brave face in public, his letters show that he hated being completely isolated for even a few days, and his uncompromising independence was only maintained at great personal cost. He welcomed artistic liaisons with flamboyant catalysts like Péladan, Jules Bois, Cocteau and Diaghilev and was probably fascinated by their immorality, however much he disapproved of it. When such links were not forthcoming, he generated his own publicity – as with the foundation of the Eglise Métropolitaine d'Art (1893–5) and his successful attempt to get his ballet *Uspud* considered for the Paris Opéra (by challenging the director, Eugène Bertrand, to a duel!). As a larger-than-life, theatrical personality he always needed to have some stage project in the offing, and in the days before television and cinema the theatre offered the greatest source of potential income for a composer. But together with his financial irresponsibility there was a bizarre streak of deliberate impracticality in Satie, and his refusal to compose descriptive music to correspond with given dramatic situations meant that none of his projects in the 1890s reached the stage. As his technique improved, it naturally became more flexible, but Satie still refused to allow the theatre to dictate terms to him and his prime concerns were the integrity of his own contribution and that it should contradict traditional expectations.

Another potential source of income was the popular song. But despite his quarter-century association with the cabarets of Montmartre (and its continuing influence on his mature music), Satie wrote relatively few original songs for this medium. Such pieces as there are belong to the years of directional uncertainty between 1897 and 1910, and mostly predate his enrolment at the Schola Cantorum in 1905. Thus, as Steven Whiting has shown (1984, 200–2), out of around 100 songs in the Harvard sketchbooks, only 28 are even likely to be original creations. And despite Satie's literary talents, only one (*Sorcière*) has a text that could be by Satie. The rest of the songs are arrangements or transpositions of works by other composers (like Paul Delmet), or of the popular tunes to which Vincent Hyspa fitted his topical ditties. For when Satie accompanied Hyspa in his engagements around the turn of the century, he seems not to have trusted his pianistic abilities in the alcoholic ambience of the *Café-concert*. Indeed, it is reported that Satie had to be locked in his room before such performances so as to remain sober. When Hyspa published his collection of fifty-one *Chansons d'humour* in 1903, only one (*Un Dîner à l'Elysée*) had music by Satie (on pp. 107–13). Thus, fulfilling a demand for cabaret music does not seem to be a valid reason why

Satie composed, and in my opinion it is of lesser importance than, say, the desire to be chic and 'Parisian' that recurs increasingly in his letters of the 1920s as he revelled in his new high society contacts.

Certainly, Satie found nothing in Arcueil to inspire him. While struggling with his opera *Paul & Virginie*, he again complained to Derain in September 1921 about the endless tedium of life in Arcueil; the daily routine of coming and going with nothing really interesting to nurture the original voice he was seeking. His depressing conclusions were that ignorance was bliss in bygone days and that progress was not necessarily beneficial.

So, to a large extent, composition must also have provided a means of escape for Satie; from everyday philistinism and all that he saw as being wrong in an immoral, materialistic society, as much as from his own highly-principled, but miserable hermeticism. His ivory tower remained impregnable only at a terrible personal cost, and his exquisite calligraphy, his obsessional drawings and devising of compositional systems, must have arisen as much from a need to fill lonely hours as from a desire to create beauty amidst ugliness and squalor. His frequent rages were, I suspect, the outward evidence of an inner compositional block – for the quantity of sketches he made far outweighs his published works. He found completing pieces far harder than starting them, and when his path forward became clear in composition after 1912, so his work rate intensified in parallel.

From the evidence of his pianist friend, Jean Wiéner, we know just how slowly Satie worked in producing calligraphic miracles that were designed as much for the eye as for the ear. 'His writing is a testimony in itself', Wiéner says (20 July 1945, 4).

> Total perfection; but it took him a good twenty minutes to write a six-line post-card. . .It happened that Satie, being at my house, wanted to write something after dinner. I left him alone (with a bottle of fine champagne nearby). . .Over half an hour afterwards, he had only started to write the address, and more often than not, it was only a question of a few lines to cancel a dinner engagement.

If fellow composers like Koechlin and Fauré were proud of their increased speed of working in later life, Satie's concern for visual perfection remained with him to the end. He first met Wiéner in 1919, so the incident he described must have taken place when Satie was in his mid-fifties. The laborious production of his scores must have taken even longer and became an end in itself, inseparable from the minute care of the compositional process. Satie admitted his slowness of composition to Bertrand Guégan, the editor of the *Almanach de Cocagne*, in November 1919. When Guégan sent him a poem to set for publication in his journal, Satie had to disappoint him because such a deeply-felt piece required much time for contemplation and could not be composed according to the time-scale he imposed.[2] It must also be said that both Satie's letters and scores, however obsessional in their neatness, still contain both corrected and unspotted errors. The very last bar Satie wrote, for instance, in the November 1924 film score of *Cinéma*,[3] contains a glaring and unintentional dissonance through a missing C♯ in the viola part in a chord of A major.

Other inner reasons why Satie composed will doubtless emerge as more is discovered about the workings of his intricate mind, but this question is far less problematic than unravelling the mysteries of where and how he composed. How Satie composed will, I hope, gradually become clear from the subsequent detailed examples which are the *raison d'être* of this study, but the 'where' question will be discussed in the remainder of this chapter.

Apart from his earliest composition, a brief Allegro for piano written on a return visit to Honfleur in September 1884, all Satie's works were written in Paris or Arcueil. The early works up to the *Sarabandes* of September 1887 were composed at his parents' homes in the rue de Marseille (1885) and the boulevard Magenta (1886–7). Both his father Alfred and his step-mother Eugénie Satie-Barnetche were salon composers of a reasonable standard, and Alfred Satie ran a small music-publishing business under whose aegis Satie's *Valse-ballet* and *Fantaisie-valse* for piano appeared in 1887.[4] Satie's brief flirtation with bourgeois salon music in 1885 may reflect a desire to please his parents. It was the sort of music he knew his father would publish, though, to give him his due, Alfred Satie also brought out Erik's five settings of the poetry of his friend Contamine de Latour[5] in 1887–8 and even the first *Gymnopédie*.[6] Here the widely-diverging opus numbers (19–20, 52 and 62 for the earliest *Valse-ballet*) should not be taken as deliberate hoaxes (see Gillmor, 1983, 109), for his step-mother displayed the same blithe disregard for chronology. Her *Brise du soir. Nocturne* published in 1883, for instance, is 'Op. 87', whereas her *Rêverie* (1888) is 'Op. 66'. All the inflated opus numbers were probably Alfred Satie's responsibility, to make his family appear more prolific and experienced than they actually were.

As soon as he could, and reputedly in the wake of an affair with a family maid, Satie left home, probably in December 1887. With 1,600 francs from his father he rented a large room at 50 rue Condorcet, Paris 9, very close to the Chat Noir cabaret where he soon gained employment as conductor of the orchestra. At the rue Condorcet Satie certainly had room for a piano, for on 20 July 1889 he advertised as a 'past pupil at the Conservatoire' for pupils to participate in 'piano classes at his home'.[7] In later life, however, such piano lessons as Satie gave were all at the homes of his pupils.[8] Here, in the shadow of La Butte Montmartre, Satie composed his three *Gymnopédies* in February–April 1888, spending much of the money his father had given him on private publications of his third *Gymnopédie* in 1888[9] and his four *Ogives* in 1889.[10] He must have retained fairly close links with his father at this time, for both editions employed his father's printers, the Imprimerie Dupré at 26 rue du Delta, Paris 9, who may also have offered him favourable terms.

Early in 1890, however, straitened financial circumstances forced Satie to move to a smaller second-floor room at 6 rue Cortot, high in La Butte Montmartre, and 'out of reach of [his] creditors' (Latour, 3 Aug 1925, 2). Here, surrounded by only 'a bench, a table and a chest' (Templier, 1969, 13), his Rose-Croix compositions emerged, including the nine *Danses Gothiques* written between 21 and 23 March 1893 'for the greater calm and tranquillity of my soul' during his tempestuous and brief affair with his neighbour, the painter Suzanne Valadon. Satie's spartan domestic circumstances were hardly more conducive to romance than they were to composition, but on a clear day he claimed he could see as far as the Belgian frontier from his window. He slept on a home-made bed consisting of three boards mounted on a trestle base (Latour, 5 Aug 1925, 3), and Santiago Rusiñol's painting of the room in 1890 shows an understandably despondent Satie sitting by an empty grate, 'au coin de son froid' as Satie put it (Fig. 2.1). Accounts vary as to whether Satie took his piano

2.1   Satie 'au coin de son froid' in his first room at 6 rue Cortot, Montmartre. Oil painting (*El estudi de Erik Satie à Montmartre, 1890*) by Santiago Rusiñol. Coll. Juan Maragall.

with him to the rue Cortot. Latour (5 Aug 1925, 3) says he did, but never played it, whereas Florent Schmitt (1913, 11) claims he never had one at all during this period. Therefore

> he usually went to his friends' homes to give himself the pleasure of hearing his music other than in his head after his long and studious composing sessions in his rooms. Thus it was that the *Gymnopédies* and *Gnossiennes* were revealed to me, and I was present when he played his first sketches for *Le Fils des étoiles* [1891].

As Satie composed entirely in his head, and there is no evidence of his ever revising a composition to make it more pianistic, it is of lesser concern than one might imagine whether he had a piano or not. He may have used the instrument to explore chordal progressions, and he certainly seems to have been anxious to play through works to friends, but the only record of him using a piano at all during composition comes in 1924, as we shall see, and here it was probably more a question of trying out completed passages of *Relâche* than of actually composing at the piano à la Stravinsky. Although he must have had a reasonable technique, his unpleasant years at the Conservatoire resulted in his playing the piano as little as possible in later life.[11] No artist's impression of his room in the 1890s reveals a piano and the only picture of Satie playing in this period (Fig. 2.2) shows him at the harmonium: an instrument he probably preferred, and for which his block-like sonorities for *Uspud* may well have been devised in 1892.

In July 1896, financial problems again forced Satie into an even smaller room at 6 rue Cortot, for which he paid his landlord (M. Bibet) 20 francs a quarter instead of 35 francs 10 centimes. This tiny ground floor room Satie called the 'placard' or cupboard – or ironically 'Notre Abbatiale', when issuing his edicts as the self-appointed 'parcier' of the Eglise Métropolitaine d'Art. It measured a mere 6 feet by 4 feet 6 inches and was 9 feet high (Latour, 5 Aug 1925, 3), with only a tiny triangular skylight to illuminate it. Here there was certainly no room for a piano, and Satie's bed and chest even prevented the door from opening: indeed, such visitors as Satie allowed to enter the room had to climb over the bed to get in. But Satie still took his portraits by Zuloaga, Comte Antoine de La Rochefoucauld, Marcellin Desboutin, Georges de Feure and Valadon with him, and gave pride of place to the gilded mirror that can be seen in Figure 2.1. 'At night', Latour recalls (ibid.), 'Satie heaped all the clothes he had onto his counterpane to keep warm, and stayed dressed down to his boots.' There does not even seem to have been room for Satie's table, but he still did the bulk of his composition here, for Schmitt recalls that 'one of the shelves served him as a writing-desk, and as an altar' for his Eglise Métropolitaine (see VI, 69). Understandably, he wrote little during this period (1896–8) but it was in these circumstances that his *Pièces froides* were written, whose title was by no means inappropriate.

Given his domestic privations, it is easy to see why Satie spent so much time at the homes of friends, and he may even have composed there too. The painter Augustin Grass-Mick recalls (1950, 7) that Satie worked at his friend Henry Pacory's home at 22 rue la Boétie, Paris 8 during this period, when the trio were inseparable. Every

2.2   Satie playing the harmonium. Charcoal drawing (*Erik Satie tocando el harmonium, 1891*) by Santiago Rusiñol, now in the Museo de Arte Moderno, Barcelona.

Friday lunchtime in the later 1890s found Satie at the bachelor flat of his friend Debussy where he was often entertained with eggs and lamb cutlets. Debussy 'possessed the secret (*the most absolute secret*) of these preparations', Satie later wrote (Ve, 51), though satisfying Satie's prodigious appetite cannot have been an easy task.

As a gourmet, he preferred simple, well-cooked dishes, but according to his brother Conrad (with whom he dined on Sundays) he could demolish 150 oysters or an omelette made of 30 eggs at a single sitting! Afterwards Debussy 'would spend whole afternoons' studying Satie's barless sketches in the 1890s, according to René Peter (1944, 71), and he frequently gave him advice about his work. Whilst Satie could in reality compose anywhere, as we shall see, the bulk of his composition before the move to Arcueil seems to have been done at his own homes in the 1890s, with visits to friends providing vital diversion and a place to discuss his works in progress.

But by 1898 Satie knew that the temptations of Bohemian life in Montmartre were impeding his composing career, and he felt the need to 'withdraw completely' and begin anew. So one afternoon in October 1898, Pacory, Grass-Mick and Satie travelled to the suburb of Arcueil-Cachan where his friends helped him rent a large second-floor room at 22 (now 34) rue Cauchy, which then overlooked 'a cottage and some trees' (Grass-Mick, 1950, 7). The location was not arrived at entirely by chance, for Pacory was born there, and the room was taken over from an alcoholic celebrity of Montmartre, Bibi-la-Purée (André Salis), a relative of Rodolphe Salis, the phlegmatic 'bonimenteur' of Le Chat Noir. Contemporary pictures in the Musée du Vieux Montmartre show a dignified tramp with an umbrella,[12] but Bibi-la-Purée was a friend of Verlaine, whose portrait was painted by Picasso and Jacques Villon – probably due to his notoriety as the 'roi de la Bohème'. He seems to have had some fairly disgusting habits, for Satie was forced into domesticity for the only known time in his life to make his new lodgings at the Maison des Quatres Cheminées habitable. As he told his brother Conrad on 8 November 1898: 'I'm here now to rub down the floor of my room with washing soda and anoint it with soft soap; when this task is completed I shall wax the aforesaid floor myself' (VI, 71). At first, Satie only spent odd nights in Arcueil, when he was attacked by 'mosquitoes, certainly sent by the Freemasons' (ibid.). Later in November, his 'pictures, mattress, chest and bench' arrived by handcart from Montmartre, with the 'precious' items following in December. But Satie was frequently back in Paris, collaborating on theatrical projects like *Jack-in-the-Box* with Dépaquit and *Geneviève de Brabant* with Latour, which occupied much of 1899.

Somehow, from somewhere, Satie acquired two grand pianos for his new room, which he placed one on top of the other, the upper one being used as a post-box for unsolicited letters and parcels. A narrow passage with a wash-basin led into the room, though Satie had to fetch any water he needed from a 'fountain in the Place des Ecoles' nearby (Templier, 1969, 26), and he rather used the passage to store the gymnastic equipment he used to keep fit. Satie soon covered up his window to keep out both the mosquitoes and the prying gaze of curious neighbours (with binoculars), and over the next quarter-century the only living beings to penetrate his bizarre sanctuary were the occasional stray dogs Satie took pity on. No further cleaning seems to have taken place, and nothing was thrown out. As Satie was a compulsive hoarder, by the time of his death the room had become an indescribable, filthy labyrinth with enough rubbish to fill two cart-loads. To judge from the reports of those who entered it in October 1925, Bibi-la-Purée's occupancy must have been like the Ideal Home Exhibition by comparison! Although Satie's precious paintings were protected by bits of newspaper, his images had become invisible beneath the grime. There were canes, old hats, shoes, wing collars, newspapers, scores and books (with dedications from friends like Péladan, Debussy, Ravel and Cocteau) everywhere. The seven identical dun-coloured velvet suits he had bought from a small inheritance in 1895 were piled on top of an empty wardrobe, whose significance in Satie's wierd existence is anyone's guess. Bredel (1982, 79) suggests that Satie may have meditated inside it, or that it was somehow linked to his fascination with magic, ritual, sorcerers and things occult that so often surfaces in his drawings and writings. The miracle is that Satie emerged each day immaculately dressed, 'as an actor steps out of the wings' (Shattuck, 1968, 181), and rumour had it that he enjoyed a long-standing affair with a laundress in Montparnasse and did not return to Arcueil as often as he claimed. Certainly it is difficult to imagine how he kept his scores and even his sketchbooks so clean if he did indeed work much in Arcueil, and the picture in reality was a sad and far cry from the cosy domesticity of Satie's drawing on a letter to Cocteau in 1917 shown on the cover of this book. The clean table must have been as much of a myth as the caged bird and the cat, though the last two may well have been symbolic. And even here Satie is dreaming rather than composing, perhaps of an ideal existence. For he often referred ironically to his servants and his estates in letters, and despite his extreme left-wing views his vision was of a luxurious, ordered existence. His drawings are full of châteaux and castles, worlds away from his self-imposed prison in Arcueil. When Georges Auriol met him in February 1924 and asked if he was still living there, Satie replied (1924, 216): 'Alas yes, my good friend. . .I am searching in vain in Paris. I need something enormous, you understand. . .30 rooms at least. I have so many ideas to accommodate!' While Satie may have joked to the last, there is still a pathetic element in his intransigence; in his inability to realize even the least part of his escapist vision. One might say that he only ever travelled to Brussels and Monte Carlo because he was so poor and because his work always came first. But for so progressive a composer there was a curiously insular and conservative streak in Satie's mentality. He hated travel and upheaval as much as he hated the telephone and other modern inventions. He never sought to record his music for posterity (as Debussy and Fauré did), he never possessed a radio or listened to one, and he even refused to use the Métro. In short, his essential world idealized the medieval past rather than the present or the future, and he showed an unexpected distrust of modern technology and the conventional concept of progress. Only as far as music was concerned did he have a futuristic vision, which more than compensated for his other deficiencies.

What then did Satie actually create in the squalor of his room in Arcueil? Firstly, his thousands of exquisite drawings on little cards, which he stored in old cigar boxes. Secondly, his articles, for we know from a letter to Constantin Brancusi that he stayed up all night recopying his article on Debussy for *Vanity Fair* on 24 August 1922.

As he reckoned on finishing 'around 7 a.m.' on the 25th, and as the article covers only eleven small quarto pages (Ve, 264), Satie could therefore still only produce about one page of calligraphed prose an hour, even when working flat out to gain money. Thirdly, some of the neat drafts of his scores, for several of these are signed and dated in Arcueil in the early 1900s. And this might well extend to the later theatrical scores written to meet deadlines on which he mentions working 'day and night' – like the orchestral scores for *Le Médecin malgré lui*, *Mercure*, *Relâche* and *Cinéma* in 1923–4. Indeed, we know he worked on *Relâche* in Arcueil, for his concierge was disturbed by Satie playing one of his apparently unserviceable pianos there during the night in the summer of 1924.[13]

So where did Satie jot down his initial ideas, and where did he work them into shape? One answer is during his daily six-mile walks from Arcueil to Paris and back – which included many stops in cafés *en route*. According to Apollinaire (cited in Volta, 1979, 128), Satie composed mostly at night, stopping beneath each street lamp to write down the ideas that came to him, in pencil, in the little folded notebooks he carried in his overcoat pocket. As Satie's initial ideas (especially after 1913) often took the form of simple melodies or arpeggios in straightforward rhythms, this is perfectly feasible. The individuality, residing in the harmony and texture, could be carefully realized later on. In 1918, the *Mercure de France* even explained that Satie's musical productivity had been retarded during the war because most of the street lamps had been put out in the necessary restrictions (ibid.). Perhaps the most celebrated account of Satie's nocturnal creation comes from the poet Blaise Cendrars (1952, 209–10), who found the composer recumbent at the foot of the Obelisk in the Place de la Concorde during a night of heavy bombardment on 13 March 1918.

> I stooped over him, thinking him dead. 'What are you doing there?' I asked him. He replied: 'I know very well that it's ridiculous and that I'm not in a shelter. But what do you know, this thing shot up in the air and I had the sensation of being at the shelter. Then I wrote some music for the Obelisk. . . It's music for the lady Pharaoh who is buried below. No-one ever thinks of her. It took this ghastly bombardment to bring me here; for the first time. Not a bad story, eh?' And he sniggered, with his hand over his beard, as he often did, his wicked eyes examining the monument. . . 'Do you know who is buried here?' I asked Satie. 'It seems it's the mummy of Cleopatra. At least, that's what I heard.' 'You don't say so', Satie replied. 'In that case I was right to write her a bit of music. Listen:
>
> Ta, tarâ, ta, ta, ta, ta, ta,
>
> Ta, tarâ, ta, ta, ta, ta. . .
>
> Fa, do-ô, sol, ré, la, mi, si – Fa, do-ô, sol, ré, la, mi.'

The result may have been something like Ex. 1, if the story is true. I have found no sign of this little march in Satie's sketchbooks, but he was preoccupied with the perfect fourth and fifth at the time of *Socrate*, so this typically bizarre anecdote cannot be so easily dismissed.

If we consider the effect of walking on Satie the composer, some fascinating possibilities emerge. Roger Shattuck, in conversation with John Cage and Alan Gillmor

Ex. 1 Music for the mummy of Cleopatra (1918)

(Cage, 1982, 25), whilst discussing the effect of deliberate boredom in Satie's music, put forward his 'pet theory' that

> the source of this in Satie, as it may have been in quite different terms in Wordsworth or Rimbaud, is the act of walking. Satie walked endlessly across Paris. . .Someone calculated that Wordsworth in his lifetime walked 24,000 good English miles. . . And Rimbaud walked everywhere; Vachel Lindsey, Mayakovsky, and there are many other instances. These are all poets or musicians who composed while putting one foot in front of the other in a fairly boring, if you want, physical act, which nevertheless has its relationship to the heart-beat and the universe. . .I think that the source of Satie's sense of musical beat – the possibility of variation within repetition, the effect of boredom on the organism – may be this endless walking back and forth across the same landscape day after day, and finally taking it all in, which is basically what Thoreau did: the total observation of a very limited and narrow environment.

This line of reasoning has much to commend it, for almost all Satie's pre-Arcueil music has a slow, or very slow, pulse while the faster, more mechanical regularity all belongs to the latter half of his career. *Parade,* with its constant pulse of seventy-six beats per minute, may thus reflect Satie's walking speed in 'slow. . .deliberate steps' (Templier, 1969, 56) as much as the human heart-beat. If Satie rarely spoke about his music to others, it must have been constantly evolving and processing itself in his mind (I should love to know in how many parts), and its absence of expressiveness and sentimentality surely reflects the drab and often dangerous areas through which he walked – 'the uncivilized quarters of la Glacière and la Santé' (Auriol, 1924, 211), or the 'smelly tanneries of Gentilly' (Templier, 1969, 22–3). Satie had an intimate knowledge of the history of old Paris, and his varied music was at one with the environments in which he moved, from the Montmartre cabarets, through the cafés of Montparnasse, to the sheer ordinariness of the long walk home through the industrialized areas in the early hours.

The elaboration of initial ideas with novel harmonic progressions must have taken place during the daytime when Satie's mind was fresher. The daily walk into Paris was a more leisurely affair, with extended pauses in favourite cafés for refreshment and composition, before Satie began the series of meetings, visits and meals in the afternoon and evening which he had arranged beforehand by letter. Much of his music was composed *chez* Tulard, a small, inexpensive café opposite the church in Arcueil. Satie transferred his allegiance there shortly after 1900 when the attentions of 'old Mother Geng' at the first cheap restaurant he chose proved too distracting to his work (Templier, 1969, 26). *Chez* Tulard, Satie had a regular table set aside, complete with the red and black inks he used at this period, and here many of his works, from *The Dreamy Fish* onwards were composed. Indeed, the neat copies marked 'Arcueil' may have originated here too, or in the bistro below his room in the rue Cauchy. As far as the notebooks were concerned, Satie's first thoughts went down in pencil, being inked over in black when Satie was sure of his inspiration. If the work was to be published he made a neat printer's copy, often in another notebook, for he preferred not to mix works from one book to another. Usually, only works for larger forces were copied on separate sheets of manuscript paper, as Satie's music was for the most part expressible on the six or seven staves his oblong notebooks offered (right up to the orchestral drafts of *Parade* and *Socrate*). The absence of food and drink stains throughout his manuscripts reflects their importance to him and the care he took over their visual appearance.[14] Templier (1969, 35), from evidence given him by Conrad Satie, says that most of the 1913–14 piano pieces (including the *Croquis et agaceries*, the *Embryons desséchés* and the *Sports et divertissements*) were composed here too, and he implies that Satie sometimes stayed *chez* Tulard most of the day.

> He would arrive at about eleven in the morning, drink a beer, smoke his cigars, chat with the other clients and suddenly bring from his pocket one of his little notebooks. Oblivious to all, he would slowly cover the score with well-formed notes. Friends would greet him, but he would not answer; yet the next day he would seriously accuse them of bad manners.

If Satie had afternoon appointments in Paris, he would move on more quickly. He hated sunshine,[15] and bad weather was a positive encouragement to him.

> At Verrières, during a certain period of Satie's life, the owner of a wine shop would always say to his wife, whenever the weather looked bad: 'Today, it will rain all day; doubtless we shall see the gentleman of Arcueil.' At noon, Satie would appear under his umbrella. (ibid., 57)

He may have composed here too.

Once in Paris, Satie patronized various establishments at different times, depending on his current friends and artistic interests. When he was not composing he was a lively conversationalist, and café society kept him up to date with the latest ideas and gossip. Although he died from cirrhosis of the liver and drank increasingly as he grew older, Cocteau rightly maintained that 'alcohol had no effect on his work' (Ve, 262). The only time he went 'over the top' was during New Year's Eve festivities in the 1920s. On 31 December 1921 he apologized to the Comte de Beaumont for missing his evening party, since post-prandial drinking at a Paris café had temporarily incapacitated him. But the fact that Satie carefully wrote the letter that evening means that he was never out of control, and the likelihood is that he preferred drinking informally with friends to a smart society party. He must have varied his drinks as much as his venues, for his favourite tipples vary between accounts. Auric says 'he boldly mixed beer and calvados' (1952, 122); Robert Caby says kirsch was his favourite (1929, 5);

whereas Sauguet says it was mixing eau-de-vie and beer that killed him (1983, 248). Satie also liked cognac and wine, and his main lament was that 'one finds in every bar people willing to treat you to a glass, but none of them will think of lining your stomach with a sandwich!' (Lanser, 1925). Thus, although Satie maintained in his 1922 article 'Painful Examples' (Ve, 56–8; W, 121–2) that he preferred brasseries (pubs), and advised young people not to frequent cafés, he admitted that 'I have done a lot of work there.' And he listed creators like Villon, Boileau and La Fontaine amongst the 'many famous people who have not wasted their time there'. Racine, for instance, wrote *Les Plaideurs* in the tavern '*Bouteille d'Or* in the place du Cimetière-Saint-Jean (now the site of the Lobau barracks)', and if this sort of behaviour was good enough for Racine, it was certainly good enough for him.

The other locale where we know Satie composed was Le Lion, a café-tabac in the place Denfert-Rochereau in Montparnasse. Here, Pierre de Massot says (1952, 125–6), Satie wrote much of *Parade* in 1916–17, and Satie's letters to Jean Guérin imply that he also worked on his recitatives for *Le Médecin malgré lui* here in September 1923. So it is reasonable to suppose that Satie also composed there in the interim, and he may well have had a table ready prepared for him there too (as he had *chez* Tulard). Other favourite cafés in this period include Spielmann's (1914f.), La Rotonde (a meeting place for the Cubists around 1916) and, in the 1920s, *chez* Graff (rue Saint-Lazare), Les Deux Mégots (place St-Germain-des-Prés), Le Bœuf sur le Toit (rue Boissy-d'Anglas) and Le Petit Napolitain (boulevard Montparnasse). But the list is endless and there is no specific information as to whether Satie composed in any or all of these. Understandably, he did not work in restaurants, but he often dined with friends like Pierre de Massot and his wife Robbie at venues such as the Grill-Room Medicis, Le Nègre de Toulouse (boulevard Montparnasse), Le Pied de Mouton (near the Gare d'Austerlitz) and *chez* Stryx (rue Huyghens), most of them appropriately near the Gare de Scéaux where Satie would try to catch his last (00.50) train back to Arcueil, if indeed he did always return there.

In reality, as we have seen, Satie could and did compose anywhere. In his pre-Arcueil years he wrote mainly in his lodgings, but after 1898 a pattern built up of notating ideas at night on foot which he then worked on in cafés during the daytime. Obviously, this is only a partial picture and I shall welcome more information on the subject. But it is safe to say that the café was the lifeblood of Satie's existence, rather than one of the 'seven deadly sins' that it represented for Péladan and his Rosicrucian circle.[16]

3

Parody, pastiche, quotation and the question of influences

In *Le Chapelier* (1916), Satie gently parodies the 'Chanson de Magali' from Gounod's opera *Mireille*[1] by adapting its melody to René Chalupt's own adaptation of an episode from The Mad Hatter's Tea-Party in Lewis Carroll's *Alice in Wonderland*.[2] Not only did the double adaptation and the incongruity of the text appeal to Satie the humorist, but he was also 'composing' an imitation of an imitation, for Gounod's celebrated duet was itself based on a Provençal folksong 'O Magali, ma bien-aimée'. Even though the choice of the 'genre Gounod' was an afterthought (like so many of Satie's best ideas), his delight in the artificial here offers a rare parallel with Ravel. Satie's first action was to set Chalupt's poem entirely to the notes of the F major arpeggio in a mechanical manner, as Ex. 2 shows, with the ticking watch reflected in the staccato

Ex. 2 *Le Chapelier*. First version, bars 1–7 (BN 9581, 16–17)

21

chords of the piano accompaniment. This type of melodic line seems to have fascinated Satie in late 1915 and early 1916. Its assertion of individuality through deliberate anonymity matched his concept of himself through his attire as a bourgeois functionary; it offered the prospect of creating boredom through insistent repetition; and it allowed the vocal line to be inexpressive and detached from its accompaniment, in which Satie could then display his quirky harmonic style to its best advantage. But perhaps because he had already used the same F major arpeggio as the melodic basis of the last of his *Cinq Grimaces* in November 1915 (albeit in a different register), or perhaps because he decided his setting was too overtly descriptive of the Hatter's ticking watch, he abandoned his first version of *Le Chapelier* with eleven bars of the piano part still unwritten.

It must have been at this point that Satie had a flash of inspiration, and realized how shocking it would be to graft Carroll's crazy world onto an operatic love-duet by that epitomy of bourgeois sentimentality, Charles Gounod. He was so sure of himself that he wrote his second version straight in black ink, adding his introductory bar (another afterthought) over the top of the last three bars of his first version.[3] The only snag was that Gounod's vocal line (Ex. 3a) did not fit Chalupt's poem beyond the first three phrases (Ex. 3a, bars 1–6), and we know that Satie considered using the remainder of the first stanza (bars 7–15) because he wrote it out below, transposed to A major and in 12/8 time. So at the changeover point he began composing himself, wickedly converting Gounod's stationary bass pedal point into a string of forbidden parallel fifths (Ex. 3b, bars 5–6) and ending his shorter version of the first stanza with a plunging sequential descent in three-note groups that is pure Satie. This perfectly matches the concept of the Hatter greasing his watch with best butter (even though this is actually the fault of the March Hare in Carroll). The second stanza takes the fifth and sixth bars of Ex. 3a as its starting point, but besides preserving Gounod's upper tonic climax (bar 12) in its rather operatic tenth bar, the vocal line is Satie's own (Fig. 3.1), with a rising sequence in bar 13 skilfully balancing the longer descent in bars 5–6. When Satie was satisfied with his concept on 14 April 1916, he copied out the vocal part for Jane Bathori to perform at the Salle Huyghens four days later (Fig. 3.1). But before the song was printed by Rouart-Lerolle the following year, Satie altered the third quavers of bars 2 and 3 (to F♯ and D respectively) and modified the 'Blue Danube' introduction (Ex. 3b) to match the first vocal entry. This was either to make his vocal line more distinctive, or to avoid possible charges of plagiarism. But the rising arpeggios in Ex. 3b suggest a link with the discarded first version of *Le Chapelier*, and it seems that a simple arpeggio was the basic musical idea behind the whole process of its composition.

Le Chapelier is as much pastiche as parody (or quotation), and anyone who criticizes Satie for technical inadequacy should also first be aware of his recitatives for Gounod's *Le Médecin malgré lui*. For Satie was perfectly capable of writing strong functional harmonies with conventional voice-leading and a sensitive regard for past styles, when he considered it appropriate. It was fortunate for the present century that this was rarely the case and that Satie attached little importance to this sort of exercise for its

Ex. 3a Gounod: *Mireille*. First stanza of the *Chanson de Magali* (Act 1)

Ex. 3b Satie: *Le Chapelier*. First stanza, second version (BN 9581, 18–19)

own sake: in the case of *Le Médecin* it was the light, almost Mozartian orchestration of which he was the most proud, and there is much individuality in both his Gounod projects.

Satie's private attitude to pastiche was, however, disapproving. He told Misia Edwards less than three months after *Le Chapelier* – with regard to a ballet based on the fables of La Fontaine, which he hoped she would sponsor – that 'these "Fables" will enable us to be very modern, because, without turning a hair, we reject *pastiche*. A fig for that!'[4] But, either due to a soft spot for Gounod (shared with his friend Koechlin), or due to the financial temptations of writing for Diaghilev (which is more likely), Satie spent the latter half of 1923 setting the spoken dialogue in Gounod's 3–Act opéra-comique[5] for a first performance in Monte Carlo on 5 January 1924.

Satie's preparation was meticulous in the extreme. First he annotated a typed copy of the libretto (BN 9595(1)). Then he copied out all the marked recitatives on

3.1   Vocal part of *Le Chapelier* (1916), copied prior to printing for Jane Bathori to sing from (Ho 43).

the right-hand pages of BN 9595(2), notating the natural speech-rhythms he was
to use on the opposite left-hand pages, numbering the bars in each section as he
proceeded.[6] Next he wrote down the ranges of the four singers (BN 9595(3))[7]
and began considering the orchestration involved. Then he began sketching the music
itself (BN 9595(4–6)), and when he was satisfied with it he copied out a vocal score
of his twelve 'scènes nouvelles' in eight separate notebooks. Finally, he prepared the
orchestral score, which has since disappeared. The passage from Act 1 scene 5 shown
in Figure 3.2 shows just how light Satie's touch was in writing pastiche Gounod.
The voice-leading is clear and logical, with the frequent dominant sevenths resolving
exactly as they should as the music moves crisply along. All the chords are carefully
(and conventionally) spaced with a clear concern for textural variety. The tenor
line (Lucas) is placed in its most effective register and is never obscured by the
surrounding accompaniment with its wealth of inventive detail. Contrary to his usual
practice, Satie uses the full nineteenth-century vocabulary of chromatic chords in his

3.2   *Le Médecin malgré lui*, vocal score of the start of Act 1 scene 5.

score (diminished sevenths, augmented sixths and fifths etc.) with perfect ease. He also develops motifs, adds little instrumental interludes, and seems to have genuinely enjoyed writing this vivacious and tasteful score. Although the word-setting is mostly syllabic, Satie indulged in the odd melisma, and even wrote a huge expressive one as his final flourish before his music joined into Gounod's octet at the end of Act 3 (Fig. 3.3).

A similar lively humour characterizes the *Sonatine bureaucratique* of July 1917, which is modelled on Clementi's Sonatina in C (Op. 36 No. 1).[8] But there is as much of Satie here as there is of Stravinsky in *Pulcinella* (1919–20), whose 'rediscovery of the past' Satie probably influenced.[9] Writing against a pre-set and familiar musical back-cloth appealed to both composers, and especially to Satie, who found composition more difficult. Indeed, it is a tribute to his constant desire to forge the path ahead for others to follow that he only indulged in one such neo-classical work. His years at the Schola Cantorum had purified his style and increased its linear strength. Just as his studies of Bach chorales and fugues had led him to seek modern equivalents for these (as in *En Habit de cheval*), so his studies of sonata form led to a re-evaluation of this in *d'Holothurie* (from the *Embryons desséchés* of 1913: see chapter 8) and the *Sonatine bureaucratique*.

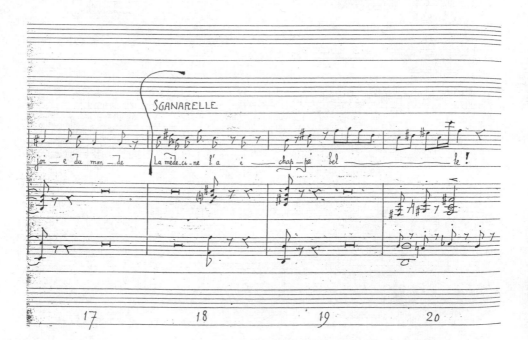

3.3   *Le Médecin malgré lui*, vocal score of the end of Act 3 scene 12.

Ex. 4a Clementi: Sonatina in C (Op. 36 No. 1). First movement, development section, bars 16–24

Ex. 4b Satie: *Sonatine bureaucratique*. First movement, development section, bars 24–36. With first version of text (as in BN 9624, 17–18)

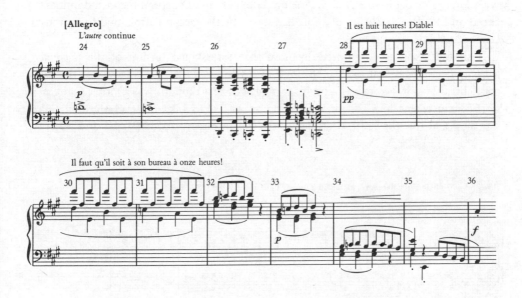

In all these cases, the modernity derives from harmonic and thematic surprises within the pre-established formal plan, and the 'development' section within the first movement of the Sonatina provides a good example of this (Exx. 4a–b). As Satie had expanded Clementi's exposition and recapitulation by half as much again (from 15 to 23 bars), he needed to add 4 bars to Clementi's 8 in the development to give an exact balance. In fact, Satie's expansion is adroitly concealed in the centre of this section, providing a deliberate element of gratuitous repetition not found in Clementi, but in keeping with Satie's non-developmental aesthetic. Thus bars 28–9 in Ex. 4b are repeated as bars 30–1, and bars 32–3 anticipate the transposition of genuine Clementi in bars 34–5 (cf. Ex. 4a, bars 20–3). The first surprise, though, is thematic. Instead of taking his own rising version of Clementi's first subject (Ex. 5b, bars 1–2) as would have been expected at the start of a Classical development section, Satie uses Clementi's subject instead. This simple transposition down a minor third (in the first two bars of Ex. 4b) must have been deliberate, for Satie follows it with his biggest shock of all, a fourfold increase in the harmonic movement (Ex. 4b, bar 26), with parallel major chords in descending octaves to boot in bar 27. To anyone who knows Classical principles well, this is one of the really funny moments in Satie, who revels in breaking up Clementi's carefully balanced phrases. And he springs yet more surprises (in the true spirit of the *esprit nouveau*) in bar 28 of Ex. 4b. First, in the abrupt change of register and tonality, which is quintessentially Satiean but wholly foreign to Clementi of course. And second, in his subtle harmonic adaptation of the original to give an implied dominant ninth followed by an added sixth (bar 29) in the same anachronistic vein. The insistent repetition of this progression drives home the irony, and in Satie's first version of the accompanying text (BN 9624) it is supposed to represent a clock striking eight. Then come further changes of register (bars 32–4) with foreign modal hints (C natural before D major, and D natural before a dominant chord on E) before normality of a sort is restored by the recapitulation, and the parody element temporarily subsides.

It should come as no surprise by now that Satie's final version of the *Sonatine bureaucratique* was only arrived at through painstaking effort. BN 9624 reveals that he chose his title long before he found his format. His first thought was a rather bombastic 6/8 movement in C major, beginning as in Ex. 6. Like most of the Sonatina sketches, and like the finished article, it stresses secondary triads (II, III and VI) in

Ex. 5a Clementi: Sonatina in C. First movement, bars 1–8

Ex. 5b Satie: *Sonatine bureaucratique*. First movement, bars 1–8 (with original text from BN 9624, 16)

Ex. 6 *Sonatine bureaucratique*. First idea for the opening bars (BN 9624, 5)

an effort to differentiate itself from its model, just as Satie avoids the Alberti bass formula throughout. What Satie did was to use Clementi primarily as a *rhythmic* model, transposing his themes and then inventing his own melodic variants of them (as in Ex. 5). For a long time he remained undecided as to whether the key of the outer movements should be F or A major, and as he had been interested in the potential of bitonality since 1913, he made various experiments with themes in F that could be harmonized in A minor. Exx. 7b–d show three of these, all based on Clementi's rhythmic 'modèle' for the finale (Ex. 7a). The third is especially interesting as its A major key signature was changed to that of F. Thus it provides a sort of half-way house between the two keys. As things are seldom straightforward with Satie's logic, the 'bitonal' version (Ex. 7b) which comes closest to the printed text (Ex. 7e) was also the first Satie devised, and he marked it 'en la maj[eur]' in consequence. Its two-bar principle of undulating I–VI harmonies over a tonic pedal (reminiscent of the contemporary *Parade*)[10] survived into the final version (Ex. 7e).

Ex. 7a Clementi: Sonatina in C. Finale, bars 1–8

Ex. 7b Satie: *Sonatine bureaucratique*. Preliminary version of start of Finale (BN 9624, 6)

Ex. 7c Ibid. (BN 9624, 15)

Ex. 7d Ibid. (BN 9624, 28). Originally written with a key signature of three sharps

Ex. 7e *Sonatine bureaucratique*. Printed version of Finale, bars 1–8

Whereas Satie adds 46 bars to the finale of the *Sonatine bureaucratique*, he removes 4 from the slow movement, which is more fluid than Clementi and in a genuine 9/8. Here Satie experimented with an arpeggio theme (plus turns) like Clementi's, before deciding that the scalar fluency – first encountered in Ex. 5b, bars 3–4 – would be more appropriate. Indeed, this idea pervades the work to a greater degree than in Clementi's Sonatina and provides an element of continuity to offset the disjunctive register changes. In many ways, Satie's slow movement looks forward to the *Nocturnes* of 1919 and may have provided the germ from which they sprang.

Ex. 8a Clementi: Sonatina in C. Finale, bars 17–24

Ex. 8b Satie: *Sonatine bureaucratique*. Finale, bars 17–28

Satie is boldest in the finale, where he juxtaposes original passages based on fourths with 2-, 4- or 8-bar chunks of Clementi. These are linked to the little story Satie concocts about the businessman's day at the office, for he hears a piano nearby playing Clementi and then reflects how sad it is (Ex. 8). Nothing develops here, and the two styles confront each other throughout, though Satie does present Clementi's running scale in parallel fifths near the end, and transposes material up a fourth (or down a fifth) to keep it in the tonic.

Satie perhaps chose Clementi, rather than a French model like Rameau, for his very lack of individuality. The clean, square-cut phrasing and absence of sustained development fitted in perfectly with Satie's own practice at the time, which also included the transposition of cells which were juxtaposed to obtain maximum contrast. But the confrontation between Clementi and the composer of *Parade* was actually reduced as Satie progressed with his Sonatina, for he first produced a complete exposition for the first movement which was altogether more aggressive, dissonant and texturally varied. A comparison between Exx. 9 and 5b shows that, whilst the outline remains the same, Satie's sparse neo-classicism was written in. The removal of the prominent secondary chords (III and VI) and the parallel fifths (Ex. 9, bar 7) from the final version (Ex. 5b), shows that Satie decided to make his opening at least 'Très Clementi' (rather than 'Très Satie'). He saved these more modern characteristics for telling effect later on.

Ex. 9 Satie: *Sonatine bureaucratique.* Early version of start (BN 9624, 12–13)

Ex. 10a Chopin: Sonata in B♭ minor (Op. 35). Marche funèbre, bars 31–8 (trio)

Ex. 10b Satie: *d'Edriophthalma* from the *Embryons desséchés*, systems 4–6

Satie's use of interpolated quotations from the masters of the past also relies on incongruity and textural contrast. They are all concentrated within the months of July–August 1913 in the *Embryons desséchés* and the *Croquis et agaceries*, and perhaps reflect the pressures on Satie of this intensely creative period when he struggled to meet the demands of his publisher Demets. The amusing directions in the at first regularly barred *Embryons desséchés*, incidentally, were added after the music was complete (BN 9590). In *d'Edriophthalma*, Satie first intended to use the main theme of Chopin's Funeral March,[11] even though only a hint of it remains in the printed version (at 'Que c'est triste!' in system 1). The decision to use Chopin's celebrated trio melody instead (Satie's 'celebrated mazurka of Schubert' passage) came only as an afterthought, for it is missing in the sketchbook. Exx. 10a–b show how Satie again uses Chopin as a model, but robs the passage of its Romantic expressiveness by making the melody move almost entirely by step, narrowing the span of the arpeggiated accompaniment to make it more monochrome, and increasing its mundanity through an insistent dominant pedal and a matter-of-fact final cadence. He further transposes Chopin's melody out of its 'Romantic' key of D flat major into the more ordinary key of C. This levelling process was surely meant to amuse rather than to antagonize, and this is also the case with the coda of *de Podophthalma* (another afterthought). Here, the insistent tonic chords recall the end of Beethoven's Eighth Symphony with sublime incongruity, for the rest of this entertaining piece is based on 'The Orangutan Song' from Edmond Audran's operetta *La Mascotte*, with a trio derived from the folksong *Il était un'bergère*!

In *Turkish Yodelling* (the first of the *Croquis et agaceries*) Satie vents his irony on Mozart's *Rondo alla Turca*,[12] whereas in *Españaña* it is Chabrier's *España* (1883) which comes under fire, with Bizet's *Carmen* transported to modern Paris in the text.[13] Thus the 'Plaza Clichy' refers to the rhythmic ostinato established in bars 29ff. of *España*, while the trombone theme of bars 218–21 precedes it at 'N'est-ce pas l'Alcade?' Here the quotations are unusually explicit and literal, perhaps owing to the high regard Satie had for Chabrier as a composer. As well as being more up-to-date in its quotations, *Españaña* includes the only brief untransposed extract I know of, for both pieces end with an emphatic F major cadence in the same register.

The real curiosity in the *Croquis et agaceries* is the *Danse maigre*, subtitled 'à la manière de ces messieurs'. Ravel's two piano pieces *A la manière de. . .Borodine/Chabrier* of the same year immediately spring to mind, but as these were not performed till December 1913, or published until 1914, it is more likely that Satie influenced Ravel than vice versa. Both, however, may share a common source in the *A la manière de. . .* pieces of Alfredo Casella (1911–13), and they are in reality all part of a long line of party-pieces stretching back to Chabrier's 'Quadrille on themes from Wagner's *Tristan*' (*Souvenirs de Munich*, 1885–6) and the Fauré–Messager 'Quadrille on themes from *The Ring*' (*Souvenirs de Bayreuth*, *c.* 1888). Satie's title *Danse maigre* may well be a parody of Cyril Scott's popular *Danse nègre* of 1908,[14] though there are no musical allusions within it. Who Satie's 'messieurs' were remains open to question, though I shall be considering the possibility that Debussy was one of them in chapter 4.

By comparison with the intriguing questions of parody, pastiche and quotation in Satie (which serve to illuminate his composing practices), the question of direct influences can be more easily dealt with. Amongst composers, the only real contender is Chabrier, and much has been made of the links between the consecutive ninths in the prelude to *Le Roi malgré lui* and those in Satie's *Sarabandes*.[15] We know from Templier (1969, 11) that Satie went to see Chabrier's opera whilst on leave from military service in May 1887, and that 'carried away by his enthusiasm for the composer's daring, Satie left with Chabrier's doorman one of his works, decorated with a superb dedication – in red ink, of course.' But why did the excited Satie wait nearly four months to put his inspiration down on paper in the *Sarabandes*? And how is it that we can also find ninths and even thirteenths without conventional preparation or resolution in his song *Sylvie* from the previous year? (Ex. 11). This first barless

Ex. 11 *Sylvie* (1886). First vocal entry

Ex. 12a Chabrier: *Le Roi malgré lui*. Prelude, bars 11–23 (1887)

Ex. 12b Satie: *Première Sarabande*, bars 1–8 (as in BN 14457, 1)

piece with its self-repeating progressions of slow minim chords seems far more likely (with the *Ogives*) to set the precedent for the later Rose-Croix music than anything in the regularly barred *Sarabandes*. On the face of it, it does seem plausible that bars 15–19 of Chabrier's prelude (within Ex. 12a) could form a precedent for the opening bars of his First Sarabande (Ex. 12b),[16] but in the Chabrier this is very much an isolated passage within otherwise functional (if daring) harmonies. An equally strong case might be put for Satie deriving his sudden register changes and blocks of contrasted sound from the juxtaposition of bars 14 and 15, or 17 and 18 of Ex. 12a; or by comparing the material in bars 15–19 to that surrounding it. And would Satie have remembered a short passage so early in the opera so precisely anyway? Then again, if we look at Ex. 12b more closely, it transpires that Satie's first chord is a major seventh on the tonic, a chord entirely absent from Chabrier's prelude, and that the bars that follow (with sevenths and ninths equally prominent) quickly lose any sense of A♭ as a key centre. Indeed, Satie reaches A major by bar 8, whilst in Ex. 12a the polarity of E major is never seriously in doubt. Rather, Chabrier's importance lay in proving to Satie that the Wagnerian path was the wrong one for a composer with wit and originality to follow.

Another possible influence on Satie's formative years was his composer friend Charles Levadé, the dedicatee of the early song *Les Anges*, the second *Ogive* and the third *Gymnopédie*. In an enquiry into the relationship between Satie and Debussy (Richard, 1932, 2), Levadé maintains that, in 1887

> It was I who corrected his first songs, which resembled pleasant creations by Massenet. I gave him harmony lessons; not for long, however, for he quickly felt a need to develop his own imagination. . . 'It was you who encouraged me to compose', Satie told me [around 1891].

But one can search in vain amongst Levadé's conventional salon compositions of the time for anything even remotely resembling Satie, or anything in Satie which shows a debt to Levadé, even though both set poems by Contamine de Latour in the late 1880s. Indeed, it was the inspiration he derived from Latour's poetry rather than the harmony lessons of Levadé which showed Satie the way forward, and it is Levadé himself who most resembles Massenet.

A similar case exists with Victor-Dynam Fumet, who Satie is supposed to have replaced as pianist at the Chat Noir in 1887. His son Stanislas claims (1954, 129) that Satie 'was infatuated with my father's music', and suggests that his 'contemporary improvisations' may have influenced Satie's *Gymnopédies* and *Sarabandes*. Both men were searching for 'purity and simplicity', and he singles out his father's *Les Enlisements d'en-haut* (?1885) as possessing 'all that appeared so new in Satie's *Sarabandes*' (ibid., 130). But despite the frequent sevenths, ninths and added sixths, most of *Les Enlisements* is far more chromatic, intensely lyrical and obviously pianistic than anything Satie wrote around this time, and the piece is closer to César Franck in style. However, the opening (Ex. 13) does have a certain static and quasi-religious aura that suggests the later Rose-Croix pieces, so perhaps Fumet is not so easily dismissed after all.

Ex. 13 Victor-Dynam Fumet: *Les Enlisements d'en-haut*, bars 1–19 (from BN Vm.[12] 10401)

The strange barring suggests that each chord was of equal importance, and that Fumet was only one step away from the fluid barlessness of the *Ogives*. But it was probably Fumet's anarchistic and mystical proclivities that influenced Satie more deeply, for both men founded their own religious cults, dabbled in occultism and yet died within the Catholic faith.

The remaining influence on Satie is Gregorian chant, of which much has been made by Léon Guichard. Certainly, Vinot's early teaching in Honfleur on the beauties of

Ex. 14 Two of the *Octo Toni Psalmorum* from the *Paroissien Romain* followed by the start of the Act 1 Prelude to *Le Fils des étoiles* (1891)

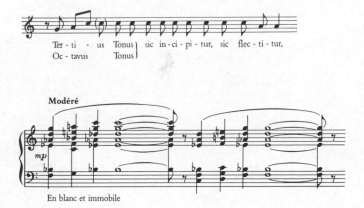

medieval music found a receptive student in Satie, who later spent much of the time (when he should have been perfecting his piano technique for the Conservatoire) studying either Viollet-le-Duc's decorations in Notre-Dame or his writings on Gothic architecture in the Bibliothèque Nationale.[17] Dom Clément Jacob maintains (1952, 88) that Satie visited the Benedictine Abbey of Solesmes, and as Debussy is known to have gone there in August 1893, the two friends may have travelled together. But, despite the elaborate parallels drawn by Guichard (1936, 335; 1973, 64–8), it does not seem to me that there are any real links between, say, the *Séquence: Victimae paschali laudes* and the first of Satie's *Trois Poèmes d'amour* (1914), other than the length of their phrases. Certainly, in the Act 1 Prelude to *Le Fils des étoiles* (1891), Satie uses a rising fourth figure which is that of the starts of the 'Tertius Tonus' and 'Octavus Tonus' from the *Octo Toni Psalmorum* (Ex. 14). And in one of his notebooks we find the words 'Plain-Chant du huitième ton (voir page 177 de mon gradual)', showing that he was well aware of these distinctions, even if his 'Gradual' was fictitious. But, just as Satie never remains in one mode for any length of time (as the *Ogives* demonstrate: see Ex. 65A), so one can search in vain in the *Paroissien Romain* for any substantive link with the Gregorian modes in his melodies. Rather, Satie absorbed the spirit of plain-song and the sort of lengths and shapes its phrases took, then composed his own free equivalents. As Patrick Gowers so rightly says (1965, 23), some of the Rose-Croix works (like the two *Préludes du Nazaréen* of 1892)

> have forms that may partly have been derived from the idea of a cantor and a choir, and some have melodies which may have been inspired by plainsong. But the differences between them and genuine medieval music so far outweigh the similarities that by insisting on the latter one merely tends to mask the true character of the music, which is, I think, only revealed by studying its techniques and, more importantly, by familiarity.

4

Satie and Debussy

> As soon as I saw him for the first time, I felt drawn towards him and longed to live forever at his side. For thirty years I had the joy of seeing this wish fulfilled. We understood each other perfectly, with no need for complicated explanations, for it seemed as if we had *always* known each other.
>
> (Satie, in an article on Debussy written for *Vanity Fair* in August 1922: Ve, 68)

From a retrospective viewpoint in 1922, Satie makes his relationship with Debussy sound idyllic, almost like a perfect marriage springing from 'love at first sight'. There can be no doubt either that the anguish expressed in his 1920 *Elégie* – 'in remembrance of an admiring and sweet friendship of thirty years' – was wholly genuine. In setting these lines from Lamartine, about the irrelevance of nature and material possessions after the loss of a single, cherished friend,[1] Satie for once brings his inner emotions to the surface in a wide-ranging vocal line of almost exaggerated expressiveness. The intense dissonances, tonal ambiguity and absolute compression are quite remarkable, as we shall see further in chapter 5. The desolation is, of course, entirely Satie's, but with the subtle suggestion that their friendship was by no means untroubled. The strangely positive resolution on a chord of C major half-way through (see Ex. 24d) only enhances the feeling of desolation elsewhere in the *Elégie*, and it is surely no accident that the song has no real ending and merely dissolves on a whole-tone chord straight after its brutal climax. Appropriately for Debussy, who identified with the neurasthenic Hamlet, 'the rest is silence'.

Given these deeply personal statements from an otherwise hermetic composer who avoided emotional commitment like the plague, it would seem likely that there was at least some truth in Marc Bredel's psychological interpretation of Satie as a repressed homosexual, whose real love was Debussy as a man rather than as a composer (1982, 84 and 90). If this were true, Satie's lack of emotional fulfilment might help to explain his paranoid tendencies. He did, after all, prefer the company of artistic young men, and he often provided music for *risqué* theatrical situations, from the exploitation of the cult of the androgyne in Péladan's *Le Prince du Byzance* in 1891 to the transvestite *Bain des Grâces* in *Mercure* in 1924.[2] But these compositions arose more from a desire to scandalize the bourgeoisie, and if there might well have been a voyeuristic side to Satie (who took a particular delight in attending the orgies of the dancer Caryathis in 1921),[3] he never allowed himself to become physically involved. Just as he hated the practical jokes he played on others to be redirected towards himself, so he even objected to Cocteau playing 'footsy' with him at dinner parties.[4] And had he been 'gay' himself he would not have disapproved of the activities of Cocteau and his circle in such an open manner. The real reason for the absence of any lasting relationships with the opposite sex, as he told Mme Conrad Satie in September 1912, was 'quite simply, the fear of being horribly cuckolded. And this would be well deserved, for I am a man that women cannot understand' (Vc). Thus Satie was, or forced himself to be, asexual, and I have it on very good authority that his 'liaison' with Debussy was entirely platonic.[5] They were like two artistic brothers, however different their aims and achievements. Or perhaps it might be truer to say that Debussy, although only four years the elder, enjoyed exercising a paternalistic role from his position of initially greater acclaim and superior technical expertise.

Broadly speaking, until Satie began to emerge from his friend's shadow after 1911, things went smoothly. But as Satie's fame grew, Debussy's incomprehension of his success caused growing friction between them, until Satie broke with the ailing Debussy over his attitude to *Parade* in 1917. Contrary to expectation, it was Satie who influenced Debussy, by and large, rather than vice versa. And not only in terms of ideas, for Debussy's modal *Sarabande* of 1894 (later transferred to the suite *Pour le piano*) surely has its roots in the *Sarabandes* of the 'gentle medieval musician, lost in this century',[6] just as there are Satiean echoes in *La Boîte à joujoux* in 1913 (see Ex. 19). Predictably, there are several allusions to Debussy in Satie's music of this period too, but other than *The Dreamy Fish* and the *Nouvelles 'Pièces froides'* there are no instances of the fiercely independent Satie experimenting with the harmonic style of Debussy, and both of these works were left unpublished through choice. Rather, it was Debussy's success with *Pelléas et Mélisande* in 1902 (and in the ensuing years of Debussyism) that gave Satie a clear plan of what to avoid after his years at the Schola Cantorum. And it was Debussyism that Satie (and Debussy) hated. As Satie wrote in *Le Coq*: 'I never attack Debussy. It's only the Debussyists that annoy me.'[7] From their example, he resolved that 'Satieism could never exist', and he came to despise the music of Ravel for its Debussyan characteristics, and perhaps, ironically, because it was Ravel's 'discovery' of Satie in 1911 that had first soured his relationship with Debussy.

The main problem in chronicling Satie's relationship with Debussy lies in discovering when and where it began. Although they were both students at the Paris Conservatoire together between 1879 and 1884, there is no evidence that they ever met there. Satie, as we saw, was adamant that their friendship lasted thirty years, which would mean that they met in 1887 rather than in 1891 when 'I was writing my *Fils des étoiles*'.[8] Thus the Chat Noir seems a more plausible venue than the Auberge du Clou, but it is even more likely that they met through the new focal point of matters *ésotérique*, Edmond Bailly's Librairie de l'Art Indépendant at 9 rue de la Chaussée d'Antin. Bailly was largely responsible for the vogue for esotericism and the occult at this time, and as his clientèle included Symbolist poets like Mallarmé, Henri de

Régnier and Villiers de l'Isle-Adam; artists like Odilon Redon and Toulouse-Lautrec; and composers like Ernest Chausson, it is natural that Debussy would have made a bee-line for Bailly's bookshop after his return from Rome in early 1887. Here, as the *ésotériste* Victor-Emile Michelet recalls, 'he arrived almost every day in the late afternoon, either alone, or with the faithful Erik Satie'.[9] 'Able to express himself freely here, Debussy let himself become strongly impressed by Hermetic philosophy',[10] and we know he was interested in Rosicrucianism whilst still in Rome from the books he ordered from Emile Baron in Paris.[11] Indeed, if Schidlof is to be believed, Debussy had already been recruited into the Prieuré de Sion (Ordre de la Rose-Croix-Véritas) in Rome, and served (probably as a figurehead) as its Thirty-third Grand Master from 1885 until his death, when he was succeeded by none other than Jean Cocteau[12] – to whom Satie transferred his main allegiance during the First World War. Pierre Mariel, in his introduction to *Axël* by Villiers de l'Isle-Adam,[13] says that Debussy 'venerated' Eliphas Lévi and his *Dogme et rituel de la haute magie*, from which 'much of *Axël*'s symbolism, including the preoccupation with the pentagram, is derived' (Howat, 1983, 169). As Debussy is known to have set a scene from *Axël* around 1888,[14] he must have been conversant with this caballistic sub-culture. It was Lévi's *Dogme et rituel* that proved a 'revelation' to Stanislas de Guaita when he was introduced to it by Debussy's future librettist Catulle Mendès in 1883 (Billy, 37), and it thus played an important role behind the foundation of the Ordre Kabbalistique de la Rose-Croix by Guaita and Péladan in 1888. Adherents to this included Mendès, Michelet, Henri de Régnier, and almost certainly Debussy and Satie, for their meetings were held in a first-floor room above the Auberge du Clou (Billy, 153). By 1890, however, Péladan's outrageous eccentricities and extravagant self-aggrandizement caused an inevitable rift with Guaita, and Péladan founded his own Ordre de la Rose-Croix Catholique, du Temple et du Graal, in which Satie assumed prominence as official composer in 1891–2. While he in no way shared Péladan's enthusiasm for Wagner, Satie did write a *Leit-motiv du 'Panthée'* (Ex. 15) as his first Rose-Croix (and only

Ex. 15 *Leit-motiv du 'Panthée'* (1891)

monodic) composition in October 1891,[15] though its prominent use of the augmented fourth and its metrical fluidity make it wholly Satiean. *Le Panthée*, incidentally, tells the story of a composer, Bihn Grallon (?I am the Grail), who is obsessed by the alchemical ideal of gold and writes a *Symphonie de l'Or*. As the impoverished Grallon works as a night-club pianist in Montmartre and features on the programmes of the first series of Soirées de la Rose+Croix[16] (in which Satie's *Trois Sonneries de la*

Rose + Croix and *Le Fils des étoiles* were first performed) it is tempting to see them as one and the same person. Grallon's admiration for Wagner and Beethoven rather reflects Péladan's own musical views at this time, though there may be an element of Debussy in the Wagnerian side, suggesting that Grallon is a fusion of the two composers. In *Le Panthée* Péladan, for once, was truly prophetic in making Grallon dream 'of escaping with his mistress to an idyllic existence on the island of Jersey' (Howat, 170–1), for this is precisely what Debussy did (with Emma Bardac) in 1904.

Whilst on the subject of gold, it is worth noting that it was Debussy who first used the Golden Section as a means of formal organization in early songs like *Zéphyr* (1881), *Rondeau* (1882) and *Spleen* from the *Ariettes oubliées* (1885–7).[17] Its sudden appearance in Satie's first *Sonnerie de la Rose + Croix*[18] in early 1892 strongly suggests that he may have been privy to Debussy's secret mysteries of creation in a way that no-one else was. Then, in Debussy's partly autobiographical play *Les 'Frères en Art'* (1897, rev. 1903), we find the painter Talancet talking about 'the lithograph of my latest painting: *Christ at the House of Gold*'[19] to Maltravers (Debussy), another painter whose views combine intellectual anarchy and pantheism. The fact that Talancet's painting has 'sold 150,000 copies' is a clear indication of Debussy's belief in the power of gold. Even as late as March 1916, we find Satie telling Henry Prunières that 'Tomorrow, I intend to peruse the "King with the Golden Mask" at Debussy's house. I couldn't do this on Saturday, although I'd seen it in good old Claude's library. It gave me the impression of being a really good sort of book, and I shall read it' (Vc). The concept of Debussy still buying any literature related to gold, and of Satie still eager to get his hands on his friend's latest acquisitions at the age of fifty, is intriguing indeed.

Satie and Debussy were by no means alone in their attraction to the occult underworld of secrecy, magic and ritual, for it also fascinated many contemporary Symbolist writers and artists, including Maeterlinck. But its influence on the then susceptible and insecure Satie was more pervasive than in most other cases. His fascination with sorcerers, magicians and the devil often surfaces in his drawings, just as his alchemical obsessions recur in his writings.[20] Both Satie and Debussy dreamed of being able to create freely without financial pressures, though neither they nor their interested contemporaries achieved their goal through occult practices. According to his sister Olga, 'Satie was a spiritist rather than a true mystic' (Myers, 1945, 202), and as Myers says (ibid.) 'This would account, no doubt, for the fact that in his "Rose Croix" period Satie was under the impression that he was working under the direct guidance of some medieval cleric whose fanatical piety he had inherited from beyond the grave.'

Satie's fascination with the medieval past, for an ideal lost world of chivalric orders, fairy-tales and Gothic castles, blended perfectly with his attraction towards the occult. Thus we find medieval castles adorning the manuscript of the first *Prélude du Nazaréen* in 1892 (Fig. 4.1), written for an allegorical play by Henri Mazel.[21] Here, the fairy-tale setting of the competing suitors for the hand of Hermosina, daughter of the enlightened Duke Baudouin, is given deeper significance by making the suitor Mario the perfect crusader from the mystical order of Nazarenes.[22] He is equated allegorically with Christ in His second coming, whilst the courtesan Impéria represents Mary

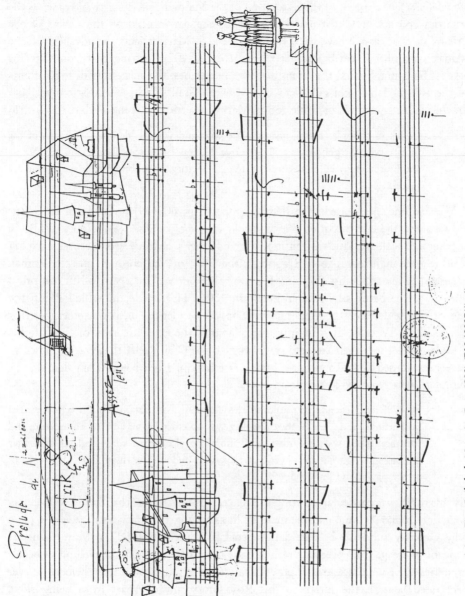

4.1 First *Prélude du Nazaréen* (June 1892) (BN 10037(1), 1).

Magdalene. The concept of the restoration of the Merovingian dynasty in France as the true descendants of Christ and Mary Magdalene was central to the beliefs of the Prieuré de Sion, as we have seen. In Act 2 scene 5, Mario rejects the advances of 'the Madeleine on her knees before her Christ' (Mazel, 107),[23] saying that 'contempt for love is the reason behind the strength of we Nazarenes, the successors of the Knights of the Round Table, and guardians of the sacred Grail' (ibid., 109). Satie must have drawn parallels with his own life too in Mario's assertion in scene 7 (ibid., 120) that

> I walk in solitude: before my path the wild and wicked hide in the depths of the forests; even the good turn aside in terror. . .Thus I advance, all-powerful but sad. . . and I surprise myself, in my true evenings of victory, by sobbing with rage behind my shield.

We also find the Merovingian King Dagobert I (*c.* 602–39) surfacing in *La Défaite des Cimbres*, the last of Satie's *Vieux sequins et vieilles cuirasses* (September 1913). In another fairy-tale of Satie's invention, a grandfather's bedtime story causes a young child to have nightmares about Dagobert, the Duke of Marlborough and the Roman general Marius attacking Boïorix, King of the Cimbri, in a surrealistic historical mix-up at the battle of Mons-en-Puelle in 1304. This battle, in which Philip the Fair of France defeated the Flemings, may appear accidental, until we remember that it was Philip IV who, at this time, was planning the extermination of the Knights Templar, and it was their treasure (perhaps even the Grail itself) that was supposed to have been buried near Rennes-le-Château (see n. 12). Even before their demise, the Templars were regarded as occult adepts, and

> by 1789 the legends surrounding the Templars had obtained positively mythical proportions, and their historical reality was obscured by an aura of obfuscation and romance. They were regarded as. . .illumined alchemists, magi and sages, master masons and high initiates – veritable supermen endowed with an awesome arsenal of arcane power and knowledge.[24]

As this myth was particularly strong in France, it is no surprise that Satie and Debussy were drawn into its aura, and the masonic links amongst its initiates may help explain why Debussy 'suddenly became Satie's benefactor' (Peter, 1944, 71). More than just a means of escape from everyday reality, Satie must have seen the unravelling of occult mysteries as a potential source of power. It must be said, however, that the occult never penetrated beneath the surface of his Rose-Croix music. Apart from being slow, hieratic and ritualistic, it is in no way descriptive of the plays associated with it, for it has its own independent and purely musical logic.

The other occult link between Debussy and Satie is Jules Bois, the author of *Le Satanisme et la magie* (Paris, Léon Chailley, 1895) and a member of the rather suspect Ahathoor Temple. This was founded in Paris in 1890 as a branch of S. L. MacGregor Mathers's hermetic Order of the Golden Dawn, the only group to formulate astrological links with the Tarot alphabet. Guaita's secretary, Oswald Wirth, described Bois as 'a delinquent in magic as well as in art' (Billy, 91), but if he was more a fascinated journalist than a true initiate into the occult, he was nonetheless a colourful figure who commanded attention, waging a press campaign against Guaita's order which culminated in 1893 in duels with both Guaita and his Rosicrucian colleague Papus (Dr Gérard Encausse). Like Péladan, Bois was fascinated by the cult of the androgyne, and both Debussy and Satie were drawn into his sacrilegious world: Debussy with his proposed incidental music for the esoteric play *Les Noces de Sathan* in 1892, and Satie with his *Prélude de La Porte héroïque du ciel* in 1894. *Les Noces de Sathan*, with Debussy's music, was announced at Paul Fort's Théâtre d'Art in *Le Saint-Graal* on 8 March 1892,[25] though given the effusive garbage he was supposed to illuminate, and the impracticality of the musical organization behind it, it is no wonder Debussy turned the project down.

Satie, on the other hand, in his desire to publicize his music, had no such qualms, and the *Prélude* is one of the finest works of his Rose-Croix period; its self-contained music makes it diametrically opposite to the perfect fusion of stage action, music and text in Debussy's *Pelléas et Mélisande*. *La Porte héroïque du ciel* has as its central character a poet sent forth by Christ on a perilous mission to forcibly supplant the Virgin Mary by the cult of Isis. For, in Bois's heretical view, Isis was the all-powerful source of life which lay concealed behind the mask of the Virgin. Perhaps, as Volta suggests (Ve, 236), this explains why Satie's 'Eglise Métropolitaine d'Art was placed beneath the sign of Jesus the Leader', and the third person in his Trinity was the Virgin rather than the Holy Ghost, putting it on a par with the Osiris–Horus–Isis trilogy of ancient Egypt (Ve, 235). But Satie showed little concern for dogma in his religious tracts, and never sought to convert others to his beliefs. The cult of Isis does, however, have other repercussions within the world of Debussy and Satie, and Debussy is known to have been still interested in Egyptology in 1908–9. The title of Bois's journal *Le Cœur*, to which Satie contributed, was a synonym for Isis, whose name originated in the sacred flame (phonetically: *is–is*). The symbolic equivalent of this can be found both in the Egyptian pyramids and in Satie's *Ogives* (Ve, 236), and in none other than the red rose of the Rosicrucian movement – which recurs in Maeterlinck as a symbol of the love between Pelléas and Mélisande, and as a *character* on the title page of Debussy's *La Boîte à joujoux*. And perhaps Debussy was so eager to collaborate with the Canadian dancer Maud Allan in 1910 because the ballet that became *Khamma* was originally called *Isis*.

Casting speculation aside, Satie's *Prélude de La Porte héroïque du ciel* did not attract the publicity he hoped it might. *L'Observateur Français* of 30 May 1894 devoted its review to Bois's play, 'which continued to promote the traditional and living symbolism of ancient sacred dramas in a modern work'. Which is a pity for, as Gowers says (1965, 18), Satie's prelude 'is one of the warmest and least aloof of the Rose-Croix works' with a relatively large number (seventeen) of well-integrated short motifs within a short time-span, and an attractive recurring cadence figure to unify it. Satie liked the piece so much that he dedicated it to himself!

Satie's contributions to the decadent androgyne cult came in the form of music for two plays by Joséphin Péladan: *Le Fils des étoiles* and *Le Prince du Byzance*.[26] For the last he wrote another prelude (now lost) and the hymn *Salut Drapeau!* (*Hail to the Flag!*) in November 1891 (see Ex. 70). This weird historical drama, set in Renaissance Italy, centres on the fatal love of Giorgio Cavalcanti (an army captain of Frederick of Sicily) for the fifteen-year-old Tonio – at first a Dominican novice, then hereditary Prince of Tarente (hence the title), then finally Princess Antonio Tarras! A thin justification for this cross-dressing is provided by earlier events: Frederick of Sicily had brought the baby daughter of the assassinated Tarras the Cruel to the Dominican monastery to be brought up as a boy who would one day reign as Prince of Tarente. Cavalcanti, at the outset of the play, has been sent to bring the child back to Frederick, but he falls in love with the androgynous Tonio, and together they decide to take matters into their own hands. With his soldiers' help, they proclaim Tonio as His Highness Tarras Antonio amid general rejoicing, and in defiance of Frederick. It is at this point in Act 2 scene 9 that Cavalcanti declaims the patriotic *Salut Drapeau!*, symbolizing the power and hereditary rights of the Prince of Byzantium. Throughout the play, the Prince asserts such masculinity as he/she has, but retribution from Frederick is inevitable, and Cavalcanti only learns on his deathbed (in defeat) that the Prince is a woman. Which is supposed to make everything all right; and is too late for Cavalcanti to be too disappointed.

It was in the context of this thinly-veiled homosexual attraction that Péladan's play was turned down, first by Paul Porel of the Théâtre National de l'Odéon in April 1890, and then by Jules Claretie of the Comédie-Française in May 1891. Porel complained that the sexual ambiguity 'would make your play terribly dangerous',[27] and Claretie thought that Péladan 'was only likely to get it staged by Prince [Ludwig] of Bavaria'! Why Satie set the *Salut Drapeau!* after these rejections remains a mystery; perhaps Péladan did not acquaint him with the facts of the case. As far as I know, *Salut Drapeau!* has never been performed in its dramatic context, which is probably just as well, for anything less evocative of the carnival atmosphere prevailing at the end of Act 2 would be hard to imagine. The curious way the piece was composed will be discussed in chapter 8.

Péladan presented *Le Prince du Byzance* to Claretie as 'my *Rienzi* in preparation for my *Lohengrin*', to which Claretie replied that 'any amount of music is no substitute for clear, precise, well-defined action. In France, dramatic art does not yet ride on the back of a swan', a sentiment which Satie heartily endorsed. Although he uses recurring motifs in all his Rose-Croix works, there is nothing at all Wagnerian in the ametrical and non-functional results. The subtitle 'Wagnérie Kaldéenne' for *Le Fils des étoiles* was a misleading afterthought which appears in neither Satie's manuscript nor Péladan's autograph scenario. Both of these (BN 10052 (1–2)) are titled 'Pastorale Kaldéenne', and the Wagnerian link appears only in the published versions. As Gowers observes (1965, 16), 'the music of *Le Fils* seems far more likely to be. . . a revolt against Wagner than a homage to him', and it is in this context that we should consider what is often claimed to be Satie's main influence on Debussy, as recalled by Cocteau in 1920:[28]

> It was in 1891 that Satie composed the music of a *Wagnérie* of Péladan, opening, without anyone suspecting it, the door by which Debussy was to enter into glory.
> Debussy frequented the Auberge du Clou at that time, in ill-repute with the artists

of the Left because he happened just to have gained the Rome Prize: he was avoided. One evening Debussy and Satie found themselves seated at the same table. They found each other pleasant. Satie asked Debussy what he was preparing. Debussy, like everyone, was composing a *Wagnérie*, with Catulle Mendès.[29] Satie made a grimace. 'Believe me', he murmured, 'we have enough of Wagner. Quite beautiful; but not of our stock. We should. . .(Here I ask the greatest attention. I have cited a phrase of Satie which was told to me by Debussy, and which decided the aesthetic of *Pelléas*). . .We should see to it', he said, 'that the orchestra does not grimace when characters enter on the scene. Look here: do the trees of the scenery grimace? We should make a musical scenery, create a musical climate where the personages move and speak – not in couplets, not in leit-motifs: but by the use of a certain atmosphere of Puvis de Chavannes.'

Think of the time [of] which I am speaking. Puvis de Chavannes was one of the audacious mocked by the Right.

'And you Satie', asked Debussy. 'What are you preparing?'

'I', said Satie, 'I am thinking of the *Princesse Maleine*; but I do not know how to obtain the authorization of Maeterlinck.'

Some days afterwards, Debussy, having obtained the authorization of Maeterlinck, commenced *Pelléas et Mélisande*.

We have to remember that, at this time of *Le Coq et l'Arlequin*, Cocteau was anti-Debussy and pro-Satie. Satie's own 1922 account, though more restrained, is essentially in the same rather biased retrospective vein:[30] it comes from a position of greater assurance than was the case in 1891:

In several of his works Debussy's aesthetics are related to Symbolism; his work as a whole is Impressionistic. Forgive me, I beg you, but am I not to some extent the cause of this? People say so.

Here is the reason why:

When I first met him, at the beginning of our liaison, he was full of Mussorgsky and very conscientiously seeking a path which was not easy to find. In this respect, I myself had a great advance over him: no 'prizes' from Rome, or any other town, weighed down my steps, since I don't carry any such prizes around on me, or on my back; for I am a man of the type of Adam (*from Paradise*), who never won any prizes – a lazy sort, no doubt.

At that time I was writing my *Fils des étoiles* – on a text by Joséphin Péladan; and I explained to Debussy how we Frenchmen needed to break away from the Wagnerian adventure, which did not correspond with our natural aspirations. And I told him that I was not at all anti-Wagnerian, but that we needed our own music – without sauerkraut if possible.

Why not make use of the representational methods of Claude Monet, Cézanne, Toulouse-Lautrec, and so on? Why not make a musical transposition of them? Nothing simpler. Are they not expressions too?

This was the profitable starting-point for experiments abounding in tentative – even fruitful – results. . .Who could show him examples? reveal discoveries to him?

> point out the ground to be explored? give him the benefit of experience?. . .Who?
> I shall not reply: that doesn't interest me any more.

As far as Cocteau's account is concerned, it contains only a grain of truth on the subject of Satie's influence. For Debussy had already spelt out the operatic aims that were to be realized in *Pelléas et Mélisande* in conversation with Ernest Guiraud in 1889. As Debussy had recently returned from seeing *Parsifal, Die Meistersinger* and *Tristan* at Bayreuth, it becomes clear that the aesthetic direction in which he was moving arose as a reaction *against* the Wagnerian conception of the Gesamtkunstwerk. Thus he tells Guiraud:

> I am not tempted to imitate what I admire in Wagner: I visualize a quite different dramatic form. In it, music begins at the point where the word becomes powerless as an expressive force: music is made for the inexpressible. I should like her to appear to emerge from the shadows and at times to return there, and she should always be discreet.[31]

All Debussy needed was his ideal poet/librettist, and to be fair to Satie (and Cocteau) it may well have been Satie's decision to set Maeterlinck's *La Princesse Maleine* in 1891 that put Debussy on the right track for, despite the statement above, Debussy was still hypocritically labouring with *Rodrigue et Chimène* at the time, which is full of allusions to Wagner, and to *Tristan* in particular. And he pressed on to complete most of it, despite Satie's advice, until he discovered *Pelléas* 'in 1893'. Thus there would appear to be a gap of nearly two years as regards obtaining Maeterlinck's authorization, rather than the few 'days' mentioned by Cocteau. But here, Cocteau is simply confusing one opera with another, which is understandable after such a long period. Satie did indeed begin work on Maeterlinck's *La Princesse Maleine* (published in France in February 1890) during the following year, for the score of a *Menuet de la Princesse Maleine*, titled in Satie's familiar Gothic calligraphy, appears in Maurice Denis's painting *Marthe au piano* of about October 1891.[32] And Debussy did write to Maeterlinck, through the intermediacy of Jules Huret (critic of *L'Echo de Paris*), to obtain his authorization to set *La Princesse Maleine* as an opera. But Maeterlinck refused this on 23 June 1891 as he had already promised the rights to Vincent d'Indy. And there the case of *La Princesse Maleine* ends as far as Satie and Debussy are concerned.

While Debussy did not employ any rhyming couplets in *Pelléas*, he did use a system of recurring leitmotifs for the main characters, against Satie's advice. And there is no evidence that he took anything from Puvis de Chavannes either. Puvis de Chavannes's simplified pastel colours and static decorative frescoes in an allegorical, moralizing vein were worlds away from the sensual, mysterious and psychologically alive atmosphere of *Pelléas*, which owes more to Turner and the pre-Raphaelites. As Anne Rey suggests (1974, 158), the 'narrative and gracile painting' of Puvis de Chavannes rather finds its 'perfect musical equivalent' in the flat and muted colours of Satie's *Socrate*.

Satie's claim that he suggested to Debussy the transference of Impressionist methods to music is dubious too. Whilst they may have discussed such concepts together, there is no evidence that Satie was ever inspired by Impressionist sources himself, and Debussy's harmonic audacities are already there in embryonic form in the Guiraud conversations of 1889. He continued to be influenced by Mussorgsky – as at the start of *Nuages* (1898–9) – and was anxious *not* to be regarded as an Impressionist anyway. His famous letter about his orchestral *Images* to his publisher Jacques Durand in March 1908 clarifies his views:

> I am attempting 'something different' – in a sense, *realities* – what imbeciles call 'Impressionism', a term which is as misused as it could possibly be, especially by art critics who use it as a label to stick on Turner, the finest creator of mystery in the whole of art!

In his *Images*, Debussy saw the everyday scenes he was evoking 'quite clearly' and he wanted them to seem as spontaneous as possible. Whilst he was as slow and careful as Satie in preparing his scores, Debussy's whole approach was radically different. Satie never wanted his works to sound as though they were improvised, or to create any sort of dream-world, and Debussy, on the other hand, had no interest in compositional systems or the effects of insistent repetition. The main difference, of course, lies in Debussy's mastery of the orchestra. If his creation of a new sound-world in the *Prélude à L'Après-midi d'un faune* (1892–4) owes nothing to Satie in terms of technique, then Satie undoubtedly played a part in making Debussy's art more French at a crucial turning-point in his career.

As their friendship developed in the 1890s, Debussy helped Satie in several ways. First, through moral support and by treating his Rose-Croix music seriously. When Satie's solo performance of *Uspud* provoked hilarity and uproar at the Auberge du Clou, Latour says (6 August 1925, 2) that Debussy alone remained 'undisturbed' by its oddity. Satie, as was later the case with *Socrate*, was ready to defy 'those who did not understand it, flatly declaring that they were nothing but ignorant and bourgeois'. Debussy's astute insight into Satie's serious motivation provided an invaluable counter-force to Satie's incipient paranoia, and the two came closer together as a result. Secondly, Debussy did his best to promote Satie's compositions, taking advantage of his growing reputation to help break down official hostility. After the failure of Satie's confrontational tactics at the Opéra with *Uspud* in December 1892, Debussy approached his friend Chausson in 1893 to try to get Satie's works played by the Société Nationale. As Satie told his brother proudly on 28 June:

> The Société Nationale (the famous Society of Franck, Saint-Saëns, Vincent d'Indy & Co.) is going to play several of my orchestral pieces this winter (they will probably choose a Gymnopédie, a Sarabande and a Gnossienne, as well as the song 'Roxane').[33] Debussy has shown some of my works to Chausson, who almost fainted, and it is that which has persuaded them to play my pieces as fragments.   (Vc)

But in the event Satie's music did not feature in the Société Nationale's 1893–4 season alongside Debussy's String Quartet and *Proses lyriques*. Satie's frustration in this period can be seen in his open letter to Saint-Saëns (published in *Le Ménestrel*) after he had again been ignored when he applied to fill the vacant seat at the Académie des Beaux-Arts left by the death of Gounod. In his guise as 'maître de chapelle de l'Eglise Métropolitaine d'Art de Jésus Conducteur', Satie wavers in May 1894 between justified indignation and paranoia:

> A feeling of justice or, in its absence, of simple politeness made me believe that my candidacy, approved by God, would be accepted by you. My distress was great when I saw that you had forgotten solidarity in Art in favour of vulgar preferences. Let those of my colleagues whom you have similarly insulted humble themselves: as for me, I will not give up my right to have at least my existence recognized. . . Your aberration can only be due to your refusal to accept the ideas of the century and to your ignorance of God, which is the direct cause of Esthetic decline.
>
> (Templier, 1969, 21–2)

Saint-Saëns did not deign to reply, and even those closest to Satie must have found his religious persona difficult to deal with. Given the odds against Satie, Debussy's faith in his eventual success seems the more remarkable. However, Satie proved to be a shrewd judge of the character and achievements of others. He later observed that the nonentities 'Messieurs Paladilhe, Dubois and Lenepveu were preferred' to him as members of the Institute 'for no reason whatsoever'.[34] Few would have regarded Théodore Dubois as Satie's musical inferior in 1894, but Satie knew exactly where he stood in the scale of events, even then. His anger arose from frustration, for those that appreciated his worth were few and far between, and throughout his life he only found a handful of friends in whom he could confide – notably Debussy, his brother Conrad, Valentine Gross, Milhaud, Henri-Pierre Roché and André Derain. As he told Saint-Saëns in 1894: 'You can accuse me of one thing only: of not knowing myself as well as I know you.' It was the constant introspection that led to the apparent distortions in Satie's personality: but viewed from the inside his perspectives seem clear and logical. In reality, he knew himself and his limitations extremely well, and was simply being modest here.

Satie did not gain a hearing at the Société Nationale until February 1897, when his third and first *Gymnopédies* were conducted by Gustave Doret in Debussy's orchestration. This was the only occasion when Debussy orchestrated the work of another composer, which helps put his esteem for Satie in its proper perspective. Had he not been associated with the enterprise, it is certain that Chausson would not have agreed to the performance, and Debussy's orchestration is the only musical event we can associate with Satie in 1896. According to Doret (1942, 98), it happened thus:

> One Monday evening, Erik Satie brought me his *Gymnopédies* for piano, luxuriously printed. Eye-glasses poised for the assault, he seated himself at the piano. But his defective playing did not display his compositions to their best advantage. 'Hang on, my old friend', said Debussy. 'I will let you hear your music.' Beneath his miraculous fingers, the *Gymnopédies* lit up with colours and nuances in an astonishing manner.
> 'It only remains', I exclaimed, 'to orchestrate them *thus*.'
> 'Quite right', replied Debussy. 'If Satie doesn't object, I will start work tomorrow.'
> You can imagine the unexpected joy of the composer.

This naive little summary rather reflects Doret's admiration for Debussy than the truth of the matter: doubtless he wanted to be associated with the creation of what became one of Satie's best-known works. For, although Satie disliked playing the piano, he was an adequate pianist, and certainly above the Grade IV standard needed to interpret his own *Gymnopédies*. Both because he was short of money, and because he wanted to learn from the process, Satie copied out Debussy's score of the *Gymnopédies* in red ink, and prepared all the orchestral parts. For anyone who claims that Debussy's orchestration runs contrary to Satie's intentions, Ex. 16 shows that Satie planned his own orchestration of the third *Gymnopédie* around 1894, with arpeggiated harp parts, divided pizzicato strings and even a voice part. But like so many of his orchestrations of this period, it peters out after only a few bars.

Ex. 16 Orchestration of the start of the *Troisième Gymnopédie* by Satie, *c.* 1894 (BN 9597(2), 1)

1896 was the year when Debussy made his most positive efforts on his friend's behalf: perhaps he had more time now that the vocal score of *Pelléas* was complete. He introduced Satie to the publisher Baudoux (who published *Le Fils des étoiles* that year), and to Jean Bellon of Bellon, Ponscarme et Cie, who later published Satie's popular songs *Je te veux*, *Tendrement* and *La Diva de l''Empire'* in 1902–4. He also defended Satie's music at social gatherings. For instance, it was at a dinner *chez* Bellon that Debussy's enthusiasm for Satie's early work helped overcome Charles Koechlin's initial incomprehension of the Rose-Croix music.[35] And at another dinner party at the home of the soprano Jane Bathori, Debussy 'vigorously defended Satie against Willy [Henry Gauthier-Villars]', adding that 'no musician had *dared* to openly attack the powerful critic of the *Echo de Paris, except Satie!*'[36] Since Debussy's famous letter to Willy about *L'Après-midi d'un faune* dates from October 1896, this dinner probably took place about this time.

On a personal level, we find Satie helping Debussy to find his new apartment at 10 rue Gustave-Doré late in 1893, and acting as a witness at his marriage to Rosalie (Lilly) Texier on 19 October 1899. Indeed, Satie, Robert Godet and Paul Dukas were the only true friends to support Debussy after his desertion of Lilly and his elopement with Emma Bardac in 1904.

The short years with Lilly, however, were vital ones as far as Satie was concerned. By early 1899 he was getting used to life in distant Arcueil, making some money accompanying Vincent Hyspa in cabarets, and only occasionally addressing his brother Conrad as 'Saint Erik d'Arcueil, Parcier et Martyre' from his 'Palais Abbatial'. Most of that summer (see Fig. 4.2) was spent working on his pantomime *Jack-in-the-Box* with his friend Jules Dépaquit. But black depression often intervened: usually it concerned the direction of his future career, in which the shadow of the more successful Debussy loomed ever-present. As he told Conrad on 7 June 1900: 'I am dying of boredom: everything I begin timidly fails with a certainty I've never before known till now. What can I do but turn towards God and point the finger at Him? I end up thinking that the old man is even more stupid than powerful' (Vl, 75). Then, on 4 February 1901, again to Conrad: 'I'm getting more and more fed up, for I can see clearly that I was not born into my proper period – a period I can't accommodate myself to, even by putting in something of myself, insofar as that is possible for me' (Vc).

At that time Satie was struggling with his unwieldy 'music for a tale by Lord Cheminot [Contamine de Latour]' entitled *The Dreamy Fish* (see Fig. 4.3). His numerous sketches and heavily corrected drafts show Satie searching for a new direction, and trying to reconcile the jaunty music-hall style of *Jack-in-the-Box*[37] with the harmonic advances of Debussy. He was also experimenting with greater rhythmic variety and fluidity, and a more traditional approach, which included a lyrical, self-contained central section (borrowed from *Geneviève de Brabant*).[38] It was the nearest Satie came to through-composition in extended paragraphs in place of his habitual motivic juxtaposition. Around 1901 he seems to have been genuinely concerned about his inability to write extended pieces, and he even tried a brief sort of development section in this strange, hybrid piece. Here, in the passage leading into the recapitulation, the shadow of Debussy looms largest in an uncharacteristic passage of luxuriant oscillating string chords (some in whole tones), and a rising climax constructed from arabesque-like woodwind figures (bars 113–20). Ex. 17 also shows that Satie was trying to think orchestrally, and another version of a later passage (bars 130–33)

4.2   Satie in the country, ?summer 1899.

4.3   Satie and ?Contamine de Latour (far right) outside a tavern in the early 1900s.

Ex. 17 *The Dreamy Fish*, sketch of bars 113–20 (BN 9587, f. 4*v*)

has giant harp arpeggios in rising sevenths and ninths in true 'impressionistic' style (BN 9587, f. 4*v*). The concept of Satie trying to imitate the revered Debussy is a touching one: it seems as if he was trying to compose Debussy out of his system, as Debussy had tried to do with Wagner in his *Cinq Poèmes de Baudelaire*. Although he must have sensed that this potential way forward was really an abortive cul-de-sac, Satie still felt obliged to try it. Perhaps Debussy had recommended such an exercise to remedy Satie's so-called deficiencies. But in trying to achieve too much at once, Satie produced an unconvincing piece, especially in its control of tonality. For all its surface activity, *The Dreamy Fish* is static, confused and more of an interesting experiment than a performable piece.

Around the turn of the century, Satie was caught in a cleft stick as far as Debussy was concerned. On the one hand, his isolation in Arcueil was such that he complained to Conrad in June 1901 that 'If I didn't have Debussy to talk to about things a bit above those common men discuss, I don't know what I should do to express my poor thoughts, if I do still express them. The artists of our day are becoming businessmen and think the same way as a lawyer' (Vl, 145). On the other hand, he was bowled over by *Pelléas et Mélisande* in 1902, which he told Conrad on 27 June was 'very chic! Absolutely astounding. This appreciation is pretty short, but how well it expresses my thoughts!' (Vc). And Satie told Cocteau later on how he had realized that 'nothing more can be done in this direction; I must search for something else or I am lost'.[39]

Debussy helpfully provided a temporary solution. Perhaps with *The Dreamy Fish* in mind,[40] he advised Satie to 'develop his sense of form' (Templier, 1969, 25), which led to the *Trois Morceaux en forme de poire*. These pieces feature in one of only three known letters to Debussy,[41] in which Satie reports on 17 August 1903 that he

> is working at the present time on a delightful work entitled *2 Morceaux en forme de poire*. Monsieur Erik Satie is crazy about this new invention of his mind. He talks about it a lot and says very good things about it. He believes it superior to everything he has written up till now; perhaps he's wrong, but we mustn't tell him so: he wouldn't believe it.
>
> You who know him well, tell him what you think about it; surely he will listen to you more attentively than to anyone, so great is his friendship for you.   (Vl, 146)

What Satie did was to work outwards from the centre, starting with the two pieces mentioned in the above letter, which became *Morceaux I* and *III*.[42] Perhaps on Debussy's advice, or perhaps because he liked working in threes, Satie added his second *Morceau* (No. 4) in September 1903 and changed the title on his manuscript (Opéra Rés. 218) accordingly. This movement was based on two cabaret songs written for Vincent Hyspa around 1899 (*Impérial-Napoléon* and *Le Veuf*), and it must have been at this point that Satie realized the potential of expanding the *Trois Morceaux* further into a compendium of his best achievements since 1890 arranged for piano duet – a resumé of his career to date, before it took off in a then unknown direction. The way the manuscript and its title page are laid out suggests that Satie then arranged the *Manière de commencement* (No. 1, also in September 1903) from a *Gnossienne* used in Act 1 of *Le Fils des étoiles* (1891), and then added the *En plus* (No. 6: a *Danse* of 1890), making five movements in all. At this stage, on the verso of page V of the *En plus*, he wrote his famous 'Recommendations' of 6 November 1903, as follows:

> I am at a prestigious turning-point in the History of My life. In this work, I express My appropriate and natural astonishment.
>
> Believe Me, despite the predispositions.
>
> Don't play around with the unknown amulets of your ephemeral understanding: sanctify your beloved and verbal phials. God will pardon you if he sees fit from the honourable centre of the united Eternity, where everything becomes known with solemnity and conviction. The Determined One cannot freeze; the Passionate One obliterates himself; the Irascible One has no reason to exist.
>
> I cannot promise more, even though I have temporarily increased myself tenfold, against all precautions.
>
> Is that not everything?
>
> I tell myself so.

This bizarre mixture of serious statement, humour, religiosity and occult references (to amulets and phials) reveals a confused state of mind that is at odds with the directness and popular appeal of the music. Satie proclaims himself in his paranoia as the God of his own small world, which suggests that it is always wise to consider his music on its own artistic merits, divorced from the paraphernalia that surrounds it.

Then Satie added a *Prolongation du même* to his *Manière de commencement*, and the *Redite* to his *En plus*,[43] bringing the final total to seven, with two pairs of balancing movements on either side of his *Trois Morceaux en forme de poire*. Of the seven movements, only the '2 Morceaux' with which he began were original compositions from 1903 designed specially for this work. The unusual title looks forward to the humorous piano pieces of 1913, and here the joke seems to have been at Debussy's expense. Vladimir Golschmann (1972, 11) reports Satie as saying that:

> All I did. . .was to write *Pieces in the form of a pear*. I brought them to Debussy, who asked, 'Why such a title?' Why? Simply, *my dear friend*, because you cannot criticize my *Pieces* in the shape of a pear. If they are *en forme de poire* they cannot be shapeless.

As 'poire' was also 'current Paris slang in 1903 for "head", and was used in the sense of "stupid head", i.e. fool' (Howe, 1948, 28n.), Satie may have been suggesting that Debussy was a fool for trying to direct him towards traditional forms. Whatever the truth of the matter, Debussy still helped Satie check the proofs of the *Trois Morceaux* in September 1911[44] when publication by Rouart-Lerolle was imminent. Satie remained proud of these 'little pieces' after the First World War, and often performed them in private and in public. At one such private performance with Pierre Bertin *chez* Roland-Manuel in 1912, his friends staged an 'oriental ballet (in imitation of *Shéhérazade*)' (Bertin, 1952, 73–4), though Satie remained blithely indifferent to their theatrical antics. And it was a performance of the *Trois Morceaux* by Satie and Ricardo Viñes on 18 April 1916 that inspired Cocteau to 'collaborate' with Satie on *Parade*.[45]

The decision to perfect his technique by study at the Schola Cantorum in 1905 was entirely Satie's own, and was made in the face of opposition from Debussy and Roussel. Like Berlioz, Debussy disapproved of academic counterpoint and thought this type of technical study could be detrimental to Satie's individuality. There is a slightly mocking tone in his dedication of his first series of *Images* in January 1906 to 'my old Satie, the celebrated contrapuntist'.[46] But that summer Debussy's mind was preoccupied by his divorce from Lilly, his new life with Emma, and the birth of their daughter Chouchou (on 30 October), so his dissuasion was less positive than it might otherwise have been. Roussel, on the other hand, put up more resistance,

> supposing him to be sufficiently acquainted with contrapuntal writing and not seeing what practical application he could make to his style through the study of four-part exercises. But he persisted, and the sober school in the rue Saint-Jacques had never known a more precise and disciplined pupil. I confess that, at the start, I felt somewhat put out, while I read his exercises through at the piano, by the presence, behind me, of this strange pupil who so little resembled the others. It seemed to me that his ironic smile intimated: 'Oh, oh! This is of course forbidden, mister professor? Really? Ah! how well this correction sounds! Here now is a truly unblemished piece of counterpoint!'[47]

On 15 June 1908, Satie was duly awarded his diploma in counterpoint signed by d'Indy and Roussel 'with the distinction "Très-bien". He has fulfilled the required conditions to devote himself exclusively to the study of composition.'[48] Proud of his licence to compose, Satie continued to develop the chorale and fugue along modern lines in original compositions. He may well have had this aim in mind even before he entered the Schola, for he told his brother in September 1911 (on finishing *En Habit de cheval*) that 'I have spent eight years in realizing this new sort of fugue' (Vc). This may help to explain why he was so determined to study with Roussel in 1905. His first definitive fugal essay came in the *Aperçus désagréables*. As this fugue is dated September 1908, Debussy must have been the first to see it, for he told his fellow-composer Francisco de Lacerda on 5 September that 'your friend E. Satie has just finished a fugue in which boredom disguises itself behind wicked harmonies and in which you will recognize the influence of the aforementioned establishment'.[49] The wicked harmonies, contorted chromatic lines and uncharacteristic syncopation in Ex. 18 show that Satie had not lost his sense of humour through his academic studies, as Debussy feared. Indeed, this fugue may have been intended as a *tour de force* to impress Debussy, for it is one of Satie's most rigorous and developed essays in this form. Regarding the treatment of fugue as more than just an exercise, Cocteau reports that Debussy advised Satie to 'Take care. You are playing a dangerous game. At your age you cannot change your skin.' To which Satie is supposed to have replied: 'If I miss my goal, so much the worse for me. It will mean that I have nothing in me' (Cocteau, 1924, 222). Although this way forward was soon supplanted by the humorous piano pieces, the modern fugue recurs at the start of *Parade*.

The *Aperçus* fugue proves that Satie could now tackle more extended compositions with success and was far from having 'nothing in him'. He could and did 'change his skin' many times, and Debussy is more likely here to have been opposing his

Ex. 18 *Aperçus désagréables*. No. 3: *Fugue*, bars 38–47

adoption of academic forms that he considered alien to his nature. No doubt he did not realize that the sectional construction of the fugue, with its methodical approach, suited Satie down to the ground, for Satie, like Ravel, was obsessively secretive about his working methods. On another level, the *Aperçus désagréables* must have been designed for Satie and Debussy to play together, for a little dialogue runs through the fugue for Debussy's amusement,[50] and they may have read it out as they went along (see Ex. 18). Being the dominant partner, Debussy would have played the Primus part:

Bar	SECUNDUS	Bar	PRIMUS
4	Smile	4	With pleasure
	–	10	Naturally
15	Since		–
23	Right [hand]	23	Without naughtiness [as the two players' right hands come close together]

25	Visible	26	From the corner
34	Necessarily	34	Much
	–	38	To be looked at [=See me]
41	Don't talk	43	Speak
45	Affected		–
50	Look out		–

and so on. Perhaps Satie turned to the piano duet in 1903–12 on Debussy's advice, both because it would force him to think more contrapuntally, and because he could easily get such works performed in a then-popular domestic format. Later he published *Parade* in duet form, as well as his 'serious fantasy' *La Belle Excentrique* (1920).

After Ravel had paved the way by rehabilitating Satie's early piano works in January 1911, Debussy agreed to conduct his orchestrations of the *Gymnopédies* on 25 March. When Debussy expressed his surprise at the success of this concert, Satie was understandably annoyed. As he told Conrad on 11 April:

> One person who isn't pleased is the good Claude. It's really his own fault; if he had done sooner what Ravel – who makes no secret of the influence I had on him – has done, his position would be different. . .The success achieved by the *Gymnopédies* at the concert conducted by him at the Cercle Musical – a success which he did everything possible to turn into a failure – gave him an unpleasant surprise.
>
> I'm not angry with him about it. He's the victim of his social climbing. Why won't he allow me a very small place in his shadow? I have no use for the sun. His conduct has antagonized the 'Ravelites' and the 'Satieists', people who have been keeping quiet in their place, but who are now yelling at each other like polecats.
>
> (Vl, 147)

Debussy's cool relations with Ravel also played a part in this, and though none of them liked the concept of factions, Satie relished the publicity it brought his music, and rightly foresaw that it would not be long before his more recent compositions enjoyed similar acclaim.

But he still had the highest regard for Debussy's music. After he had been to see the ill-fated *Le Martyre de Saint Sébastien*,[51] he told Conrad on 29 May 1911 that 'M. Gabriele d'Annunzio gave us a very incomplete piece, poor man. A very select and numerous audience. Your brother was very hot. Very beautiful interpretation. Claude's music was very successful; it saved the situation' (Vc). Given the 'situation' between the two composers, and the fact that by no means all of *Le Martyre* is first-rate Debussy, this was a generous review. Whether Satie addressed his comments to Debussy too is not known, but it is likely that Satie kept many of his true thoughts about his august mentor to himself. In 1912, according to Roland-Manuel (1952, 10), Satie 'exasperated Debussy by promising him that his next publication would be a piece called 'The Bottom of the Barrel [*Sous la futaille*]'. No-one who loved music could dream of such a thing, in Debussy's opinion. But Satie did, as BN 9632 shows, though he did change the title to *Avec camaraderie* before adding it as the fourth of his *Préludes flasques (pour un chien)*. But if Debussy was the 'camarade' in question in

4.4   Debussy and Satie in Debussy's studio at 80 Avenue du Bois de Boulogne, Paris 16 (now the Avenue Foch) in 1910.

this jolly dance, and did force a change of title on a reluctant Satie, the *Préludes flasques* were never published in Satie's lifetime and very little of the music was altered with the title. Perhaps Debussy's anger was fuelled by hearing of another Satie title *Le Vent dans la 'futaille'*,[52] which was intended as a parody of his own 1909 prelude *Le Vent dans la plaine*.

Relations probably became closer in 1913 as Debussy sensed his own insecurity in the light of Stravinsky's ascendant star, and because Debussy approached Satie's world more closely in his children's ballet *La Boîte à joujoux*. Satie loved children and wrote some delightful *Enfantines* in 1913 which show how well he understood their fantasy world and the sort of music children would enjoy playing. He was like an elder brother to Debussy's daughter Chouchou, who called him Kiki. They often played together with 'bows and arrows', and when they ventured on the manicured grass in the Avenue du Bois de Boulogne, Debussy (ever the father-figure) would scold them both.[53] In *La Boîte* in September–October 1913 we find Debussy taking extracts from the popular Classics,[54] as Satie had done earlier in his *Croquis et agaceries*, and using snippets from French popular songs,[55] as Satie had done in his *Descriptions automatiques* that April, and in his *Embryons desséchés* two months later. Both composers used extracts from Gounod's *Faust* during September 1913, and it is hard to believe that they did not discuss their projects together. However, Satie's *Chez le Marchand d'Or* (the first of the *Vieux sequins et vieilles cuirasses*) was completed by 9 September, whereas Debussy did not begin his second tableau of *La Boîte* (with its references to Gounod's 'Soldiers' Chorus' one-third of the way through) until 6 September at the earliest. The most intriguing parallel of all comes near the end of this tableau in a row of chromatically ascending major seconds (Ex. 19b) from about 20 September. Ex. 19a shows an extract (also in reality in triple time) from Satie's *Españaña*, completed on 25 August. The chord onto which Ex. 19b emerges (with its repeated staccato quavers) is strikingly similar to the final bar of Ex. 19a too, and the only differences lie in the length of Debussy's run of major seconds and in the dynamic levels.

At the same time, Satie made numerous allusions to the composer he most admired in his 1913 piano pieces, as a sort of homage. Due to their context, the results never sound at all Debussyan, and there is no case of straightforward borrowing. The points for comparison are given in Exx. 20–3, most of them being concentrated in *Regrets des Enfermés*, the last of the *Chapitres tournés en tous sens*. Perhaps Satie regarded

Ex. 19a Satie: *Españaña*, systems 7–8 (25 August 1913)

Ex. 19b Debussy: *La Boîte à joujoux* (Tableau 2), reduction 34, bars 1–10 (*c.* 20 September 1913)

Ex. 20a Satie: *Danse maigre*, final system (2 June 1913)

Ex. 20b Debussy: '*Les sons et les parfums tournent dans l'air du soir*', start (Preludes: Book 1 No. 4, 1 January 1910)

Ex. 21a Satie: *Regrets des Enfermés*, systems 12–13 (5 September 1913)

Ex. 21b Debussy: *Images oubliées*, No. 3, bars 48–50 (1894)

Ex. 22a Satie: *Regrets des Enfermés*, system 10 (1913)

Ex. 22b Debussy: *Nuages*, bars 1–2 (1898–9)

Ex. 23a Satie: *Regrets des Enfermés*, end (1913)

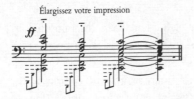

Ex. 23b Debussy: *Pour le piano*, No. 1: Prelude, end (1901)

Debussy as an imprisoned man after his ostracizing marriage to Emma Bardac, like Jonah and Jean-Henri Masers de Latude, whose stories he tells in this piece. It is based on the folksong *Nous n'irons plus au bois*, which had similarly obsessed Debussy from his song *La Belle au bois dormant* (Vincent Hyspa: 1890), through the third of his 1894 *Images* and *Jardins sous la pluie* (1903) to *Rondes de printemps* (from the orchestral *Images*) in 1905–9. *Regrets des Enfermés (Jonas et Latude)* is dedicated to Mme Claude Debussy, perhaps ironically, though Satie's other dedications to Debussy and his family[56] contain no such positive musical references.

In 1913 Satie's growing confidence can also be seen in his review of Debussy's ballet *Jeux* in the *Revue musicale SIM* of 15 June (Ve, 134–5). Since its première a month earlier, the impact of *Jeux* had been eclipsed by the scandal of Stravinsky's *Rite of Spring* on 29 May and, to be fair, Satie's satire was directed at Nijinsky's setting and choreography, not Debussy's score. Satie knew that Debussy disliked Nijinsky's Dalcrozian methods and mathematical approach, and the dancer clearly knew little about the game of tennis around which his slight scenario revolved. The movements he invented more resembled those of golf, and the bouncing ball that Debussy evoked so graphically in his score was nearly as large as a football, which provoked much mirth on the opening night. So Satie's review is consistent with his declared policy of 'never attacking Debussy', and he even signed it 'Swift' to be on the safe side. What Satie actually thought of Debussy's score remains unknown, but the tone and style of the following review are unmistakable:

> *Summer sports*. Several readers have asked about the rules of Russian tennis which will be all the rage in country house-parties this season. They are as follows: the game is played at night on floodlit flower beds; there are only three players; the net is done away with; the ball is replaced by a football and the use of the racquet is banned. In a pit at the end of the court one conceals an orchestra which accompanies the games. The purpose of this sport is to develop an extreme suppleness in the movements of the wrists, neck and ankles; it has the blessing of the Academy of Medicine.

In fact, Satie's review probably amused Debussy, who had been disappointed by the lack of impact of his attempt to 'bring *rhythm* alive in a musical atmosphere'.[57] He had sought to dissociate himself from Nijinsky's contribution in this same article in *Le Matin* on the day of the première.[58] Whilst his cinematographic approach, the tendency towards a constant pulse, and the use of twenty-one short motifs (few of which recur) may suggest parallels with Satie's own methods, the way Debussy develops his motifs into larger units, and his polyrhythmic inventiveness and subtle orchestral palette yield wholly different results. Satie, on the sidelines of a masterpiece, must have been overawed by Debussy's technical achievement in *Jeux*, but at the same time he knew that vast orchestras, the sensual evocation of stage action, and the bourgeois concept of the diverting entertainment represented the end of an era. Roland-Manuel says (1952, 9) that, as early as 1910, Satie 'considered Debussy as a musician of the past. Ravel illustrated the present, whilst the future was promised to Albert Roussel.' Satie later came to down-grade his opinion of Ravel, and to substitute Stravinsky for Roussel, but his opinion of Debussy remained constant. In this he was backed by Diaghilev, who employed Satie and Stravinsky rather than Debussy for his future Ballets Russes commissions. Indeed, Satie's restrained orchestral forces, clear-cut sonorities, and cabaret-derived ambience themselves came to represent the future in French art, leaving much more to the listener's imagination.

During the War, Satie (who served in the Home Guard in Arcueil) came to regard Debussy's patriotism and lamented inability to help the national cause with suspicion. The contrast between their life-styles was partly to blame, though Debussy, despite his affluence on the surface, was deeper in debt than Satie. Jealousy and isolation also played a part in Satie's outburst to Paul Dukas on 18 August 1915 that 'Debussy bathes at the seaside in Dieppe. . .He understands nothing of the War. For me, this war is like a sort of Apocalypse, more idiotic than real. Happily we shall not be present at this grandiose, but stupid and inhuman *final* ceremony' (Vc). But, in this case, Satie misunderstood the true depths of Debussy's feelings. Debussy's creativity was reduced to a minimum by the worsening crises of 1914, and as early as 8 August he had told Durand that he was 'nothing more than a wretched atom hurled around by this terrible cataclysm, and what I'm doing seems to me so miserably petty! It makes me envious of Satie and his real job of defending Paris as a corporal.'[59]

Debussy's frustration increased as he developed rectal cancer during the winter of 1915–16. Satie often visited him to try to cheer him up as he became 'more and more serious'.[60] We find him playing 'backgammon with poor Debussy' all afternoon on 6 January 1916,[61] and telling Dukas after another such visit in March that 'our great friend seems rather better. He is constantly in great suffering, however. But let us hope! yes, hope!' (Vc). On 20 November, Satie told Cocteau how much he was troubled by Emma Debussy's letter about her husband's state of health, but by then Satie was working flat out on *Parade* and could spare less time to visit his ailing friend.

In early 1917 Debussy rallied sufficiently to complete his last major work, the Violin Sonata. However much he disapproved of the direction Satie's career was now taking, he still took an active interest in it, even attending the rehearsals of *Parade*. It was during one of these that Debussy must have voiced the opinions that caused the break between them, for on 8 March Satie sent the following curt letter to Mme Debussy: 'Decidedly, it will be preferable if henceforth the "Precursor" stays at home, far away. P.S. Painful teasing – and at a rehearsal too! Quite unbearable, anyhow' (Vl, 148). Debussy nonetheless attended the scandalous première of *Parade* at the Théâtre du Châtelet on 18 May where, according to Pierre Bertin (1971, 77), he joined in the general furore, shouting 'Be off with you, you're too ugly!' to Picasso's Cubist Managers in their ungainly costumes. It sounds as if he objected to the staging rather than to Satie's music, and what his criticisms in this direction were can only be surmised. No doubt his main objection was to the whole concept of this 'ballet réaliste': as an anarchic farce that was totally insensitive to the political situation at the time. The holocaust on the Western Front was at its worst, with hundreds of Frenchmen dying daily in seemingly futile advances against the German lines on the river Aisne. Russia had just defaulted, and Allied morale was at a low ebb; and to be faced with a Russian ballet company performing such trivialities, with Russian soldiers in the audience (at Diaghilev's invitation) was an affront to any Frenchman, especially the sensitive Debussy. Despite Diaghilev advertising the première as being for the benefit of various war charities, the public (a mixture of high society, and artists from Montmartre and Montparnasse on complimentary tickets) was understandably hostile, for political as much as for artistic reasons. The perpetrators of *Parade* were branded as Boches, which in Satie's case took a long while to live down, and greatly troubled him. It must have been inconceivable to Debussy that Satie could so divorce his music from his own life, and from the political events surrounding him. But in judging Satie, Debussy also passed judgment on his music, and this Satie could never forgive. His inexorable path forward took precedence over personal loyalties (as his close friend Roland-Manuel was also to discover after he criticized *Socrate*), and his 'ten months of hard labour' on *Parade*[62] could not be allowed to pass in vain. Satie's preoccupation with the libel case brought against him by Jean Poueigh after *Parade* meant that the rift with Debussy went unhealed until Debussy was on his deathbed. The fact that Satie, for the only time in his life, relented is a tribute to the strength of their friendship. As he told Henry Prunières on 3 April 1918: 'You know of Debussy's death, of course. I wrote to him – fortunately for me – a few days before his death. Knowing that he was doomed, alas, I didn't want to remain on bad terms with him. My poor friend! What a sad end. Now people will discover that he had enormous talent. That's life!' (Vl, 150). On reading Satie's apology, Debussy simply muttered 'Sorry!', though in the end each composer arrived at a better understanding of how the other had suffered.

For Satie, Debussy's passing had an effect parallel to that of Schoenberg's death on Stravinsky. Whilst Stravinsky felt able to approach serialism without a backward glance after 1951, Satie in 1918 was at last able to complete his symphonic drama *Socrate* and have it performed without fear of criticism from the source he dreaded most. It might uncharitably be said that Debussy's death had more influence on Satie's music than any event during his lifetime, and that its liberating effect allowed Satie to become a more serious composer in *Socrate* and the *Nocturnes*. But, in reality, much of *Socrate* was composed while Debussy was alive. So his death was really only part of a chain of events in which Satie's growing circle of friends had played a more significant role since 1911. Nothing was allowed to detract Satie from his forward path, and he only really took stock of the emotional effect of Debussy's passing in his *Elégie* two years later. An extreme case of a delayed reaction, perhaps.

I cannot agree with Ned Rorem (1981, 16) that 'Satie never did anything that Debussy didn't do better', because the two composers' achievements never really overlapped, and because the pieces in which Satie tried to imitate Debussy were never published by him. As Louis Laloy said (1928, 258–9):

> A tempestuous and yet indissoluble friendship bound Debussy to Satie. Or rather,
> it was like one of those family hatreds which was aggravated by the repeated shock

of incompatible traits, without destroying the deep sympathy of the characters that was due to their common origin. . .A musical brotherhood; yet a rivalry of musicians.

How much they really had in common, besides a love of things English, and a desire to carry French music into the twentieth century against all odds, is debatable. But for an arch enemy of Satie's, Laloy provides a pretty fair summary. Even so, we should leave the last word to Satie in 1922 (Ve, 68):

> My poor friend! And to think that if he were still alive, we would today be the worst of enemies. Life – and the 'Debussyists' – would have taken it upon themselves to separate us, and to sow the seeds of hate between us. We were no longer on the same road; our horizons were continually shifting. So?. . .
>
> Our long friendship would have been ruined for evermore.

5

Satie's compositional aesthetic

During the composition of *Mort de Socrate* in the latter part of 1917, Satie made a unique and completely serious statement about the nature of his art on the cover of the notebook concerned (BN 9611). It is typical of the paradoxical Satie that this most impersonal and detached of works is accompanied by his most deeply personal statement. But perhaps the composition of the vital part of what he knew would be his main claim to future respect forced him to concentrate his mind. And his recent break with Debussy had increased his sense of independence and his seriousness of purpose. *Socrate*, without doubt, entailed a thorough examination of the principles underlying his art, and the result was 'Subject matter (Idea) and Craftsmanship (Construction)'.[1] Its centrality to the whole question of how Satie composed merits its full reproduction:

> Craftsmanship is often superior to subject matter.
>
> To have a feeling for harmony is to have a feeling for tonality.
>
> The serious examination of a melody will always make an excellent *harmonic* exercise for the student.
>
> A melody does not imply *its harmony*, any more than a landscape implies its *colour*. The harmonic *potential* of a melody is infinite, for a melody is only an expression within the overall Expression.
>
> Do not forget that the melody is the Idea, the outline; as much as it is the form and the subject matter of a work. The harmony is an illumination, an exhibition of the object, its reflection.
>
>   *   *   *
>
> In composition, the various parts, between themselves, no longer follow 'school' rules. 'School' has a gymnastic aim, nothing more; composition has an aesthetic aim, in which taste alone plays a part.
>
> Make no mistake: the understanding of grammar does not imply the understanding of literature; grammar can help or be set aside as the writer pleases, and on his responsibility. Musical grammar is nothing but grammar.
>
> One cannot criticize the craft of an artist as if it constituted a system. If there is form and a new style of writing, there is a new craft.
>
> To speak of 'craft' requires great care and – in any event – great learning.

Who possesses such learning?

The error arises in that a great many artists lack ideas in general, and even specific ideas.

Great Masters are brilliant through their ideas, their craft is a simple means to an end, nothing more. It is their ideas which endure.

What they achieve is always good and seems natural to us.

The craft of Bach is not a contrapuntal exercise. Craft, in an exercise, should be defective; in composition, it is perfect.

Who established the Truths governing Art? Who?

The Masters. They had no right to do so and it is dishonest to concede this power to them. Everyone has had professional cases to complain about. Look at Rodin, Manet, Debussy, etc. But the Masters are not seized by the police, nor by ushers or other magistrates.

* * *

Become artists unconsciously.

The Idea can do without Art.

Let us mistrust Art: it is often nothing but virtuosity.

Impressionism is the art of Imprecision; today we tend towards Precision.

In his first section, Satie is clearly reacting against the Conservatoire tradition of harmonizing a given melody, at the same time as stating his beliefs about the relative importance of melody and harmony in his own compositions. Satie had first-hand experience of Conservatoire methods from being an 'auditeur' in Antoine Taudou's harmony class in 1883–4,[2] and he may also have attended Ernest Guiraud's composition classes in 1891 on Debussy's recommendation. His hatred of this reactionary corrective institution burst forth on several occasions. In the first version of his ballet *Uspud*,[3] he writes (beneath a prayer for the dead) on 17 November 1892: 'I entered your classes as a child. My spirit was then so gentle that you could not understand me. . .by your lack of intelligence you have made me hate the clumsy art that you teach; by your implacable austerity you have long since made me despise you.' Satie achieved a measure of retribution through a wicked article on Ambroise Thomas in *L'Œil de veau* (Ve, 17), where his achievements as Conservatoire Director and composer take second place to Satie's fury over a lost umbrella. But the whole concept of reverence for the Masters of the past and the slavish adherence to academic rules still irked Satie in 1917. Although he had had to harmonize Bach chorales at the Schola Cantorum in 1906–7 (see Exx. 31b and 32), Roussel's approach had been freer and more contrapuntal, and there is no implied criticism of his teaching here.

In the layout of his credo, Satie may have the Schola's *Cours de composition musicale* in mind, with its tendency towards down-to-earth summary statements and italicized key-words. Here, in the section on harmony,[4] we find assertions such as:

Harmony is the simultaneous issue of several different melodies.

Musically, *chords* do not exist, and harmony is not the *science of chords*.

> The study of chords *in their own right* is an absolute aesthetic error, for harmony
> springs from melody, and should never be separated from it in application.
> The affinity between sounds reveals itself both *melodically* and *harmonically*.

D'Indy's philosophy may be different, but the assured presentation of ideas is markedly similar. Indeed, it is a tribute to the Schola's enlightened methods that it could develop craftsmanship without stifling originality, as its many composer–pupils show. Its foundation in sound technique based on a thorough knowledge of the Masters of the past might well serve as a model for the teaching of today.

First and foremost, Satie's article reveals the primacy of melody in his art. This constitutes the idea behind the work, traces its outlines and conditions its form and content. The work that emerges from it is illuminated by its harmony, which is tonal in origin. In cases like Satie's songs where two melodic lines are involved – the voice and the upper accompaniment line – it was invariably the latter that came first and conditioned the content of the song. Although Satie may have had a basic idea for the vocal line, or planned its rhythm in advance, the voice part was fitted around the accompaniment, rather than vice versa – in direct contrast to the nineteenth-century French concept of the *mélodie*. This concept can even be found in a large-scale work like *Socrate*. Thus, we should first look for a melodic logic behind Satie's juxtaposition of the musical cells from which most of his works are constructed. To return to the 1920 *Elégie* for Debussy, a relatively straightforward case, Satie began by planning the rhythm of the vocal line (bars 1–6) on a monotone e^1. It seems from this, and from Ex. 24a, that he intended to centre the song in E minor, although C major is the only key reached in the final version (Ex. 24d), which appears to begin and end on the (?neapolitan) centre of F. Ex. 24a, a series of undulating parallel fifths, was Satie's first 'melodic' thought. This survived to condition the form and content of the whole *Elégie* through transposition – for Satie frequently reused his cells at different pitches, favouring transpositions of a perfect fourth or fifth. He then 'illuminated' his basic idea (Ex. 24a) by harmonizing it in different ways (Ex. 24b), numbering the cells as they were to appear in his final version (Ex. 24d). This produced the monothematic form in four three-bar units as follows:

A	A1	A	A2
	(A, down an octave and a fifth, reharmonized)		(An incomplete form of A1. Notes 1 and 3 only)

The contrast between the sections, as so often in Satie, is one of register, with the textures reflecting the motivic form in this supremely economical song. A2 gave Satie the most trouble, both because of the tonal ambiguity he wanted for the end of the song, and because of his concern for logical voice-leading. His three preliminary attempts at A2 can be seen in Ex. 24c, which harmonize notes 1 and 3 of A1, and show e^1 as the leading-note to f^1, the bass note with which the song began. The cadential bass line, decided on during stage 3 of Ex. 24c is, however, a red herring. Although it exactly mirrors the bass line at the end of A1 (Ex. 24d, bars 5–6), the dissonant climax in bar 11 and the whole-tone disappearance in bar 12 ensure that F is never established as a tonal centre.

Lastly, Satie composed the anguished vocal line, the object of the whole exercise, but only after he had established the form and content to his satisfaction from its basis in a simple undulating idea. The vocal line, in turn, went through two different versions (see Ex. 24d), with Satie composing the angularity into it with Lamartine's poem and his own emotional tribute to Debussy in mind. The only thing that is at all conventional in Satie's compositional process is the right hand link Satie added later between A1 and the return of A in bar 6. After his disorientating modulation to C (Ex. 24d, bars 5–6), this again suggests F (minor) and leads to the f¹ in the left hand (bar 7), which is again contradicted by the implied basis on E of the upper voices. One might say that this main phrase of the song was bitonal, with the upper voices in a phrygian E minor and the lower voices (in octaves) in F major. But so subtle is Satie's control of tonal ambiguity that the two voices coincide on a first inversion chord of E minor in bars 3 and 9, confirming that E minor is the main tonal centre after all, despite the apparent equality of the lines that make up motif A. The logical conclusions which Satie expects us to draw are that everything ends where it began,

Ex. 24 *Elégie* (September 1920)

a. The initial idea (BN 9576, 8)

b. The 4 cells (BN 9576, 8–9)

c. The 3 stages in the emergence of cell 4 (BN 9576, 8)

Ex. 24 (*cont.*)

d. The complete song, also showing the first version of vocal line (BN 9576, 10–11)

and that bars 10–12 of Ex. 24d extend into unresolved infinity through the implied completion of motif A2 by whatever means. Whilst the parallel fifths and whole-tone chords may be seen as a tribute to Debussy, the bitonal approach, absolute economy and the sonorous left-hand octaves identify Satie as the author. These last are the only Germanic feature in Satie's otherwise French art. But perhaps they rather derived from his years as a cabaret pianist?

Another example from the previous month in 1920, the *Marche Franco-Lunaire* from *La Belle Excentrique*,[5] shows both how varied Satie's music was in his later years, and the lengths to which he was prepared to go to make his harmony a 'reflection' of the melody (which he still used to control the form). From 1913 onwards, Satie often chose actual popular melodies, or his own equivalents of them, for his 'outlines'. They were usually scale- or arpeggio-based, with regular phrasing. While the melodies made the music outwardly accessible, Satie's unpredictable harmonies 'exhibited' them in an individual way. One disappointing conclusion is that Satie was less adventurous rhythmically than one would expect for such a precursive composer, and his sensitive harmonic ear seems to have been his greatest gift.

Ex. 25 *La Belle Excentrique*. 1: *Marche Franco-Lunaire* (1920)

a. First version of opening melody (BN 9605(2), 8–9)

b. Final version of opening melody (BN 9605(2), 10–11, completed from printed version)

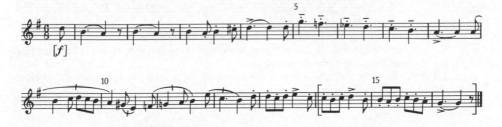

In the case of the *Marche Franco-Lunaire* the melody outlines the simple ritornello form (with two episodes) as follows:

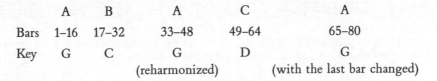

	A	B	A	C	A
Bars	1–16	17–32	33–48	49–64	65–80
Key	G	C	G	D	G
			(reharmonized)		(with the last bar changed)

As Satie's compositions hardly ever emerged through-composed, or in their final printed orders, it comes as no surprise to find him writing the episodes (B and C) first. He even finalized their instrumentation *before* composing the ritornello (A), though he had a clear idea of where everything fitted beforehand for he numbered the bars individually (as above) as he went along. The cabaret-style melody for A arrived in only two drafts (Exx. 25a–b), and the main problem with the first draft (Ex. 25a) seems to have been that it was too low-pitched to make a striking initial impression. Perhaps it also stayed too close to the basic keys of G and D and did not offer Satie the harmonic possibilities he required. It also ended inconclusively, which threatened to undermine the clear formal plan. So, rather than modify it, Satie wrote a second version (Ex. 25b) with more incisive rhythms and internal contrasts, and a wider range of modulations. The fact that Ex. 25b stops three bars short of the end is not significant: Satie knew how to finish it by sequential extension and simply did not bother to write it out.

Ex. 25 *(cont.)*
The genesis of bars 1–4 of the *Marche Franco-Lunaire*. All the following sketches from BN 9605(2) are in pencil, unless otherwise indicated

c. (p. 11) (Part of a first draft of bars 1–8, immediately below Ex. 25b)
f. (p. 10) (In bar 2 Satie discovers the parallel octave conception of the final version, and in bar 1 the idea of putting the accompaniment above the melody)
g. (p. 12) (Satie discovers the parallel octave conception of bar 1 with the C♮ above the melody, cf. Ex. 25ab)

i. (p. 12) (Satie discovers the basis of bars 3–4 by making a textural contrast to a simpler version of bars 1–2. In bar 4 the alto line is eventually transferred to the bass)

Ex. 25 (*cont.*)

k. (p. 12) (Satie discovers the F♮/F♯ succession, but in bar 2 rather than bar 1. He reverts to parallel octaves in bar 1)

l. (p. 13) (Satie comes a stage closer to the final version by reverting to the process begun in Ex. 25g)

m. (p. 13) (The F♮/F♯ succession appears in bar 1)

p. (p. 13) (Satie comes a stage closer to the final version of bars 3–4. The addition of dynamics looks promising, but the net result is still too diatonic and conventional)

q. (p. 12) (Satie discovers all the elements of bars 3–4 and inks them in in black, including the trombone part. He is still dissatisfied with bars 1–2 and crosses them out here)

Ex. 25 (*cont.*)

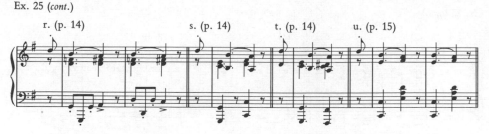

s. (p. 14) (Satie works on bar 1 only, but comes no closer to fulfilling his intentions)

t. (p. 14) (ibid.)

u. (p. 15) (Satie goes back to square one, cf. Ex. 25c)

v. (p. 15) (The rare diminished sevenths suggest an element of desperation as Satie reverts to solving the problem of bar 1)

w. (p. 15) (Satie discovers the G♯ he will later transfer to bar 2)

x. (p. 15)/y. (p. 15)/z. (p. 15) (Satie works on the voice-leading in the upper parts of bar 1. In z he finally gets the effect he wants through the superposition of fifths and fourths, and is now ready to write his final version)

aa. (p. 15, top RH corner) (Satie is satisfied at last with bars 1–2 and adds instrumental indications, though this process in itself takes three further stages to incorporate the woodwind, due to the complexity of the voice-leading)

aa. (p. 15, top RH corner)

ab. The final version of bars 1–4 arranged for piano duet (as in the Eschig printed score)

Then his real problems began, of how to find just the right texture and harmonies for the opening. Again, typically, he got bars 3–4 fixed in his mind (see Exx. 25i, p and q) long before he solved the puzzle of bars 1–2. The twenty-five attempts he made (Exx. 25c–ab) demonstrate better than any other example I know all the points made in the first section of 'Subject matter and Craftsmanship'. Above all they show how a 'melody does not imply *its harmony*'; that 'the harmonic *potential* of a melody is infinite'; and that 'craftsmanship is often superior to subject matter'. Again, rather than working on any of his drafts for the March, Satie kept starting afresh, discovering stage by stage (but with many digressions) the elements that would satisfy him in the final version. Thus the process of discovery would seem to have been a subconscious one. Before he reached the final stages, Satie was thinking in terms of two hands at a piano (as he usually did) and in terms of pure music. These examples also demonstrate how ordinary his first thoughts often were, and the extent to which his harmonic idiosyncrasy was worked on and into a composition. Whilst Satie always displays an immaculate concern for voice-leading, he often conceived his outer parts in parallel motion, as if deliberately flouting the 'school' rules regarding parallel fifths and octaves (see Ex. 25f). This did not arise purely from a desire to shock, for parallel fifths are a feature of the intimate *Nocturnes* of 1919 too, and much of his later style centres on the intervals of the second, fourth, fifth and seventh.

Ex. 25 shows Satie's drafts in their most likely compositional order in BN 9605(2), 10–15.[6] Within reason, anything seems to have been possible except a root position tonic chord of G major at the start. As Satie struggled to find just the right level of dissonance to accompany Caryathis's first striking appearance on stage as *La Belle Excentrique*, we can see that the harmonic effect had to be arrived at through contrapuntally explicable means. If the accompaniment crossed the melody in the opening bar for linear reasons, this could be adjusted later through the instrumental balance. It in no way detracted from the melody as the outline and guiding factor behind the composition, but it played a large part in the unexpectedness Satie was seeking.

Ex. 25 is by no means uncharacteristic: being a straightforward theatrical entertainment did not mean that Satie took less care over *La Belle Excentrique*. Indeed the 'serious' *Nocturnes* had emerged with far less soul-searching the previous year. And it was not only music designed for the theatre that enjoyed such scrupulous care. Whilst the 'Ragtime' theme for *Parade* underwent fifteen revisions (eight reharmonizations and seven trial orchestrations) when it recurred in altered form in the finale, Satie also made thirteen versions of the tiny 8-bar song *Ta parure est secrète* (the last of his *Trois Poèmes d'amour*) in his quest for perfection in simplicity.[7] In these songs, the vocal line is paramount and conditions the form and content. But as it alters from sketch to sketch, whilst preserving the same rhythm, we can see that the 'melody is the Idea' in this case. In each 8-bar song, every bar sets Satie's own 'magic words' to the same rhythm of six quavers and a crotchet (see Ex. 26), taking advantage of French as an unstressed language in the process, and poking fun at the vocalized mute 'e' in sung French at the end of each line. For his poems, Satie took the verse-form of the medieval French *Chanson de geste*, with its monorhyme stanzas (*laisses*), and adapted it to modern ends. Satie never took anything literally from the past; so just as the vocal lines look like plainsong in Ex. 26 but only preserve its spirit, so the verse-form of the thirteenth-century *trouvères* is modified from the customary ten or eight syllable lines to seven, and Satie joins these lines by consonance rather than assonance.[8] In Ex. 26,

Ex. 26 *Trois Poèmes d'amour*, No. 3: *Ta parure est secrète* (the textual additions come from BN 9615(1), 16–19)

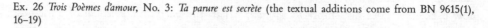

bar 1 recurs as bar 7 (together with its text), giving an overall ternary form through the vocal line. This is even clearer in the other two *Poèmes d'amour* of 1914, where the first two bars return as the last two. In the printed version of Ex. 26, the mocking preface about the ultra-Romantic poet with 'eyelids fluttering like leaves' and all the humorous textural accretions were removed (even down to the marking 'Avec tendresse' and the dynamics), so that the song should appear as simple and dead-pan as possible. The curious chromatic flourishes (at odds with the prevailing modality) in Ex. 26 bars 3 and 7, incidentally, were added at the final proof stage; for there is no sign of them in Satie's sketches. Here (in BN 9593(2) and 9615(4)) *Ta parure est secrète* passes through a variety of harmonizations and trial textures, even emerging as a waltz in some of the intermediate stages. The sectional, cellular approach is clearly an organizing principle, as it was in the *Elégie*, and the oscillating chords of Ex. 26 bars 1–2 occur in each of the three songs, playing a unifying role secondary only to the undulating vocal line. In this respect the harmony serves as an 'illumination' of the melody, an 'exhibition' of its objectives; and in a case like bar 8 of Ex. 26, it might be said to be its 'reflection'.

Thus Satie, whose aesthetic principles were clear even before he wrote his 1917 credo, was fully aware of the respective roles of melody and harmony, and of what could be achieved with them through a modern interpretation of (or a conscious reaction against) the principles of the past. He shows how both musical and literary 'grammar' is 'nothing but grammar' by adapting elements from it as he 'pleases and on his responsibility'. If the forms he uses are simple, then it is because the interest lies elsewhere. As there is a 'new style of writing' – a cellular jigsaw of abrupt contrasts, but with an overriding melodic logic – then 'there is a new craft'. And after his years at the Schola Cantorum, that 'craft' paid increasing heed to contrapuntal principles in realizing its dissonant aims. Although Satie delighted in devising musical systems, as we shall see, the composer in him with his 'aesthetic aim' always took precedence over the systematician, and the contrast between adjacent works like *La Belle Excentrique* and the *Elégie* for Debussy shows how adaptable Satie's 'craft' was. Certain principles do recur, as I have begun to show, but Satie was always anxious to stay ahead of his imitators, and like Debussy he tried to make each new work into a new concept. In Satie's view it was their willingness to continue writing within accepted traditions that would stop composers like Massenet, Ambroise Thomas and Saint-Saëns from ever being considered as true Masters. In their music craft became an end in itself: a substitute for 'general and even specific ideas'. And if one might not, in the last analysis, class Satie among the master-craftsmen of all time, then, on his own terms, he was surely a Master of ideas – both general and specific. He thought that the Masters of the past should have been locked up for trying to establish the 'Truths governing Art', an opinion he shared with Stravinsky. Indeed he began his 1922 article on Stravinsky with the words: 'I have always said – and I shall keep repeating it long after my death – that there is no such thing as Artistic Truth (no unique Truth, that is).'[9] For Satie, music was totally flexible and the composer discovered his own individual truths at various stages during his career. What appeared to be a truth at one stage might appear false at another (and this is a very real problem when trying to assess Satie the composer). Only the Idea ultimately survived, and it could 'do without Art' and all the empty virtuosity which the unenlightened majority mistook for Art. By 1917, Debussy and the imprecise evocations of Impressionism belonged to the past, and speaking as a figurehead for the next generation, Satie could say, with justification, that the essence of the *esprit nouveau* was 'precision'.

6

Satie, counterpoint and the Schola Cantorum

Satie's attitude to counterpoint as the essence of craftsmanship was briefly discussed in the previous two chapters, and it was his growing awareness that he could not progress without a sound contrapuntal basis to his technique that led him to enrol at the Schola Cantorum in October 1905. While he had achieved a degree of satisfaction with the *Trois Morceaux en forme de poire*, the extent to which his self-borrowing increased in the years 1901–3 was not a healthy sign. He did not know how to develop the greater flexibility achieved in the *Pièces froides* of 1897, and the prospect of a future devoted to popular waltzes and cabaret songs must have seemed bleak and unfulfilling. If the theatre ultimately led Satie back to his cabaret roots in the war years, he was only able to achieve his serious objectives with the expertise acquired at the Schola behind him.

So what did Satie actually learn at the Schola Cantorum between 1905 and the award of his glowing certificate in counterpoint in June 1908? As we saw in chapter 4, Satie was not deterred by Roussel's qualms about the need for such a course given his age and experience. As Satie told Robert Caby, quite simply, during his final illness in 1925: 'There is a musical language. One must learn it.'[1] But with only his cabaret work and a few piano pupils to support him, enrolling at the Schola entailed much financial sacrifice, and in BN 9637, 51 we find Satie drafting a letter to obtain some form of State aid. As he explained: 'I am a poor artist, much affected by the difficulties of life.' In all probability the kindly Vincent d'Indy (the founder of the Schola in 1894) waived all or some of the usual fees, and he may even have helped Satie from his own personal fortune. And so Satie began his studies with Roussel at the beginning of the academic year 1905–6.[2] In fact, he probably enrolled for the whole of d'Indy's *Cours de composition musicale*, of which the counterpoint course was an initial part, as we shall see.

Roussel's classes each Monday and Wednesday morning were highly organized and to the point.[3] Satie presented his beautifully calligraphed exercises in red and black ink with commendable regularity: Roussel carefully corrected them and made helpful suggestions. Above all, Roussel was sympathetic to Satie's character and problems and he made swift progress, especially in 1906–7. The fact that he was three years older than his teacher, who was himself still studying at the Schola, only increased the rapport between them, which was founded on mutual respect. Fortunately, most of

Satie's Schola notebooks have survived,[4] and Darius Milhaud later used them as teaching models for his own courses in America (Sasser, 1949, 6).

Satie began with strict counterpoint in two parts. As he progressed quickly through the different species, he forced himself to use the unfamiliar C clefs and learned from his mistakes – especially as far as writing fluid bass-lines was concerned. In early December 1905, Roussel let him loose on free two-part counterpoint, and the competent (if unexciting) result can be seen in Gillmor, 1988, 136. By Christmas Satie was working in three parts, and by 4 April 1906 in four (Ho 1, 17) – adding three of his own parts to the 'chant donné' (or cantus firmus) in semibreves set by Roussel, and again progressing through the various species. By late September, Roussel thought that Satie might be ready to progress beyond the first three species, and allowed him to write his first piece of free four-part counterpoint (Ex. 27), though its numerous corrections suggest that this confidence was rather premature. Beneath the general comment 'Fairly good', Roussel made the following additional trenchant observations:

1   Avoid *over-wide melodic leaps*, which lead you to inevitable part-crossing. Avoid too much melodic deviation – rather use suspensions.
2   Make the melodic line *more supple*.
3   *Distribute your rhythm* better – *avoid bundles of notes* followed by too sudden inactivity.

As elsewhere, Satie writes the given cantus firmus and the clefs in red ink, with his own additions in black: Roussel's corrections, in contrast, are in spidery pencil. During October 1906, at the start of Satie's second academic year, Roussel worked hard to correct the fundamental problem that there was '*too much harmony* and *not enough counterpoint*' in Satie's work – as his comment on the free 4-part exercise for 3 October shows (Ho 1, 26–7). His next such piece on 22 October (Fig. 6.1) shows Satie still taking liberties with 6–4 chords (bar 2), making daring use of passing notes (bar 3), and doubling the note of suspension in the lower parts (bar 7), amongst other things. Roussel's corrective essay ran as follows:

> All this has *too harmonic* a feeling. Clearly, you are too thoughtful in combining notes to put them on any beat, even on weak ones. You should sustain the *melodic movement* of each part more. In your hands, the melodic movement proceeds by leap, and does not have the easy and natural feeling that one should seek in counterpoint. But, in every case, *it's very musical*.

The problem was the age-old one of thinking vertically rather than horizontally, and Satie's invaluable first drafts for some of his 1906 exercises (Ho 7) show that he did indeed approach them harmonically at this stage. When the cantus firmus was in the bass, he added harmonic figuring to it, which he then elaborated in the upper parts, and when the cantus firmus was in the soprano, alto or tenor he still began by adding a figured bass – removing the figures, of course, before presenting his exercise for Roussel's approbation. Surprisingly, it was only in chorales (like Ex. 32) that he did not employ the fundamental bass method (see Ho 7, 24–5).

But Satie made strenuous attempts to improve the fluidity of his bass lines, and the

Ex. 27 Counterpoint exercise, dated 'Lundi 1er Octobre [1906]' (BN 9638, 40–1). Transcribed into G and F clefs, with Roussel's pencil corrections added

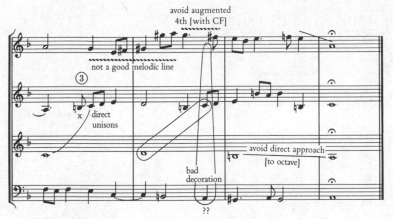

① Don't begin with movement and then stop it.
② Defective doubling because it involves the leading-note.
③ Causes friction, to be avoided because it is badly approached.

Ex. 28 Counterpoint exercise, dated 'Mercredi 14 Novembre [1906]' (BN 9639, 6)

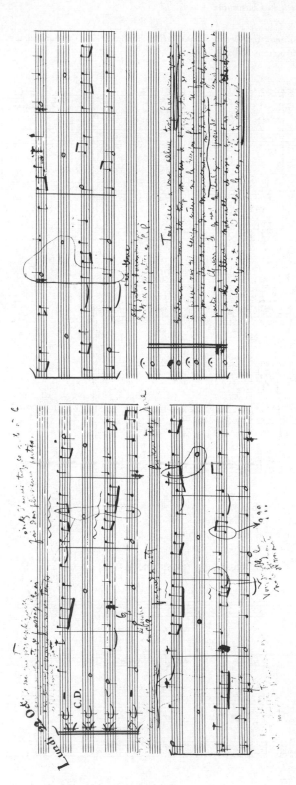

6.1   Satie's counterpoint exercise for Roussel presented on 22 October 1906 with Roussel's
      corrections and comments on its inherent musicality and overly harmonic character
      (Ho 1, 28–9).

melodic equality and smoothness of his upper voices, and on 14 November 1906 he produced a 'good' piece of 4-part counterpoint, requiring only three minor amendments. The start, including one such correction, is given as Ex. 28. This shows Satie rather happier using strict species counterpoint: here the alto uses the third species, the tenor the fourth, and the bass the fifth (beneath the soprano cantus firmus). Satie also seems to have taken Roussel's advice from his previous class to heart: 'Less decoration, more passing notes',[5] and Roussel seems not to have minded about the accented auxiliary note in bar 4 of Ex. 28 (alto, third crotchet), or the clash on the third crotchet of bar 5 between the alto and the bass. He must have encouraged Satie to produce such dotted rhythms across the middle of the bar (bass, bar 5), for they frequently occur in his work, however dubious the resulting suspension may be by sixteenth-century standards. But this was a contrapuntal exercise and not a piece of style composition.

Ex. 29 Canonic exercise, dated 'Mercredi 20 Février [1907]' (BN 9639, 18–19)

By January 1907, Satie was writing strict counterpoint in five real parts, and proudly indicating (in red ink) the presence of his canonic upper voices (the first to be added) in his exercise of 20 February (Ex. 29) – though Ho 7, 32–3 reveals that he was still using a figured bass in his preliminary draft. Although the canon only persists for four bars (at the major second below), and results in several unisons which Roussel was quick to highlight in pencil, Satie also manages to involve the first tenor part in the canonic process in bars 3 and 4 with some skill, and in the correct place in the bar. The triplet figure that begins the canon is derived from the opening of Roussel's 'chant donné', and Satie's upper lines are now better shaped and flowing, with fewer awkward digressions. Only the bass line, after a promising start, is not integrated into the contrapuntal whole. Consecutive fifths and octaves have by now disappeared, and the only other faults Roussel points out are the 6–4 chord at the start of bar 3 and the absence of movement in the middle of bar 6. Satie, who liked working in short, self-contained sections, must have found 8-bar exercises like Ex. 29 a congenial challenge to his ingenuity.

By April 1907, Satie had achieved the desired goal of producing skilful counterpoint in six voices, and what would appear to be only his third such exercise on 24 April (Ex. 30) shows a masterly handling of two imitative points derived from the cantus firmus by diminution. The tenor part in the lower pair of voices uses all but the last note of the given theme in bars 1–3, whereas the upper parts use the second half in quavers, in imitation at a bar's distance. Satie's skill with flexible voice-leading, part-crossing, and the balance between the vertical and the horizontal is now considerable. Roussel's correction to the bass line in bar 2 is questionable, for it makes the imitative point less precise in favour of a slight harmonic improvement. But he neatly removes the parallel octaves in bar 3 and ensures an even flow of quaver movement by adjusting

Ex. 30 Counterpoint exercise, dated 'Mercredi 24 Avril [1907]' (BN 9640, 24–5)

Ex. 30 (*cont.*)

the tenor line. And in bar 4 of Ex. 30 he makes the first soprano entry clearer by removing one of Satie's favourite octave leaps in the crossing second soprano part. But again, one might say that Satie's original line had a more distinctive shape, and that Roussel's correction produced two leaps in the same direction in the second soprano. Therefore, by now, their relationship seems more equal, and not simply that of a master correcting an errant student.

The progression from two-part species counterpoint to writing imitative 'contrepoints fleuris' in six parts was not all that Satie achieved between 1905 and 1907. As well as varying the keys and lengths of Satie's exercises, and co-ordinating his Monday and Wednesday classes so that Satie could rework the same 'chants donnés' in different parts, Roussel introduced such disciplines as invertible counterpoint, canon and the realization of Bach chorales. His initial approach to Bach chorales in November 1906 was harmonic, and a comparison between Bach and Satie's versions of *Nun ruhen alle Wälder* (Exx. 31a–b) shows that Roussel placed little importance on

Ex. 31 Chorale: *Nun ruhen alle Wälder*, start

a. Harmonized by J.S. Bach (Riemenschneider No. 289)

Ex. 31 (*cont.*)

b. Harmonized by Satie in 1906 (BN 9617(1), 26)

slavish stylistic imitation. Although the harmonic direction is broadly similar, Satie begins each phrase with rests, and his cadences avoid the dominant seventh (root position) approach that Bach habitually favoured. Roussel encouraged Satie to produce flowing independent lines, regardless of such anachronisms as the doubled seventh resolving upwards (tenor, bar 2, beats 2–3), the minims in bar 1, and the vast gaps between alto and tenor (bar 3). As with Satie's use of Gregorian chant, it is the spirit rather than the letter which is preserved, and he must have liked Roussel's liberal approach, with its modal use of flattened leading-notes and its acceptance of unprepared suspensions and chords like the added sixth. A year later, in December 1907,

Ex. 32 Chorale: *O Haupt voll Blut und Wunden*, harmonized by Satie on 18 December 1907 with the melody in the tenor (BN 9639, 38)

Satie's approach is more contrapuntal from the basis of greater experience: the chorale melody now serves as another 'chant donné'. Ex. 32 shows the start of his second attempt at the Passion chorale *O Haupt voll Blut und Wunden*. Whilst Satie's cadences still find no parallels in Bach, the imitative soprano line in the first phrase is ingenious. Roussel's fussy correction to the bass line at the start is, to my mind, inferior to Satie's version.

Towards the end of 1907, we find greater individuality creeping into Satie's counterpoint, as for instance in his daring chromatic canon at the fifth of 16 October (Ex. 33). After the leading part ends in bar 7, Satie introduces his favourite sonorous bass octaves and adds a grandiose little coda ending on the dominant. Having proved that he could write a strict canon, Satie felt free to express himself through a simple contrast that provides a perfect foil to his chromatic canon. The coda is not entirely guileless, however, for its inner part derives from bar 2 of Ex. 33, and its counter-balancing solidity suggests that Satie must have anticipated Roussel's criticism that the 'canon

Ex. 33 Canonic piece, dated 'Mercredi 16 Octobre [1907]' (BN 9639, 29)

modulates too much' and contains too few 'complete harmonies' (that is, thirds and sixths). The final chord, incidentally was converted from G minor to G major by Roussel.

But between the end of January 1908 and his June exam Satie's contrapuntal work at the Schola degenerated. Perhaps Roussel was unable to teach him, due to other commitments,[6] for the few corrections in Satie's notebook for this period (BN 9641) are in another hand, possibly that of Auguste Sérieyx, who had only graduated himself in 1907. Perhaps Satie felt he had progressed sufficiently to pass his exam, or perhaps he was preoccupied with his cabaret work – for we find him apologizing to d'Indy on 3 May 1908 for submitting his exam work late (see Fig. 6.2). 'I beg you to believe that it was not my fault', Satie pleads, 'and I entreat you not to penalize me for it.' D'Indy, being an enlightened teacher and an understanding man, did not treat Satie harshly, though had he looked at his work in 1908 he might well have wondered how Satie passed so highly that June. It would seem that Satie and his new counterpoint professor did not 'hit it off'. Being demoted to simple three-part counterpoint did not help, and Satie's untidy, misaligned, and sometimes unfinished work is untypical of him. Ironic titles like *Fâcheux exemple* (29 January) and *Désespoir agréable* (12 February)[7] suddenly appear, and after the latter, Satie must have had a 'severe reprimand', for his presentation temporarily improved. Sérieyx, if indeed it was he, bothered little

Arcueil le 3 Mai 1908

Cher Maître —
      Excusez-moi de vous faire
parvenir mon travail d'examen avec
un tel retard .
      Je vous prie de croire qu'il
n'y a pas de ma faute, et vous supplie
de ne pas m'en tenir rigueur.
      Respectueusement.

Erik SATIE

6.2   Letter to Vincent d'Indy, 3 May 1908 asking him not to penalize him for his late
         entry in the counterpoint exam.

about written advice, however much it was needed. But one feature that appears in
this period is an increase in syncopated rhythms, as at the start of the otherwise unin-
spired *Fâcheux exemple* (Ex. 34). Whether Satie was being awkward or not, these
rhythms were transferred into the fugue of the *Aperçus désagréables* that September
(see Ex. 18). Apart from the *Danse de la Brouette* in 5/4 time in *Relâche*, Satie did not
indulge in rhythmic irregularity, so perhaps we should be grateful for his brief
unsettled period at the Schola Cantorum.

Ex. 34 *Fâcheux exemple*, dated 'Mercredi 29 Janvier 1908', start (BN 9641, 4)

While introducing a concert by the Nouveaux Jeunes in 1918 (Ve, 81), Satie modestly maintained that 'I have always been a bad student – a dunce. But I can tell you that I worked hard with d'Indy, and that I have excellent memories of the seven years I spent with that good and straightforward man. I also worked for three years with Albert Roussel, with whom I have remained friends.' Satie's technical facility may not have matched that of his teachers, but the earlier examples in this chapter show that he was certainly no dunce. By and large, he worked slowly and assiduously at the Schola and approached his work with the enhanced commitment of a mature student. The many examples of strange mixed-clef pieces (like Ex. 35) in his notebooks are not

Ex. 35 Start of a mixed-clef piece, *c.* 1909 (BN 9651, 30)

parodies of the Schola's strict notational demands,[8] but an ingenious method of familiarizing himself with the C clefs he was required to use in his exercises. Ex. 35, designed to improve his facility with the soprano clef, probably dates from as late as 1909, and if the old clefs were a persistent challenge, Satie never drafted his exercises in the more familiar G and F clefs first. What Satie did possess was an excellent musical ear, and his regular dictation exercises show no sign of alterations. He had become so proficient at dictation by December 1909 that he found time to harmonize the first 8 bars of his 12-bar exercise (given out in five phrases for notation in the alto clef) while waiting for the other students to catch up. It is characteristic of Satie's harmonization in Ex. 36 that he ingeniously avoids the expected key of C# minor, casting the piece in E major/minor with a bass pedal E at the start. His concern for continuity between phrases even led him to make two versions of bars 4–5, of which the second is shown in Ex. 36. The sudden bass octaves in bars 3 and 8 and the modal cadence in bar 8 betray Satie as the author, and show that the accompaniment was not part of the dictation.

Satie's 'seven years' at the Schola Cantorum mean that he must have enrolled as a composer for d'Indy's complete *Cours de composition musicale* in 1905. His notebooks reveal that he attended parts of the first three courses at least, probably as an *auditeur*, though much of his work was for Roussel's *Cours complet de contrepoint* which formed

Ex. 36 'Dictée pour le 31 Déc. [1909]' (BN 9651, 46–8)

part of the 'Enseignement du premier degré'.[9] The second stage of the 'degré' was divided into four courses, which seem to have run concurrently in two-year cycles. Satie took the parts of these that most interested him without sitting the formal examinations, and each course had a theoretical and a co-ordinated practical element. The most likely scenario is that Satie participated in elements of courses 1 and 2 with d'Indy while he took his counterpoint course with Roussel. This would explain why it took him three years to complete this preliminary part instead of the usual two. From his notebooks it would appear that Satie studied the following elements from d'Indy's 'premier cours' between October 1905 and June 1907: rhythm, melody, harmony, notation, tonality, modulation and the evolution of music to Renaissance times, with a special study of the motet. The practical element of this last aspect consisted of analysing and composing motets, and Satie's incomplete and subjective analysis of Palestrina's *Assumpta est Maria* survives in BN 10033(10). Like Debussy, Satie was emotionally moved by the 'transparent style' of this 'seraphic musician', who he saw as being 'always close to God; his manner is sacred; his genius is beneficent. Here we can see the delightful son of our sweet religion; of wonderful, imperishable Catholicism.' All of which suggests that Satie liked the Schola's emphasis on the great religious masterpieces, however much he resisted discussing them in technical detail. He also began a four-part setting of 'Ave Christe immolate' in sixteenth-century imitative style (BN 9647, 22–3), but this only lasts a few bars.

Then between October 1907 and June 1909 Satie studied fugue and canon, suite form and the development of sonata form from d'Indy's second course. The practical side was mostly involved with writing fugues and analysing and composing sonatas. In Satie's workbooks we find extensive notes on the various forms involved in writing a sonata (BN 9643); and in BN 9643, 9649, 9650 and the neat copy in BN 10033(11), Satie's own *Petite Sonate* written for d'Indy in 1908–9. As with the *Passacaille* of 1906, Satie worked in short cells joined together by means of numbered bars, so his sonata was not through-composed. Satie tried to concentrate as many features as possible within his single 82-bar movement,[10] which has a slow introduction, two contrasting subjects (recapitulated in the tonic), and a short fugal development section in 12/8 time (with two episodes) which incorporates elements of a slow movement. Satie's anarchic side surfaces in Ex. 37, where he marked the bridge passage into the second subject 'ironiquement' in his final draft, eliciting the comment from d'Indy: 'It's very clever. . .too clever for you. . .it shouldn't be necessary to work so ironically.' When Satie sketched this passage in BN 9650, 9 he arrived at the last three bars through the decoration of a series of chords (see Ex. 37), a process he was often to return to in later

Ex. 37 *Petite Sonate* (1908–9), bars 25–32, bridge passage (BN 10033(11), 3)

years. True to form, Satie originally intended these bars to be numbered 22–4, and they only became bars 30–2 after he had inserted bars 1–6 and 15–16 to make a more substantial slow introduction. The anodine, neo-classical first subject begins in bar 17 (originally bar 9): d'Indy found it 'not bad at all. There is personality here and this is what pleases me.' Its start is given in Ex. 38a, and its rhythmically varied inversion formed the basis of the contrapuntal 'development' section, whose start is given as Ex. 38b. D'Indy thought that Satie should have prepared this 'in advance with the

Ex. 38 *Petite Sonate*

a. Bars 17–18, first subject (BN 10033(11), 2)

b. Bars 44–5, start of middle section (BN 10033(11), 4)

theme in its original form, without which one can't perceive its significance and this passage seems pointless'. It is certainly not the sort of rigorous cellular development d'Indy might have wished for. Satie's one attempt at this uncongenial procedure (Ex. 39) was quickly rejected; its uncharacteristic drive made it unsuitable for his simple *Petite Sonate*. Even in this stormy passage, we can see Satie resorting to repetition and transposition rather than further development after just four bars, and the

Ex. 39 Rejected sketch for the development section of the *Petite Sonate* (BN 9650, 4)

whole exercise must have further served to convince him that Germanic procedures were neither suitable nor desirable for his talent.

Between October 1909 and June 1911 (or early 1912) Satie concentrated on the study of orchestration with d'Indy, beginning with the composition and orchestration of minuets and trios in the autumn of 1909, and detailed studies of the ranges and characteristics of the various instruments in December (BN 9651). This aspect will be discussed in chapter 7. This third course also included a study of variation form (including the chorale variation) with Auguste Sérieyx (see BN 10033(4)), and Satie's own chorales from this period[11] show him at a mid-way point between Bach and the dissonant chorales of *En Habit de cheval* (1911) or the opening *Choral inappétisant* from the *Sports et divertissements*. Here, Satie was developing the chorale along modern lines, and its appeal again lay in its short, self-contained phrases. As Satie observed after his *Choral hypocrite* in the *Choses vues à droite et à gauche* of 1914: 'My chorales match up to those of Bach; the only difference being that they are rarer and less pretentious.' D'Indy seems not to have forced Satie into analysing Beethoven, Wagner, Liszt and Franck, which were staple fare for other Schola pupils in their final years. Rather we find him analysing the seventh fugue from Bach's *Art of Fugue* (BN 10033(2)) and an up-to-date song like Ravel's *Noël des jouets* of 1905 (BN 10033(9)) which show how d'Indy kept abreast of the latest compositions of his contemporaries.

Satie's notebooks suggest that his main interests were orchestration and fugue during his final years at the Schola. He did not continue with the fourth and final course in which pupils wrote operatic scenas, sacred and secular oratorios and lieder in the rue Saint-Jacques, and d'Indy wisely put no pressure on him to do so. He seems to have terminated his studies in early 1912 because his own career was beginning to take off at last, rather than because he found the rest of the course uncongenial or irrelevant to him. *En Habit de cheval* offers the best example of Satie integrating Schola teaching with his own composition, and in it he also worked out his own individual concept of orchestration. If the direct influence of the Schola seems slight, its underlying effect in superior craftsmanship and a new linear approach was considerable. Besides strengthening his technique, it provided the basis from which he could develop his own concepts of the chorale and fugue – his reinterpretation of the past with modern sensibility, seen in the opening pages of *Parade*.

As we have seen, Satie's fugal studies began in 1907, and drafts of fugal expositions exist alongside three-part cantus firmus exercises (together with notes on suite form) in BN 9648. Similarly, we find sketches for a fugue in C minor together with four-part realizations in BN 9646. Despite copious notes and analyses, none of Satie's exercies fugues is complete, though he excelled in inventing episodes, expositions and counter-expositions as separate entities. A typical example, which occupies much of BN 9663–4, is the Fugue in E♭ (?) minor. Its exposition (Ex. 40), with a regular, contrasted counter-subject neatly overlapping the phrasing of the subject, shows how fluid Satie's contrapuntal writing could be in a chromatic context. Only the third entry (at the top of BN 9664, 4) is barred, and Satie may have devised the modal subject himself, for it turns back on itself like the *Fugue litanique* from *En Habit de cheval*, or

Ex. 40 Exposition of the 'Fugue' in E♭ minor (BN 9663, 8–9: first two entries (unbarred); BN 9664, 4: third entry (barred))

the *Fugue à tâtons* from the *Choses vues*, and is non-modulating. Ex. 40 clearly needs a codetta to bridge the awkward gap between the entries, but Satie never indulged in these, and it was probably because he found the subject too fluid and traditional that he abandoned it. Satie's own subjects that result in finished fugues (however loosely structured) tend to be deliberately trite, repetitive and unpromising – and call to mind the fugal finale of Mozart's *A Musical Joke* (K. 522). Telling Satie to 'stick to the rules of the past', as d'Indy did,[12] was like a red rag to a bull, though it is doubtful if Satie aimed to parody tradition in *En Habit de cheval*, for his short-winded elliptical subject for the *Fugue litanique* caused him considerable problems before he completed the fugue to his satisfaction in 1911.[13] The reasoning behind his selection of one version in preference to another is by no means obvious in this case, but the dull, liturgical drone of its subject remains fixed throughout as a challenge to his ingenuity and a reminder of the way in which he was reinterpreting fugal form.

Lest anyone should think that a principle has been discovered here, Satie explored many different fugue subjects before he found the one that was right for his *Fugue à tâtons* in 1914. He persisted for nearly 50 bars in a first, through-composed draft (very rare) of this *Groping Fugue*, whose subject (Ex. 41a), appears just as repetitive and unpromising (and therefore just as likely) as his final subject (Ex. 41h).[14] When this draft dissolved into a violin cadenza full of glissandi, Satie simply abandoned it. But to get even this far, he had already tried at least six other subjects. The first was another non-modulating subject ending with the folksong *Au Clair de la lune*, which is slightly obscured by beginning on the second bar of a four-bar phrase (Ex. 41b). Then he considered the folksong complete as his subject, before appending a reference to it to a more promising chromatic start. This time the accentuation was correct, but the folksong was slightly altered (Ex. 41c). Here Satie got as far as an answer and a

Ex. 41 The emergence of the fugue subject for the *Fugue à tâtons*, No. 2 of the *Choses vues à droite et à gauche (sans lunettes)* (1914)

a. BN 9573(2), 1

b. BN 9573(1), 6

c. BN 9573(1), 8–9

d. BN 9573(1), 10

e. BN 9573(1), 12

Ex. 41 (*cont.*)

f. BN 9573(1), 14

g. BN 9573(1), 19

h. Final version of the start of the *Groping Fugue*

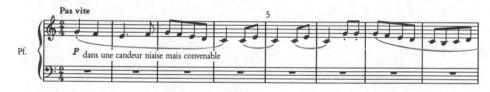

modulating counter-subject, which offered a superb example of chromatic 'groping' at the end. But again it was dismissed as too conventional (or too interesting?). Satie then experimented with another repetitive subject (still in G) which, with its chromatic counter-subject, looks more like a piece of strict counterpoint for the Schola (Ex. 41d). He even tried out harmonies for this subject, plus an entry in the relative minor and a stretto. So he must have thought it had more potential than Ex. 41c. Then he tried Ex. 41e, complete with counter-subject and figured bass; then the revealing Ex. 41f, which shows him starting with the answer and counter-subject in the dominant and working back to the subject.

At this stage he abandoned the *Fugue à tâtons* and wrote a 31-bar chorale-like move-ment (Ex. 42) for violin and piano, the first movement of the *Choses vues à droite et à gauche (sans lunettes)* to be completed. It appears here in print for the first time. This dissonant movement fits in well with the three other movements Satie chose to publish and no-one I have played it to can suggest why Satie in the end omitted it. Its open strings and basis on G balance the opening *Choral hypocrite*, just as the two quasi-fugal movements in C balance each other. Its ideal position would thus seem to be as the third of the *Choses vues*, before the *Fantaisie musculaire*, but the fact that it is untitled is

Ex. 42 Unused third (?) movement for the *Choses vues à droite et à gauche* (BN 9573(1), 16–18) © Biblio-thèque Nationale, Paris, 1990

Ex. 42 (*cont.*)

a bad sign. The real reason for its rejection was probably not concerned with musical quality at all, but arose from Satie's fear of repeating himself after *En Habit de cheval*, which had also used two pairs of interlocking chorales and fugues. And so the desire to be always moving forward superceded Satie's natural instinct for balance, though as Oscar Wilde observed (in a manner perfect for Satie) 'the truth is rarely pure and never simple'.

Returning (refreshed?) to his fugue, Satie tried a subject in the final key of C (Ex. 41g), abandoned it, and then wrote the last two bars of the *Choral hypocrite* (BN 9573(1), 19) which preceded the rest of the movement! He then hit upon what is virtually the final version of bars 16–33 of the *Fugue à tâtons*. Next he wrote the sub-dominant entry of the subject (bars 44–57) *before* finalizing the initial subject and answer in the tonic (Ex. 41h), to join onto his first thought, the *episode* beginning in the middle of bar 16. And in between these last two stages came the draft with which this saga began (Ex. 41a), which ran to more than half the length of the printed version before being discarded. The last passage to materialize in the *Fugue à tâtons* was the 'Grande episode' (bars 58–65) linking the sub-dominant entry to the final page (with its dominant pedals and stretto by inversion). But if all this appears to be an odd way to proceed with a composition, it is typical of Satie, and the *Fantaisie musculaire* (the last of the *Choses vues*) acquired its title and mock-virtuosic concept long before Satie hit upon a note of its final version – which, this time, began with its fugue subject (bars 9–14), but became less strictly contrapuntal as it proceeded.

Another example of Satie making a composition less contrapuntal as it progressed is *Spleen*, the second of the 1923 song-cycle *Ludions*. To evoke Fargue's image of 'an ocean of ill-will sitting on a dismal bench in an old public park' Satie first devised an idea in invertible counterpoint (Ex. 43a, bars 1–4), involving a rare use of the harmonic minor scale. When he reached the surprise in Fargue's poem (as the figure turns out to be 'a plump and worthless blond'), Satie made the music more dynamic and then brought it to a halt in bar 8 after the words 'that I grow tired of'. Here the first version ends, and Satie undoubtedly realized that he had made his grand statement in Ex. 43a, bars 5–6, which would undermine the coming words about 'this cabaret of Nothingness, which is our life' which he intended to be his main climax. So he began again with the final chorale-like version in sonorous crotchet chords (in a notebook in *F-Pfs*, 6–7). This enabled him to speed up the movement into angry quavers when he got to the 'cabaret of Nothingness' so relevant to his own existence (Ex. 43b). He still kept the same, pre-planned vocal rhythm for the first three lines (the basic idea behind the song), but he altered the shape of the voice part, improving the prosody as he did so by setting 'triste' to a single quaver in bar 4. In the published version of the end (Ex. 43b), Satie breaks into triplets to give impulse to his climax, in which the 'cabaret du Néant' takes pride of place as it first climaxes in the high, insistent vocal line and then in the final C major chord of the accompaniment – a contrapuntal achievement of another kind. The sudden plunges in the accompaniment in Ex. 43b lend weight and drama to the apotheosis in the context of the restraint elsewhere. The difference in the text between bar 7 of Ex. 43a and bar 2 of Ex. 43b may indicate that Satie, like

Ex. 43a First version of *Ludions*, No. 2: *Spleen* (BN 9594, 8–9)

Ex. 43b Final version of *Spleen*, last 4 bars

Debussy, learnt his texts before setting them, but sometimes remembered details inaccurately. Equally, Fargue may have sent Satie a revised text at a late stage. But the emphatic way in which Satie changed the last bar from 'Qu'est la vie' to 'Qu'est notre vie' during the drafting of his final version (MS in *F-Pfs*) confirms that he made the alterations on his own initiative.

One piece that did survive in its initial contrapuntal conception, however, was the *Sonnerie pour réveiller le bon gros Roi des Singes (lequel ne dort toujours que d'un œil)* written for the first (October 1921) issue of Leigh Henry's journal *Fanfare*. Satie, being 'short-sighted from birth',[15] was fascinated by eyes and their power, and his mischievous, expressive eyes were often mentioned as his most salient feature. Sauguet (1945, 4) says that they still 'preserved their liveliness and intelligent maliciousness' on the day before his death in 1925. But Satie's obsession with the single eye is altogether stranger. The plot of his surrealist play *Le Piège de Méduse* revolves around Astolfo's ability to 'dance on one eye'. And Satie, like the 'good old King of the Monkeys', reported in 'The Musician's Day' that 'My sleep is deep, but I keep one eye open.'[16] Other physical actions are associated with one eye too, and particularly in 1921 at the time of the *Sonnerie*. If a critic 'laughs, he only does so with one eye, whether it's the good one or the bad one', Satie wrote in the journal *Action* that August.[17] Whilst most of his one eye references appear humorous on the surface – like Satie only 'drinking with one eye open'[18] – the underlying concept of the power of an all-seeing eye is nonetheless there, with its Egyptian/occult connections, and its links with the evil eye of the devil. In the text of *Méditation*, the last of the *Avant-dernières pensées* of 1915, the devil is mistaken for the wind of Genius passing by, who gazes on the poet/creator 'with an evil eye: a glass eye'. Satie, who believed himself haunted by the devil, was the poet in question.

To return to Satie's *Fanfare*, we find him beginning by relating his two trumpet parts through a strict canon at the third by inversion (in D major). His first version (at the top of Fig. 6.3) was mostly arpeggio-based and its upper part reached its dominant goal one bar too early, leaving its canonic imitation high and dry on the subdominant in bar 8. Rather than work on this, Satie began again with the same contrapuntal con-

6.3   First version of the *Sonnerie pour réveiller le bon gros Roi des Singes* (1921) (BN 9670, 6).

ception (Fig. 6.3, system 2). By making his upper line more varied and chromatic he achieved his dominant objective in bar 8 with ease, before switching to invertible counterpoint in bars 9–12. Bars 9–10 were originally a fourth lower, and bars 11–12 a fifth higher (crossed out). But Satie must have seen in a flash that by transposing them he could bring them into line with each other, and not make bars 11–12 stand out as the highest in the piece. After writing the straightforward bars 13–16, he at last realized that the second trumpet was consistently too low for its range, but that by transposing the whole *Sonnerie* 'en fa majeur' he could solve his problems and get a brighter sounding march into the bargain. Thus in a single revision Satie put everything right. All that remained was to copy out the final transposed version (Fig. 6.4) and send it off to his friend Leigh Henry.[19] As a demonstration of contrapuntal expertise integrated without ostentation into a living composition, the *Sonnerie* verifies Satie's 1917 view that 'The craft of Bach is not a contrapuntal exercise. Craft, in an exercise, should be defective; in composition it is perfect.'

6.4   Final version of the 1921 *Sonnerie* (MS in *US-NYpm*).

7

Orchestration versus instrumentation

The New Grove Dictionary defines orchestration as 'the art of combining the sounds of a large complex of instruments to provide a satisfactory blend and balance',[1] with the emphasis being on the size of the standard symphony orchestra rather than the imaginative skill with which it is handled. Instrumentation, on the other hand, is a more general term 'meaning the study of the characteristics of the various instruments, as well as the way instruments are selected and combined in a composition'. Straightaway in Satie's case there are problems. What he learnt at the Schola Cantorum should be classed as instrumentation, even though it was a course in orchestration. Also, Satie always referred to his finished work as orchestration, even though most of his pre-orchestral drafts look like instrumentation (with each note carefully arrowed to the instrument concerned). But then so do the pre-orchestral drafts of Charles Koechlin, who was widely acclaimed as a master of the craft, and was chosen by Fauré to orchestrate his *Pelléas et Mélisande* suite in 1898, and by Debussy to complete the orchestration of *Khamma* in 1912. Although Debussy was renowned for his orchestration, and Fauré was perfectly competent at it (as *Pénélope* shows), both composers shared an unenviable record of leaving this vital task to others. They regarded the creative process of composition as separate and all-important, and this is partly explainable by the fact that orchestration was not taught as an art at the Paris Conservatoire during this period: it was assumed that students would pick up the necessary skills during composition classes, or through private study. Satie, on the other hand, was always experimenting with textures; he often composed with particular instrumental combinations in mind; and he usually had a clear conception of the finished product he was aiming for before he began composing. His orchestral scores, on average, were produced three times as quickly as his music could be composed, and the evidence suggests that he found the process easier and more enjoyable. He was proud of the results too, especially in later life. For instance, he told Diaghilev on 1 December 1923 that the orchestration of *Le Médecin malgré lui* was 'progressing marvellously', and after its première he told Paul Collaer excitedly on 5 January 1924: 'Excellent orchestra – very pleased with my orchestration. It sounded "chic"' (Vc). As much of Satie's orchestration time was deployed in slowly copying his immaculate scores, we can only conclude that the process of scoring itself was relatively quick and assured. If Maurice Dumesnil (1942, 855) calls Satie's orchestration 'thin and deficient', there are plenty of more authoritative sources that praise it. Louis Durey (1930, 164) – who was no particular friend of Satie's – found the orchestration of *Parade* 'rich in resources, direct in expression', saying 'exactly what it means to say'; whilst Darius Milhaud (1927, 24) singled out the score of *Relâche* for special praise. 'This score amazes me', he enthused. 'One always finds a richness in the writing, an imaginativeness in the gestures, and a discretion in the lyricism that lend his work its character of authenticity and perfection.'

If Satie conceived his music more in terms of the chamber or cabaret orchestra than the full symphony orchestra, then this was allied to his conception of his precursive role as a composer. That he could handle a large orchestra with perfect ease is shown in *Parade*, and here he was writing for the forces available in Diaghilev's Ballets Russes. Had Satie been involved in a less prestigious collaboration, he would have written a different type of score. And in the case of d'Indy's orchestration classes, we should remember that the distinction between instrumentation and orchestration was not one that was made at the time. Composers were judged simply as good, passable or bad orchestrators. Satie, well aware of such distinctions, advised musicians to 'kill yourselves rather than orchestrate as badly as Florent Schmitt. . .What horror, my God!. . .What horror!'[2]

As Satie cannot be compared with either the Germanic or the Impressionistic orchestrators of his day, his orchestration must be assessed on its own merits, and on the basis of what he was trying to achieve by orchestral means. He certainly achieved the 'satisfactory blend and balance' required using 'a large complex of instruments' in *Parade* for instance. There can be no doubt, however, that the expertise of the later ballets was hard-won, and that it was not until after his studies at the Schola Cantorum that Satie felt fully at ease with the instruments of the orchestra. But at the same time Satie was never guilty of writing impossible parts for his players in later life (as Ravel was); his sureness of inspiration meant that he never revised his orchestration once it was finished[3] (as Debussy did); and he was certainly never guilty of overscoring (as Richard Strauss and Wagner were). If Satie avoided complexity, rhetoric, drama and sentimentality, it was because he saw such post-Romantic characteristics as alien to the modern aesthetic. His 'new spirit' of simplicity and his habitual use of smaller ensembles should again not be seen as Satie making a virtue of his technical limitations. He was perfectly capable of using conventional forces in a conventional style when he chose to, as *Le Médecin malgré lui* demonstrates. Having said that, it is still a wise creator who can 'cut his coat according to his cloth', and a still rarer being who can make that coat unlike any that has gone before, and tailor it so that it is still admired long after his death.

1890–1909

The most important orchestral principles that Satie established in the early 1890s were the 'static sound décor' in *Le Fils des étoiles* and the blocks of contrasted sound in *Uspud*. For Péladan's first Soirée de la Rose-Croix in March 1892, the programme

(BN Rés. Vma 174(8), 2) announced that 'Monsieur Erik Satie has composed three preludes for harps and flutes, of an admirably Oriental character, which, before each act, prepare the spectator impatiently for the tableau he is going to see.' According to Templier (1969, 13–14), Satie's music for *Le Fils des étoiles* 'proved to be far above the heads' of his audience 'and was met by an icy silence'. Probably the only impatience it generated was for it to be over. As no score exists, and there are no instrumental indications in Satie's manuscript reduction,[4] we can only conjecture how Satie distributed his parts for flutes and harps. The main motif, which begins the Act 1 Prelude with Satie's famous fourth chords,[5] for instance, might have been scored as in Ex. 44.

Ex. 44 Start of the Act 1 Prelude ('La Vocation') to *Le Fils des étoiles*, as it might have been scored for the 1892 première. The ringed scale degrees show the impracticable harp re-tunings

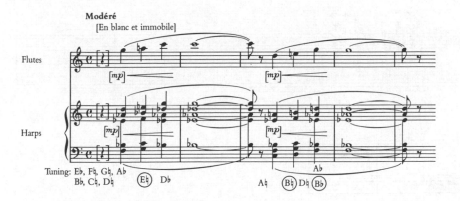

But immediately there are problems. If Satie knew anything then about Erard's double-action pedal harp (which seems unlikely), he would have realized he was asking for the impossible, even on the most sophisticated harp available at the time. Even with the flute melody taking care of the Ab–A♮–Ab change in bar 1 of Ex. 44, the second chord still requires the harpists to retune immediately from Eb to E♮, which would cause an ugly twang if there was no break between the chords – and Satie's phrasing mark indicates that this was meant to be the case. The E♮ cannot be played enharmonically as Fb because there is already an F♮ in the second chord. A similar instance occurs with the ringed changes in bar 3, and the only solution would be to have a second harp playing the second chords in bars 1 and 3, which would again break up Satie's smooth line. Even if this was the case, the harp sound would die away far too quickly in bars 2 and 4 at the slow tempo indicated. So, even in the very first bars of *Le Fils des étoiles* there are such impracticalities as to suggest that Satie conceived this music simply with a typical 'antique' sonority in mind. The way he uses a Greek chromatic mode in *Uspud*, or creates a frieze-like sonorous background in the orchestral accompaniment in *Socrate*, suggests that his idealized vision of the past was that of ancient Greek civilization. The setting of *Le Fils des étoiles* in Chaldea in 3500 BC was of no more importance to him than what his harpists would actually play at the première. Perhaps the whole score was played on the piano, as Ravel did when he revived the Prelude in 1911. But the curious thing is that the *Trois Sonneries de la Rose+Croix* are known to have been performed with instruments at the same concert, for Robert Caby possesses a printed copy marked by Satie in red ink as 'corrected to conform with the orchestral parts' (presumably for trumpets and harps). But as no score or parts for the *Sonneries* has survived either, we can only imagine what happened at the Galerie Durand-Ruel in March 1892. Undoubtedly the atmosphere at rehearsal was less 'blanc et immobile' than Satie's music, in whatever form it emerged.

Ex. 45 A passage near the end of Act 1 of *Uspud* (BN 9631, 19)
'He [Uspud] takes up a larger stone which explodes with a bang; flames burst forth and from their midst the stars escape.'

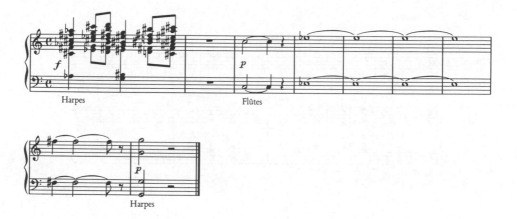

Later that year, in the short score of *Uspud*,[6] the various motifs are indicated to be played on either flutes, harps, string quartet, or flutes and harps together. Again the writing is grossly impractical for harps, and Satie must have had bass flutes in mind if Ex. 45 was to be performed as indicated. This example from the end of Act 1 also shows how divorced the music was from its dramatic text, and the 'Grande convulsion de la nature' two pages later is similarly static and unperturbed. If, as Gustave Doret says (1942, 98), Satie performed *Uspud* as a solo venture at the Auberge du Clou, he probably did so at the harmonium (rather than the 'piano') using different stops for the changing sonorities (see Fig. 2.2), and reading out the text between the musical sections. Even if we find Satie changing scoring in mid-motif (or even in the last bar of a section, see Ex. 45), the concept of contrasting blocks of sound is clearly established here, and again Satie associates flutes with harps in an 'antique' conception, but never combines either of them with the strings.

The harp also features as the basis of Satie's only complete, dated orchestral score from this period, the 54-bar *Danse* of 5 December 1890, otherwise scored for flute, oboe, clarinets (in Bb and A), bassoon and four timpani.[7] Here the principle of devising an original combination suited to a specific piece begins, and the pianistic harp part is rather more practical. The start (Ex. 46) shows Satie trying to cross a *Gymnopédie*

Ex. 46 *Danse* (5 December 1890), bars 1–8 (Ho 48, 1–2)

in common time with the modally ambiguous melody of a *Gnossienne,* and in common
with much of his later scoring the woodwind take much of the melodic material, with
absolute clarity resulting from the absence of any unison doubling. There is even a
touch of instrumental colour in the additional flute line in bars 7–8 of Ex. 46, in which
the doubling in thirds on second flute was later crossed out. Neither this, nor the first
clarinet part survived in the later transcription for piano duet in the *Trois Morceaux en
forme de poire.* Prior to his studies at the Schola Cantorum, Satie does not seem to have
known how low timpani could reasonably go, and here it was the continuo role of the
harp that took away many of his orchestral responsibilities and allowed the *Danse* to
be completed.

    When Satie came to orchestrate his *Pièces froides* in 1897, on the other hand, it was
his uncertainty over both the form his accompaniments should take, and the forces
necessary to realize them, that led to so many rejected trials. For in BN 9575(1–2) and
Ho 55 there are as many as nineteen different starts for what were to be *Deux Pièces
froides* for orchestra (the first of the *Airs à faire fuir* and the second of the *Danses de
travers*). As Satie told Louis Lemonnier on 22 March 1897, my orchestrations are 'going
opportunely, in a small way. I'm going to play you these symphonic pieces on the
tormented slide-trombone and make you block up your ears' (Vc). Joking aside, the

orchestrations certainly were proceeding 'in a small way', for the farthest Satie got was a mere nine bars,[8] and he must have spent at least as much time calligraphing the different instrumental lists and clefs in red ink as he spent writing the notes in black. He experimented with strings without violas, strings without first violins (as in Ex. 47), fuller versions with brass and timpani, and so on. The only feature common to all these trials is the presence of cellos and the absence of oboes and, of course, trombones. Ex. 47 gives one of the first drafts of the second *Danse de travers*, with its

Ex. 47 Trial orchestration of the start of *Danse de travers* No. 2 (BN 9575(1), 7: ?1897)

curious double-bass pizzicati entering after the beat. It shows Satie adding instruments like the cor anglais and second violins as he went along. But before deciding what to do with the lower strings in bar 5, Satie abandoned this version for another, which he hoped (wrongly) might prove a more suitable combination. In fact, devising just the right combination for his *Pièces froides* forever eluded Satie, and involved more work than their original assembly from a series of numbered phrases. But we know that Satie took orchestration very seriously at this stage in his career, for Robert Caby met three Conservatoire musicians earlier in his life who recalled that Satie often arranged for small groups of professional musicians to try through his orchestral efforts.[9] Satie, incidentally, always wrote his instruments at their transposed pitches; hardly ever used abbreviations; used one continuous barline across all the instruments; and usually worked from the top of the score downwards.

He did, however, attain greater success around the turn of the century with his cabaret orchestrations, which are eminently practical and full of delightful touches. The standard 'brasserie orchestra' of the epoch (which Satie used) consisted of flute (doubling on piccolo), clarinet, bassoon (or tuba), horn, cornet à pistons, trombone, percussion (side drum, bass drum and cymbals) and strings. Sometimes, as in *Poudre d'or* (?1901), Satie used piccolo and flute, two clarinets, two horns, two cornets and

three trombones, but this must have depended on the forces available in the venue
for which it was intended. In this particular case (BN 10060), the list of individual
parts shows that the strings tended to be top and bottom heavy, with five desks of first
violins, one desk of seconds, one desk of violas, two desks of cellos and one double-
bass. Ex. 48, the first 8 bars of the verse (or 'couplet') of *La Diva de l''Empire'* (1904),[10]

Ex. 48 Start of the first verse of *La Diva de l''Empire'* (BN 10065, f. 3r, with vocal part added from
BN 10064, 2)

Ex. 48 (cont.)

shows Satie's cabaret orchestra style at its most inventive and varied. The strings
provide both the melodic and the harmonic basis, with doubling up between the
second violins and violas (especially in divisi passages) because of the small number of
players involved. The strings, incidentally, always use divisi rather than double-
stopping. As in virtually every bar Satie orchestrated, the woodwind are always present

– even if it is only the bassoon standing in for the cello when the latter doubles the violin line at the lower octave (Ex. 48, bar 1), or the clarinet doubling the first violins at the lower octave in the refrain. Here, as elsewhere, the flutes and clarinets are used for melodic reinforcement, whilst the horns sustain inner parts and the other brass add weight and emphasis, or bring out inner harmonic parts when there is no risk of obscuring the voice (cornet, bars 2 and 4). The percussion does not enter without the brass, though the reverse sometimes occurs (as in Ex. 48, bars 6 and 8). The piccolo is saved for extra brilliance in introductions and codas, and Mozartian *forte/piano* contrasts replace any subtler dynamic gradations. Apart from the second violins and violas no part doubles any other at the same pitch, and each part is placed in its most effective range. The orchestration is practical and varied, with minute attention to detail, and Satie prepared vocal and piano solo scores for most of his popular compositions, as well as writing out the instrumental parts himself. He even copied out his own 'Tableau personnel des instruments' about this time (Ho 65), a neat but much-worn document which suggests frequent reference to a master-list. The ranges of the orchestral instruments are extremely conservative – the flutes, for instance, go from f^1 to e^3; the clarinets from a to d^3; the oboes from d^1 to g^2; the trumpets from c^1 to e^2; and the first violins only as high as e^3 – but this was almost certainly because Satie was aiming for a safe, practical orchestration which would sound well after limited rehearsal, and in which the high sounds of the respective instruments would not cause any undue prominence of a particular tone-colour, or distort the essential musical character of the piece concerned.[11]

The reason why Satie's cabaret orchestration was so much more assured than any of his other scoring at the time lay in his familiarity with its forces and practices since his early days as a conductor at the Chat Noir. He was also less self-conscious with the music he wrote for this preordained medium. He wrote attractive melodies like *Je te veux* and *Tendrement* with relative ease, and agonized far less over them than over 'serious' works like the *Pièces froides*. Through the advocacy of Vincent Hyspa and the 'Queen of the Slow Waltz', Paulette Darty, Satie became better known for his popular songs than for his other music. Indeed, his friends in Arcueil-Cachan in 1909–10 thought that this was all he did, much to Satie's annoyance. It was not until Satie allied his 'serious' compositions with the familiar forces of the cabaret orchestra that he began to achieve a greater degree of satisfaction and fluency. This only came about with *Les Pantins dansent* in 1913; in short, through his growing attraction towards the theatre.

Satie did, however, make one attempt to score for full orchestra around 1901 in what would appear to be a 'serious' context. This is *Le Bœuf Angora* (*The Angora Ox*) which, like *The Dreamy Fish*, is music for a story by Lord Cheminot (alias Contamine de Latour).[12] The heavily corrected score (BN 10062) bears witness to Satie's tremendous struggle with its orchestration, though like all his scores it still manages to look attractive in its red and black calligraphy. Here Satie used a standard larger orchestra of piccolo, two flutes, oboe, cor anglais, two clarinets in A, two bassoons, two horns in F, two trumpets in C, three trombones, tuba, timpani, side drum, bass drum and strings. Only *Parade*, with its Eb clarinet, cornet, harp and extra 'noise-making' instruments, is larger. *The Angora Ox* is incomplete, running to 73 bars, of which the last 8 (in triple time in a new key) may not necessarily be continuous. The final bars are, however, more clearly scored, and Satie reused them in the *Trois Morceaux en forme de poire*, as we have seen.[13] Satie seems to have sought advice with the main part of this thick experimental score. On BN 10062, f. 4v, the tuba part (which Satie uses as a duplicate double-bass) is corrected in another hand by someone who knew more about the instrument (Ex. 49). The hand is not Debussy's, and to me it looks like that of Charles Koechlin, who had also known Satie since the early 1890s. He may have advised other changes too, for the uncharacteristic doublings and thicker, more 'professional' textures seem closer to Koechlin's post-Romantic style than to Satie's.[14] Details such as the descending chords on clarinet, horn and strings which are put onto

Ex. 49 *The Angora Ox*, bars 61–5, showing ?Koechlin's revision of Satie's tuba part (BN 10062, f. 4v)

pianissimo trombones (bars 15–16), the addition of the timpani part (replacing the tuba on f. 3r, bar 5), and the minims with their stems on the right-hand side all suggest Koechlin.

Thus in the two 'Lord Cheminot' pieces, Satie was trying to find a way forward by experimenting with the more technically advanced styles of his composing friends Debussy and Koechlin. In *The Dreamy Fish* he tried Impressionistic harmonies and development, and in *The Angora Ox* he tried fuller, colourful orchestration. That only two such large-scale pieces exist is a tribute to his quickness to realize that he was backing down a blind alley, and that his future lay elsewhere, however long it might take him to find it.

1909–1917

It was not until 1909–10 that Satie acquired the basic technical training in orchestration that he needed. Two Schola notebooks have survived from this period: Ho 25 probably represents the first notes Satie took down in October–November 1909 on the ranges and capabilities of instruments, whilst BN 9651 is marked 'IIIe Cours (1909 – Décembre)' and deals with the way instruments blend with each other in practical application. It seems strange that the skilful orchestrator of *La Diva de l'Empire'* should have felt the need to take down so much rudimentary information at the age of forty-three, much of which could be found in existing treatises on the subject. But Satie was obsessively methodical, and he must have thought that if he wrote down everything d'Indy said he would be able to answer any questions that arose later on. Stranger still, Satie does not seem to have noticed the contradictions between one notebook and the other, which suggests that if d'Indy was responsible for the December 1909 course, the earlier introduction (Ho 25) was by someone else. Thus in Ho 25 we find:

Ex. 50a (Ho 25, 2)

whereas BN 9651, 23 offers a more sensible and detailed approach that takes account of the flute's penetrating power in the lower register – though neither the flutes (nor the oboes) seem to have been allowed to use their lowest notes by d'Indy:

Ex. 50b (BN 9651, 23)

To paraphrase Gertrude Stein: 'A flute is a flute is a flute', and poor Satie must have been confused by some of this information. Why, for instance, should the cor anglais and the flute 'never' be doubled at the unison, whilst the cor anglais and clarinet 'work well' thus (BN 9651, 35)? Why should the oboe and bassoon be 'good' in octaves, yet the oboe and horn 'bad' (ibid., 38)? Perhaps it was this long regimented list of problems over unison doublings (ibid., 35–7) that account for their rarity in Satie's later orchestration? Another effect of d'Indy's teaching was to make Satie suspicious of using the French horn. 'It's an instrument I despise', Satie told Roland-Manuel (Vc) (when planning to use only two of them in *En Habit de cheval* in September 1911). For d'Indy had expressed all manner of dubious reservations about its doubling potential, and had filled Satie's mind with the restrictions of natural horns, as follows (ibid., 27):

Ex. 51 (BN 9651, 27)

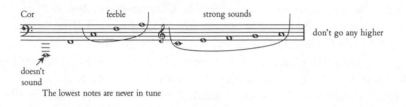

Fortunately, Satie later came to realize for himself the blending potential of this perfect filler of inner parts, and he used two chromatic horns to flexible advantage in *Parade*. We find them, for instance, in their 'feeble' range on OS 38 and 68,[15] with the first horn higher than recommended on the melody in OS 21–2. But even so, the horns are used less than one would expect, and there are never more than two of them, so d'Indy's teaching was only beneficial here insofar as it encouraged Satie's sense of restraint.

The other d'Indy maxim that Satie remembered, and again quoted to Roland-Manuel in 1911, was that three trumpets meant 'the end of the world' (Vc). Although d'Indy himself habitually used three trumpets in C,[16] he seems to have induced Satie to use only two (in C) for the rest of his career. 'More of them are never necessary', Satie told Roland-Manuel (Vc). But on the whole d'Indy's coaching from his own greater experience gave Satie confidence and much of his advice was profitably taken to heart, especially where it confirmed Satie's existing practice. Thus we find him frequently doubling violin melodies at the lower octave on clarinet (as in the 'Ragtime' theme of *Parade*, OS 49), making flexible use of the bassoons, generally using instruments in their best registers, and carefully placing the main harmony notes in fuller scoring – following d'Indy's advice that 'the writing has an influence on the sonority'. A good example of this can be found in the opening chorale of *Parade* (Ex. 52), whose distinctive sound has as much to do with its spacing as with its harmonies.

Ex. 52 *Parade*, opening *Choral*, bars 1–8 (Salabert, OS 2–3)

During the summer of 1911, Satie struggled to reconcile theory and practice in *En Habit de cheval*. Its pairs of fugues and chorales emerged for piano duet between June and 6 September, and when Satie took his work in hand to show Roussel (including the recent exposition of his *Fugue de papier*), he reported with delight to Roland-Manuel on 4 August that 'the whole thing entertained him. He has sided with me over this new conception of the fugue, especially the expositions. He loved its little harmonies' (Vc). On 9 September Satie sold the duet version to the publisher Aléxis Rouart, and between then and the end of October he wrestled with the orchestration.[17] From the drafts in Ho 31–2 we can see that Satie devised different combinations to suit each movement,[18] with the fullest scoring being used to make an impressive effect in the opening chorale – which includes new instruments (for Satie) like the sarrusophone and the contrabass tuba. In the last two movements Satie reduced his scoring, and he used the cor anglais in preference to the oboe in movements 2–3 (perhaps in defiance of d'Indy), though both instruments appear in the final *Fugue de*

papier. Satie seems to have liked the distinctive timbre of the cor anglais, for it features in most of his later works.

From incomplete pages in the Harvard manuscripts, we can gain a fascinating insight into how Satie prepared his orchestral scores. First he ruled unbroken bar lines, usually eight per page. Then he wrote the list of instruments to be used on each page alongside the staves. Then came the noteheads, followed (as in late Handel) by the tails and stems. Lastly, he added the dynamics and phrasing. In the case of the *Fugue litanique* (Ho 32) between letters B and C, Satie wrote the woodwind parts before the strings, working from the top of the page downwards. In the *Fugue de papier*, he left the start of the exposition till last (bars 1–9), perhaps because it involved simple instrumentation for strings, or perhaps because he was more interested by the orchestral challenge of the fugue once it got under way. In the final score of the opening chorale there is more doubling than usual, especially when Satie sought to make a massive tutti of the final three bars (Ex. 53). Although, as elsewhere, he adds no notes to the duet version during orchestration (as Debussy or Koechlin would have done), his Schola training led him to balance his tutti by using complete harmonies in each orchestral group, and even to introduce double-stops in the violins (an extreme rarity). Only the flute parts in the final two bars are redundant, due to their low pitch and their doubling by horn and trumpets. In this case Satie would have been better off using the oboes he specifically rejected. The clarity he later achieved by selecting and balancing precisely the right instruments needed to make an effect can be seen by comparing Exx. 52 and 53. The effect is just as weighty and impressive in *Parade* with only twelve instruments above the lower strings as it is with sixteen instruments plus violins in *En Habit de cheval*. Besides putting the melody line on the instruments that count in Ex. 52 (two trumpets and trombone, instead of flute, trumpets and violins in Ex. 53), the whole conception of Ex. 52 is simpler and more effective, showing how far Satie had progressed in the intervening eight years.

In the aftermath of *En Habit de cheval*, Satie went through a period in 1912 when he described himself as a 'phonometrographer' – one who measured the loudness of sounds by subjective comparison. This was not just a joke with which to begin his 'Mémoires d'un amnésique'[19] and usher in his 'fantaisiste' period, for we find him begging Emile Vuillermoz 'to present me as a phonometrician and not as a musician' at an SMI concert. He also told Roland-Manuel on 1 April 1912 that 'I'm not writing music, but phonometry – it's better' (Vc). This was partly a smoke-screen in the uncertain period before Satie finally found a way forward with the *Véritables Préludes flasques* in August 1912, but it also grew out of the careful process of balancing sounds and dynamics in *En Habit de cheval*, and of weighing possibilities one against the other. This seems more likely than Templier's explanation (1969, 76) that Satie was making 'fun of himself for the insistent rhythm which characterized a number of his earlier works', and reading between the lines it seems that Satie thought his Schola training was in danger of making him into 'an acoustical workman without any great understanding'.[20]

The last obvious sign of this training comes in the *Chanson canine*,[21] where Satie's

Ex. 53 *En Habit de cheval*, No. 1: *Choral*, bars 11–13 (Salabert, OS 4 bars 3–5)

fluid two-part invention took a wrong turning in bar 2, and was only completed to his satisfaction when he reverted from attempted through-composition to a more congenial assembly of separate cells. The dissonant individuality and the unusual beaming of the phrases across the barlines (for visual rather than aural effect) were both written into the prelude deliberately. This was a sure sign to Satie that a new approach was needed, and it came through the issue of a 'severe reprimand' to all pedagogic teaching in the first of the *Véritables Préludes flasques*. Even d'Indy is included under this umbrella, for the first bass entry of this toccata is marked 'The voice of the master' (BN 9618, 4).

Once Satie could laugh at the Schola and himself he was back on course, and this is nowhere more evident than in the 'seven tiny dances' for Jonah the monkey which separate the scenes of his bizarre play *Le Piège de Méduse* in 1913. The anarchic world of the myopic Baron Medusa is partly that of Satie himself, though he was furious with Pierre Bertin for mimicking him when the play reached the stage in 1921.[22] Polycarpe, the butler, who initially dominates Medusa, and is anxious to get off to a billiards match (and later to be married) surely contains an element of Debussy. In his miniature dances, Satie found a new world of simplicity and humour which can be seen in No. 4, a Mazurka with a delightful, deflating coda (Fig. 7.1). Here, the players all laugh at Satie's exaggerated cross-phrasing and cadence, much as the orchestra laugh at Shostakovich's Leningrad Symphony in the *Interrupted Serenade* of Bartók's Concerto for Orchestra, but in cameo, of course. In *Le Piège de Méduse* Satie chose only the instruments he needed; three strings balanced by three wind. Then he added almost as many percussion instruments again (bass drum, two cymbals, triangle, tambourine and tarolle) a trend of 'exteriorizing his thought' that stretches through to *Cinéma*, his final chamber score – where the percussion parts were also added later (in larger notes) to enliven the surrounding texture. As well as being the first Surrealist play, *Le Piège de Méduse* also contains the first use I know of a prepared piano: at its private première in 1914[23] (in its original keyboard version), Satie 'slid sheets of paper between the strings' and the hammers to produce a mechanistic effect (Chalupt, 1952, 41).

Satie's other theatrical venture in 1913 was *Les Pantins dansent*, a strange, disembodied 'poème dansé' written for a Metachoric Festival devised by Valentine de Saint-Point. From a press controversy with Paola Litta in *Le Figaro* and the *Revue musicale SIM*, we learn from Mlle Saint-Point herself that 'in my *Métachorie*, music and dance are equal partners, both uniquely and similarly dependent on the Idea, that is to say the idea evoked in the poem or drama. . .Instead of being exclusively dependent on music, Metachory is not its slave but its equal, both being dependent on the [poetic] idea and subjected to strict architecture: that of the geometrical line and of number.'[24] Litta had accused Saint-Point of taking her Metachoric concepts from his book *Déesse nue*, which he claimed to have sent her on 23 July 1912. But as Saint-Point was quick to point out: 'Litta considers "the dance as an expression of the music". As people have seen, I interpret a poem and not the music, and the music is inspired by the poem and not "conceived choreographically", as M. P. Litta would wish it. . .Metachory is conceived in the modern spirit. . .it needs a creative musician. . .its direction is intellectual and not sentimental.'

7.1   *Le Piège de Méduse* (1913). Orchestral score of Dance No. 4: Mazurka (Ho).

It is easy to see why the whole concept attracted Satie with its modern spirit of participation and intellectual aims. Both the composer and the dancer were to be separately inspired by a common poem with their creations combined on stage, in a concept far different from the free choreographic improvisations to well-known pieces by contemporary dancers such as Isadora Duncan, Maud Allan and Loïe Fuller. In fact,

The Puppets are Dancing is a rather maudlin, self-indulgent and repetitive poem in six verses in which the author predicts her death during a festival, her inner emotions and black depression contrasting with the artificial gaiety of the puppets cavorting around her.[25] Although atmospheric, it does not match up to Saint-Point's lofty ideals.

Satie was actually inspired to write two different interpretations of *The Puppets are Dancing*, both in 2/4 time. Their approximately equal lengths (82 and 76 bars), and their jerky, *staccato* textures and disappearing codas indicate that they belong together, but Satie cannot have intended the regular 4-bar phrases of his final version to each fit one line of Saint-Point's poem (see n. 25), for the music would then finish at the first line of stanza 5. So the poem and music *must* have been performed independently within an overall duration of 1½ minutes. The return of bars 1–4 as 69–72, and bars 5–8 as 65–9 may have been intended to reflect the way stanza 1 returns as stanza 6 (with bars 73–6 as the disappearing coda). In the first version, on the other hand, there is a separate 8-bar introduction, but with bars 9–24 similarly returning as a modified (and rescored) *da capo* in bars 57–72 (after which a 2-bar extension again leads to a vanishing coda in bars 75–82).

The first version, which I have reconstructed from Satie's sketches,[26] must have been too jaunty, expressive and harmonically unambiguous to create the effect Satie wanted, though it was perhaps Valentine de Saint-Point's opinion that led to its rejection, given the fact that Satie virtually completed it in short score and was not given to synchronizing his music with stage events anyway. Apart from its striking, dissonant introduction, the scoring is sparse and varied, with a substantial role given to the harp. Ex. 54a shows a return of the main rondo theme (characteristically arpeggio-based) given to the bassoon with low trumpet accompaniment, and this is followed by a delightful scalar episode, which may have been rejected as too flowing and extroverted. It is abruptly interrupted by the harp in a manner unique to this piece, just before the *da capo*. The parallel passage in the final version (Ex. 54b)[27] is more abstract tonally and other-worldly: its melancholy regularity contrasting with the longer melodic sentences of Ex. 54a. Satie's favourite melodic outline of the augmented fourth figures naturally in bars 1 and 5–6 of Ex. 54b, in contrast to the conjunct familiarity of Ex. 54a.

In 1915 Satie acquired his only composition pupil, a wealthy industrialist named Albert Verley, who manufactured perfumes at his own factory in the Parisian suburb of Neuilly. Perhaps Verley was introduced to Satie by his brother Conrad, who was also a chemical engineer. Like so many scientists, Verley's main love was music, and the two *Pastels sonores* which he published privately in 1916 show that he was a talented composer in an evocative, 'Impressionistic' manner. In January 1916, Satie made a piano duet reduction and an orchestration of the second of these *Pastels: L'Aurore aux doigts de rose* (*The Rosy-Fingered Dawn*). As with Debussy and his orchestration of the *Gymnopédies*, this was the only occasion when Satie orchestrated the work of another composer, and given the sensuous, descriptive nature of the music, he must have done it for money. Verley, it would appear, wanted to be known by the leading composers of his day, for Satie's published duet version of *L'Aurore*[28] is dedicated to Ravel, and an extract

Ex. 54a *Les Pantins dansent*, first version, bars 33–56 (BN 9604, 18–19, 21)

Ex. 54a (*cont.*)

Ex. 54b *Les Pantins dansent*, final version, bars 33–40 (based on the extract cited in Schmitt: *Montjoie!*, 1913, 12)

from Verley's ballet *Le Masque de la mort rouge* is dedicated to Paul Dukas (Gillmor, 1988, 138). According to Vladimir Golschmann (1972, 12), it was Verley who sponsored the Concerts Golschmann (which launched his conducting career) after Satie had introduced Golschmann to Verley as an expert repetiteur in 1917. Satie also tried to interest his friend Edgard Varèse in America in his orchestration of *L'Aurore*.[29] After its completion, he wrote on 6 February 1916:

> I am sending you a strange piece by A. Verley – one of my good pupils – a piece I have reduced to four hands and orchestrated; or rather, I have orchestrated it and reduced it to four hands. I *recommend* this piece. It is a *real* collaboration. Read this work with your usual lucidity, mon Gros Père. You will like its naive and tender simplicity. Verley is a delicate colourist whom you can present to your American friends.
>
> (VI, 105)

In *The Rosy-Fingered Dawn*, Satie uses substantial forces with extreme economy in what amounts to a kaleidoscopic chamber scoring.[30] Exx. 55a–b give the representative opening and its duet reduction, which is so literal that one would never guess it came last without Satie's testimony. There are no unison doublings whatsoever in the orchestration, even down to the first trombone replacing what one would expect to be a cello line in bar 7 of Ex. 55a. Satie never uses all the instruments together, but conversely the strings and wind hardly ever play alone. The way Satie mixes the sounds can be seen in Ex. 55a, with its very distinctive opening for high clarinet and cor anglais, which Debussy would surely have put on solo strings (as at the start of his *Première Rapsodie* for clarinet and orchestra). But even though Verley's piano piece has Debussyan echoes, this was the last thing Satie wanted to evoke in his orchestration. This may appear thin in the context of the piece and its style, but Satie's concern with balance and detail show him to be no mere instrumentator in this instance. In bar 6 of Ex. 55a the strings are carefully bowed and muted to avoid accentuation, so that the flute melody will come through clearly. The trumpet is removed on the third quaver of bar 8, both to aid the diminuendo and so as not to obscure the rising line on the second violins. The viola line in bars 3–5 is unmuted and marked 'bien chanté' so that it will stand out, and so on. Satie's duet reduction is equally inventive and practical, with the Seconda surrounding the Prima in its bitonally spelt opening, and a cross-hand effect ensuring an accented F♯ in the Prima part in bar 9. Perhaps the nearest Satie ever came to what might be termed creative orchestration comes in Ex. 56, where the violas support the added harp *glissando*, and a touch on the tambourine marks its climax in six-part divided strings supported by a *pianissimo* roll on timpani. Satie clearly knew about such colouristic effects, even if he never used them in his own music. It is a tribute to his integrity that he remained so close to his own individual concept of orchestral transparency, whilst still revealing Verley as the 'delicate colourist' he knew him to be.

To a certain extent, Satie's orchestral restraint in *Parade* and *Socrate* arose from the methods he employed in preparing their scores. In these more complex cases (as with Debussy in *Jeux*) he made separate orchestral drafts. But these were still in the oblong

Ex. 55a Verley, orch. Satie: *L'Aurore aux doigts de rose*, bars 1–9 (BN 10034, 2–3)

Ex. 55a (*cont.*)

Ex. 55b Satie's duet reduction of Ex. 55a (BN Fol. Vm.¹² a. 471)

pocket-books he used for composition, which had only six (or at most seven) staves per page. Like Verdi in his early operas, Satie arranged his instruments in order of descending pitch rather than in conventional family groupings here. Whilst the restricted space ensured the sparseness he wanted, it also led to complications. Indeed, it is doubtful whether he could have heard the instrumental combinations he created at all easily when clarinets suddenly became violas doubling cellos, or horns shared the same stave with trombones, or the trumpets were added on an empty stave above the piccolos. All of these occur on the first page of Figure 7.2 as the giant wave overwhelms the stricken Titanic in Part 2 of *Parade*. But with a few minor changes to the

Ex. 56 *L'Aurore aux doigts de rose*, bars 20–1 (BN 10034, 7)

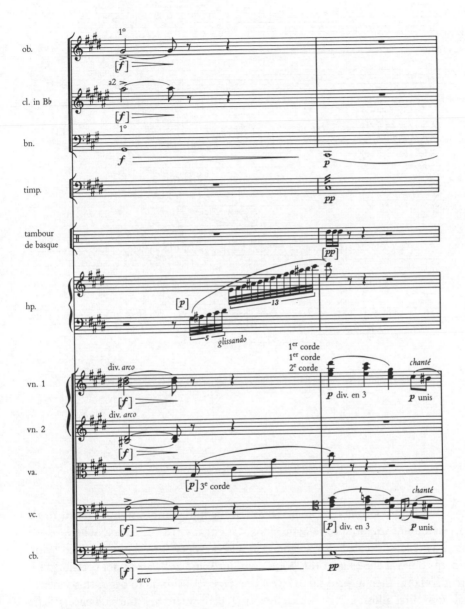

violins, the addition of a doubling harp part (bars 6–9), a pulsing timpani pedal in quavers, and a 'sirène grave', Figure 7.2 became the final version (OS 61–3) without too much apparent difficulty. In fact, orchestrating his bitonal wave caused Satie far less trouble than making it materialize musically, and in general he avoided such complex passages.

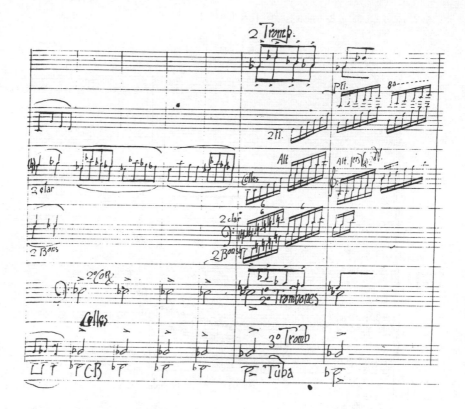

7.2   The giant wave overwhelms the Titanic in Part 2 of *Parade* (1917) (BN 9602(2), 18–19).

As we saw with *La Belle Excentrique* (Ex. 25), the initial impression his music made was of paramount importance to Satie. This was equally true of *Parade*, where, as we also saw, Satie later decided that a chorale should be added – to show the 'box' being opened up to reveal the cabaret (or 'boîte') within;[31] just as Picasso's red curtain (with its circus scene) is then opened up to reveal the stage set behind. To begin this series of optical and aural illusions (in which the true performers are the audience), Satie wanted something striking in its simplicity. He originally began with the undulating idea which now comes in bar 9 (Ex. 57). This in itself represented the ninth stage in a process of progressive simplification of the accompaniment to a melodic idea that remained unchanged throughout. Then, as he was nearing a final version, Satie must have suddenly realized that Ex. 57 would sound much better as a contrast to a sonorous chordal opening (Ex. 52). This arrived, by comparison, in just two stages.

The first (Ex. 58a) proved too short, too widely spaced, and too close to the undulating passage to follow, in that it used the same theme as its bass. The second version (Ex. 58b) must have come as a flash of certain inspiration, for it was written at great speed, directly in ink in the top left-hand corner of the same page, as a series of fourteen chords, to which Satie added rhythms and barlines later. Ex. 58b was still linked to Ex. 57 in that its first two bars began on the focal note e^1, and the melody of its third bar was the same as that of the first bar of Ex. 57. But the whole process had become more subtle in an instant, and Satie was so sure of this opening that he added instrumental indications there and then. A comparison between Ex. 58b and Ex. 52 will show that it was transferred directly in this form, apart from the lower octave doubling of the trumpet theme on two horns (Ex. 58b), which Satie realized would reduce the orchestral clarity.

Ex. 57 *Parade*, opening *Choral*, bars 9–12 (Salabert, OS 3: 1919)

Ex. 58a *Parade*, first version of the start of the *Choral* (BN 9602(4), 20)

Ex. 58b Ibid., second version (cf. Ex. 52) (BN 9602(4), 20)

1917–1924

'In writing *Socrate*', Satie told Paul Collaer in May 1920, 'I thought I was composing a simple work, without the least idea of conflict' (Vl, 155). Its title 'symphonic drama' would appear to be a misnomer, until one realizes that it is symphonic insofar as its main motifs all appear in the orchestra, and dramatic insofar as it describes the events leading to the drama of Socrates' death in its final part. There can be no more potent example of Satie's 'cult of restraint' than this sparse chamber score, which he actually planned as *musique d'ameublement* in 1917. Yet its detached, monochrome effect arises rather from its low dynamic level, slow pulse, and motivic preoccupation with the bare interval of the perfect fourth than from its orchestration. In most places the recitative-like vocal line was grafted onto an already complete musical argument, and Satie's sketches show that his motifs were conceived complete with their harmonies – like the four rising modal triads that symbolize the ill-fated Socrates in Part 3. Nonetheless, the motifs are primarily linked by a linear logic, which is assisted by the orchestration. Here, the abrupt block-like contrasts between phrases in *Parade* have, by and large, disappeared, to be replaced by an almost Fauréan basis in the strings, with comments and additions from the nine other instruments. As Poulenc observed in 1920 (Collaer, 1974, 2), we see in *Socrate* 'the beginning of horizontal music which will succeed perpendicular music. It is this self-same criterion that *Socrate* owes its limpidity, which is like running water.' A good example can be found in the *Portrait de Socrate* (Ex. 59).[32] Here the oboe part leads into the violins in bars 2–3; the strings into the descending scale at figure 9; and the scale into the chord in the final bar, all with commendable smoothness and logic. There is even an overlap of phrases on the harp in the final bar (cf. Ex. 54a), and two bars of strings on their own before figure 9. Ex. 59 should be compared with the continuous Exx. 52 and 57 to see the essential difference between *Socrate* and the juxtapositions of *Parade*, and in Part 2 of *Socrate* there is even a 12-bar passage with no wind whatsoever.[33]

The scales (mostly rising) as links between the phrases recur in each section of *Socrate* as a force for continuity and unity. Socrates' rising tetrachord (which dominates the latter half of Part 3) is, of course, an aspect of this, 'insinuating itself into the listener's imagination as a kind of musico-poetic symbol of the serene and stoic death of the great philosopher' (Gillmor, 1988, 223). But Satie's earliest sketches (BN 9623 (1)) show that he did not discover his rising series of chords (VS 35) until he reached the point he realized should be the recapitulation (VS 54 bar 9, with its sudden drop from *fortissimo* to *piano*). This led to a second series of drafts (with vocal line) in BN 9611, which enabled Satie to complete his masterpiece. Prior to this discovery there had been no orchestral introduction to *Mort de Socrate* at all, and we find Satie inserting his rising fifths (marked 'Entrée – 4 fois. La basse en dehors') into the margin of BN 9611, 4, then superposing its descending continuation in ink over several earlier pencil versions beneath his unchanged vocal line for the first phrase (now bars 5–6). He then shifted his earlier accompaniment to this phrase (in its fourth version) two bars sideways, providing him with what now became bars 7–8, which was subtly

Ex. 59 *Socrate*. 1: *Portrait de Socrate* (Eschig, OS 17: cf. VS 9 bar 11 – 10 bar 4)

Ex. 59 (*cont.*)

linked into the fourth-based motif in its simplest form in bars 9–10. The hard-won result can be seen in Ex. 60. Here the flute line in detached crotchets helps to accentuate what is actually the main (bass) line of the rising motif of Socrates, and again we can see how the orchestra is essentially string-based with a careful concern that each motivic fragment in the assembly leads logically into the next by linear means.

In the latter half of *Mort de Socrate* (VS 54 bar 9 onwards) the insistent repetition of the Socrates motif suggests the inexorability of the philosopher's fate. Just as the Mélisande motif remains unchanged in Debussy's opera, but is presented in a variety of changing textures that reflect the developing psychological situation, so Satie uses all his imaginative powers to present the Socrates motif in a wide variety of harmonic and orchestral contexts. As Phaedo describes how Crito is ordered to bring the poison for Socrates, the motif marches across the woodwind in fifths (bars 180–3; VS 57 bar 8–58 bar 2) against its own decoration in quavers on the lower strings, in a process Satie had subtly introduced in bars 5–6 of Ex. 60. Then, as Phaedo, the philosopher's pupil, describes how they break down and cry as Socrates drinks the poison, Satie introduces

Ex. 60 *Socrate*. 3: *Mort de Socrate*, bars 1–10 (Eschig, OS 60–1: cf. VS 35)

Ex. 60 (*cont.*)

falling fifths (on the first violins) against the motif in its descending form to suggest their falling tears (bars 225–8; VS 61 bars 2–5). Then, as Phaedo describes how the poison begins to take effect and Socrates' 'body freezes and stiffens', Satie, with supreme economy, introduces a poignant countermelody to the motif on oboe, then on cor anglais, separated by an entry on the trumpet (Ex. 61). Such an obbligato is rendered the more effective by its rarity elsewhere; by its proximity to the (soprano) vocal line; and by the C♮/C♯ clashes between the motif and its countermelody. Within a deliberately restricted compass, Satie uses small expressive gestures to telling effect, each gesture having been honed down to its bare bones, but still shining through the transparency of the surrounding texture. For the dramatic effects one might expect during Socrates' death itself, Satie substitutes seventeen bars of bare fifths on two shifting pitches (A and B), whose simple dignity transports the tragedy onto a higher plane. The last two bars, virtually for full orchestra, were an inspired afterthought added at the proof stage, for none of the three alternatives found in the sketches

Ex. 61 *Mort de Socrate* (Eschig, OS 103–4: cf. VS 67 bar 5 – 68 bar 2)

(BN 9623(3), 3) satisfied Satie. He was determined to avoid the expected tonic of A, and two of his sketches actually end on C (as an upward resolution of the A/B alternation of the previous bars). His final solution (Ex. 62) was ingenious in the extreme, for it both left the drama suspended in mid-air on an implied second inversion of B minor, and also brought it back to the point where everything began, on an F# pedal in the bass.[34] The abrupt shift to B had been prepared six bars earlier (VS 71 bar 2), but

Ex. 62 *Mort de Socrate*, last 4 bars (Eschig, OS 109: cf. VS 71 bars 6–9)

now the biting augmented fourth (B/E♯) added weight to the tragedy, and its incomplete resolution onto F♯ ensured that the effect of Socrates' death lingered on after the music simply stopped. Suddenly adding a fuller orchestra in the middle of Ex. 62 even suggested a new departure towards more exalted regions.

Satie's final ballets of 1924 add little that is new to the picture of Satie as an orchestrator, and the score for *Le Médecin malgré lui*, which Satie was so delighted with, has unfortunately not come to light. In *Mercure*, which is unusually extrovert for such a short ballet, Satie reverts to a slightly augmented version of the cabaret orchestra of *La Diva de l''Empire'* (see Appendix), keeping, as always, to his limit of two horns and two trumpets, and here using only a single trombone. The scoring is mixed throughout, apart from the *Bain des Grâces*, which is a rare reverie for strings alone. The 'brilliant overture' is less fully scored than one might expect, and its brilliance derives more from its syncopation and active bass line than from any abrupt juxtaposition of orchestral textures. After the experience of *Socrate*, Satie attached great importance to linear continuity in *Mercure*, and one very interesting feature in Tableau 3 is the way Satie combines the themes of the *Polka des lettres* and the *Nouvelle Danse* in the succeeding movement *Le Chaos* (No. 12) in two-part counterpoint between wind and strings (the first 'Gaiement' and the second 'Très expressif'). Satie intensifies this truly orchestral concept (Ex. 63) by making the wind *staccato* and the strings *legato*, with each

Ex. 63 *Mercure*. No. 12: *Le Chaos*, bars 5–9 (OS in *F-Pfs*, coll. Henri de Beaumont, 69)

group doubled in three octaves. But it is the Polka on the wind that dominates in the context, because Satie introduces and ends his 'representation of chaos' with transposed and rescored versions of the introduction and coda of the original Polka.

In *Relâche* the orchestra is even smaller (see Appendix), and the continually mixed 'cabaret' scoring more restrained. The percussion accentuation is sparing, with the tarolle and cymbals only being employed for ten bars in the final number. Indeed, Satie's judicious selection of instruments is such that the whole band never plays together – there are no timpani, percussion or oboe in the final bars, for instance. Favourite devices, such as doubling the first violins and cellos in octaves, or blending the clarinets with the violas and the bassoons with the double-basses, still persist, but there is very little unison doubling, and no string double-stopping for extra sonority. The orchestration is used to reflect the form, in that the many recurring passages have the same scoring, and the use of orchestral contrast between phrases is more noticeable than it was in *Mercure*. Satie uses terraced dynamics frequently to ensure the correct balance in performance, and in the *Danse de la Brouette* in Act 2 he makes this unusual 5/4 movement more unusual by varying the dynamics rather than the scoring to achieve his sectional contrasts. Again, we can see that Satie was aware of such possibilities, but saved them for special occasions.

During the composition of *Mort de Socrate*, as we saw in chapter 5, Satie observed that 'Impressionism is the art of Imprecision; today we tend towards Precision', and this was precisely what he achieved in orchestral terms. With absolute economy he selected only the instruments vital to each different work to give the transparency, linear clarity and simple directness that were his ultimate aims. If he used the single woodwind of the cabaret orchestra more than the full symphony orchestra in his later works, it was by then not because he was more familiar with it, but because its sounds were more appropriate to his goals of restraint and modernity. *Parade* shows that he could handle the full orchestra with absolute confidence, and the fact that one only has to hear a few bars to identify Satie as the author is a tribute to his imaginative skills as an orchestrator. His orchestration always sounds well, and that sound is a unique and unforgettable one. As Satie told Poulenc before Diaghilev's revival of *Parade* in May 1919: '*Parade*, on Sunday [18 May], will prove that I can orchestrate as well as anyone else. For many, this work was only good when played on the piano. What a myth!!' (Vc). In *Parade* there is never any question of mere instrumentation; its sounds were wholly new and made an indelible impression on Stravinsky and the generation of Les Six. Indeed, there can be no better summary of Satie's own achievements than those he praised in Stravinsky in 1922 (Ve, 64):

> His method of orchestration is new and fearless. He never orchestrates in a 'fuzzy' way; he avoids 'orchestral pot-holes' and 'haze' – which causes the loss of more musicians than navigators. He goes where he wants to.
>
> Note that Stravinsky's orchestration is the result of a deep and precise knowledge of how to write for instruments. The whole of his 'orchestra' is based on instrumental timbre. Nothing is left to chance, I tell you. What is the source of his sumptuous 'Truth'?
>
> Regard him as a remarkable logician, unerring and energetic; for he alone has composed with such magnificent power, such certain assurance, such constant will-power.

8

Questions of form, logic and the mirror image

Satie rarely spoke about form, and never about the logic behind the way his compositions were assembled. His only advice to other composers was to 'be brief', and his own exemplary brevity has been compared with that of Webern, who shared Satie's inner necessity for 'concision and understatement. . .independent of historical factors' (Lajoinie, 39). Just as each note for Webern was an expressive entity of equal importance, so Satie told Robert Caby on his death-bed that 'no-one will be able to say later on that I have written a note which has no meaning, or which I have not carefully planned' (Caby, 1929, 4). If Satie never used mirror canons and palindromic variations, as Webern did in his Symphony (Op. 21), he was no less concerned about mirror images, formal reflections and proportional balance. In fact, he had an obsession with numerology second only to that of Berg and was forever counting his bars.

As Satie said in 1920: 'I have always striven to confuse would-be followers by both the form and the background of each new work' (Ve, 45), and this he successfully did in a variety of ways. His attitude to the way music existed in time and space, like an architectural structure, was entirely new. 'Before I compose a piece, I walk round it several times, accompanied by myself', he wrote of the *Aperçus désagréables* in 1913 (Ve, 143). And he told Paul Collaer that if his second and third *Gymnopédies* or *Sarabandes* appeared to him as good as the first, it was 'the absolutely new form' he had invented that 'was good in itself' (Collaer, 1955, 136). Which was rather like viewing the same sculpture by his friend Brancusi from three different angles. As Shattuck says (1968, 141): 'There are obvious grounds for comparison of this procedure with that of the Cubists. They investigated the complexity in time and space of a simple object studied simultaneously from several points of view.' But as always, Satie was first off the mark with his contemplation of the static sound-object. His use of extensive repetition enhanced the relevance of minute variation when it occurred, and it usually excluded any need for conventional development or recapitulation. Extended Classical forms were reinterpreted rather than adopted verbatim, and Satie rather favoured simple ternary or rondo structures. Sometimes, as in *Parade*, these were combined with an ingenuity that is as impressive as that of Debussy in *L'Isle joyeuse*. For Satie was not concerned with through-composition and the normal perception of music 'getting somewhere' through functional forms and harmonies. He was more interested in exploring the effects of monotony and boredom, and in the potential of the miniature and of unitary form. His concern lay in the way our perception of time could be expanded and telescoped, and how music could function as a spatial element in time.

Concepts of time and space

In real life, as Satie observed to the film director René Clair in 1924, 'time passes and will not pass again'. But through his music, Satie found numerous ways to cheat the passage of time. The ubiquitous slow pulse and chains of block chords in the Rose-Croix pieces create an impression of timeless immobility; even to the extent that it does not seem to matter where a piece begins or ends. The absence of any climax, or movement towards a goal, and the way that progressions recur imperceptibly, gives the impression of a timeless creation revolving in space. While Satie did not experiment systematically with multiple sound-sources as Varèse did, his later concept of the vocal line of *Socrate* being alternated by four sopranos represents a step in this direction. So too does his *Musique d'ameublement* of 1920. Here, as Milhaud recalls (1952, 105): 'In order that the music might seem to come from all sides at once, we posted the clarinets in three different corners of the theatre, the pianist[s] in the fourth, and the trombone in a box on the first floor.' But again, the concept of music as a sonorous backcloth, endlessly repeating short fragments whilst everyday life continues around it, is of greater importance than any anticipation of stereophonic effects. Satie's shouts of 'Go on talking! Walk about! Don't listen!' had the reverse effect to that intended. As soon as the audience switched from their own individual time-scales to that of the music, the whole experiment was ruined.

Ex. 64 *Vexations* (*c.* 1893) (MS in coll. of *F-Pfs*)
NOTE DE L'AUTEUR: Pour se jouer 840 fois de suite ce motif, il sera bon de se préparer au préalable, et dans le plus grand silence, par des immobilités sérieuses.

Perhaps the best example of Satie cheating time comes in *Vexations* (Ex. 64), where the 840 repetitions of a short, self-repeating piece can take between twelve and twenty-four hours, depending on the interpretation of the tempo marking 'Très lent'. As Gavin Bryars relates in his article '*Vexations* and its Performers' (1983, 12–20), the piece can have strange, hallucinatory effects on both performer(s) and audience; especially on the former, who have to contend with Satie's abstruse enharmonic notation which spells chords 13 and 33 differently, even though they are one and the same. The identical right-hand parts of chords 1, 10 and 12 (or 18, 27 and 29) in Ex. 64 are all spelt differently too. This, together with the atonal and ametrical nature of *Vexations*, forces the player to concentrate throughout the repetitions and not rely on memory. It is perhaps not surprising that few of the performances Bryars lists have been complete, for with the bass theme repeated between each 13-beat harmonization, it recurs 3,360 times. The second harmonization is a mirror image of the first, with the upper parts inverted, and all but chords 2 and 19 involve Satie's favourite interval of the tritone. As the same VIIb chords occur in *Bonjour Biqui, Bonjour!* of 2 April 1893, and both pieces have inscriptions in the same type of ink and end with an iambic rhythm, it is probable that Satie's vexations are those expressed in the latter part of his difficult relationship with Suzanne Valadon, that is to say, somewhere between April and early June 1893. The bass theme, incidentally, contains eleven notes of the chromatic scale with only five notes repeated; a sort of early attempt at serialism. The missing note (G#/Ab) occurs four times in the accompaniment to make the chromaticism total.

It seems churlish to suggest that Satie did not know exactly what he was doing when he wrote *Vexations*. He probably envisaged a single performance taking one minute, with 840 repetitions taking exactly fourteen hours. Any shortfall was made up by the period of silent meditation recommended beforehand. From the evidence of the manuscript,[1] Bryars suggests (ibid., 12) that the watered-down ink of the title and directions implies that they were added after the music (in darker ink) was complete. But as Satie would have been copying this final draft from a sketch (now lost), and because he often resorted to this economy measure, there is no convincing proof that the music predates the conception of *Vexations*. Indeed, with the careful precautions against memorization built into the music, a reverse hypothesis would seem more likely.

Much of what Satie was trying to achieve in his early works can be seen in his four *Ogives* of 1886, which share the same unitary conception and ametricality as *Vexations*. In the first *Ogive* (Ex. 65), Satie's material consists of a plainsong-type theme in octaves (A), divided into two mirroring halves. These are both modally ambiguous, beginning on E and ending on D. Satie makes them into a complete piece simply by harmonizing A in two ways. First, in *fortissimo* parallel octaves with root position chords alternating with first or second inversions (Ex. 65: A1). Second, in quiet root position chords with the outer parts tending to move in contrary motion (A2). Another repeat of A1 (not shown in Ex. 65) ends the piece, and this A–A1–A2–A1 pattern is followed in the other three *Ogives*.

As the main element which varies in the *Ogives* is the lengths of their phrases, their

Ex. 65 *Ogive* No. 1 (1886). The arrows show the chordal variants between A1 and A2

(Repeat A1 to finish *Ogive*)

form might be said to be 'chronometric. . .a function of time and duration' (Gillmor, 1988, 36). Thus ten beats are answered by fourteen in No. 1 (Ex. 65); nineteen by twenty-one in No. 2; with twenty telescoped into eighteen in No. 4. But, as with all Satie's logical systems, there are deliberate flaws built in to prevent imitation. The third *Ogive*, for instance, has its phrases in single spans of twenty-four crotchets, and the arrows in Ex. 65 show how the chordal links between A1 and A2 are broken in four places. There are similar instances in the other *Ogives* of major chords becoming minor, or vice versa,[2] but just when a logical truth seems imminent, the fourth *Ogive* alone carries its single change of chord in A2 into the final statement of A1.[3] And it might reasonably be said that Satie is indulging the eye rather than the ear here: for, given the very slow tempo, it would take a very acute listener to notice these dispersed variants without prior warning. The most noticeable aspects are the fact that only A2 is not in octaves, and the abrupt changes of texture and dynamics between each statement of the plainsong theme. Thus the form is as conditional on these parameters as it is on time and repetition. As Professor Gillmor concludes (1988, 36): 'We find in Satie's music a concentration upon unfamiliar relationships of time and space that relate to certain pre-Renaissance (and non-Western) conceptions of musical form while at the same time looking forward to the early music of John Cage and the hypnotic sound world of the minimalists.'

As regards direct references to passing time, all Satie's pictorial descriptions of chiming clocks belong to his later years. A clock strikes eight in the original text of the *Sonatine bureaucratique*, for instance (see Ex. 4b), whilst another strikes thirteen (twice) in the *Affolements granitiques*.[4] As most of his barless piano pieces of 1913–15 were conceived with regular bar lines, it is true to say that Satie's later music was more precise and metrical; it belongs to the immediate present (rather than the distant past) and shares its time-scale. Thus, by and large, regular phrasing and tonal clarity replace the early experiments in assymetrical fluidity and modality. In the Rose-Croix works such rhythmic interest as there is was often grafted onto the initial chains of crotchet chords. After 1912, rhythm plays a larger role, and perhaps Satie remembered the opening sentence of d'Indy's first lecture at the Schola Cantorum,[5] which defined rhythm as the main element in creating 'order and proportion in time and space'. For despite his iconoclasm, Satie was fascinated by the possibilities of creating his own orders and proportions. But having said this, rhythm and timbre never became Satie's predominant concerns in composition, as they did in contemporary works like Debussy's *Jeux* or Stravinsky's *The Rite of Spring*. And perhaps their example offers a reason why this was so.

Punctuation form in the Rose-Croix music

In the 1890s Satie's experiments were mostly with harmony and form. In Rose-Croix pieces like the two *Préludes du Nazaréen* (1892) and the *Prélude de La Porte héroïque du ciel* (1894), Satie invented what Patrick Gowers has christened 'punctuation form' (1965–6, 18).[6] To bring order to his assembly of motifs, Satie took the ingenious step of turning to literature for a solution. The result can be seen in the first Nazarene prelude, where the musical 'prose' is constructed from four motifs (Ex. 66: A–D), which are articulated at irregular intervals by a distinctive 'punctuation' phrase at three different pitches (Ex. 66: 1–3). The phrase and its two transpositions recur four times in strict rotation like commas, with a double statement of 1 (as a sort of full stop) to end the piece. Figure 8.1 shows how the prelude divides into four sections and a brief coda. Thus, what appears to be a repetitive, meandering piece in fact proves to be a highly organized and logical creation. Just as punctuation phrases 2 and 3 are transpositions of 1 down a perfect fourth and up a tone, and 3 equals 2 up a perfect fifth, so the only transpositions of motifs B–D involve precisely the same intervals. In this way, the punctuation mirrors the musical prose. Further, the motifs are each differentiated from the other by their transpositions: B transposes only up a fourth; D transposes up a tone and up a fourth; whilst C adds transposition up a fifth to include all three pitches. Motif A is kept separate from B–D by remaining untransposed, and by only appearing in sections 1 and 4. As the first part of section 2 (up to § in Fig. 8.1) is recapitulated as section 3, surrounded by two statements involving A, the whole piece might be said to be in arch, or mirror form.

Ex. 66 First *Prélude du Nazaréen* (1892): motifs and punctuation phrases (BN 10037)

The latter half of the section marked 'development?' only contains two brief aspects of this – the alteration of the first chord of C (at * in Figure 8.1, the exact centre of the prelude), and the brief extension of the start of C at the end of the section (by descending sequences). Three smaller mirrors (marked by square brackets in Figure 8.1) using motifs C and D are formed in sections 2 and 3, and as one of these falls in the centre of what should be the development, Satie's aim was rather to interlock these central sections, again distinguishing the second mirror by its different transpositions. The cadential independence of the punctuation phrases can be seen in their exclusive use of the dominant 7th, 13th and 9th,[7] and also by the way that different transpositions punctuate the same 'prose' material when section 1 returns as section 4. Nonetheless, all four sections contain one complete cycle of punctuation phrases.

Section 1 (Exposition I)
A – 1 – A + extension – 2 – A – 3
solo

Section 2 (Exposition II)   §

B – B – C – 1 – D – C – 2 – D – C – D + D – C – 3
solo   up a   up a   up a   up a   last 2   up a
                          tone   tone   4th   tone   chords   5th

(Development?)   *

B – C – D – C   – D – C
up a   up a   up a   up a 5th, first   up a   start only, extended
4th   4th   4th   chord changed to 4th   by falling sequence
                     VIIb (exact centre
                     of prelude)

Section 3 (Recapitulation I)

1 – B – C – 2 – D – C – 3 – D – C – D + D – C
              up a   up a   up a   up a   last 2   up a
              tone   tone   4th   tone   chords   5th

Section 4 (Recapitulation II)   + Coda)
1 – A – 2 – A + extension – 3 – A – 1 – 1 + 7-part D minor
      solo   chord

8.1   Motivic plan of the first *Prélude du Nazaréen* (1892).
       (1–3 above are punctuation phrases; all 4ths and 5ths are perfect).

As far as the musical prose is concerned, continuity is provided by the oscillating
figure bracketed in motifs A–C (Ex. 66). This grows to dominate motif C, which in
turn dominates the centre of the prelude in sections 2 and 3 and becomes its overriding
image. Given the modal ambiguity of the prelude, Satie had trouble finding the right
pitch to end on. Figure 8.2 shows that he first chose an E minor chord after the first
punctuation phrase in the coda (treating the F 9–7b chord as a sort of neapolitan
sixth). He then decided to extend his coda by repeating the punctuation phrase.
First he resolved this onto an octave G (treating the F♮ in the bass as a modal flattened
leading-note), before deciding on D minor as his final solution. In so doing, Satie took
a broader view of the prelude, for motifs A and B begin and end on A (the dominant
of D minor), and motif A (the last to be heard) began with a D minor chord. It was
probably while he was working this out that Satie drew the Gothic turret directly
above the final cadences, and the one solution he did not consider (of course) was to
resolve his dominant 9th on F onto its expected tonic of B♭ major.

Most of the changes to BN 10037(1) involve making the punctuation phrases exact
transpositions of each other,[8] so it seems likely that the cyclic repeating pattern was an
afterthought – like all his best ideas. His method, in this and other manuscripts of the

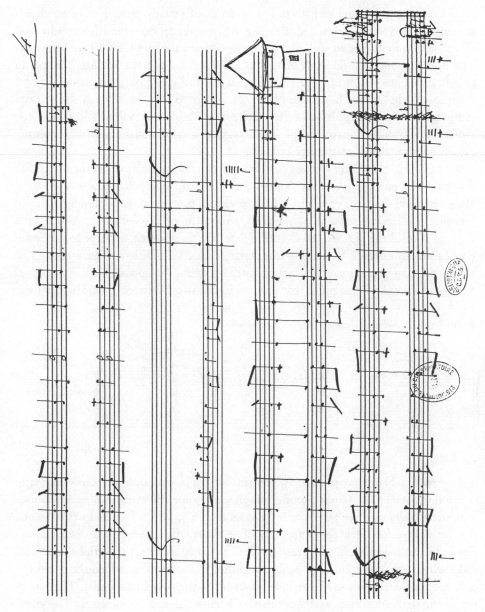

8.2   First *Prélude du Nazaréen* (BN 10037(1), 4).

period, was to copy out each section as a series of equally spaced crotchet chords to which the rhythms were added (as in Fig. 8.2, system 3). Between the staves he used ledger lines only for middle c^1, and he usually copied the right-hand part before the left, as is suggested by the start of system 4. Here Satie got the left-hand correct in punctuation phrase 3, but inadvertently put in the final chord of punctuation phrase 1 first in the right-hand as he changed from one system to another. We can also see him jumping one chord ahead in the right-hand part at the end of system 1 in Figure 4.1, while the left-hand is correct; all of which suggests a calculated and abstract approach to composition at this early stage in his career.

It is possible that Satie derived his idea for literary music from Péladan's *Le Fils des étoiles* the previous year. As Gowers says (1965–6, 15), Péladan was 'a fanatical Wagnerian and used one genuine old text in various places and with cunningly altered interpretations as an attempt at a literary equivalent of the *leit-motiv*'. When Jules Claretie rejected the play for the Comédie-Française on 3 March 1892, he told Péladan that *Le Fils des étoiles* 'is something like literary music'.[9] Doubtless Péladan passed this information on to Satie, and it is not altogether fanciful to suppose that it sparked off a chain of thought in his mind that resulted in the two Nazarene preludes that June.

Ex. 67 Second *Prélude du Nazaréen*: punctuation phrases

The second Nazarene prelude is perhaps the most extraordinary and enigmatic creation of Satie's Rose-Croix period, though it has some stiff competition. It too uses four strict cycles of three punctuation phrases (Ex. 67), which rise up in thirds until the last is a perfect fifth above the first. The punctuation phrases are distinguished from the surrounding musical prose by their cadential nature, their triplet rhythms, and their five-part harmonies (a dominant ninth, followed by an added sixth and the only root position triads in the prelude – apart from the two final chords). They are as straightforward and direct as the remainder is elliptical and tautologous. The chromatic prose consists of major, minor, augmented and diminished triads all notated as four-part first inversion chords moving in contrary motion. As can be seen from Figure 8.3, each short phrase ends with a minim, but the crotchet and quaver groupings are subtly varied elsewhere so that no two phrases are exactly the same, even though chord progressions of varying lengths repeat both immediately and at a distance, with transpositions and reharmonizations also being employed to confuse the issue.

Satie begins with the cantor-choir formula of presenting the main motif and harmonizing it. He then introduces the first punctuation phrase and continues with

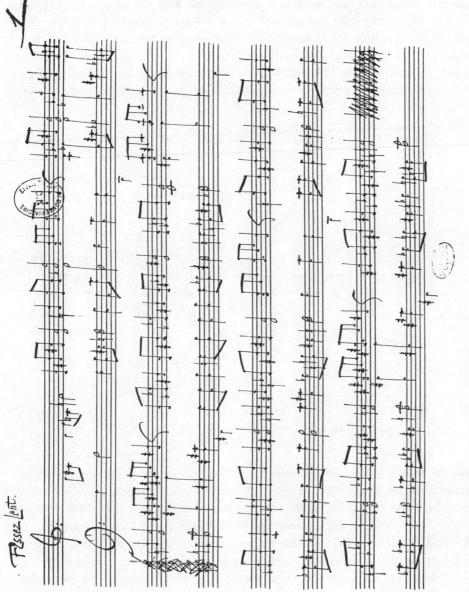

8.3   Second *Prélude du Nazaréen* (BN 10037bis, 1).

the first part of the main motif up a perfect fourth (Fig. 8.3, system 1). After this, nothing follows any strict pattern, as far as I can ascertain, apart from the punctuation phrases. There appears to be a sort of arch shape organized around the tripartite central phrase, which works in proportional counterpoint to the four-part division through the punctuation phrases. This is shown by the brackets on the left-hand side of Figure 8.4, and fits the version of the prelude published by Rouart-Lerolle in 1929. However,

Number of phrases	Number of crotchet beats	Total number of crotchets	Number of chords	+Punctuation phrase
4	4 + 4 + 4 + 4 solo / harmonized	16	8	1
2	4 + 6	10	10	2
2	8 + 4	12	14	3
2	8 + 6	14	15	1
2	6 + 5	11	12	2
*[3	5 + 6 + 5	16	17	2]
1	7	7	8	3
3	5 + 5 + 5	15	15	1
1	6	6	6	2
2	5 + 8	13	15	3
3	6 + 6 + 4	16	19	1
1	7	7	9	2
2	6 + 5	11	11	3
3	3 + 6 + 4 (final chord)	13	11	-

8.4   Phrasing in the second *Prélude du Nazaréen* (1892).

due to the numerous internal repetitions, the publishers (quite understandably) omitted the last five chords of Figure 8.3, system 3, and this means that the starred entry in square brackets in Figure 8.4 must instead be incorporated into the plan, so destroying its overall mirrored structure. Perhaps Satie would have omitted these five chords if he had revised the prelude for publication during his lifetime (just as he left five bars out of the second *Sarabande* in 1911),[10] but this is only wishful thinking. What does seem likely, however, is that the rhythmic groupings may have been the last thing to be decided upon, with deliberate assymetry and obfuscation in mind. For if we compare the second half of the prelude with the first, there are substantial chunks of material recapitulated in similar positions, suggesting that it is a subtle A+A1+coda construction. Exx. 68a–b show two such passages, with the quaver patterns indicated above the chords to make the comparison easier. The material is the same, and proof of this is provided by the rare augmented chord at *, which is changed in the same place in both Exx. 68a and b. The other internal repetitions (shown in square brackets below the music) give some idea of the complex interrelationships involved in this enigmatic piece, which would need a chapter of their own to demonstrate in full.

Ex. 68 Second *Prélude du Nazaréen* (BN 10037bis)
a. Passage between punctuation phrases 2 and 3
b. Passage between punctuation phrases 8 and 9 (which are the same as 2 and 3)

It seems likely from the way the same two punctuation phrases are used in different places in Exx. 68a and b that they were inserted arbitrarily, after the musical prose was complete. We can see a punctuation phrase similarly bisecting a repetition of the same motif in Figure 8.3 (end of system 2 and start of system 3), and further evidence to support this hypothesis is provided by the crossed-out chords at the end of Figure 8.3. Here Satie continued with the next phrase and forgot the intervening punctuation phrase (which appears at the top of the next page).[11] Similarly, the previous punctuation phrase in Figure 8.3, system 4 pursues the preordained pattern of rotating pitch-levels regardless of the chords surrounding it.

Thus, while the punctuation phrases provide formal sign-posts in the prelude, they remain detached, abstract creations, on another plane from the reasoned argument of Joyce-like semantic complexity that they intersect. As Gowers recommends (1965–6, 19): 'the way to listen to this piece is to let the punctuation phrases slip by almost unnoticed and concentrate on the chain, thinking of it as far as possible as a whole, rather than as sections divided by a response in the manner of a litany'.

Compositional logic in other Rose-Croix pieces

An even stranger case of Satie's attitudes to composition, form and logic is the hymn *Salut Drapeau!*, whose background was outlined in chapter 4. In Péladan's play *Le Prince du Byzance*, Cavalcanti's rabble-rousing speech in Act 2 scene 9 is in three prose paragraphs, which he adapted into unequal verses for Satie to set (BN 10053). But all he did in fact was to remove the repetition of 'Salut!' from the start of paragraphs two and three, and change the final line to 'Symbole généreux, Idéal collectif'.[12]

I can think of no better example than *Salut Drapeau!* of what Constant Lambert describes as 'formal logic which is independent of all dramatic and narrative element' (1934, 120). For in this haunting, disembodied hymn Satie pursued a preordained musical plan seemingly regardless of his text, and wholly without concern for its patri-

Ex. 69 a. The Greek chromatic mode
b. The transposition used by Satie in *Salut Drapeau!* and *Uspud* (starting up a major ninth on the fifth note of a.)

otic context in Péladan's drama. For reasons unknown, Satie chose a transposition of the ancient Greek chromatic mode (Ex. 69) as his melodic basis, and it is more likely that he arrived at it through research than by chance. This mode provides the clue to the curious way he set Péladan's irregular verses, and Ex. 70 shows that he spread three verses over four repeats of a rigid musical sequence of forty-four crotchets, which start at the points marked a–d.[13]

Ex. 70 *Salut Drapeau!* (2 November 1891) (BN 10053)

Ex. 70 *(cont.)*

Ex. 70 (*cont.*)

Voi - le gon - flé - e par tou - tes les poi - trines,   or - gueil - leux

la - ba - rum,   Aile é - plo - yé - e des fou - les pal - pi -

tantes,   Tu por - - tes dans ton vol, le des - tin d'u - ne

race.   Sym - bo - le gé - né - reux,   i - dé - al col - lec -

tif.   Sa - lut Dra - peau!

(coda repeats introduction)

Satie quite naturally began with verse one, where the vocal line (as the surface of the accompaniment) is set entirely to the Greek mode, following the principle that each syllable is set to a crotchet (except the very first), and that each line ends with a minim and a crotchet rest. Only the accompaniment between the lines breaks the pattern, introducing A, C and F naturals that are not in the Greek mode. Satie must then have discovered that verses two and three did not fit the pattern established in verse one, and as he wanted the final appearance of 'Salut Drapeau' to coincide with the first four notes of his repeating pattern, he almost certainly worked *backwards* from this point, adjusting the gaps between the verses accordingly in his three-into-four plan. The appearance of the nine ringed notes (A, C and F) only in verses two and three (Ex. 70) serves to confirm this theory. It did not seem to matter to Satie that the minims at the end of each line often clashed with the accompaniment, or that the syllabic dis-tribution was correct during the lines, but not at their ends ('poi-*trines*'; 'pal-pi-*tantes*'). In fact, Satie did not bother to split the words into syllables at all in his draft (BN 10053), and this caused his only miscalculation (in verse three). Rather than apportion two notes to 'race' and break his pattern of having no mute 'e's at the ends of lines, he put a two-crotchet melisma on 'Tu *por*-tes' where it was less noticeable (at * in Ex. 70). Otherwise, rigid adherence to his logical system was paramount, though he must have been pleased with the way that the final 'Salut Drapeau' overlapped into the repeat of the introduction as the coda. Whether he was poking fun at Péladan's inflated and indifferent blank verse in his awkward vocal lines is, of course, another matter.

Another example of writing a piece first and adjusting its external form later comes with the *Danses Gothiques*, which Satie composed between 21 and 23 March 1893 as a mental escape from the intensity of his affair with Suzanne Valadon. The score (BN 10048) contains nine un-dance-like dances, with quasi-religious or self-pitying titles like *A propos de Saint Bernard et de Sainte Lucie* (No. 4), or *Pour les pauvres trépassés* (No. 5). But the ten motifs involved, which are transposed, split up and juxtaposed in various orders, show that Dances 4 and 7–9 begin in mid-motif, which means that the titles were positioned after the music was written (as one long piece). But this alterna-tive form of adding punctuation to the musical prose was not entirely arbitrary, for Dance 5 is substantially longer than those surrounding it, and provides a central focus for the set in which all the motifs (except the eighth) reappear. Its length almost exactly balances that of the opening dance too, in which the first six motifs are introduced.

Satie's other notable experiment in form comes in the *Air de l'Ordre*, the first of the *Trois Sonneries de la Rose + Croix* of 1892. Here Satie combines elements of sonata form with proportional symmetry based on the principle of the Golden Section, as Professor Gillmor was the first to discover (1988, 87–9). In Figure 8.5, A is a chain of thirty-six crotchet chords (mostly root position triads), whilst A1 is a decoration in octaves of the melody of A. They appear together in A2 (an octave higher), where Satie again uses register as much as material to differentiate his sections. As we saw in chapter 4, it was probably Debussy who introduced Satie to this technique of propor-

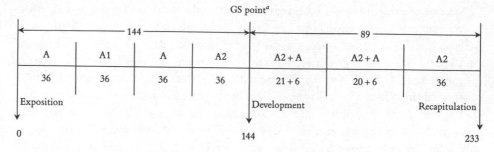

8.5   Golden Section form in the *Air de l'Ordre* (1892).

tional organization, which derives from nature and was known to the ancient Greeks and to earlier composers like Machaut and Dufay. It was much used in painting and architecture, though its conscious reapplication to music was quite new in the early 1890s. As might be expected, Satie's use of the Golden Section was more straight-forward than Debussy's, and it runs in parallel with the sonata form divisions rather than in proportional counterpoint with them. But whether he used the technique consciously or not, the symmetrical and Golden Section proportions are still there in Satie's *Sonnerie*. The rarity of anything resembling development or sonata form else-where in Satie's music suggests that the construction of the *Air de l'Ordre* was precisely calculated, and the way he used one form in the service of the other refutes any allega-tions of technical incompetence that have since been laid at his door.

Sonata form and the question of development

The two sections of 'development' in the *Air de l'Ordre* are interesting because Satie uses material from the middle of both sections A2 and A (see Fig. 8.5). True to form, he adds no new harmonies or thematic material, but rather he presents what has been heard before in new guises by elongating certain notes, altering the phrasing, repeating some chords, and varying the registers, as can be seen in Exx. 71a–c. Ex. 71a shows the passages used from A2 and A, and as everything derives from the chain of thirty-six chords found in A it is logical that the two passages Satie chooses are harmonically continuous (beats 10–23 of the chain; then 24–7) even though they come from differ-ent sections. For once Satie is liberal with his dynamic markings, and in Ex. 71 the same material is never presented twice at the same dynamic level, suggesting that nothing is accidental in this carefully balanced *Sonnerie*,[14] which is at the same time a work of great beauty, poise and feeling.

In other Rose-Croix works like *Le Fils des étoiles* or *Uspud*, where an element of

Ex. 71 *Trois Sonneries de la Rose + Croix*. No. 1: *Air de l'Ordre*
a. Section A2, beats 10–23, plus section A, beats 24–7
b. Development 1 (A2+A: 21+6 beats)
c. Development 2 (A2+A: 20+6 beats)

development might be said to occur (in Satiean terms), it is rather a case of providing rhythmic and harmonic variants of the basic motifs, or juxtaposing them in new combinations, either wholly or in part. The nearest Satie comes to providing a passage with any of the forward thrust or continuity associated with development comes in Act 2 of *Uspud* (Ex. 72b). Here he takes motifs 2 and 5 from Act 1 (Ex. 72a), both

Ex. 72 *Uspud* (1892)

a. Motifs 2 and 5 from Act 1 (see Ex. 69b)

b. Extract from Act 2 (BN 9631, 28–9)

based on the Greek chromatic mode used in *Salut Drapeau!* (Ex. 69), and extends them through fragmentary repetition. Indeed, it might be maintained that motif 5 was a variant of motif 2, were they not presented as separate entities in Act 1 as part of a larger group of five such motifs based on the same scale. But a closer examination of Ex. 72b shows that the only real aspect of development is the reharmonization of part of motif 5 in the second phrase, and that the continuity is shattered by the silent bar in the centre. Any sense of forward thrust is further undermined by the change of metre to 3/4 soon afterwards. In addition, Satie carefully reiterates the 'very slow' tempo marking at the start of what is only a short, self-contained section, with pauses before and after for narration. And, as one might expect, the relatively dramatic music (for Satie) is wholly at odds with its text, which tells of 'The reappearance of the Christian Church, white as snow and transparent as crystal. Lotuses spring up beneath her feet.'

The question of Satie's capacity for development is, however, a crucial one as far as his reputation is concerned, for to most Western critics a cellular composer whose cells do not generate momentum, or rigorously develop in any way, is deemed a failure. Charles Koechlin (1927, 14–15) believed Satie was perfectly capable of Germanic development, but simply chose not to perpetuate this method in a 'long sonata or some thundering symphonic poem' that was alien to his aesthetic. In support, Koechlin cites the case of Debussy, who had been accused of being unable to develop material in *Pelléas et Mélisande* by reactionary critics who missed the point of what he was trying to achieve. Rather, as Koechlin says elsewhere (1924, 201), Satie's attitude to development was to question why it needed to exist at all. As a reaction to this sort of obligatory expansion, he honed down his material into a 'super-condensed form', which had the perfection of a Japanese netsuke or haiku – as in the *Sports et divertissements*. Little by little, Koechlin observes (ibid., 196), Satie 'rid himself of recapitulation and restatement. He prunes, discards the redundant, suppresses tied notes, condenses, and reduces the musical dialogue to an absolute minimum (most often in only two parts).' Whether there was anything deliberately redundant in the Rose-Croix music is, of course, debatable, though it is true that the tautology and induced monotony of long works like *Uspud* disappears after Satie's years at the Schola Cantorum. From his experiments in devising extended constructions with a minimum of motivic material, Satie moves to a position wherein material and form are more concisely balanced. The generally faster tempos of the later works greatly enhance their concision, and here Satie exerts more discipline on his natural talent as an inventor of starts and textures. As Cocteau astutely observes in *Le Coq et l'Arlequin* (trans. Myers, 1926, 18): 'Satie is the opposite of an improviser. His works might be said to have been completed beforehand, while he meticulously unpicks them, note by note' – a process more akin to de-composition.

In later life, Satie became increasingly scathing of conventional development and the 'cellule génératrice'. He told Roland-Manuel around 1912 (1952, 10–11) that 'poor Schumann does not know how to develop material', and he complained in *Le Coq Parisien* in 1920 about the heaviness of Beethoven's craftsmanship, 'which is something that very few people seem to understand' (Ve, 45). Apart from the *Sonatine bureaucratique*, Satie made only one further exploration of the parodistic potential of sonata form in his later years, and this was in *d'Holothurie*, the first of the *Embryons desséchés*. Here his brief 'development' is divided into two halves.[15] The first suggests a variety of nearly-related keys and the rising start of the second subject, but cleverly states neither of them. The second part, which Satie describes as being 'like a nightingale with toothache', is a parody of a brief Rossinian transition (a composer he admired). It merely decorates a dominant seventh on D over a range of four octaves as a single line, and goes straight into C (not G) for the exact, untransposed reprise. For what Satie was most interested in doing in this mockery of sonata form was to write a movement ending in G major (complete with its Classical parody coda), but in which both the first and second subjects were in C major and were texturally undifferentiated. Numerous pauses, or musical question marks, punctuate this little toccata, as if Satie keeps asking us to think what the whole principle of sonata form is about, with its traditional dependence on contrast and tonality. At the end of the proofs (BN Rés. Vma 161), incidentally, Satie drew a malicious, disapproving six-legged spider, which suggests that he knew exactly what he was doing beneath the innocuous and entertaining surface of this early neo-classical experiment.

For the second subject of *d'Holothurie*, Satie chose a popular song, *Mon Rocher de Saint-Malo* by Loïsa Puget which, as a melody, resolutely implies G major. Before he decided to maintain the semiquaver movement behind the first (deliberately nondescript) subject into the second, Satie intended to make the sort of textural contrast implicit in an opening Allegro – for all four trial harmonizations have an accompaniment in quavers or longer notes. The first (Ex. 73a) shows that Satie's initial response to a melody was often along traditional lines, which means that the sparse, slightly dissonant two-part counterpoint that prevails in this period was written into the works in question. Here Satie uses conventional four-part chromatic harmony, demonstrating the scrupulous concern for voice-leading instilled by the Schola Cantorum. He even uses the circle of fifths at the end of Ex. 73a, which nonetheless avoids the G major implications of the melody throughout – in anticipation of his 1917 dictum that 'the harmonic *potential* of a melody is infinite'.

Ex. 73 *Embryons desséchés*. No. 1: *d'Holothurie* (1913). Harmonizations of the second subject: *Mon Rocher de Saint-Malo* by Loïsa Puget (BN 9590, 2–7)

Ex. 73 *(cont.)*

(p. 7 systems 2–3)

d.

(final version, Eschig score, p. 2)
[Allez un peu]

e.

[*P*]   Quel joli rocher!

Satie then decided to maintain a two-part texture in his second subject, though Ex. 73b shows that he still intended it to begin in E minor. This version was probably abandoned because of its modulation to G at the end, and again Satie's initial response is to harmonize in conventional thirds and sixths, rather than in the characteristic fourths, fifths and sevenths of the final version.

The third version (Ex. 73c) is in G major throughout, and Satie even added a key-signature, but thought better of it. Such retrogressive versions are common with Satie, who usually began afresh rather than correct them. The fourth version (Ex. 73d) at last introduces the concept of the *perpetuum mobile* accompaniment, even if it is still in quavers. Again the harmonization is in G, but we can see an indication of the final version in the perfect fifths on the first three crotchet beats, and in the way the lower part begins on C.

D'Holothurie is typical of Satie in that the greatest transformation took place between the penultimate sketch (Ex. 73d) and the final published version (Ex. 73e). Here Satie kept the accompaniment in C at the start, and was even forced to change Loïsa Puget's melody slightly (at 'x') to assist his tonal plans. The important note F♮, establishing C at the expense of G, appears often in the final version, and B♮ is conspicuous by its absence in the fourth-based cadences at the end of Ex. 73e. And with this ambiguous version Satie was finally satisfied. Whilst keeping the shape of a sonata form movement, he had reinterpreted every conventional aspect of it, even down to ending in a different key from the start and introducing new material in the coda (the popular sing 'Je n'ai pas de tabac').

Motivic construction

With so much rethinking of conventional forms and so much experimentation, composition was inevitably something of a hit-and-miss affair for Satie. Thus, within the Rose-Croix period, taut little motivic constructions like the *Eginhard* prelude (A A1 B C B D B C A2) and the *Préludes du Nazaréen* coexist with sprawling uncertainties like the assortment of movements in the *Messe des pauvres* (1893–5) as we know it.[16] Similarly there is more motivic material in the two-page *Prélude de La Porte héroï-que du ciel* than in the whole of *Uspud*, a 3-Act ballet with thirty-five pages of music. Even though motifs are in short supply (12 in all) and the 5 Greek-mode motifs are interrelated in *Uspud*, Act 2 closes with the introduction of two new motifs and ends on the same chord that begins Act 3. The logic behind such decisions is often impossible to fathom, and Gowers's formal plan of *Uspud* is almost as complex as the score itself (Ph.D. 5376, 136). Even in much shorter pieces the ordering can be just as inscrutable and seemingly perverse. Take for instance the *Prélude en tapisserie*, an archetypal motivic jigsaw puzzle of eighty-one bars in which six ideas and their variants were assembled as shown in Figure 8.6. The dotted lines below simply indicate

```
Motif  A  -  B  -  A  -  C  -  D  - | A  -  B1  -  E  -  D  (up a 5th)  -  B2  -  A  (up a 4th)  -  A  -
Bars   1     3     5     7     11   | 12    14     16    20                  21      23                  24

C1  -  C1  (up a 4th)  -  E  (down a major 3rd)  +  extension  - | B1  (down a maj. 6th)  -
26     31                 35                         37          | 40

C2  -  B3  -  F  -  F  (up a 4th)  - | C3  -  D  (down a minor 2nd)  -  E  (up a min. 3rd)  -  B4  -
42     45    47    49               | 51     55                          56                    60

C2  (up a maj. 3rd)  +  extension to E  (up a 4th)  -  E  (down a min. 3rd)  +
62                      65                              67

new extension  -  C4  -  G  -  G  (up a 4th)  +  final chord  (open 5th on C)
69                72    76    78                 80–1
```

8.6   Motivic construction in the *Prélude en tapisserie* (1906) (All 4ths and 5ths are perfect).

where Satie's *a tempo* markings occur, and I can discern no overall logic in this construction, other than the way it begins with A as a recurring rondo motif. A–C all start with a dotted quaver/semiquaver rhythm (that of C being an afterthought), but beyond this (and the prevailing 2/4 metre) there seems to be no definite plan. (Unless there is a link with Act 2 of *Uspud* in the late appearance of motif G?) Whilst Satie's works were seldom composed in their published orders, the *Prélude en tapisserie* is about the most bizarre case I know of, for it began at the end with bars 72–5 and ended with bars 3–4 (motif B). Indeed, Satie was even forced to use two different coloured numbering systems in assembling the motifs so that he was not confused himself,[17] and even the appropriate title *Tapestry Prelude* only emerged near the end of the sketches.

A similar impenetrability surrounds the *Danses de travers* (1897), an early example of minimalism in which all three slow, quiet dances share the same rhythm, texture and melodic shapes, and are difficult to tell apart. Possibly Satie had the arpeggiated textures of Schumann or Fauré in mind here, and one would never imagine that their construction was in any way complex. But Satie wrote eleven numbered segments and a host of unclassified ideas for the first dance alone, before settling on the five he wanted to use.[18] The manuscript suggests that his original preference was for a single, more varied dance, with a clearer formal plan in which cell 1 recurred as cell 10, cell 2 as cell 11, and cell 3 as cells 6 and 8. It was probably his decision to write two more dances in the same manner which led him to avoid a recapitulation of the opening cells within the first. As only the third dance has a held chord at the end, it would seem that Satie meant them to be continuous, with the passage doubled in octaves in the second dance (p. 12, system 4) recurring in a similar position near the end of the third (p. 15, system 4) in a cyclic manner.

In my last motivic example, I hope to show the logic behind the emergence of part of *Mort de Socrate* in 1917. Apart from the fixed start ('Depuis la condamnation de Socrate'), the orchestral part emerged ahead of the vocal line, which was flexibly wedded to it (as we saw earlier). Satie made numerous sketches for the orchestral motifs in both BN 9623(1) and his later draft (BN 9611), gradually whittling down his more 'symphonic' first thoughts into their simplest possible expressions, and then ordering them into longer paragraphs by means of letters or numbers. In pp. 49–53 of *Mort de Socrate*,[19] the orchestral part was assembled in two halves, without any sign of the vocal line. The less complex second half (VS 51 bar 5–53 bar 7) was the first to emerge, in the form of four motifs (each repeated four times). These were conceived in the order given in Ex. 74 and then numbered '1–3–4–2' to give the order found in the

Ex. 74 *Socrate*. 3: *Mort de Socrate*, the motifs found in the Eschig VS 51–3 (BN 9623(1), 16)

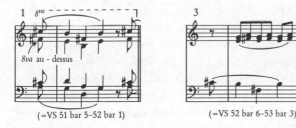

(=VS 51 bar 5–52 bar 1)   (=VS 52 bar 6–53 bar 3)

Ex. 74 (*cont.*)

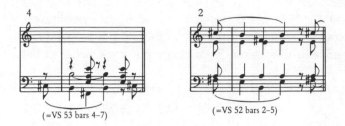

(=VS 53 bars 4–7)   (=VS 52 bars 2–5)

vocal score. Thus motif 1 produced VS 51 bar 5–52 bar 1; its harmonic variant at the lower octave (motif 2) produced VS 52 bars 2–5; then motif 3, using the main fourth-based idea in the bass, gave VS 52 bar 6–53 bar 3; and lastly, another variant with an inner pedal and offbeat quaver chords gave VS 53 bars 4–7.

Then on pp. 16–18 of the same notebook, Satie worked out the more varied and harmonically complex passage prior to this (VS 49 bar 1–51 bar 5), arranging its six motifs of one, two or four bars in length (with only the fourth repeated) by means of letters. Predictably, the order of composition was not that of the printed score, and we can see this passage emerging in Satie's notebook as follows:

D	B	A	E		Dbis	C
VS, 50	49	49	51		50	49 bar 7–50
bars 2–5	bars 3–6	bars 1–2	bars 1–5		bars 6–9	bar 1
(see Ex. 75)			(joining into Ex. 74)			

But this time the genesis was by no means as smooth. The repeated motif D came first, but went through three stages before Satie decided on its correct pitch. First it began an octave and a semitone up (Ex. 75a), repeated four times. Then Satie decided on a version which transposed the motif up a perfect fourth each time (realized from Satie's notes as Ex. 75b, with the eventual end of C and the continuation as Dbis given too). Then Satie marked the first bar of D 'au mi♭ maj[eur]' to produce the four-bar repeated passage found in the vocal score (Ex. 75c). Incidentally, it is interesting that Satie conceived this passage in a major key, when we might perhaps more readily imagine it as being in C minor with a flattened seventh, or in the transposed Aeolian mode. The reason is, almost certainly, that Satie did not see the link between bar 1 of Ex. 75b and bar 2 of Ex. 75c as being any sort of dominant–tonic relationship. Contrast in key and register between self-contained motifs was a guiding principle in the composition of *Socrate*. Satie probably realized that Ex. 75b, bar 2 (starting in D) made a less striking continuation from the Lydian mode on G found in the last bar of motif C (Ex. 75b, bar 1), and also that his rising passage in Ex. 75b made too smooth a link into motif Dbis in terms of pitch. It also implied a chromatic modulation through an augmented sixth (Ex. 75b, bars 5–6) which was alien to the harmonic style

Ex. 75 *Mort de Socrate*, the genesis of motif D (BN 9623(1), 16)

of *Socrate*. The abrupt register change achieved in Ex. 75c was important to Satie as it was coupled with a change in rhythm and one of the dynamic changes from *piano* to *forte* which characterize *Mort de Socrate*. Satie's original idea (Ex. 75a) would have made too smooth a tonal transition into motif Dbis (V7c–Ib in E major), as well as giving a less striking register change than we find in the final version. Thus, in this instance, we can begin to deduce some of the logical choices that led Satie to reject Exx. 75a and b and decide on Ex. 75c. At this point all that remained was to find a suitable vocal line.

Proportional reflections and mirror images

Proportional reflections and mirror images recur throughout Satie's *œuvre*, from the *Gymnopédies* to *Relâche*. As Satie was largely a nocturnal creature it is not altogether fanciful to suggest a comparison here with the mirrored vision of nocturnal mammals. For, as we have seen, Satie's beautiful Gothic calligraphy was designed to delight the eye at least as much as his music was meant to delight (and surprise) the ear. His complex logical patterns are often more easily discernible by the eye too, and his obsessions with numerology, bar counting and structural reflections partly help to explain his slowness as a composer. For, whatever the situation for which he was writing, Satie was concerned that his music should be perfectly proportioned (as Debussy's was) and able to withstand minute critical analysis.

At the root of Satie's calculations lay the 'golden number' three, whose trinitarian symbolism pervaded Masonic ritual, including that of the spurious Rosicrucian movements to which Satie adhered. In Mozart's Masonic opera *The Magic Flute* we find a key signature of three flats and a rising series of three rising chords complete on three trombones at the start of the overture, with three times three chords ending the exposition. In Satie too we find three *Sarabandes*, three *Gymnopédies*, and the humorous piano pieces of 1913 arranged in nine groups of three (including the *Trois Nouvelles Enfantines*). When, in the Rose-Croix period (1891–5), these groupings disappear (apart from the *Trois Sonneries*), we find the trinitarian aspect transferred to the harmonies. Chains of 6–3 chords dominate works like *Salut Drapeau!* (Ex. 70) and the second *Prélude du Nazaréen* (Ex. 68), whilst chains of 5–3 chords (two thirds superposed) dominate the *Trois Sonneries* (Ex. 71). Works like the *Prélude de La Porte héroïque du ciel* involve mixtures of the two, with here some addition of extra thirds to the dominant chord in the form of sevenths and ninths. We also saw dominant aggregations up to the thirteenth in the punctuation phrases to the Nazarene preludes (Exx. 66–7), and even Satie's famous immutable fourth chord (Ex. 14) is constructed with three notes in each hand, with the right hand always containing a tritone. Satie's fascination with the tritone is bound in with all this numerology, a classic example being *Vexations* (Ex. 64), where all the chords are notated as 6–3s, and the upper parts are almost all tritones. It is surely no coincidence too that each half of *Vexations* contains eighteen chords (six times three), with the upper parts in the second half being a mirror image of those in the first.

Another intriguing early case of mirror reflection comes in the *Gymnopédies*, which are not as identical as they appear. First, their lengths diminish progressively (78, 65 and 60 bars),[20] and Satie was clearly counting the bars in his manuscript (BN 8537(1–3)). Then the fact that the second *Gymnopédie* did not appear in print until seven years after the others (see Appendix) and was not orchestrated by Debussy, suggests that Satie was in some way unhappy with it. Indeed, the manuscript reveals that Nos. 1 and 2 were originally meant to be a mirroring pair. The first *Gymnopédie* is made up of two exactly balancing 39-bar halves, with a 4-bar variant in the second (cf. bars 33–7 and 72–6). Its 4-bar introduction is not balanced by a 4-bar coda; whereas in the second *Gymnopédie* there was originally a 4-bar coda and no introduction. And in the case of the sixteen bars that recur almost exactly in the two balancing sections of the second *Gymnopédie* (cf. bars 3–19 and 38–54), Satie altered the melody of the *first* half in a revision. The variant thus appears in the first half of the second *Gymnopédie*, and in Satie's first draft both passages were identical.[21] Both aspects make the second *Gymnopédie* a mirror of the first, though at some stage between 1888 and 1895 Satie added a 4-bar introduction to the second *Gymnopédie*, so that all three began in a noticeably similar manner.

The most straightforward kind of formal reflection is, of course, ternary (ABA) form. Whilst we find this in the second *Morceau en forme de poire* in 1903, it is mostly the province of the simpler post-war *esprit nouveau* music, like the *Grande Ritournelle* of *La Belle Excentrique* and the *Premier Menuet* of 1920. In Satie's later music there is a general tendency towards self-contained sections[22] with less intricacy than we find in that of the 'Esoterik Satie'[23] before the move to Arcueil. Thus, rather than the ABA1 structure of the last two *Embryons desséchés* (in which the B section functions as a trio), we find in the *Airs à faire fuir* of 1897 an altogether more complex ternary structure covering all three pieces in the set. Near-perfect symmetry is provided by a beat count of 188–108–187, and apart from their codas, the first and third *Airs* contain exactly the same material. The only other difference is that beats 1–28 of No. 1 are transposed in No. 3: first down a fourth (beats 1–16), then up a fifth (beats 17–24), then down a tone (beats 25–8). An 8-beat repetition (No. 1, beats 29–36) is cut out in No. 3 to balance the difference in length between their codas (6 and 13 beats). Why Satie allowed such tiny (and easily remedied) flaws to stand in his large-scale mirrors remains a mystery to me. He often made substantial changes as late as the final proof stage, but in the *Airs à faire fuir* all he revised in 1912 were the dynamics (in No. 1) and the amusing texts.[24] His concern for detail can be seen in Figure 8.7, when he feared that Ricardo Viñes might play a wrong note at the start of *On joue*, the last of the *Véritables Préludes flasques* at their première on 5 April 1913. The note in question was corrected in subsequent editions, and we can only conclude that the one beat difference between the first and third *Airs à faire fuir* simply escaped his scrutiny, or that he was not quite as good at arithmetic as one would have expected.

Different kinds of proportional and formal mirrors (again with slight flaws) occur in pieces as diverse as the cabaret song *Je te veux* and the first two *Nouvelles 'Pièces froides'*. In the expanded orchestral version of *Je te veux* in C major (BN 10058), the plan is as shown in Figure 8.8. Had Satie added a further reprise of C to the end of his new trio, or substituted C for D1, the mirror would have been perfect as regards both material and section lengths. The regular phrasing of the song naturally assisted this sort of symmetrical proportioning, and it is interesting to find a first version of the text in BN 10057, which suggests that Satie had to ask Henry Pacory to water down his rather explicit song before it could be published.[25] The revisions to even this first version (in Satie's hand) suggest that he may have contributed to the lyrics himself.

In the *Nouvelles 'Pièces froides'* of 1907, Satie's musical reflection involves two harmonizations of the same melody in *Sur un mur* and *Sur un arbre*, rather like a 'chant donné' exercise from the Schola Cantorum in a more lyrical vein. The 8-bar melody (bars 3–10) may rather have come from a contemporary Schola dictation (cf. Ex. 36). It is repeated at the same transposition in each piece, though its third appearance is cut off after three bars to make way for a return of the introduction as a balancing coda.[26] A parallel passage between *Sur un mur* and *Sur un arbre* (Exx. 76a–b) shows Satie still experimenting in private with Debussyan sonorities and using the whole-tone scale both melodically (bars 11–12) and harmonically. In Ex. 76a in particular, the texture and choice of chords strongly suggests early Debussy, and only the sonorous bass octaves in bar 14 and the unexpected 6–4 chord at the end of the phrase hint at

8.7 Letter to the pianist Ricardo Viñes, 26 March 1913, correcting a mistake in the first edition of the *Véritables Préludes flasques*, at the start of No. 3: *On joue* before the première on 5 April (*F-Pfs*).

Introduction	Refrain A	Couplet B	Refrain A1	Trio C	C	D	D1	C
Bars: 5	32	32	32	16	16	16	16	16
Key: C major		G	C	F		Bb		F

Refrain A	Couplet B	Refrain A1	Codetta
32	32	32	5
C	G	C	

8.8   Formal plan of *Je te veux* (?1897).

Ex. 76 *Nouvelles 'Pièces froides'* (1907)

a. No. 1: *Sur un mur*, bars 11–14

b. No. 2: *Sur un arbre*, bars 11–14

c. *Sur un arbre*, bars 3–8

Ex. 76c. (*cont.*)

Satie as the author. Similarly, in *Sur un arbre* the first appearance of the recurring melody (Ex. 76c) shows Satie trying out Fauré's style in his search for a new direction, complete with off-beat semiquavers (bar 5), arpeggiated textures, logical voice-leading, and a typical Fauréan cadence at the end preceded by a climax on an augmented fifth (bar 7). Once again, Satie is proving that he is well aware of the harmonic styles of his contemporaries and can reproduce their characteristics at will if he chooses. Indeed, one even suspects that he may have been a repressed Romantic at heart. Only in the more austere *Sur un pont*[27] do we find more characteristic touches, like the cheeky whole-tone chords which end the piece after the opening two-part contrapuntal exercise has returned in inversion. This again confirms that the *Nouvelles 'Pièces froides'* were experimental offshoots from Satie's exercises at the Schola Cantorum, and he was wise not to publish them during his lifetime.

Wilfrid Mellers was the first to comment on Satie's mirror structures in *Parade*, and they have understandably generated much analytical comment since.[28] In 1942 (218), Mellers observed that 'Satie's music to *Parade* is the most "cubist" of all his compositions. Here the recreated "order" is so symmetrical that each single movement, and the sequence of movements that make up the whole, is built on a mirror structure that gives the work its remote and objective self-sufficiency.' This is most succinctly expressed by Figure 8.9[29] in which the arrows indicate recurring material Figure 8.9 shows how mirrors are created by the identical entrance and exit music framing each of Parts 1–3 in ternary form, whilst around them the 'Red Curtain' fugue and the repetitive Managers' theme form an outer mirrored shell. At the centre, the longest second part is couched in ternary within ternary form, with the frenzied dance of the Little American Girl and the sinking of the Titanic framing the memorable Ragtime section, which is appropriately the exact heart of the ballet in proportional terms. This is, in fact, still the case in Satie's original conception (the 1917 piano reduction) whose 560 bars were bisected by the start of the Ragtime at bar 277. In this shorter version, the mirror concept is even clearer. The opening Chorale (bars 1–19) and the Finale (bars 572–676) were added in 1919, and Satie only completed the orchestration of the rest on 8 May 1917, just ten days before Diaghilev's première at the Théâtre du Châtelet. At the same time, the additions enhance the score considerably.

INTRODUCTION

Bars

1 – 19   *Choral*
20 – 34   Fugal *Prélude du Rideau rouge*
35 – 44   Transition
45 – 86   'Entrée des Managers' (3/8, 2/4, 3/8, 2/4)

The PARADE. Part 1: *Prestidigitateur Chinois*

87 –104   Entrance of conjurer
105–199   Conjuring tricks (disappearing egg: 105–83/breathing fire: 184–99)
200–217   Exit of conjurer

Part 2:   *Petite Fille Américaine*

218–225   Entrance of American Girl (cf. 144–8)
226–295   Dance of American Girl (inspired by silent films)
296–319   'Ragtime du Paquebot' (the Titanic) in ABA form
320–335   Trio (B)
336–343   Reprise of bars 312–19 (A)
344–364   The sinking of the Titanic (with giant wave effect)
365–380   'La voix' (bars 369–77 were originally a short song: 'Tic, Tic, Tic, le Titanic s'enfonce, allumé dans la mer')
381–388   Exit of American Girl

Part 3:   *Acrobates*

389–412   Entrance of acrobats
413–524   Acrobats perform (subdivided: 413–64, 465–92, 493–524 in a sort of ABA form, with B being a smooth section between two brittle ones)
525–549   Exit of acrobats

550–571   'Suprême effort et chûte des Managers' (2/4, 3/8: metre order reversed, and new ostinatos added)

Part 4:   *Final* (condensed reprise of Parts 2, 3 and 1)
2   572–587   Condensed reprise of 230–51
     588–603   Reprise of 'Ragtime': 296–311 (reharmonized in G, theme in bass)
     604–607   Varied reprise of 284–7
3   608–623   Varied reprise of 421–8, 409–12, plus augmentation of 413–14
1   624–655   Reworking of ostinato section 105–63 (cf. 105–8 and 630–33)

656–676   Final appearance of Managers' theme (2/4 section only, extended)

677–684   *Suite au 'Prélude du Rideau rouge'* (counter-exposition)

8.9   Formal reflections in *Parade* (final version, 1919).

The opening Chorale (Ex. 52) gives *Parade* a more imposing start, besides presenting the generating cell (a rising fourth plus a falling semitone) in bar 3. This provides a perfect foil for the ethereal appearance of the main 2/4 part of the Managers' theme in augmentation (Ex. 57), and this theme assumes a rondo function in the fuller form of *Parade* through its triple recurrence at strategic moments (Ex. 77). Then the Finale

Ex. 77 The Managers' theme from *Parade* (a diminution of Ex. 57). It appears in this form in bars 57f, 550f and 656f (Salabert, OS 10f, 93f, 111f)

recalls material from each of Parts 1–3, telescoping rather than developing it, and presenting the already familiar in new contexts through cellular reordering and reharmonization. Although there are fourteen identifiable themes in *Parade*, only the Ragtime theme from Part 2 is recalled, and then only in the bass for sixteen bars with a new counter-subject, new harmonies and a new key. It is as if Satie is confirming that the oscillating ostinatos that dominate *Parade* constitute its true thematic material. This is wholly appropriate to its role as a musical backcloth to a theatrical spectacle, from whose dramatic antics it largely claims exemption – both as *musique d'ameublement* and in its objective structural balance.

The beauty of Satie's plan was that once he had his broad conception of the whole, the constituent parts could be composed and assembled in virtually any order. After Picasso joined the team in August 1916 and gave Cocteau's impractical vision the transfusion it needed – principally through the introduction of the Cubist Managers – Satie was able to work swiftly. By 1 September he had finished the Chinese conjurer's music, and he seems to have used the three balanced parts as a basis from which to work outwards. For the last item to appear in the original plan was the *Prélude du Rideau rouge* (his 'Homage to Picasso') on 12 December. Indeed, we should be careful about reading too much into *Parade* as a complete musical organization, for Satie was quite happy to perform the three parts he had written in piano duet form at a concert in the rue Huyghens on 19 November 1916.[30] Its form then expanded outwards, as we have seen, and finally in April–May 1919 he gave it its final form for a revival, at Diaghilev's request.[31] 'This retouching is more important than I at first believed', he told his patron Misia Edwards (Vc, original letter in *US-NYpm*), and its exact nature is revealed here for the first time.[32] Satie also wrote in the manuscript of his added Finale in 1919 (BN 17677(5), 6) that 'the "Counter-exposition" of the Fugue [OS 115] is to be suppressed in the theatre, but kept in in concert performance'.[33] Which only adds to the problems of establishing a definitive version of *Parade*.

The self-sufficiency of the three main parts of *Parade* means that they are actually interchangeable, and in the 1917 piano reduction the 'Petite Fille Américaine' is 'No. 3' and the 'Acrobates' 'No. 2', suggesting that the order was changed during the final rehearsals. This would make the ordering of the reprises in the Finale an exact mirror of the order of the three parts, and would put the most substantial part last as the climax of the ballet. But again, we should be wary of reading too much into this, for the *Trois Poèmes d'amour* of 1914 were wrongly numbered 1–3–2 by Satie, deliberately,[34] and the final ordering of *Parade* is superior with the Ragtime as its centre. It also improves the artistic arrangement of the Finale by not recalling the material of the Little American Girl immediately after it has been performed, with only the reprise of the Managers' theme in between. It is tempting to see Satie the composer supplanting Satie the logician here. But once again we should be careful, for Satie's early drafts show that he intended the Acrobats' performance to come last all along. If the parts were changed round temporarily during rehearsal, it was probably done by others, just as the 'noise-making' instruments were imposed by Cocteau on a reluctant Satie. The page in question (BN 9603(4), 16) shows the link between the 'Petite Fille Américaine' (last bar) and 'Acrobates' (Fig. 8.10). It also shows that Satie first intended to link the sections together smoothly through the voice-leading, and that the constant pulse of seventy-six beats per minute was another inspired afterthought.

Whilst palindromes and literal mirror reflections probably did not interest Satie (or were too difficult for him to manage), there are still some intriguing instances of musical reflection in *Parade*. The generating cell of C–F–E (Ex. 52 bar 3) also outlines the main tonal areas of the ballet (C and E), as for instance in the 'Red Curtain' fugue (C) followed by the 'Entrée des Managers' (E and C alternating), or in the Ragtime (C), or the central section of the Acrobats' performance (over an organ pedal E in OS 81–3, which Satie sometimes proudly played himself for Diaghilev). F as a bass pedal point is saved for the main theme of the Acrobats (OS 73–4), and it is in this third part that the derivation of both themes and ostinato patterns comes most consistently from the fourths and seconds of the generating cell (as in Ex. 78). The main agent of dissonance is provided by the tritone found in the original extension of this cell (Ex. 57 bar 2). It can be seen at its most striking in the bitonal passage in C and F♯ at the start of 'Acrobates' (Ex. 78), and the tritone is also used to provide maximum contrast between subsections (as in bars 112–13, 319–20 or 633–4),[35] coming into its own as a generator of harmonic tension in the last part of the Finale (from OS 106 onwards).

Although *Parade* has a basic pulse throughout, which makes proportional relationships between the different metres easy to calculate, there is no evidence of a strict overall scheme, or any use of the Golden Section. Obviously the repeated sections balance exactly, and the central Ragtime is constructed so that its trio and reprise exactly balance the initial theme (48 = 32 + 16). It is also tempting to think that Satie made his opening Chorale sixty units long to balance precisely the sixty units of the 'Entrée des Managers' (bars 45–86). The Chorale is also exactly twice as long as the 30-unit 'Red Curtain' fugue (bars 20–34), which is balanced by the thirty units of the 'Suprême effort et chûte des Managers' at the end of Part 3, and by the fifteen units in the final 'Red Curtain' fugue. This may have been connected with the one-bar-to-a-second plan suggested by Figure 8.10, but it is more likely that it was only a means of distinguishing the outer shell from the rest of the material, in which regular phrases of four or eight bars produce mostly multiples of eight in the section lengths.

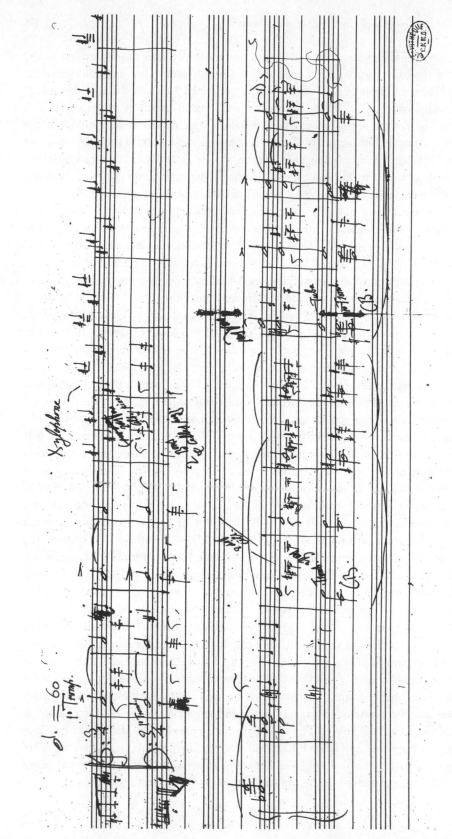

8.10 The start of Part 3 (*Acrobates*) in *Parade*, showing the link with Part 2 and the slower metronome marking (BN 9603(4), 16–17).

Ex. 78 *Parade*. 3: *Acrobates*, bars 5–8 (Salabert, OS 69–70)

The strange case of *Relâche*

In chapter 3 we saw Satie setting an extract from The Mad Hatter's Tea-Party in 1916 and planning to make *Alice in Wonderland* into a ballet with Louise Norton (later Mme Varèse) in 1921. As Louise Varèse noted in her appropriately titled *Looking-Glass Diary* (1972, 161): 'He was the only Frenchman, he said, who understood English humor. . .and the only composer whose music "understood" Alice.'[36] We do not know precisely when Satie discovered the topsy-turvy world of Lewis Carroll's Alice stories, but there are striking parallels between Satie and the eccentric Oxford don, whose brilliantly absurd creations conceal a wealth of intriguing logical problems and literary parodies beneath their innocuous surface. Both men adored children; both enjoyed inventing imaginary worlds, numerical systems, puns and puzzles; both enjoyed playing chess, backgammon and billiards; and both were fascinated by concepts of time and space, magic and mirror images.[37] Just as the whole of *Through the Looking-Glass* is based on a chess game, so we find Satie working out elaborate chess problems in his notebooks,[38] and Tweedledum's 'contrariwise' logic invites comparison with Satie's own. As evidence that Satie's music indeed 'understood Alice', I should like to look finally at the only musical product of Francis Picabia's 'instantanéiste' movement, the ballet *Relâche*. Superficially its aim, as a late flowering of Dadaism, was anarchic and subversive, accompanied by the slogan 'rien + rien = *Relâche*'. But underneath an escapist surface of popular tunes in a music-hall idiom, Satie's final challenge to his enemies[39] was a remarkable exercise in logic whose mirrored structure reflects years of experimentation.

Ironically, it was rather the wall of reflecting onstage mirrors blinding the audience in Act 2[40] that provoked the scandal of *Relâche* when it finally reached the Théâtre des Champs-Elysées on 4 December 1924.[41] The deliberate provocation of the authors did not help matters either. Lurid onstage posters telling the chic society audience that 'Those who aren't satisfied are authorized to fxxx off' only fuelled the riot, and it is small wonder that the critics were hostile and only praised René Clair's film (which divided the performance). Satie, who was no stranger to chaotic Dada 'happenings', delighted in being the focus of public attention, like his friend and co-author Francis Picabia. It is doubtful whether he knew that their appearance on stage in the conductor Roger Désormière's little 5CV car would be his last,[42] and it seems likely that his health only deteriorated rapidly once the excitement of *Relâche* was over. Up until then the anticipated battle had kept him at the peak of his ingenuity.

Relâche was, in fact, the very opposite of the deliberate artistic suicide it has been claimed to be, and Satie saw it as the start of a 'new period'. He had been largely responsible for keeping the original project – a ballet by Blaise Cendrars called *Après-dîner* – alive, and he had brought in Picabia to revise it into *Relâche* when Cendrars left for Brazil late in 1923. Satie had begun to collaborate with Cendrars before *Le Médecin malgré lui* was complete, or before *Mercure* was even thought of. So, far from being a rushed job and the inferior fling of a declining composer, *Relâche* was, in Satie's eyes, the most important theatrical project of his career; his path into the future, and his opportunity to show that Dadaism did not necessarily preclude reasoned structural planning.[43] He saw his score, as always, as a self-sufficient objective entity that would have the strength to withstand its milieu, just as *The Rite of Spring* had survived the scandal surrounding its première in 1913.

The only real surprise is that Satie had not received a commission from Rolf de Maré's Ballets Suédois before this. For, during its short rivalry to Diaghilev's Ballets Russes for the championship of the theatrical avant-garde between 1920 and 1925, the wealthy de Maré had the foresight to commission such ballets as *L'Homme et son désir*, *Les Mariés de la Tour Eiffel*, and *La Création du Monde*, which were choreographed by his overworked leading dancer Jean Borlin. Even before the success of *La Création du Monde* (by Milhaud and Cendrars) on 25 October 1923, de Maré had asked Cendrars to devise a new ballet for his 1924–5 season, and Satie, who had presented the composers of L'Ecole d'Arcueil during this same gala evening,[44] must have seemed the obvious choice as its composer.

Cendrars's scenario for *Après-dîner* cannot be easily dismissed as far as *Relâche* is concerned, and Satie may have played some part in its formulation.[45] The nine subdivided scenes in its single act offered wide opportunities for 23½ minutes of specified music, ranging from Turkish and Spanish dances (Nos. 5 and 6) to a dream sequence

(No. 8), which anticipates the *Apparition du Chaos* in Tableau 3 of *Mercure*. More importantly, it introduced the concept of an interlocking musical structure, for the 'Waltz of the Revolving Door' ('Valse de la Porte tournante') introduced in No. 2, recurs in Nos. 3–5, 8 and 9 in different guises, and a classical pavane in No. 6 recurs in No. 7.

But whilst a *Danse de la Porte tournante* turns up in Act 1 of *Relâche*, there is little other evidence from Picabia's point of view that his scenario was derived from the earlier one. An atmosphere of colourful frivolity reigns in both, but Picabia's two-act conception, separated by a filmed interlude, was quite new. Although Satie fulfilled Picabia's broad requirements – such as music for the men undressing and the wheelbarrow dance (*Danse de la Brouette*) in Act 2 – he considerably expanded and revised the proportions of Picabia's ten minutes of specified music,[46] just as René Clair expanded on his brief from Picabia in filming *Cinéma* and the opening *Projectionette* sequence in June 1924. Thus, for instance, Nos. 18–20 in Figure 8.11 below were supposed to take only '15 seconds' in Picabia's scenario, whereas in Satie's score they occupy almost four minutes (longer than Picabia's schedule for the entire second Act). Similarly, by introducing and developing Cendrars's conception of recurring movements, Satie converted Picabia's hasty assemblage of ideas into an integrated musical structure. Thus, the music for the *Entrée de la Femme* (No. 4) and the *Entrée des Hommes* (No. 8) returns with their reappearances in Act 2 (Nos. 14 and 13). Both recur in transposition and the former is in augmentation as well. The further reappearance of the *Entrée de la Femme* in its original form (but in a further transposition) as No. 21: *La Femme rejoint son fauteuil* then completes one of several interlocking sequences. Similarly, material from the *Danse de la Porte tournante* recurs in both the *Danse de la Femme* (No. 10) and the *Danse de la Couronne* (No. 19), which also focus on the leading female dancer (Edith Bonsdorff). In fact, only the *Danse de l'Homme et de la Femme* (No. 16) in Act 2 comes close to being a self-contained number, and even this shows some links in its introduction and undulating chromatic theme with No. 7. The mirrored structure between the two Acts is only broken by material from No. 12 recurring in varied form in No. 17 (within the second Act), and by No. 18 recurring as No. 19, in a subtle metrical transformation from 5/4 to 3/4 time.[47] The whole interlocking plan can be seen in Figure 8.11, which also shows how Satie's carefully planned movement lengths were adjusted during the process of composition.

Lest anyone should suspect that Satie was merely making things easy for himself with all this recurring material, only 6 of the 863 bars in *Relâche* recur exactly in the same key. This happens when the start of No. 2 comes back as No. 20, and it only involves a themeless undulating ostinato in F major. Moreover, in No. 2 the music was used to accompany Satie's bouncing appearance onto the roof of the Théâtre des Champs-Elysées in the opening *Projectionette* sequence of René Clair's film, whilst in No. 20 the same music is used in a dance to make an abrupt contrast with the A major ending of No. 19.

Several interesting observations emerge from a comparison of Satie's plan for *Relâche* and the finished product (see Fig. 8.11, right-hand columns). First, he was concerned that the two Acts of the ballet should balance each other as exactly as possible in

Movement titles

ACT 1	Number of bars in OS	Number of bars in plan
1. Ouverturette	52	52?
2. Projectionette	28	28?
3. Rideau	8	8?
4. Entrée de la Femme	20	20?
5. Musique	32	24
5a. Danse sans musique	–	–
6. Entrée de l'Homme (Borlin)	38	32
7. Danse de la Porte tournante	52	64 + 64 (Valse)
8. Entrée des Hommes	34	32
9. Danse des Hommes	30	32
10. Danse de la Femme	64	32
11. Final	68	32
	Total: 426	420

Film *Entr'acte* (separate score titled *Cinéma*)

ACT 2		
12. Musique de Rentrée	38	64
13. Rentrée des Hommes	48	32
14. Rentrée de la Femme	40	32
15. Les Hommes se dévêtissent	32	32
16. Danse de l'Homme et de la Femme	60	64
17. Les Hommes regagnent leur place et retrouvent leurs pardessus	40	24
18. Danse de la Brouette	32	64
19. Danse de la Couronne	52	32
20. Le Danseur dépose la Couronne sur la tête d'une spectatrice	43	32
21. La Femme rejoint son fauteuil	20	32
22. La 'Queue' du Chien [Petite Danse finale]	32	20
	Total: 437	428

8.11   The mirrored structure of *Relâche* (1924).

length, and with the inclusion of the time taken by the *Danse sans musique* in Act 1, one might say that he achieved his aim. Second, although almost all of the individual numbers emerged differently (and more irregularly) in the score, the overall proportions of the Acts of *Relâche* were only minutely different as a result, which is an even more remarkable achievement. Third, during composition Satie expanded musical numbers towards the end of each Act at the expense of those *en route*, in order to add musical weight to their climaxes. Thus, the *Danse de la Porte tournante* and the following *Valse* (each sixty-four bars in the plan) were compressed into a single 52-bar movement in Act 1, whereas the *Danse de la Femme* and the *Final* were more than doubled in length. Satie also planned his tonal scheme carefully so that the Act 1 movements oscillate a third above or below the 'principal key' of G major, whilst in Act 2 he employs a wider range of keys (again, all major tonalities) as the ballet develops towards its conclusion in D major (the key in which it began). Satie's sketches

(BN 9622(1–6)) show him (unusually) composing mostly in performance order with relatively few second thoughts, which is a tribute to his structural pre-planning and the continuity of his inspiration. There are some delightful touches too, like the reference to the Chinese conjurer's music in *Parade* (OS 17, fig. 7) at the end of the *Projectionette* sequence (Reduction, end of 6). This afterthought was added on an extra stave in BN 9622(1), 11, and Satie deliberately delayed the rise of the curtain for three vital bars to accommodate it. He was so pleased with the effect that he repeated it (in different keys) at the end of No. 9 and as the curtain falls in No. 22 – the last of his mirror images.

Care should be taken not to confuse the pre-planning of section lengths and keys seen above with what appear to be minutely detailed plans for Satie's final theatre works. Figure 8.12 is, in fact, a plan for the layout of each of pages 1–17 of his orchestral score for *Cinéma*, with the customary eight bars to a page. It again shows Satie's obsession with totalling the number of completed bars in each section as he progressed. Similar plans exist for *Mercure* and *Relâche*,[48] and each bar of each section is numbered individually in both the piano reduction and the orchestral score of *Relâche*. Something which is unique to *Relâche*, however, is the strange set of graphs found in the Harvard collection (Ho 83), which were made whilst Satie was beginning to prepare the orchestral score in late August and September 1924. Figures 8.13–16 show four of twenty-one such graphs, some of which (like Figures 8.13–14) are copies of each other. A first glance at Figure 8.14 would suggest that it had something to do with the layout of the orchestral score too, perhaps the number of instruments involved on successive pages. But a check with this score shows that this is not the case, and closer scrutiny reveals that Satie was taking the complete ballet as a fixed axis and trying to rationalize its two halves into proportionally divided mirrors of each other through a scale plan. Thus the lines marked '8' in Figure 8.13 divided the whole into eight equal (measured) segments, those marked '7' into seven parts, and so on.[49] The double line at the centre (where the film *Cinéma* occurs) is marked '2, 4, 6, 8' because these divisions all coincide at this point. The same is true of the coincidence of '4' and '8' halfway through each Act. In Figure 8.14 (a neat version of Figure 8.13) each dividing line is also given a different (and proportional) length. The inverted plan in Figure 8.13 is merely a simpler version of the plan above and was not intended as a mirror image of it, despite appearances. Unfortunately, the number of mirrored plans Satie tried out suggests that his attempts to rationalize *Relâche after* the music was complete were unsuccessful. He tried tenths (Fig. 8.16) and even ninths and fifths (Fig. 8.15), where there is some evidence too of bar counting in the margin.

But how does all this correspond with the music itself? To take a couple of basic calculations: the half-way point in Act 1 (bar 213) is a descending bass chromatic scale two bars before letter E in No. 7 (Reduction, 13), whereas the half-way point in Act 2 gives the last bar of No. 16. Although this is also in G major and is preceded by a descending chromatic scale in the bass in 3/4 time, the thematic material surrounding it is quite different, and there is no other link between the dances concerned. A division of each half into three parts yields no profitable results either, except that in

8.12 Plan for the orchestral layout of the orchestral score of *Cinéma* (1924), pp. 1–17. (BN 9678, page A).

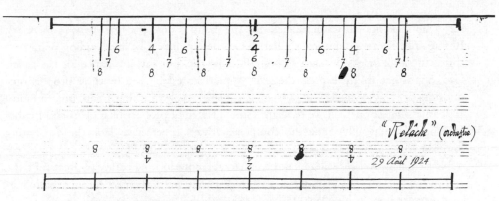

8.13 Plans for the proportional division of *Relâche* (Ho 83, second series, f. 3*v*).

8.14 Ibid. Second series, f. 3*r*.

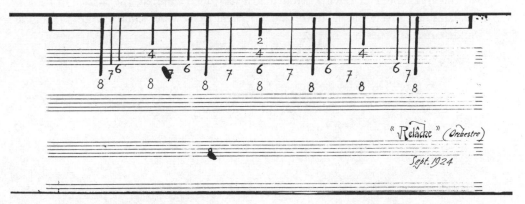

8.15 Ibid. First series, f. 8*r*.

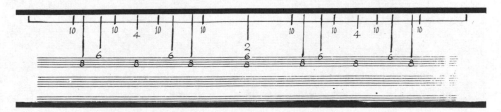

8.16 Ibid. First series, f. 7*r*.

Act 1 both points fall within dances for the men, as does the first division in Act 2. But again there are no musical similarities at these points. The last dividing point into thirds in Act 2 marks the start of No. 19, it is true, but this is a dance for the *female* lead. So, as one might expect, the only similarities established by these proportional divisions are coincidental. Unless there is something obvious that I have missed (and I welcome suggestions), all we have are some intriguing proportional plans and further evidence that, happily, Satie the composer always superceded Satie the calculating logician.

Nevertheless, *Relâche* still remains a remarkable interlocking edifice of great subtlety, and in the final analysis its unity derives from purely musical considerations. Satie may well have striven in his plans 'to confuse would-be followers by both the form and background' of this 'new work', and it must be said that he succeeded in this. But, as in the *Alice* books of Lewis Carroll that he so much admired, the surface of *Relâche* remains deceptively simple, direct and entertaining, however 'contrariwise' the logical undercurrents beneath it may be.

9

Compositional systems and other sources of inspiration

According to the conductor Maurice Dumesnil (1942, 849), Satie advised young would-be followers of his in the 1920s to '"Walk alone, do the opposite of what I do. . .I always write my compositions three times, and I change plenty from one version to another", adding, with a twinkle in his eye, "The two rounds – and the final!"' Whilst it is uncharacteristic of Satie to make this sort of admission, Dumesnil's reported observations have a ring of truth about them, and are more than mere elaboration with the benefit of hindsight.[1] Satie conceived most things in threes, and the comparison of composition to a boxing match is by no means inappropriate. Even beginning the contest could cause problems, and given the 'contrariwise' logic we saw in chapter 8, it should come as no surprise that Satie was forever inventing systems of composition, even if few of them were adhered to for any length of time in practice. Almost all of them were aids to harmonic organization, yet most of them sprang from a melodic or scalar basis. More importantly, Satie enjoyed inventing them, and he seems to have felt a strong need for organizing systems, popular melodic models, or visual and literary stimuli throughout his career.

The titles of Satie's works are no indication as to whether a system was employed or not. Usually his simplest titles accompany his most serious works, as with *Socrate* or the *Nocturnes*, though only the latter spring from an identifiable system. Neither is complexity a guide, for we find a highly organized plan behind the *Enfantines* of 1913. In fact, the only conclusion that can be drawn is that the systems of the earlier years were the only ones that produced complete compositions. As he grew more experienced his approach became more flexible and the system became just one of many means to an end.

Satie's early collaborator Contamine de Latour was the first to draw attention to Satie's compositional systems in a series of retrospective articles in *Comoedia* in 1925. Referring to Satie's Bohemian period in Montmartre, Latour says (3 August 1925, 2) that his

> musical education was very incomplete. He put together all the factors he possessed and devised a private formula, declaring everything else to be non-existent and even invisible in worthwhile musical expression. He was in the position of a man who knew only thirteen letters of the alphabet but who had nevertheless decided to create a new literature with only these means, rather than admit his inadequacy. As

audacity, it remains unsurpassed, but Satie considered it a matter of honour that he should succeed with his system. 'I'm obliged to make *tours de force* to get down a single bar', he confided to me.

The earliest system, to which Latour is probably referring, comes in a Harvard sketchbook from around 1892. Amongst sketches for the *Messe des pauvres*, we find a series of thirteen two-chord progressions (Fig. 9.1) classified by whether their melodic line rises or falls by a second, third or fifth. So 'the melody is the Idea, the outline' even here. The harmonies are a mixture from the contemporary Rose-Croix vocabulary: augmented and diminished triads spelt as 6–3s (the latter being presented as VIIb chords), and second inversion triads (mostly minor). The cells that Satie marks as 'terminations and points of rest' are as non-finite as the others, except insofar as they end with minim chords. But so does cell 2 in Figure 9.1, which is identical with the 'termination' found in cell 12. Equally, cells 1 and 11 are the same, and cell 13 is a transposition of cell 5. Thus we can see repetition built into the system, ready to generate yet more repetition in any subsequent composition.

Ex. 79a The middle section of the *Fête donnée par des Chevaliers Normands* (*c.* 1892), constructed from the 13 cells shown in Fig. 9.1 (Ho 62, f. 3*v*)

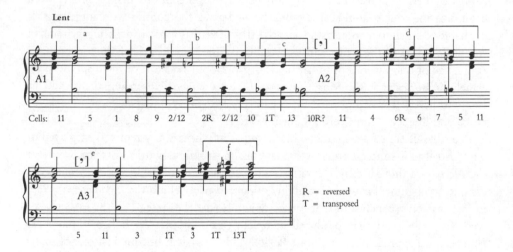

In the same sketchbook Satie uses these cells as the musical basis for what became the *Fête donnée par des Chevaliers Normands en l'Honneur d'une jeune Demoiselle (XIe siècle)*, probably in 1892.[2] Ex. 79a shows the first stage in this process, with Satie relating every chord to every other, rather than working only with separate two-chord cells. Each of the three phrases (A1–A3) begins with cell 11 from Figure 9.1, and Satie makes some of the progressions palindromic (marked a–f in Ex. 79a), though this is largely the result of the way the cells overlap. But even in this straightforward example, Satie the composer supplants Satie the systematician at the end, where cells 3 and 13

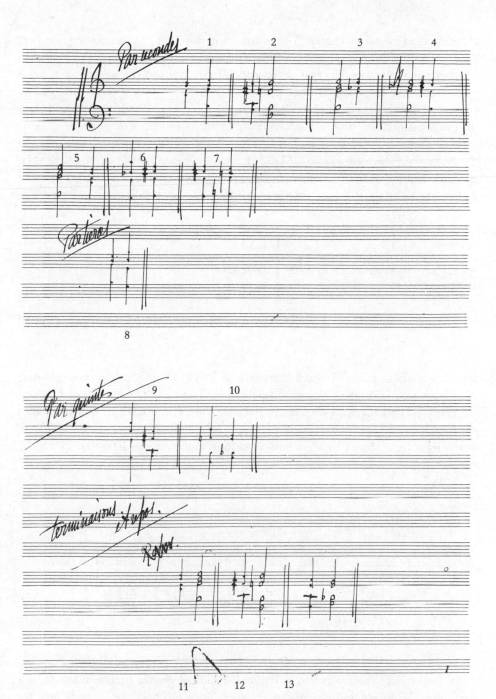

9.1   Compositional system with 13 harmonic cells divided into melodic categories in
      Ho 62, f. 2r and v (c. 1892). The cell numbers are added by the author.

are transposed to make a climax. The treatment of cell 3 (at *) is interesting, for here Satie breaks the guiding principle of contrary motion, changes the rhythm to two crotchets, and transposes the first chord up a minor third and the second up a major third. However, the transpositions and reversals here are few, and as Gowers says (1965–6, 11): 'This makes it more likely that the piece was actually synthesized from the progressions than that these were merely an analysis of it.'

Once Figure 9.1 had been finalized, most of the actual composing was over. In the *Fête donnée*, the three phrases (A1–A3 in Ex. 79a) were made to answer their own 'eleventh-century' quasi-plainsong melodies as the central section, surrounded by more massive statements of the three phrases as a single unit. The plan is given in Figure 9.2,

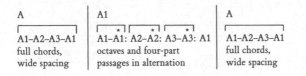

A	A1	A
A1–A2–A3–A1	A1–A1: A2–A2: A3–A3: A1	A1–A2–A3–A1
full chords,	octaves and four-part	full chords,
wide spacing	passages in alternation	wide spacing

9.2   Plan of the *Fête donnée par des Chevaliers Normands* (*c.* 1892).

with the phrases of Ex. 79a starred. As well as having internal palindromes (or mirrors), each section contains its own formal mirror by repeating A1 at the end, just as the complete opening section recurs as the last. The printed edition, which converts the fourth chord of A2 in the outer sections to a straight G minor, is wrong. The d³ in the right hand should be e³ on both occasions, as it is in BN 10050(1).

Ex. 79b An earlier attempt to construct a piece from the cells shown in Fig. 9.1 (Ho 62, f. 3r)

Cells: 9   2   2R   2 10 13R   8T   9T 12T   1T 4T 6RT   2R 2 10 13R

An earlier piece constructed from Figure 9.1 showed greater rhythmic and cellular flexibility, and Satie's possible reasons for rejecting it can help our enquiry into the workings of his compositional mind. First, whereas Ex. 79a uses all thirteen cells of Fig. 9.1, Ex. 79b omits cells 3, 5, 7 and 11, and Satie may have considered it inferior for this reason. The extent to which cells were reversed and transposed must have served to confirm this decision.[3] Second, although Ex. 79b is unified by the recurrence of the phrases marked 'a' and 'b', it lacked the tripartite definition of Ex. 79a which would facilitate symmetrical expansion into a complete piece. Third, Ex. 79b was too varied rhythmically for the sort of timeless quasi-medieval piece that Satie had in mind at this time. As chords 1–10 (the first part of Ex. 79b) are in black ink, chords 11–15 in purple ink, and the chords after the bar line in black ink with purple beams, it seems likely that Satie worked on his earlier draft on more than one occasion. So he must have thought it had potential.

This early experiment at systematizing the compositional process yields other conclusions too. First, what appear to be arbitrary progressions of unlinked chords in Satie's Rose-Croix music are, in fact, quite the reverse. Second, apart from a single use of cell 8 in Exx. 79a and b, the controlling melody always moves by seconds and fifths, and it was these intervals (together with their inversions, the seventh and fourth) that were to dominate Satie's work at the expense of the conventional third and sixth. Third, the Debussyan principle of each work being a unique entity did not apply as rigidly to Satie. We have already seen him borrowing from earlier works in the *Trois Morceaux en forme de poire* and *Relâche*, and a variation of this principle applies to the Rose-Croix works of 1891–5, which suggests that they should be considered as a corpus rather than as separate cases. For the cells of Figure 9.1 recur in *Uspud* (Ex. 80a)

Ex. 80 The cells of Fig. 9.1 used in other Rose-Croix pieces:
a. *Uspud* (1892), Act 2 (BN 9631, 26)

b. *Danses Gothiques*, No. 1: *A l'occasion d'une grande peine* (1893). Start, motif 1 (BN 10048, f. 4r)

and the *Danses Gothiques* (Ex. 80b) in 1892–3, though there is more transposition and less overlapping of cells here. In *Uspud*, Ex. 80a comes as a later harmonization of the motif which opens the ballet in octaves, and is the only one of the twelve motifs to use these harmonic cells. Whereas of the nine motifs (and their variants) in the *Danses*

Gothiques, Nos. 1–2 and 7–9 all contain progressions found in Figure 9.1, though only motif 1 (Ex. 80b) and motif 9 are wholly constructed from them. The resultant short-windedness of this introspective and abstract approach did not worry Satie in the least. In fact, making a lot out of a very little had a high priority at this time. In the case of *Uspud*, the contrast between the wealth of bizarre ideas in the libretto and the extreme economy of the music is stark. As Latour observed (6 August 1925, 2): 'Satie carefully gathered all the extravagances possible in his determination to amaze the public. For this libretto, Satie composed a half-dozen musical phrases which he pompously called "his score".' And of the twelve motifs used, five were based on the Greek chromatic scale found in *Salut Drapeau!*, and another was derived from Figure 9.1, as we have seen. So Latour's estimate of Satie actually composing a 'half-dozen' new 'musical phrases' is more accurate than it might at first appear. As Gowers has shown (1965–6, 2), a limited number of musical ideas and chord-types dominate all Satie's Rose-Croix music, which should be regarded as a wholly serious attempt to create a new, systematic musical language from what was then a position of limited technical expertise.

Satie's enquiring mind was, of course, always open to new possibilities. The four *Gnossiennes* composed between 1889 and 1891 had taken him in a more exotic direction, incorporating the hypnotic effects of repetition from the Javanese gamelan, and the acciaccaturas and melodic style of the Romanian folk ensembles, both of which had impressed him at the Universal Exhibition of 1889. The *Gnossiennes* also mark the return of barless music and the first use of the witty communications to the pianist that were to become a trademark. Another systematic experiment, found on the back of the sixth *Gnossienne* of January 1897 (BN 10054 (2)) shows Satie taking the Northumbrian folksong *The Keel Row* (later used by Debussy in *Gigues*) and using it as the basis for a composition of his own. His process of transformation can be seen in Ex. 81. Here, for once, Satie begins with the rhythm (Ex. 81a), and then adds the familiar tune, naturally without bar lines (Ex. 81b). The numbering above the rhythm in Ex. 81a seems to have been a guide to the way the harmonies repeat in Satie's complete piece (Ex. 81c),[4] though given the chromatic transformation of the melody it is not surprising that only the starts of the first two phrases follow the original plan. What is more unusual is that Satie reduces the number of repeating chords from fourteen to ten. He was clearly experiencing harmonic problems, for a first version of

Ex. 81 The *Keel Row* sketches (1897)
a. The rhythm, with numbered harmonic indications (BN 10054(2), f. 2v, system 1)

b. Satie's version of *The Keel Row* (BN 10054(2), f. 2*v*, system 3)

c. Second attempt at a chromatic transformation of *The Keel Row* (BN 10054(2), f. 1*v*)

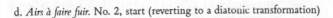

d. *Airs à faire fuir.* No. 2, start (reverting to a diatonic transformation)

Ex. 81c contains blanks at the starts of phrases three and four which are only filled in the final version. Although Satie left Ex. 81c unpublished and never expanded it into a longer piece, a more diatonic version of it became the second of the *Airs à faire fuir* in March 1897 (Ex. 81d). Some traces of Ex. 81c can be seen at the points marked 'x', though the result is altogether simpler and more tonal, and there is even a rare conventional V7–I progression between phrases one and two, which is repeated between the balancing phrases three and four. The whole *Air* is made up of three statements of the *Keel Row* theme in varying transpositions (plus the ubiquitous coda), as shown in Figure 9.3:

Form	A		A1		A2		+ Coda
Phrases	1 2 3 4		1 2	3 4	1 2	3 4	new material, leading
	(Ex. 81d)		down a min. 3rd	down a perfect 4th	as A	down a min. 3rd	into *Air* No. 3

9.3   Plan of the second *Air à faire fuir* (1897).

Apart from an incomplete harmonic scheme in BN 9618, 2 for the *Véritables Préludes flasques* (which helps to explain the prevalence of arpeggiated 6–5 chords in *Sévère réprimande*), the next compositional system that I have discovered is for the *Menus propos enfantines* of October 1913. Here the care he took to find just the right formula for these simple children's learning pieces is quite amazing. Satie first composed the set known as the *Trois Nouvelles Enfantines*,[5] but decided that they were too sophisticated and chromatic for absolute beginners. Moreover, their wide pitch range involved changes of register and fingering difficulties. He then embarked on the *Menus*, planning to use different metres and five-finger scales in each of the three pieces. The three consecutive white-note scales (Ex. 82a) were each one note lower than the other. During composition Satie must have realized the possibility of writing three sets of three pieces of graduated difficulty, so he rejected the *Menus* he had already written using scales 2 and 3 of Ex. 82a, and used scale 1 only, achieving variety by putting his central piece up an octave. In the *Enfantillages pittoresques* he then introduced his three different five-finger scales (Ex. 82b) and more varied rhythms; and in the *Peccadilles importunes* he placed more emphasis on mild dissonance, by making the left hand in the first piece and the right hand in the second cover the interval of the tritone (Ex. 82c). But he still kept the second piece the highest in pitch to match the pattern of the other two sets. Although these little two-part pieces (with occasional chords) sound rather similar, Figure 9.4 shows how carefully graduated they actually were. The *Peccadilles importunes*, incidentally, form a textural mirror of the *Enfantillages pittoresques*, and the final *Peccadille* returns to the same scale with which the *Menus* began. In addition, Satie's rejected sketches show how concerned he was to preserve the interest of his beginners. Two early versions of *Menus* No. 3 (*Valse du Chocolat aux Amandes*) in

Ex. 82 The five-finger scales used in the *Enfantines* (October 1913)

Title	5-finger scales used	Register	Metre	Texture		
Menus propos enfantines	f–a¹	low/8va up/ low	2/4; 4/4; 3/4	Single notes (1 chord to end No. 3)		
Enfantillages pittoresques	e–g¹/f¹–a²/ g–b¹	low/high/ low	2/4; 4/4; 2/4		3rds, 4ths and 5ths	
Peccadilles importunes	b–d²/d¹–f²/ f–a¹	middle/high/ low	2/4; 4/4; 2/4		2nds, 3rds, 4ths, tritones and 5ths	

9.4   The organization of the three sets of *Enfantines* (1913).

BN 9612, 14–15 and 19 were rejected because they were either too repetitive or too short-winded melodically. Then whole stretches of the final version of this waltz were crossed out because they used more than one note in each hand. Even though the final version is so simple, it was still composed in tiny segments which arrived in the wrong order and were assembled by numbered bars (BN 9612, 16–18). One of these rejected sketches, incidentally, shows Satie instinctively adding fingering as in a normal C major scale, instead of the easy fingering given in Ex. 82a, No. 3. Satie quickly realized his error, but it may have been in so doing that he decided to limit the *Menus* to the more natural first scale of Ex. 82a, and save the tritone compass for the *Peccadilles*. All of Satie's published pieces can, of course, be played solely by numbers, once the hands have been placed in the correct positions and the simple rhythms learnt. But as a means of introducing children to the piano and maintaining their interest both visually and aurally, their only real rival is Bartók's *Mikrokosmos*.

Satie's final compositional systems appear in the five *Nocturnes* for piano of August–November 1919 which, together with *Socrate* and the *Premier Menuet*, are his only later works which show no cabaret influence. He was no doubt aware that rondo forms were the most suitable for his talents at this stage in his career, and here the basic idea is that of a slow 12/8 movement, with a harmonically unpredictable left hand beneath a lyrical melody. This melody recurs in decorated form as the rondo element, often separated by more sonorous episodic material which again reveals Satie's almost Brahmsian fondness for low bass octaves. Satie conceived the first three *Nocturnes* as a group in D major, to which *Nocturnes* Nos. 4 and 5 were added later. A letter to Valentine Hugo of 24 August 1919 (Vc) shows how delighted he was with their progress:

> I am coming to the end of my Third Nocturne.[6] I am dedicating it to you. The three of them are not at all bad. The first serves as a prelude; the second is shorter and very tender – very nocturnal; the third, *yours*, is a more rapid and dramatic nocturne, a little longer than the first. Between the three of them they form a whole with which I am very pleased – though the first is the least good.[7]

The five published *Nocturnes*, which became more chromatically enigmatic as Satie got used to his format, only tell part of the story however. The notebooks include many rejected openings, as well as a virtually complete sixth *Nocturne*,[8] which was advertised on the covers of the *Fourth* and *Fifth Nocturnes* when they were published by Demets in 1920. Satie, in fact, planned at least seven of them, as Figure 9.5 shows. But by the time he had published five, Satie must have thought that it was time to pass on to other things. The *Fifth Nocturne*, for instance, is mostly in uncharacteristic thirds and sixths and shows no signs of being derived from the second-, fourth- and fifth-based harmonies of Figure 9.5, even though it is in F major.

In Satie's plan for the *Second Nocturne* we find the following directions: 'Harmony. By major seconds, perfect fourths and fifths. Sometimes these intervals can be *augmented* or *diminished. Never* use the octave, especially the perfect octave. (Use the fourth in preference to the fifth).' With this goes the intervallic plan shown in Ex. 83a, demonstrating Satie's order of preference for harmonies beneath the various degrees of

9.5   Harmonic system (in F major) for *Nocturnes* 5–7 (1919) (BN 9609(2), 21).

Ex. 83 *Second Nocturne* (1919)

a. Intervallic plan (BN 9666, 5)

b. Bars 1–4 (Eschig edition)

the D major scale, from the second, fifth and sixth degrees (at the top of the list), to the fourth and seventh degrees (at the bottom). The seventh degree, or leading-note, was singled out for special avoidance, though why Satie should have disliked the fourth degree (rather than the conventional dominant) is a mystery. The same reservations can be seen in Figure 9.5. But even in the simple opening bars of the *Second Nocturne* (Ex. 83b) we can see Satie breaking his own rules four times in the interest of musicality, at the points marked 'x'. First he introduces a sixth on the eleventh quaver of bar 2, perhaps to balance the shape of the left-hand figure in quavers 2–3 and 5–6. Then he introduces another sixth on the ninth quaver of bar 3, to give a smoother left-hand part. He also introduces unisons on quavers 3 and 6 in bar 4, making the c#¹ into a sort of inner pedal and reinforcing the 'very bad' leading-note – although in this case it does not lead to a tonic harmony. We can also see by comparing Exx. 83a and b that it is the intervallic conception that is paramount, rather than the precise pitch of the left hand in relation to the notes of the D major scale. It looks as if even this simple system was a spur to Satie's inspiration rather than a strict model for composition, and it shows that his approach to composition in later life had become more flexible and assured.

Ex. 84 A rejected nocturne (1919: BN 9609(2), 10–11)
a. The harmonic plan
b. The resulting nocturne, bars 1–4

What is even more interesting is a rejected nocturne (BN 9609(2), 10–11) which is an elaboration of an unusual four-part harmonic progression with no intervallic preconceptions, again suggesting that Satie needed some sort of plan to get him started, and that his two-part openings were the result of paring down a more solid and sonorous musical thought to a linear, more enigmatic statement. Ex. 84a gives the harmonic progression, each chord of which provides the basis for half a bar of Ex. 84b. Satie tended to think in parallel rather than contrary motion at this stage in his career, but it may have been the consecutive 'perfect octaves' in the second half of bar 2 that led to the rejection of this nocturne.

The majority of Satie's other compositional systems for the Nocturnes do not link up as well as the above example, however. Another unfinished nocturne (BN 9609(4), 6–8) is made up from a series of one-bar phrases found on pp. 1–4 of the same notebook. Here Satie takes four simple melodic cells and harmonizes them on various degrees of specified major scales,[9] with the cells then juxtaposed as only he knew how. The underlying melodic idea was stepwise movement and each 12/8 bar ends with a quaver rest. But the more complex and ingenious the system, the more likely Satie was to reject its end-product,[10] for the draft of this nocturne ends after twelve bars. Ex. 85a

Ex. 85a Cells for an unfinished nocturne, arranged in 4 melodic categories (BN 9609(4), 1–5)

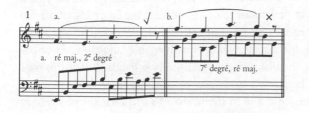

shows specimens of cells in each of the four melodic categories, which Satie either ticked for use or marked with a cross as unsuitable. They ably demonstrate again how 'the harmonic *potential* of a melody is infinite'. The degrees of the scale indicated by Satie seem to derive from the prominent note in the lower part (cells a–d, f–g) and in some cases (cells a–b) this is also the first note stated. This invites comparison with the plan for the *Second Nocturne* (Ex. 83a), but Ex. 85a shows that only 7 beats concur with this (cell a, beats 1 and 3; cell c, beat 1; cell d, beats 1 and 3; cell f, beat 1 and cell g, beat 3), so Satie's aim here is rather to consider each bar as a harmonic unity. The reasons for rejection of twelve of the twenty-two harmonic cells Satie devised for this nocturne are impossible to establish without recalling him from beyond the grave. There are several cells (besides cell e) that seem to be rejected for being in contrary motion, but then cell i is accepted whilst cell e is rejected. Similarly, whilst cell a might reasonably have been used in preference to cell b, because the latter is cast on the 'very bad' seventh degree, other equally promising cells on the 'good' first and sixth degrees are rejected. Cells f and g, for instance, look equally viable, and the only possible criterion for rejecting cell g is the distance between the two hands. But if this was the case, why were cells b and h rejected in favour of cells a and i? It does seem, however, that continuity of the melodic line in the midst of swift changes of key was Satie's overriding consideration from the way the cells were assembled at the start of the nocturne (Ex. 85b). This is made up from cell a (in D), cell c down a perfect fifth

Ex. 85b Start of the Nocturne constructed from the cells in Ex. 85a (BN 9609(4), 6)

T = transposed

(in G), cell i (in B♭), cell d down a tone (in C), and cell f down a major sixth (in F). But there is no strict rotation of cells in the four melodic categories. Indeed, category four, which seems to offer the promising source of contrast, does not return after bar 3. Cells not included in Ex. 85a (which put the melody in the bass) do feature in bars 6 and 12 of the nocturne, but even a plan of abrupt textural change every three bars is not adhered to, for in bars 9–10 the first two bars of Ex. 85b return in decorated form, suggesting that the only plan common to all the nocturnes was their simple rondo structure.[11]

Ex. 86 Chromatic scales in perfect fifths and fourths (BN 9609(4), 3)

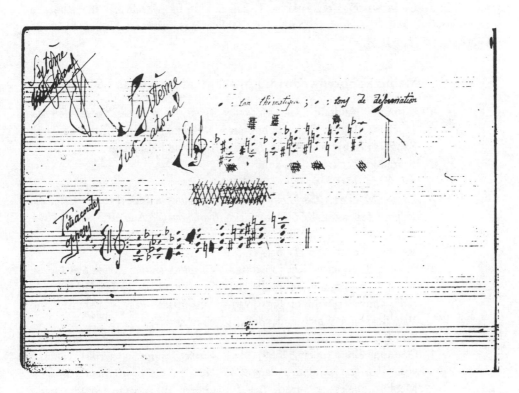

In the midst of all these cells we find four chromatic scales combined in contrary motion in parallel fourths and fifths (Ex. 86). These, predictably, play no part in the surrounding nocturne, and Satie's later notebooks abound in such schemes for organizing total chromaticism in polytonal harmonic combinations (sometimes around a focal tonality). He even formulated a 'Système sur-atonal' in 1917 (Fig. 9.6), though there is

Fig. 9.6 *Système sur-atonal/Tétracordes opposés* (1917) (BN 9624, 4).

no sign of it in the *Sonatine bureaucratique,* in whose notebook it occurs. Whilst the principle of the 'ton thématique' (in red ink, starting on middle c[1]) and the other 'tons de déformation' (in black ink) is easy to understand here the concept of certain combinations being 'consonant' whilst others are 'dissonant' is not. Even Satie thought better of this, and crossed these distinctions out. The other fourth-based system in Figure 9.6 has its 'Tétracordes opposés' constructed in two rows of interlocking minor sevenths (in black and red ink). They both reflect Satie's fascination with unconventional scales as the basis of harmony, but neither of them progressed from theory into practice. The nearest Satie came to doing this was in a first sketch for the independent *Fourth Nocturne* based on scales in superposed fourths (BN 9609(1), 8). But the sketch only lasts one bar, and was quickly superceded by the freer final version using parallel fifths instead (for which no known plan exists). Thus there is no evidence of these ambitious chromatic schemes reaching any sort of musical fruition, and I believe that they were rather the figments of Satie's fertile creative imagination, like the endless Gothic castles and occult advertisements he was so fond of designing in his isolated introspection in Arcueil.

Satie found a simpler and more productive source of inspiration in popular melodies, especially in the humoristic piano pieces of 1913–14. The sources for most of these recur frequently in writings on Satie, so I shall not do more than list them here in chronological order (as used by Satie) in the five categories established by Léon Guichard (1973, 68–74).

1 Melodies borrowed from operas and operettas

1 Edmond Audran: *La Mascotte* (operetta, 1880). 'The Orangutan Song', sung by Fiametta in Act 3. Refrain: 'Enn'tremblez donc pas comm' ça', bars 5–8.

Embryons desséchés No. 3: *de Podophthalma* (4 July 1913). Page 9 system 1 and elsewhere.

2 Aimé Maillart: *Les Dragons de Villars*[12] (operetta, 1856). 'Ne parle pas, Rose, je t'en supplie!' Sylvain's Romance from Act 1, bars 1–3.

Chapitres tournés No. 1: *Celle qui parle trop* (23 Aug 1913). Page 1 systems 2–3 and elsewhere.

3 Robert Planquette: *Rip* (operetta, 1884). 'C'est un rien, un souffle, un rien'. Choral refrain of Rip [Van Winkle]'s aria which ends Act 1, bars 1–3.

Chapitres tournés en tous sens No. 2: *Le Porteur de grosses pierres* (25 Aug 1913). Page 4 system 1 and elsewhere.

4 Gounod: *Faust* (opera, 1859). 'Le veau d'or est toujours debout!' Mephistopheles' aria from Act 2, bars 1–3.

Vieux sequins et vieilles cuirasses No. 1: *Chez le Marchand d'Or* (9 Sept 1913). Page 3 system 1 and elsewhere.

5 Gounod: *Mireille* (opera, 1864). Duet for Mireille and Vincent in Act 2, first stanza. See Ex. 3a.

Trois Mélodies No. 3: *Le Chapelier* (14 April 1916). See Ex. 3b.

6 Ambroise Thomas: *Mignon* (opera, 1866). 'Connais-tu le pays, où fleurit l'oranger?' Mignon's Romance from Act 1, voice part, bars 9–16.

Musique d'ameublement: 2d Entr'acte (Un salon), bars 1–8 (1920). (Bars 9–12 may have been based on bars 22–4 of this Romance.)

2 Material borrowed from symphonic works

1 Beethoven: 8th Symphony (1812), end of finale.

Embryons desséchés No. 3: *de Podophthalma* (4 July 1913). Coda, p. 11.

2 Chabrier: *España* (1883). Bars 29–30, 218–21, 518–19 (end).

Croquis et agaceries d'un gros bonhomme en bois No. 3: *Españaña* (25 Aug 1913). The text here refers to Bizet's *Carmen* (1875).

3 Debussy: *Nuages* (1898–9). Bars 1–2. See Ex. 22b.

Chapitres tournés No. 3: *Regrets des Enfermés* (5 Sept 1913). Page 8 systems 1–2. See Ex. 22a.

4 Saint-Saëns: *Danse macabre* (1874). Descending second theme, bars 50–7.

Musique d'ameublement: 2d Entr'acte (Un salon), bars 13–20 (1920). (The first entr'acte: *Chez un 'bistrot'* may be Satie's version of the student song 'Gaudeamus igitur', which ends Brahms's *Academic Festival Overture* (1880).)

3 Material borrowed from piano works

1 ?Debussy: *Minstrels*. Bars 34–5, or 45–6 (1910).

Croquis et agaceries No. 2: *Danse maigre* (2 June 1913). Page 5 end of system 3.

2 ?Debussy: *La Cathédrale engloutie*. End (1909).

Ibid., p. 5 start of system 4.

3 ?Debussy: '*Les sons et les parfums. . .*' Bars 1–2 (1910). See Ex. 20b.

Ibid., p. 7 system 5 (start). See Ex. 20a.

4 Chopin: Sonata in B♭ minor (Op. 35), Funeral March (1837). Main theme and trio.

Embryons desséchés No. 2: *d'Edriophthalma* (1 July 1913). See Ex. 10.

5 Mozart: Sonata in A major (K. 331, 1781–3), Rondo alla Turca. Third strain.

Croquis et agaceries No. 1: *Tyrolienne Turque* (28 July 1913). Page 3 system 2–p. 4 system 1.

6   Debussy: *Pour le piano*, No. 1: *Prélude*. Final bars (1901). See Ex. 23b.

Chapitres tournés No. 3: *Regrets des Enfermés* (5 Sept 1913). Page 9 system 4. See Ex. 23a.

7   Debussy: *Rêverie*. Bars 23–6 (1890).

Sports et divertissements: *Le Bain de mer* (11 April 1914). Start.

8   ?Debussy: *The Little Nigar*. Bars 5–8 (1909).

Ibid., *Le Pique-nique* (19 April 1914). End of system 1–start of system 2.

4   Melodies borrowed from popular songs or children's songs

1   Chorus of 'Hello! Ma Baby' by Howard and Emerson (1899).

Used as model for *Le Piccadilly* (1904), bars 9–24.

2   'Maman, les p'tits bateaux qui vont sur l'eau, ont-ils des jambes?' Children's song.

Descriptions automatiques No. 1: *Sur un vaisseau* (21 April 1913). Page 2 system 4.

3   'Dansons la Carmagnole'. French revolutionary song.

Ibid., No. 2: *Sur une lanterne* (22 April 1913). Page 4 system 2 onwards. Here, the title probably comes from the refrain of another revolutionary song: 'Ah! ça ira, ça ira, ça ira! Les aristocrates à la lanterne!'

4   'Mon Rocher de Saint-Malo'. Popular song by Loïsa Puget, to words by her husband Gustave Lemoine, c. 1830–40.[13]

Embryons desséchés No. 1: *d'Holothurie* (30 June 1913). Second subject, p. 2 systems 1–4; p. 4 system 4–p. 5 system 1. See Ex. 73e.

5   'Il était un'bergère'. French folksong.

Ibid., No. 3: *de Podophthalma* (4 July 1913). Trio, p. 9 systems 3–5.[14]

6   'Nous n'irons plus au bois'. French folksong.

Chapitres tournés No. 3: *Regrets des Enfermés* (5 Sept 1913). Page 6 system 3 onwards.

7   'Marlborough s'en va-t-en guerre, mironton, mironton, mirontaine' and 'Le Bon Roi Dagobert avait son culotte à l'envers'. French popular songs, the first of c. 1722.

Vieux sequins No. 3: *La Défaite des Cimbres* (14 Sept 1913). Two songs used in alternation throughout (e.g. Marlborough, p. 9 systems 1–2a; Dagobert, p. 9 systems 2b–3).

8   'La Marseillaise'. French revolutionary song by Rouget de Lisle, c. 1792.

Sports et divertissements: *Les Courses* (26 March 1914). At 'Les Perdants'.

9   'Au Clair de la lune'. French folksong.

Ibid., *Le Flirt* (29 March 1914). At 'Je voudrais être dans la lune'. Compare Exx. 41b and c, also from 1914.

10 'That Mysterious Rag' by Irving Berlin (1911).[15]

Used as rhythmic model for 'Ragtime du Paquebot' in *Parade*, Part 2 (1917).[16] The first theme provides the central section (OS 54–7), and the second theme the outer sections (OS 49–54; 57–9).

11 'Sing a Song of Sixpence'. English nursery rhyme.

Tenture de Cabinet préfectoral (*Musique d'ameublement* for Mrs Eugène Meyer (Junior)) (28 March 1923). Bars 1–4.

12 'Compère Guilleri'. French popular song.

Ludions No. 5: *Chanson du chat* (May 1923). Vocal line.

13 'Le Marchand du navet' and 'Savez-vous planter des choux'. French popular songs.

Relâche (1924). No. 1: *Ouverture* (reduction, pp. 1–3 from letter A); No. 6: *Entrée de l'Homme* (ibid., 10–11); No. 20: *Le Danseur dépose la Couronne* (ibid., 41–2).

14 'Air connu' cited by Xanrof in *Flagrant délit* (*Chansons sans-gêne*, 1890, 80).

Relâche. No. 8: *Entrée des Hommes* (reduction, 14–15); No. 13: *Rentrée des Hommes* (ibid., 26–7).

15 'Cadet Rousselle'. French popular song.

Relâche. No. 11: *Final* (ibid., 21–3); No. 15: *Les Hommes se dévêtissent* (ibid., 30–1).[17]

5 Material borrowed from military sources

1 Side-drum and fanfare patterns

Descriptions automatiques No. 3: *Sur un casque* (26 April 1913). Page 7 systems 1, 3 and 5 (in the last case cf. Debussy: *Minstrels*, bars 81–5).

2 'As-tu vu, la casquette, la casquette?' (*La Casquette du père Bugeaud*) (1847). This song is itself based on *Aux champs (en marchant)* of 1812.

Vieux sequins No. 2: *Danse cuirassée* (17 Sept 1913). Entire melody line.

3 Fanfare patterns

Sports et divertissements: *Le Réveil de la Mariée* (16 May 1914). At 'Levez-vous!' (after a reference to 'Dormez-vous?' from *Frère Jacques*).

4 Fanfare patterns

Relâche (1924). No. 12: *Musique de Rentrée* (reduction, 24–5, from letter A); No. 17: *Les Hommes regagnent leur place* (ibid., 35–6).

What is most interesting in the above lists is the way Satie mostly uses evocative *fragments* from popular sources. In most cases these derived from his well-thumbed copy of Pierre Larousse's *Grand Dictionnaire universel*. This is somewhat akin to Douanier Rousseau using popular illustrations from *Le Petit Journal* or *Bêtes sauvages*[18] as models for his own fantastic and naive paintings, and there is a two-dimensional quality to much of Satie's humoristic music too. But, like Rousseau, Satie transformed his sources during the creative process, and like Handel he repaid his borrowing with interest – as can be seen in his ingenious treatment of Audran's banal 'Orangutan Song' in *de Podophthalma*. In return, Satie also invented melodies which later became popular. Like the prefiguration of *Tea for Two* which begins *Le Golf* in *Sports et divertissements* (see Fig. 10.3). Whether Vincent Youmans knew of this when he wrote his musical *No, No, Nanette* in 1925 is another matter.

All Satie's operetta quotes come from works that were popular in the 1880s, which his father probably took him to see when he lived in the family home in Paris. And it comes as a true Satiean irony that Robert Planquette's *Rip* was diverting audiences from *Relâche* in a revival at the Gaîté Lyrique in December 1924, and that Puccini's death on 29 November that year took up much of the press space normally available for theatre coverage. Perhaps Satie was fortunate in this, for most of the reviews of *Relâche* that were published were hostile.

The reasons why Satie turned to popular sources so extensively during 1913–14 were fourfold. First, they helped him to sustain the unaccustomed bout of creativity that followed the sudden demand for novel groups of pieces from his publisher Demets. Second, they gave these humorous piano pieces greater popular appeal. Third, guessing their sources provided a sort of musical quiz that helped sustain public interest after their initial vogue had faded: the way Satie succeeded in this respect can be seen from the number of editions these pieces enjoyed in subsequent years. Lastly, popular sources helped Satie rediscover his path forward by taking some of the responsibility for inventing original material from his shoulders. For many, these pieces represent Satie at his best, and the best of the best are the *Embryons desséchés*, a compendium of popular sources that still sound fresh and funny whenever they are performed – which is no mean achievement.

10

Composition and the other arts

For Satie, the *esprit nouveau* that transfused the artistic life of Paris during and after the Great War proved an unmixed blessing. It promoted the existing cross-fertilization between the arts; brought about a social levelling; and stimulated the patronage of the avant-garde by high society. Naturally, the horrors of the war affected Satie as deeply as any other contemporary artist, but the phoenix it produced in *l'esprit nouveau* could not have arisen at a better time. For, long before Guillaume Apollinaire had become the self-appointed spokesman of the Cubists, Satie had made himself an expert on all forms of contemporary painting.[1] Whilst his own artistic talents lay in imaginative design and calligraphy – and, like Paul Klee, he was an exquisite rather than a great artist – Satie always preferred talking about art rather than music. Indeed, he considered that 'it was painters who taught me the most about music' (cited in Volta, 1982, 8). Similarly, his enquiring mind kept up with the latest developments in poetry and literature, and his ironical writings outweigh his published music, in quantity if not in quality. As far as social levelling was concerned, Satie had the happy gift of being able to communicate easily with people in all walks of life, and he revelled in his new role as the avant-garde mascot of high society when Cocteau championed him as the musical epitomy of the *esprit nouveau* in *Le Coq et l'Arlequin*. Without any hint of snobbishness, Satie strove on the one hand to make his music 'chic', Parisian and surprising to please his new patrons, and simple, self-sufficient and balanced on the other, to satisfy his own criteria.

If it might seem in retrospect that the *esprit nouveau* was designed with Satie in mind, the truth is that it was. Both this and the term 'surrealism' were coined by his friend Apollinaire in his article on *Parade* which appeared in *Excelsior* on 11 May 1917, and a week later in the programme of the ballet itself. Here is the relevant passage (as translated in Steegmuller, 1970, 513–14):

> This new union – for up until now stage sets and costumes on the one hand and choreography on the other were only superficially linked – has given rise in *Parade* to a kind of super-realism [sur-réalisme]. This I see as the starting-point of a succession of manifestations of the *esprit nouveau*: now that it has had an opportunity to reveal itself, it will not fail to seduce the élite, and it hopes to change art and manners from top to bottom, to the joy of all. For it is only natural to wish that arts and manners should attain at least the level of scientific and industrial progress. . .Picasso's

Cubist sets and costumes bear witness to the realism of his art. This realism, or this Cubism, whichever you prefer, is what has most deeply stirred the arts during the last ten years.

Satie, like Apollinaire in *Les Peintres cubistes* (1913), possessed an uncanny instinct for backing winners in a volatile artistic world that had more than its fair share of charlatans. He planned ballets with Derain, collaborated directly with Picasso on *Mercure*, got Braque to provide the illustrations for *Le Piège de Méduse*, and helped Man Ray produce his first 'Ready-Made' sculpture, and so on. With his insight and taste (plus a little capital), Satie could have become wealthy as an art-dealer and collector. But if Satie was just as aware of what was going on around him in his early career, it was his meteoric projection into the limelight by Ravel and Cocteau which gave him what he desired most, and put him on equal terms with the giants of the Parisian artistic scene. In this respect, it comes as no surprise to find Satie attending Apollinaire's lecture on *L'Esprit nouveau et les poètes* at Jacques Copain's Théâtre du Vieux Colombier on 26 November 1917. Indeed, Satie even memorized passages from it, or obtained a copy of the text, for we find him quoting extracts from it in his *Conférence sur les 'Six'* in Brussels in April 1921. Passages like the following echoed his own contemporary aesthetic: 'The New Spirit will dominate the world. . .The New Spirit exists in surprise. . .It is through surprise. . .that the New Spirit distinguishes itself from all the artistic and literary movements that have preceded it' (Ve, 89). Given Apollinaire's goal of stimulating surprise and a sense of wonder in a jaded society through art, Diaghilev's command to Cocteau to 'Astonish me' with *Parade* falls easily into context. So too does the infinite care Satie took to give his later works an arresting opening (see Ex. 25). In his 1921 lecture, Satie also declared that 'For me. . .The New Spirit is above all a return towards classical form – with modern sensibility' (Ve, 89), even though the classical principles of clarity, contrast and structural balance had never really been absent from his music. But this statement does show that even a detached and impersonal work like *Socrate* was bound up with The New Spirit, which can be seen to be equated with the 'cult of restraint' and with Cubism in Satie's eyes; for he told Henry Prunières on 3 April 1918 that *Socrate* also represented 'a return to classical simplicity with a modern sensibility. I owe this – very useful – return to my 'Cubist' friends. Bless them!'[2]

1886–1905

Satie's early career in the cabarets of Montmartre brought him into close contact with writers and painters rather than composers, and thus set the broad pattern for his later life. Apart from Debussy, who shared and fostered his catholic tastes, Satie made no enduring friendships with professional musicians of any calibre during this period. One of his circles of friends were those who painted his portrait between 1891 and 1895: the Catalan artists Ramón Casas and Santiago Rusiñol y Prats,[3] the Basque artist Ignacio Zuloaga y Zabaleta, as well as French painters like Marcellin Desboutin, Suzanne Valadon, Comte Antoine de La Rochefoucauld, Augustin Grass-Mick, and the Dutch Symbolist painter and designer Georges de Feure. Before they reached Satie's treasured collection, these portraits became widely known through numerous exhibitions, and they kept Satie's striking Bohemian image alive in the public eye – dandified, nocturnal and often slightly tipsy. Indeed, Satie was more often to be found in art galleries, artists' studios and Salons d'Exposition than he was at concerts, and he often chose these venues for the premières of his works. Thus his first incidental music (for *Le Fils des étoiles*) was heard at the Galerie Durand-Ruel on 19 March 1892, whilst his *Trois Sonneries* had been performed there nine days earlier at the inauguration of the first Salon de la Rose+Croix, amidst Symbolist paintings by Alexandre Séon, Carlos Schwabe and others.

In the early 1890s, it was Santiago Rusiñol who recorded Satie's first statement of his aesthetic. This was

> to realize in music what Puvis de Chavannes has succeeded in doing in painting, notably to attain extreme simplification in art. To say in two words what a Spanish orator could only express in long eloquent phrases, and to pervade his work with an indefinable something that would allow the listener to follow, according to his own capabilities, the way traced out for him, which runs straight ahead, adorned with harmonies and full of feeling.[4]

Thus Satie sought to equate his pared-down music with the single static image of a painting, and we have already seen him advising Debussy in 1891 to 'create a musical climate where the personages move and speak – not in couplets, not in leitmotifs: but by the use of a certain atmosphere of Puvis de Chavannes' (cited in Cocteau, 1924, 221). This helps to explain his experiments with time and space in the *Ogives* and the concept of music as a scenic backcloth, an immobile sound-décor in *Le Fils des étoiles*. It also explains why Satie's music for Henri Mazel's *Le Nazaréen* or Péladan's *Le Prince du Byzance* takes no heed of its theatrical context.

The problem in Satie's statement (as recorded by Rusiñol) concerns the way we perceive music as being 'full of feeling'. Whereas Satie intended to achieve this through his choice of harmonies, with the guiding melody tracing the way ahead for 'the listener to follow', he did not equate the ebb and flow of emotional tension with music's power to develop and dissolve climaxes. In contrast to Mallarmé's jealousy of the power of music, or Rimbaud's attempts to transfer musical effects to poetry, Satie aimed to rid music of its expressive connotations and render it flat, pale and fresco-like in the manner of Puvis de Chavannes. For Satie 'boredom was mysterious and profound'; repetition and objectivity were to be encouraged not despised. If Rimbaud experimented with words as units without syntactical relationship but with purely evocative value, then Satie (despite his motivic constructions) was still concerned with linear continuity, just as the lines in Puvis de Chavannes' frescoes created a harmonious whole.

Templier (1969, 11) finds a musical representation of Puvis de Chavannes' paintings as early as 1888 in the *Trois Gymnopédies*, though these can be attributed to literary sources too. Satie claimed they were inspired by reading Flaubert's *Salammbô*, and here there is another link with Debussy, who also considered Flaubert's Carthaginian novel as the basis for an opera (or a symphonic commentary) in 1886. But it is hard to find any links between this full-blooded Romantic tragedy and the gently undulating *Gymnopédies*, whose more likely source would seem to be Contamine de Latour's contemporary poem *Les Antiques* (see Appendix). Flaubert does, however, provide another linking thread in Satie's early career, for all the evidence suggests that *Uspud* was a parody of *La Tentation de Saint Antoine* (1848–56). Among the striking parallels are its desert setting, long lists of saints and animals, tripartite division, and isolated central character. Also, Latour reports (6 August 1925, 2) that *La Tentation* was Satie's favourite bedtime reading at this time. Henri Rivière's first great shadow theatre success at the Chat Noir came with a version of *La Tentation* too, with music by Satie's friend Albert Tinchant and Georges Fragerolle. This was first performed on 28 December 1887 and would certainly have been seen by Satie. Then at the Auberge du Clou (to which Satie decamped in 1891) one of the shadow theatre specialities was a humorous version of the temptation of St Anthony, which ended with his decision to leave his retreat and follow a more sensual existence. So it is quite likely that *Uspud* was itself designed for this new cult medium, which so impressed both Satie and Debussy. However, Satie's only known contribution to the shadow theatre – a *Noël* with words by Vincent Hyspa and scenery by Miguel Utrillo (1892) – has unfortunately not survived.

Besides writing the music for *Uspud*, Satie made a substantial contribution to its weird surrealistic libretto. Indeed, the whole project is more likely to have been his idea than that of Latour. The extravagance and occult symbolism of the longer first version[5] suggests that Péladan still exercised an influence over Satie, even after the much publicized break with him in August 1892.[6] The apocalyptic side, however, may have come from Latour, for this tendency in his poetry can be seen in the extract from *Damnation* (*La Perdition*) which originally prefaced Satie's first *Sarabande* in 1887 (BN 14457):

> Suddenly the heavens opened and the damned fell,
> Hurtling and colliding in a gigantic whirlwind;
> And when they were alone in the sunless night,
> They discovered they were wholly black. Then they blasphemed.

Again, this bears no more resemblance to the music it apparently inspired than does this extract from the end of Act 1 of *Uspud* (trans. in W, 130):

> uspud picks up stones and throws them at the christian church; the
> stones change into balls of fire. uspud's fury. he takes up a
> larger stone, which explodes with a bang; flames rise up and from
> their bosom the stars escape. great convulsion in nature.

The revolutionary idea of printing entirely in lower case here (an anticipation of the poetry of e.e. cummings) was Satie's own visual invention, and the above extract comes from the large *Uspud* brochure which he published privately in 1893.[7]

Satie's collaborations prior to his association with Cocteau in 1915 were all with minor literary figures: even in later life the texts he worked from (*Socrate* excepted) were of little merit in themselves, despite their authors being better known. This, of course, enhanced their potential for an original contribution from Satie, and perhaps therein lay their appeal to him. While Satie and Latour were 'two beings having the same affinities' (Latour, 3 August 1925, 2), their collaborations between 1886 and 1893, and between 1899 and 1905 must rather have arisen from the closeness of their friendship and circumstances than from Satie's admiration for Latour's poetry. When he was not trying to be apocalyptic, Latour tended to be sentimental and platitudinous, as in the opening verse of *Chanson*, which Satie set in 1887:

> Bien court, hélas, est l'espérance
> Et bien court aussi le plaisir,
> Et jamais en nous leur présence,
> Ne dura tant que le désir.

Perhaps Satie's vamped accompaniment slyly mocks Latour's superficiality, though the vocal line is more eloquent.[8] It was not until the *Trois Mélodies* of 1916 that Satie produced songs of distinction to the poems of others. In between came numerous collaborations for cabaret use with friends such as Henry Pacory, Vincent Hyspa, Dominique Bonnaud and Numa Blès. Charming as songs like *La Diva de l'Empire'* may be, they were hardly chosen for their literary merits, and Satie often omitted the words, even in his fair copies.[9] In some cases, like the lost operetta *Pousse l'amour* with Maurice de Féraudy and Jean Kolb, Satie collaborated in the hope of making money, for he referred to it in scathing terms in letters to Paulette Darty. In others, like the pantomime *Jack-in-the-Box* with the future first mayor of Montmartre, Jules Dépaquit, the object seems to have been a congenial diversion from the miseries of Arcueil in 1899. Only *Geneviève de Brabant* with Latour, which may have been conceived for the shadow theatre in Montmartre in the same year (or in 1900), seems to have been thought through as a modern (and bizarre) recreation of the legend of Saint Genevieve from its earlier sources.[10] Again the attraction to Satie may have resided as much in the role he could play in shaping the libretto as in the possibilities it offered for music, for he only provided a score lasting about ten minutes for a play of over an hour's duration. With impracticalities such as this and those encountered elsewhere (as in *Le Fils des étoiles*), it is small wonder that most of Satie's early theatrical projects never reached the stage during his lifetime. His plans for a three-act opera with Albert Tinchant, for instance, called *Le Bâtard de Tristan*, was only a joke at Wagner's expense, even though it was announced for the Grand Théâtre de Bordeaux in *Le Courrier du soir* on 22 July 1892. Similarly, the various offshoots from *Uspud* planned with Latour in 1893[11] never stood a chance of materializing. Satie was really more interested in inventing the genealogy of the Uspud clan (with a Proustian fascination) than he was about setting their imaginary exploits to music.

From the work of the collaborators Satie chose, it is easy to see why he was most influenced by painters. In fact, the only 'perfect collaborator' he found was Plato, and in *Socrate* he used the nineteenth-century translation of the *Dialogues* by Victor Cousin rather than a recent one by Mario Meunier. The one disappointment is that he never joined forces with the imaginative humorist Alphonse Allais, another Montmartre habitué who was involved in establishing Le Chat Noir. But perhaps in the inventor of germ warfare, microfilmed newspapers and abstract painting[12] Satie saw a rival genius to his own and stayed clear of musical involvement with him. Satie's friend Pierre de Massot (1924, 2) called Satie 'un Allais musical', and his own anecdotes owe much to his friend from Honfleur, especially those signed 'Virginie Lebeau' in *La Lanterne Japonaise* in 1888–9.[13]

Satie used numerous pseudonyms in his long writing career, including 'Chamfort' (1888), 'L'Homme à la Contrebasse' (1913–14: a reference to the cover picture of the *Revue musicale SIM* to which he was contributing), 'Swift' (1913–14), and 'Ursulin des Pierres' (1922).[14] During the Poueigh scandal after *Parade* in 1917, he often referred to himself as 'Monsieur Sadi' or 'Monsieur Satt-hie', but like Allais he was furious if anyone turned the tables on him. Allais often signed himself 'Francisque Sarcey' when he imitated the earnest style of the well-known Parisian drama critic, but he complained vigorously when a similar parody appeared in a Paris journal. So too did Satie when a series of nine 'Commandements du catéchisme du Conservatoire' appeared in the *Revue musicale SIM* on 15 February 1914 signed 'Erit Satis'.[15] 'I am in the habit of signing what I write', he told the editor Jules Ecorcheville on 8 March. 'Those who know me are aware that the kind of sentiment expounded in these *Commandements* is not mine, nor that of any writer of taste.'[16] His demand that this letter of denunciation should be printed, however, fell on deaf ears, and uncharacteristic commandments like: 'Dieubussy alone shalt thou adore,/ And copy perfectly' and 'Perfect harmony shalt thou not desire/ Except in marriage alone' have now entered Satie literature as genuine,[17] as Satie feared they would. So, although Satie often indulged in irony, puns and fantasy, or in later articles did not choose to develop the serious points he made from time to time, every word in every article he signed was carefully considered. Indeed, they contain more truth and less fantasy than might appear to be the case, and there is always method behind the apparent madness.

Satie's break with Péladan in 1892 should not be taken to imply a complete rejection of his artistic ideals, any more than Satie's short association with him implies adherence to Wagnerism or the cult of the androgyne. Rather, Satie was attracted to a potential source of publicity, with the Rosicrucian side, the occult symbolism and Péladan's deification of Puvis de Chavannes coming as bonuses. Satie did not share Péladan's enthusiasm for Italian masters like Raphael and Leonardo da Vinci; nor is there any evidence that he was attracted (as Péladan was) to the poetry of Verlaine; or, curiously, to the Symbolist paintings of Gustave Moreau. But it does seem likely that Satie admired some Catholic religious art, for when his Catalan painter friends somehow acquired two pictures by El Greco in January 1894, Satie proclaimed that these were a perfect embodiment of what his recently founded Eglise Métropolitaine d'Art de Jésus Conducteur had set out to achieve. Its aim, according to Rusiñol, was 'to attack society by means of painting and music'.[18] Thus in his first *Cartulaire* of May 1895,

Satie passes judgement on his former associates in the Péladan camp as follows (W, 46): 'The annual gathering of painters and sculptors, generally called Salons, have once again borne witness to the aesthetic decadence and degradation of Art, which has become the agent of western corruption.' But he was still able to praise those painters like Georges de Feure and Marcellin Desboutin who had executed portraits of 'Our Dear and Venerable Parcener', as 'Monsieur le Pauvre' now styled himself. And he was pleased to attend a banquet in honour of Desboutin at the Restaurant Coquet in the boulevard Clichy on 8 June 1895. The tickets for this were designed by none other than Georges de Feure (Vy, 33).

Another aim of Satie's Eglise Métropolitaine was to attack his enemies either in the critical press – like Henry Gauthier-Villars (Willy), or in the theatre – like Aurélien Lugné-Poë, director of the Théâtre de l'Œuvre. Surprisingly, Satie attacks Willy for his ignorance of Wagner, who he defends elsewhere in his *Cartulaires*. But, true to form, he and Willy remained deadly enemies. They even came to blows at the Concerts Chevillard on 10 April 1904, when it was Satie who was led away by the Municipal Guard, even though it was Willy who struck Satie first. Satie's intransigent pursuit of his enemies and unforgiving nature remain his least attractive features. His moral self-righteousness in isolation meant that there was nothing communal or altruistic about his Metropolitan Church of Art, but to be fair Satie never sought to convert anyone to his cause. More than anything, his church provided an excuse to return to the medieval world he loved, with architectural designs and fake plainsong 'copied in the Gothic style of Our Forefathers; which is a durable form pleasing unto God'.[19] Satie seems to have been most concerned with the short *Dixit Dominus* from his *Messe des pauvres*, for the music of *Intende votis supplicum* (published by the Librairie de l'Art Indépendant in 1895) is none other than that which appeared posthumously as its second movement (wrongly titled *Dixit domine*). Satie made another Gothic score of an earlier, less chromatic version of this movement,[20] though neither of these richly harmonized organ scores would fool any scholar for long.

Satie's Metropolitan Church was also founded partly to occupy (or perhaps to purify) his mind after his earthly liaison with Suzanne Valadon in 1893. As a talented painter, Valadon (the mother of Maurice Utrillo[21]) was encouraged by Renoir, Degas and Toulouse-Lautrec, for whom she posed as a model. No doubt Satie's circle of artistic friends widened during their affair, as much as through the Librairie de l'Art Indépendant where he met the young writers Gide, Valéry and Claudel. Satie also kept up his links with Péladan's wealthy patron, Comte Antoine de La Rochefoucauld. He contributed a prelude to his protégé Jules Bois's esoteric play *La Porte héroïque du ciel*,[22] as well as a *Gnossienne* to La Rochefoucauld's journal *Le Cœur*. In 1894 La Rochefoucauld also painted Satie's portrait in neo-Impressionist style, which was praised by Alfred Jarry.[23] In 1896 we find Marcel Proust mentioning Satie as an example of an avant-garde composer in his collection of short stories and poems *Les Plaisirs et les jours* (1896, 92), and Proust must have followed Satie's precursive career with interest, for we find him writing to Cocteau in May 1917 praising the dance of the Little American Girl in *Parade* as 'so moving. . .it puts on the brakes and gets moving again so marvellously. What concentration there is in all this, what nourishment for this age of famine.'[24] Whilst Satie's career as a miniaturist is worlds away from the masterpiece-of-a-lifetime concept of *A la recherche du temps perdu*, there is a marked similarity between their approach to their respective arts. As André Maurois observes: 'Proust constructed his work by bringing the material to a high temperature, and then "running" the various fragments into the molten mass, or, let us say, by bringing these fragments into juxtaposition so as to form a mosaic in accordance with a pre-established design.'[25]

Whilst far more evidence will surely come to light about Satie's artistic contacts and projects in the shadowy years around the turn of the century, there can be no doubt that his cabaret activities and his love of café society provided a vital antidote to his introspection and uncertainty as a composer. Drawings and paintings by his close friend Grass-Mick show him in the company of Jane Avril, Georges Courteline and Toulouse-Lautrec at the Café des Princes in 1899, or listening to Frédé playing his guitar at Le Lapin Agile in 1905 in the company of the novelists Roland Dorgelès and Romain Rolland, and the low-life poet Jehan Rictus. Although Satie claims to have suggested to Debussy the potential of applying the representational methods of Monet, Cézanne and Toulouse-Lautrec to music, there is little evidence that he sought to do so himself. Like Péladan he mistrusted the aims of the Impressionists, and preferred realistic clarity and transparency to blurred colours and hazy outlines. We have already seen similarities between his art and that of Douanier Rousseau, though Satie was a cerebral rather than a primitive artist, for all his purity of vision. Perhaps the best comparison, however, is with Gauguin, whose decorative art with its flattened surfaces had so little to do with academic practice. Yet 'this amateur amongst great artists. . .created out of his own technical inadequacy an art so revolutionary that much of what happened in the twentieth century is unthinkable without the example of his pictures'.[26] As Satie was so fond of saying: 'Vivent les Amateurs!'[27]

1905–1924

(a) Literature and poetry

Again, little is known about Satie's contacts with painters and writers during the interregnum years at the Schola Cantorum. But as his links with the cabaret weakened in 1909–10, so his interest in journalism, his *violon d'Ingres*, grew. Initially, he set out to serve his local community by contributing unsigned propaganda for local events and societies to *L'Avenir d'Arcueil-Cachan*. He participated in some of these himself as a member of its Patronage Laïque.[28] In Arcueil he was known as a composer of popular songs, an image he seems to have been anxious to encourage, for he imported well-known friends like Paulette Darty and Vincent Hyspa to perform his works before admiring audiences in the autumn of 1909.[29] It was in this period that Satie developed his interest in the cinema, for we find numerous ecstatic advertisements for

'M. Ollinger-Jacob, the famous Director of the *Largest Cinema in the World*' at 60 rue Emile-Raspail. Satie describes him as 'a real magician', his highest accolade.

In 1912 the pattern for the final part of Satie's career began to take shape. His disinterested encouragement of promising young composers began with Roland-Manuel, and he started contributing articles to *L'Œil de veau* and the *Revue musicale SIM*, as well as establishing the formula for his humoristic piano pieces with the *Véritables Préludes flasques*. Besides publishing Satie's 'Observations d'un Imbécile (Moi)', Roland-Manuel's short-lived journal *L'Œil de veau* also brought Satie into contact with Le Groupe Fantaisiste, young poets who admired the ironical work of Toulet and Laforgue. One of their number, Francis Carco, also contributed to *L'Œil de veau* and his poems were set by Satie's friend Robert Montfort, another isolated composer who had shared his love of things mystic and medieval since around 1904.[30] After a referendum in *Gil Blas* had elected Paul Fort as 'Prince of Poets' in 1912, a group of Satie's young supporters (Montfort amongst them) tried to run a similar campaign to get Satie elected 'Prince of Musicians' that July. Although this initiative failed, it added to the growing publicity surrounding Satie, as had the premières of *En Habit de cheval* and Roland-Manuel's orchestration of the *Prélude de La Porte héroïque du ciel* at the Salle Gaveau on 17 June – a concert Satie felt he was too poorly dressed to attend!

As a result, Satie's music was taken up by the publisher Demets and we find him classing himself 'amongst the "fantaisistes"' in his autobiographical sketch for Demets in 1913. Here he was referring not only to the whimsical titles of his 'humorous' piano sets (which usually preceded their composition), but also to the commentaries that accompanied them (which were often appended later). Naturally, the music exemplified the French 'fantaisiste' spirit of lightness and subtle irony too, as a modern equivalent of the *esprit gaulois*. Indeed, some of Satie's commentaries are really prose poems, like *La Balançoire* (*The Swing*) from the *Sports et divertissements*:

> C'est mon cœur qui se balance ainsi.
> Il n'a pas de vertige.
> Comme il a des petits pieds.
> Voudra-t-il revenir dans ma poitrine?

or *La Chasse* from the same collection:

> Entendez-vous le lapin qui chante?
> Quelle voix!
> Le rossignol est dans son terrier.
> Le hibou allaite ses enfants.
> Le marcassin va se marier.
> Moi, j'abats des noix à coups de fusil.

In his *Heures séculaires et instantanées*, Satie forbade 'anyone to read the text aloud during the performance', adding that 'Ignorance of my instructions will bring my righteous indignation against the audacious culprit. No exceptions will be allowed.' So it seems that all such additions were to amuse the pianist alone, as a sort of aid to meditation or to understanding the pieces concerned. Whilst Marcel Duchamp or Picabia in-troduced words into their paintings, only Satie employed a simultaneous counterpoint of poetry, music and drawing within a single composition. This, together with their Japanese concision and immaculate calligraphy, is what makes the *Sports et divertisse-ments* such a remarkable achievement. In their original conception in 1914, Satie worked to a different set of twenty pencil drawings by Charles Martin to those printed in 1923 by Les Editions Lucien Vogel et du Bon Ton. Evidently, Martin felt a need to take account of artistic developments in the interim, and provided a second set of illus-trations in 1922 which are just as witty, but show the influence of Cubism.[31] It is thus quite understandable that the details of Satie's texts should be at odds with Martin's pictures, with only the original titles corresponding. Fortunately, however, ten copies with both sets of plates (plus an extra early plate for *Le Pique-nique*) were printed in 1923 by Vogel for the Librairie Maynial, which had bought the material after the initial dissolution of Lucien Vogel and Cie.[32] Copy No. 7 of this extreme Satie rarity is now in the collection of Heidi Nitze in New York, and she has kindly allowed me to reproduce the 1914 and 1922 designs for *Le Golf* (Figs. 10.1 and 2) which show how Satie's text (in Fig. 10.3) did in fact fit Martin's 1914 illustration. The '"caddie" follows the golfer, carrying the "bags". The clouds are surprised' by the turf the Colonel throws up, and as he makes his 'swing, his "club" bursts into pieces'. Only the 'Scotch Tweed' is missing and the '"holes" trembling with fright'.

10.1   Charles Martin: first illustration (1914) for *Le Golf* in *Sports et divertissements*.

10.2   Charles Martin: second illustration (1922) for *Le Golf*.

10.3   The music for *Le Golf* (1914).

In other cases too, like *Le Bain de mer*, Satie's text is far closer to the 1914 than the 1922 Martin illustration. In the 1914 version there is a lady who has fallen beneath an enormous breaking wave, whereas in the 1922 version the sea is calm and the lady appears to be diving into a boat, much to the consternation of the man rowing it. So Satie's humorous text ('The ocean is wide, Madame. . .Don't sit down at the bottom. . .Here are some good old waves. They are full of water') fits only the first version. Indeed, it does not seem that Martin made any attempt to match his 1922 illustrations to Satie's poetic vignettes. In this piece, however, his little triangular wave design at the start of the music does seem to be directly related to Satie's rolling left-hand arpeggios, so it is possible that these also date from 1914 and that Satie drew inspiration from them in his music.

Le Golf was the last of the sports that Satie illustrated in music. Getting everything exactly right involved him in five progressively shorter attempts at the text,[33] and no less than nine attempts at the music. Like the other *Sports et divertissements*, his sketches all had regular bar lines (here in 2/4 time) which were then removed for visual effect in the printed version. Satie began with the perky dotted rhythm found in the prelude to *Jack-in-the-Box*, which he must have associated with Scotland, and ended up with a more 'asthmatic' version of the Colonel which prefigures *Tea for Two* at the start (Fig. 10.3), as we have seen. Although Satie may not have set out to provide musical (and verbal) equivalents to all the events in Martin's picture, he clearly had its central image of the old Colonel and the disastrous swing of his club in mind. For this was the first thing that Satie fixed musically (during his fourth attempt), and the only element from the first sketches (in BN 9627(9)) to survive into the final version. Ex. 87

Ex. 87 *Sports et divertissements: Le Golf*, first version (BN 9627(9), 16–17) (Originally bar 13 was an exact repeat of bar 12)

Ex. 87 (*cont.*)

shows this complete early version with its Scottish dance rhythms. Satie may have rejected it because it was too short to fill the large printed page he envisaged, and the final version (Fig. 10.3) lasts for the equivalent of twenty-five bars. It is possible, of course, that Martin devised his 1914 pictures from Satie's finished pieces, but from the evidence of *Le Golf*, I believe the reverse scenario to be equally likely. After all, Satie was only approached by Lucien Vogel (via Valentine Gross, then one of his illustrators) after Stravinsky had turned the project down. And Charles Martin also worked as an illustrator for Vogel's *Le Gazette du Bon Ton*, from whence the project originated. So Vogel probably selected the subjects for illustration (with Martin's help) sometime in late 1913, and Martin would surely have known about them before Satie in any event. It is also possible that Martin and Satie worked independently on their respective contributions, but again I seriously doubt if this was the case, given the care with which Satie approached his other later collaborations.

In the midst of these sketches for *Le Golf* Satie was planning other sets of piano pieces. These include *Les Globules ennuyeux* (*Boring Globules*) and *Les Etapes monotones* (*Monotonous Day's Marches*). Neither set was composed, but Satie wrote texts for the first. The opening piece (*Regard*) begins with a Verlaine parody ('Son regard est une tiède parure') and ends up talking about an umbrella made of 'porcine silk which has the appearance of a tomato'![34] This surrealistic fantasy is comparable to the strange texts of the *Heures séculaires et instantanées*, in which a story is told in disjunct images, like a contemporary poem by Apollinaire. To see Satie experimenting with visual, poetic and musical images simultaneously is a testament to the breadth of his artistic vision. If the music was always his priority, he was almost as skilled in the other branches of the arts, and was equally concerned that they should be represented in his *œuvre*, which found its natural fruition in the theatre. Thus we find him writing the first surrealist play *Le Piège de Méduse* in 1913, whose nine anarchic scenes are divided by fragmentary dances for Jonah the monkey. Or writing his own contemporary versions of thirteenth-century troubadour poetry for the *Trois Poèmes d'amour* the following year.

Satie's concern for the eye as much as the ear even stretches to the texts of his late lectures, which look like a literary equivalent to Apollinaire's *Calligrammes*,[35] though

... Scarlatti & Rameau sont nés la même an-
née ___ 1683 ___
    l'un, à Naples ;.... l'autre, à Dijon :....
      ......
..Ce fait prouve qu'ils ne sont pas "jumeaux",.. si
j'ose dire ....

       ....
.... Bach ___ que l'on appelle toujours
le "vieux" Bach ,... était encore jeune lorsqu'il
mourut :...
   ...il n'avait que 65 ans ___ ce qui
n'est pas vieux ,...en somme ......

      :·········
..... Byrd & Rameau ___ lui ___ sont morts dans
la force de l'âge .:.....
   .... ils avaient 81 ans ___
     ......"chacun",... bien entendu ...

   !!!!!!!
... On remarquera que de ces musiciens ,... ceux
qui ont eu ,...ce qu'on appelle ,....la vie dure,
sont :......
...Byrd ,..Rameau ,...Monteverde ,. Scarlatti &
Gluck ....

10.4   *Préambule*, p. 3 for a concert by Marcelle Meyer on 17 January 1922 (Ho).

precedents for these can be found in the emblematic verse of Lewis Carroll (such as the 'Mouse's Tale' in the shape of a mouse's tail in chapter 3 of *Alice in Wonderland*). But Figure 10.4, which is part of a 'preamble' to a concert given by Marcelle Meyer in 1922,[36] does in fact have a practical purpose too: it was designed for Satie to read aloud, with the numbers of dots indicating the pauses (and their length) in his opening speech. Nonetheless, they add greatly to the visual effect of the manuscript, and Satie's only lecture on the evolution of music is more remarkable for its calligraphy than for its historical content.

Satie was always an avid reader and, like Apollinaire, he would spend whole days in the Bibliothèque Nationale devouring books on similar subjects, from medieval legends to the esoteric. He was an authority on the past history of Paris, and from his excellent memory he would regale any companion he happened to have on his long walks across the city with appropriate information on the sites they passed.

In later life Satie became even more interested in contemporary poetry, setting texts by Cocteau and Radiguet in 1920 and being especially attracted to the short *cocasseries* of Léon-Paul Fargue, whose *Ludions* perfectly matched his own aphoristic style. That he never attempted to set any of Apollinaire's poetry is curious, but perhaps Satie avoided it because of the contemporary settings by Poulenc and Honegger.[37] With his wide circle of literary friends he was often sent poems to set, but he was extremely selective and acutely aware of what was right for him at any particular time.[38] In all, he wrote fewer songs than one might expect, and saw the theatre as a greater attraction (and potential source of income). Once he had Diaghilev's ear with *Parade*, he devised many ballet projects of his own. But again, although his favourite reading was the tales of Hans Andersen, it was the fables of La Fontaine that he chose for the scenario he proposed to Diaghilev and Misia Edwards in July 1916.

The dominating literary figure in Satie's life between 1915 and 1923, however, was Jean Cocteau. On the positive side Cocteau gave Satie more publicity than he had ever dreamed of, projecting him as the personification of the new modern spirit of simplicity and French nationalism, with its roots in popular melody and its inspiration in the music-hall, cabaret and circus. Through *Parade* and *Le Coq et l'Arlequin* (1918), Satie was elevated from the bad boy of music to a cult figure in an élite society hungry for sensation, his meteoric rise being assisted by Stravinsky's absence from Paris between 1914 and 1920. On the negative side, Cocteau wasted a great deal of Satie's valuable composing time, and it should be remembered that he could not read music and had an instinctive rather than a balanced understanding of the art. Their first project, incidental music for *A Midsummer Night's Dream* (planned for the Cirque Médrano in 1915 with the Cubist painter Albert Gleizes) came to nothing, with Satie's *Cinq Grimaces* remaining unpublished during his lifetime. Satie was only able to get anywhere with *Parade* once Picasso had joined the team, and he resisted the inclusion of Cocteau's noise-making instruments. Then much of 1920–3, which should have been Satie's most productive years, were taken up with the abortive opera *Paul & Virginie*, to a libretto by Cocteau (with contributions from Radiguet). Indeed, it was only after breaking with Cocteau in Monte Carlo in January 1924[39] that Satie was wholly able to be himself, moving further to the left as Cocteau moved to the right. It might reasonably be said that Cocteau's publicity made Satie headstrong, and that association with this flamboyant interfering egotist set Satie on the path towards what most critics assessed as artistic suicide in 1924, which the final break intensified. Further, it did not require much critical acumen to find gaping holes in Cocteau's arguments in *Le Coq et l'Arlequin*, which in truth were as simplistic as the simplicity they advocated. His lack of historical perspective placed Debussy and Wagner in the same musical category, and he was equally unobservant about Satie when he said that his music was more French than that of Debussy, or that it was Satie's music which evolved rather than Debussy's. His cardinal errors are that 'Satie does not pay much attention to painters and does not read the poets', and that Satie 'clears, simplifies and strips rhythm naked' (trans. Myers, 1926, 18), when rhythm was never Satie's priority and he did little more than borrow the existing rhythmic patterns of the *Café-concert*. As David Bancroft observes of *Le Coq et l'Arlequin* (1967, 115):

> To blame the public for being continually *en retard* of its generation, and equally to blame them for creating a cult when they do manage to catch up with the art of their time – this was not part of a musical cause at all in Cocteau's case, but rather it was expressive of his masochistic hostility towards the public for their rejection of *Parade*, and of his ill-concealed frustration at being no longer pampered by them as he was during the *prince frivole* period.

Thus, although Satie did derive benefits from his liaison with Cocteau, the public association of him with the philosophy behind *Le Coq et l'Arlequin* ultimately did him more harm than good. Indeed, it may partly have been an attempt to set the record straight that led Satie to write so many articles in 1920–4. The most notable examples of him doing this are his 1922 articles on Debussy and Stravinsky, and it is significant that Satie told Marcel Raval that year that 'Cocteau came to bring me his book "Secret professionnel", but I don't have any of his other novels.'[40] Radiguet's writings, on the other hand, were found beside his hospital bed after his death.

One major source of enlarging and maintaining his circle of artistic friends was the left-bank bookshops that Satie loved to frequent – notably those of Adrienne Monnier, Sylvia Beach and Pierre Trémois. At Monnier's La Maison des Amis des Livres (7 rue de l'Odéon), one of the first performances of *Socrate* took place on 21 March 1919, when Satie accompanied Suzanne Balguerie in the *Portrait de Socrate* after an introduction by Cocteau. *Chez* Monnier Satie borrowed (rather than bought) books, but more importantly he met authors such as Ezra Pound, Gertrude Stein and James Joyce. He had been introduced to Stein by Henri-Pierre Roché, the future author of *Jules et Jim*, and she became an ardent admirer of his music after hearing Virgil Thomson play *Socrate*. Satie corresponded with her and attended her soirées from 1920 onwards, and as Volta says (Vy, 68): 'through the continuous use of the present tense and the suppression of transitional material, the work of this writer has been compared to Satie's music'. Satie also tended to write in the present tense too, for by then it was the present and the future that concerned him rather than the past. As Satie never missed any sort of 'happening' if he could possibly avoid it, he was almost certainly present amongst the crowd that packed Monnier's bookshop to hear the first readings from Joyce's *Ulysses* in December 1921 – in a French translation by Valéry Larbaud. We find Satie, Joyce, Pound, Picasso Man Ray and others at George Antheil's deliberately riotous concert at the Théâtre des Champs-Elysées on 4 October 1923, which was arranged to publicize the Ballets Suédois' new season. Satie (in a box with Milhaud) applauded violently at the end of Antheil's *Airplane Sonata* and as Antheil recalls (1945, 109), at the end of *Mechanisms* 'I suddenly heard Satie's shrill voice saying, "Quel précision! Quel précision! Bravo! Bravo!" and he kept clapping his little gloved hands' as the police moved in to arrest some of the more demonstrative rioters. Unbeknown to them, the whole event was being filmed and had been organized by Margaret Anderson, the editor of *The Little Review*, at whose salon Satie renewed his acquaintance with Ezra Pound. *L'Inhumaine*, the film in question (starring Maeterlinck's ex-mistress Georgette Leblanc) still exists.

Satie also frequented Sylvia Beach's bookshop Shakespeare and Company in the nearby rue Dupuytren, where Joyce's *Ulysses* was first published. On finding that Beach wrote only business letters, Satie 'said that this was the best kind of writing; you had something to say and you said it' (Beach, 1960, 159). Satie too could be eminently terse when he wanted to be. When he fell out with Fargue in 1923 (after he inadvertently forgot to name him as the author of the *Ludions* at their private première on 30 May), Satie demanded an apology in extremely blunt terms.[41] But all he got was more abuse, despite their earlier closeness (for the usually formal Satie uses the familiar 'tu' form here, something he never did with Cocteau). Indeed, Satie had been a member of Fargue's circle of 'Potassons', who would gather in Monnier's bookshop to hear his witty and obscene stories. As 'Potasson' was the name of Fargue's fat cat, Satie's final *Ludion*, the *Chanson du chat*,[42] was adopted as the *Marche des Potassons* by his admirers (Volta, 1988, 24).

When his friend Pierre Trémois opened his bookshop at 14 rue de l'Université in 1922, Satie eagerly contributed articles to his first six *Catalogues* between March and November that year. These are essays on such subjects as Bookishness, Reading, Publishing, the alchemist Nicolas Flamel, and Writing in Cafés ('Painful Examples').[43] The most important is that on Publishing, because Satie was acutely concerned with the way his musical thoughts were 'exteriorized', and because it helps explain his fascination with well-printed books. 'A literary publication', he says (Ve, 54),

> appears more brilliant, more logical, more 'genuine' than its cousin the musical publication. . .its value, very often, tends to rise towards a high value, to the 'rare' class.
>
> In a word, the book is a 'genuine' object – a kind of jewel, a type of work of art. It is complete.
>
> A musical work. . .has none of these precious external features; it appears like a sort of brother to academic books – an ugly brother.
>
> Take Albéric Magnard, who published a great number of important works, dressing them up to look like an 'atlas'. . .His example – a very 'deliberate' one in this case – shows how little importance he attached to the notated 'exteriorization' of his

thought, and underlines the difference which exists between literary and musical publications.

Satie, like Debussy (but unlike Magnard) played a positive role in designing editions of his works, and here he suggests that music 'should be put in print in some quite different way' as 'engraving is so awkward physically'. Unfortunately he does not elaborate on this point, but we can perhaps see why he deliberately removed conventional bar lines and key-signatures from his later music for single performers, for he considered that the 'variable nature of musical notation spoils the "patina" of musical works. Times destroy the meaning of the "symbols": clefs, accidentals etc.' Therefore Satie sought to make his own publications as close as he could to the literary models he admired, hence the 'historical background' in the form of added texts or stories. His ideal solution was the reproduction of his original manuscript in red and black ink, as in the *Sports et divertissements*. But the opportunity for this sort of expensive collaboration between the arts was extremely rare. It was perhaps to make this publication a commercial possibility that Satie is said to have initially refused Vogel's commission because the fee offered was too high: whereas Stravinsky had earlier refused to collaborate because the (higher) fee he was offered was too low!

(b)   Painting, sculpture and theatrical collaborations

In one of his sketchbooks Satie observed that 'Musical evolution is always a hundred years behind pictorial evolution' (cited in Ve, 158), and it was from painters that he derived most influence in his quest for modernity. To continue the list of premières associated with artistic events,[44] his *Trois Mélodies* were first heard in conjunction with an exhibition of modern painting *chez* Mme Bongard[45] in a Satie-Granados concert on 30 May 1916, when both Matisse and Picasso contributed original engravings for the programme. Similarly, the première of the *Trois Valses distinguées du précieux dégoûté* took place on 19 November 1916 during an 'Instant musical d'Erik Satie' which inaugurated an exhibition of paintings by Matisse, Modigliani, Kisling, Picasso and others at the Société Lyre et Palette, together with the first French exhibition of negro sculptures.[46] Satie dedicated the 'Entrée des Managers' in *Parade* to Kisling, and its 'Red Curtain' prelude to Picasso, and it was *Parade* that first brought Picasso's talents to the service of the theatre, just as the writer and artist Francis Picabia was drawn into its world in *Relâche* through Satie's activities as a professional catalyst. To complete the picture, Satie's *Musique d'ameublement* first appeared in conjunction with an exhibition of children's drawings[47] at the Galerie Barbazanges in 1920, and his *Quatre Petites Mélodies* were first heard as a group at the Galerie Georges Giroux in Brussels in April 1921.[48]

As is well known, Satie's concept of 'furnishing music' derived from Matisse, who 'dreamed of an art without any distracting subject matter which might be compared to a good armchair'.[49] The term applies to much of Satie's music from 1916 onwards. Matisse was the principal member of the Fauve group (active 1905–8), notable for their flat patterns and violent use of colour: one of Satie's closest friends, the hard-drinking, down-to-earth André Derain, was an original member of this group. We find Satie encouraging Derain as 'the greatest painter of the Fauvist period' when he thought his career was over in 1912, and again persuading him to continue painting after the War. So it is small wonder that Derain considered that 'it was Satie who saved me as a painter'.[50] Satie worked with Derain on a number of projects in 1921, including the opera *Paul & Virginie, Supercinéma* for the Ballets Suédois and *La Naissance de Vénus* for Diaghilev. This, and Satie's unfinished piece for violin and piano *L'Embarquement pour Cythère*[51] were both inspired by paintings (by Botticelli and Watteau respectively). According to a letter to Derain on 8 September 1921, *La Naissance de Vénus* was scheduled to accompany Stravinsky's *Les Noces* in Diaghilev's Spring 1922 season at the Paris Opéra, and in March 1922 he told the Comtesse Edith de Beaumont that 'At Derain's all three of us talked about this *initial* choreography: starting off with the choreographer, which is very *new* and has never been done before. I'm the one who suggested this idea to Massine.'[52] Unfortunately Satie did not elaborate further on how his new conception might be put into practice, but it shows his lively interest in all aspects of the theatre in his final years.

In 1923 Satie planned two more ballets with Derain: *Concurrence* and *Couleurs*. No details are known about them, and the latter might seem unlikely as Derain became more traditionalist after 1919 and worked principally in sombre browns and olive greens. Satie's ballet plans originated mostly during the summer months when he was stuck in Arcueil while his friends (like Derain) were holidaying in the South of France. So it is understandable that Derain seems largely to have ignored Satie's letters spurring him into action, though it is thanks to these that we know how varied his artistic interests were. Satie's two derelict pianos, incidentally, were bought by Derain and Braque as memorials after his death, and it was Satie who was responsible for Braque's first work as an illustrator, the woodcuts for *Le Piège de Méduse*.[53] This was published under the patronage of Daniel-Henry Kahnweiler, a well-known dealer in Cubist paintings, in 1921.

Satie's interest in Futurism was more peripheral than might be expected from a later active participant in Dadaism. The chief reasons were probably its Italian origins (with Russolo and Marinetti) and its concentration on noise rather than music. But Satie did show some interest in the Futurist movement around 1913, when he attended the 'Lundis de *Montjoie!*'. These soirées were organized by the director of the revue *Montjoie!*, Ricciotto Canudo, and by Valentine de Saint-Point, author of the *Manifeste de la Femme Futuriste* (Ve, 294). Thus *Les Pantins dansent* of November 1913, written for Saint-Point's Metachoric Festival, is associated with Futurism, and so was the *Revue musicale SIM* to which Satie contributed (as 'L'Homme à la Contrebasse') in 1913–14. His article 'Water Music', for instance, shows an attitude of enthusiasm mixed with irony. 'The mysterious frontiers which separate the worlds of noise and music are tending increasingly to be obliterated. Musicians are annexing these unknown territories that are so rich in surprising sonorities with increasing satisfaction', Satie begins (Ve, 140). But he typically ends up joking about 'the joy of the Water Companies' at all the potential outdoor festivals, and about 'the first concert for two obligatory taps and orchestra', anticipating Nicholas Slonimsky and Gerard Hoffnung. Indeed, Satie seems to have been far more excited by the possibilities of synaesthesia at this time, as proposed by Rimbaud and primitively executed in the colour-keyboard of Scriabin (see Ve, 141).

It was Diaghilev (in his wish to remain in the forefront of modern advances) who seems to have imposed the Futuristic elements in *Parade* on an impressionable Cocteau, and he also commissioned décors from the Italian Futurists Balla and Depero for other ballets in 1916. It was a pity that Satie never saw the single performance of Balla's *Feu d'artifice* in Rome on 12 April 1917 (during the rehearsals for *Parade*), for Balla 'transformed the entire theatre into an all-embracing synaesthetic ambience by means of the time-controlled spatial interaction of sound, moving three-dimensional abstract colored forms and colored lights that played on and off stage' (Martin, 1978, 92). But doubtless Picasso told Satie about Balla's Futuristic innovations, and his 'plastic complexes' probably influenced Picasso's 'poses plastiques' in *Mercure*, whilst the concept of overwhelming lighting effects recurs in *Relâche*, perhaps on Satie's initiative.

Some of the responsibility for the noises and onomatopoeic nonsense syllables in Parts 2 and 3 of *Parade* must lie with Apollinaire's *L'Antitradition futuriste* (1913), which together with Marinetti's *Il Teatro di Varietà*[54] influenced Cocteau while he was elaborating his scenario for *Parade*. Satie even set some of Cocteau's 'trompe l'oreille' sounds in his sketches,[55] though the actors with megaphones were dispensed with for both practical and aesthetic reasons before the 1917 première. So too were the sirens, typewriters etc. now commonly regarded as an integral part of the unique sonority of *Parade*. They were scheduled for inclusion in the Paris Opéra revival of May 1920, but due to opposition from both Satie and Cocteau this never took place. Some of the sound-effects were restored in the triumphant revival on 21 December 1920 at the Théâtre des Champs-Elysées, but Satie did not comment on them until after they were incorporated in full in 1923. Then he told Diaghilev in no uncertain terms, on 19 June, that 'I don't much like the "noises" made by Jean. But there is nothing we can do here: we have before us a likeable maniac.'[56]

Given the tone of this letter, we should be wary of Cocteau's attempt to link the external noises, or 'fragments of reality' in *Parade* to the *papier collé* and *objets trouvés* techniques of Synthetic Cubism. Perhaps he sought to make them seem more up-to-date by divorcing them from their original links with Futurism. Whilst it is Satie's noises and Picasso's Managers that have led to descriptions of *Parade* as a 'ballet cubiste', rather than a 'ballet réaliste' (as it is titled), Cocteau was not above putting words into Satie's mouth. In the following extract from *Vanity Fair* (1917, 106), his aim was to assert himself as a collaborator of equal importance to Picasso and Satie, by showing (wrongly) how Satie wanted to incorporate his ideas rather than those of Picasso:[57]

> 'I only composed', says Satie modestly, 'a background to throw into relief the noises which the playwright considers indispensable to the surrounding of each character with his own atmosphere. These imitated noises of waves, typewriters, revolvers, sirens or aeroplanes, are, in music, of the same character as the bits of newspapers, painted wood-grain, and other everyday objects that the cubist painters employ frequently in their pictures, in order to localize objects and masses in nature.'

For all its dubious authenticity, there is a fragment of truth in this elaborate justification of Satie's aims in composing *Parade*. The score *was* intended as a background, but it was Picasso's scenic effects rather than Cocteau's flimsy scenario that were uppermost in Satie's mind. And Satie *was* concerned with the way that the Cubists' altered perception of everyday objects was changing the course of twentieth-century art towards abstract conceptions. But it was the earlier phase of Analytical Cubism (1909–12) which I believe interested him most, with its reordering of objective reality in new structures and forms through the subjective vision of the artist, and not the textural trappings of Synthetic Cubism (1912–14). Satie wrote in 1922 (Ve, 37) that it was painters like 'Manet, Cézanne, Picasso, Derain, Braque and others' who were at the forefront in liberating art from the 'worst practices' of the past. 'At their own risk, they have saved Painting – and artistic thought at the same time – from complete, permanent and universal devastation.' Following Cézanne's concentration on geometrical forms in nature, the reaction against Impressionism had been completed by Braque and Picasso in their rejection of decorative arabesques, sensuous colours and conventional perspective. Their non-imitative art, with its linear approach and flattened surfaces, synchronized well with what Satie was trying to achieve in music. From the structural advances of Analytical Cubism, Satie realized that a new reality could be created in *Parade* by the way that simplified blocks of sound (mostly constructed from non-expressive ostinatos) coexisted in time and space. There is no use of the 'wrong-note' harmony we find later in the music of Les Six. As Constant Lambert says (1934, 118–19):

> His progressions have a strange logic of their own, but they have none of the usual sense of concord and discord, no trace of the *point d'appui* that we usually associate with the word progression. They may be said to lack harmonic perspective in much the same way that a cubist painting lacks spatial perspective.

Satie's transparent orchestration matches the colouristic restraint of the Cubists, just as the self-sufficiency of *Parade* matches that of an 'assassinated' object in a Cubist painting by Picasso or Braque. The absence of rhetorical argument and any sense of development linked with a narrative plan gives *Parade* an abstract quality, and brings Satie's similar experiments with surface texture to the fore. At the same time, Satie's interlinking and balancing of his blocks of sound can be compared on a basic level with paintings like Picasso's *L'Arlésienne* (1912), which showed a figure in profile and full face simultaneously; or with an influential early work like *Les Demoiselles d'Avignon* (1907), which concentrated on formal compression and geometric shapes at the expense of colour. Indeed, Richard Axsom (1979, 52) calls *Parade* 'the *Demoiselles d'Avignon* of the dance world' – the first truly modern ballet; just as Gertrude Stein maintained that 'the pure period of cubism, that is to say the cubism of cubes, found its final expression in *Parade*'.[58] The additional perspective of time and the amalgamation of other Cubist elements in the theatre makes this conclusion the more relevant.

As Satie's primary concern was to apply the principles rather than the minutiae of Cubist art to music, I believe that it is misleading to look for detailed equivalents of

Parade in contemporary paintings. It is equally misguided to equate his simplicity and clarity in both vision and attainment with any sort of naivety on Satie's part. Indeed these elements come only from the distillation of complexity through mature experience, and amid the abstract theorizing which characterizes so much of the writing about Cubism in its various stages of development, there was a positive need for the uncluttered vision that Satie's friends saw him as possessing. As Fernande Olivier, Picasso's mistress in his Montmartre days (1904–12), says (Vy, 65):

> The only person that I heard argue clearly and simply about Cubism was Erik Satie. I believe that he alone, if he had written on Cubism, could have made it easily comprehensible. But he would doubtless have done it in such a manner that the painters concerned would have disowned it. It would have been too clear!

The parallel between Satie's disinclination to write about Cubism and his refusal to discuss the way he composed suggests that the two were of equal importance in his mind. He followed Picasso's career with interest, and as he owed his 'return to classical simplicity' in *Socrate* to his 'Cubist friends', it is not fanciful to see in *Socrate* a combination of the linear, monochrome flatness of early Cubism with Picasso's attraction towards the Classical style of Ingres after 1915, with all the restraint and stylization that this implies. Lambert aptly compares *Socrate* with the printer's art too (1934, 121), wherein 'the lettering is graceful, the margins well proportioned, and the occasional decorative capitals have a grave charm, but there is no alternation in style and make-up because one page happens to be more tragic in content than another'. Satie, as we have seen, attached great importance to the way music was printed, and an indication of how good he might have been in explaining the intricacies of Cubism can be found in his 1922 article on Stravinsky, where he discusses his novel use of the mechanical pianola by means of some apt graphic analogies (Ve, 40). 'The difference in technique between the pianola and the piano makes one think not so much of the distinction between Photography and Drawing, as of the reproduction methods of lithography in comparison with direct strokes on paper. For, to summarize, the lithographer plays the pianola, whilst the artist himself plays the piano.'

Satie's own drawings represent a coherent corpus worthy of serious consideration, in which design and invention achieve a perfect balance. Whilst they are illustrative rather than Cubist, the flattened perspective is usually present and many of them contain fantastic geometrical designs, as well as curious, imaginative texts. Bryars (1976, 316) usefully compares this 'use of isolated facts as a means of giving a picture of a whole state of affairs' with Satie's music, 'where ideas are seldom, if ever, developed and are only stated in their logically-primitive form'.[59]

Satie's collaboration with Picasso continued in 1923 with a *divertissement* entitled *La Statue retrouvée*, written for a masked ball (*L'Antiquité sous Louis XIV*) at the home of his new patron, Comte Etienne de Beaumont, on 30 May (see Fig. 10.5). This amounted to less than three minutes of music for organ, consisting of a brief 'Entrée'; two individual quests ('Recherches') for a lost statue; the discovery of the statue ('A deux (vers la statue)'); and an organ postlude (with added trumpet at the end).[60] This late score is reproduced here in full for the first time as Ex. 88. It is hardly first-

10.5   A masked ball at the Hôtel of Comte Etienne de Beaumont, 2 rue Duroc, 1923, showing
        the Count and Anna de Noailles.

rate Satie, but it marks his final collaboration with Cocteau, who devised the brief
scenario around the newly-restored eighteenth-century organ in the Beaumonts' music
salon in the rue Duroc. But even here they had an argument, for Satie wrote to the
Comtesse de Beaumont on 26 December 1922 that 'I'm very surprised to see that Jean
shares the prejudice of the masses against the organ. . .Odd, isn't it?. . .Yes. I very

Ex. 88 *Divertissement: La Statue retrouvée* (1923) (BN 9608, 2–9) © Bibliothèque Nationale, Paris, 1990

Ex. 88 (*cont.*)

much hope to win him over to our cause – our good cause. Yes. The organ isn't necessarily religious and funereal, good old instrument that it is. Just remember the gilt-painted merry-go-round' (Vl, 161). Then in February 1923 Satie brought in Picasso to design the scenery and costumes, and in April he introduced Massine to help with the dignified choreography, thus completing a reunion of the team who had collaborated on *Parade*. The dancers probably included the Comte and Comtesse de Beaumont, Mme Olga Picasso[61] and the Marquise de Medicis, so it is not surprising that Satie's score (Ex. 88) is stately and uncomplicated, with each chord individually numbered to correspond with a step in the quest for the statue. In mid-May rehearsals began, and Satie was finishing the final number (Ex. 88, letter D onwards) for Mme René Jacquemaire.[62] At the last minute, however, she was replaced by the irrepressible Mme Daisy Fellowes (niece of the Princesse de Polignac), with whom Satie was infinitely delighted. 'At last! I find an interpreter with some *initiative*', he told the Comtesse on 24 May (Vc), and he added a trumpet solo to her final number and a 'special episode' for her (the 'Entrée' in Ex. 88) between that date and the slightly delayed première on 30 May. Despite its simple nature, the final number (letter D) went through three complete revisions before Satie was satisfied with it (BN 9607, 10–11) and the 'Entrée' two revisions. The first bass-line of the 'Entrée' (in square brackets) shows Satie replacing cadential progressions with parallel fifths between the outer parts. Both this and the way the harmonies keep moving chromatically until the last moment in the very individual cadence (Ex. 88 bars 3b–4: with the accompaniment above the melody) are typical of Satie's final years.

Then in the first half of 1924, Picasso, Massine and Satie again collaborated on *Mercure*, this time for Comte Etienne de Beaumont's Soirées de Paris, a series of chic, but ill-organized spectacles that borrowed their title from the review founded in 1912 as a vehicle for Apollinaire's talents. For this 'purely decorative' ballet, Picasso wrote the scenario as well as devising the scenery and costumes, and Satie infinitely preferred this direct collaboration with the artist, which cut out Cocteau as the troublesome intermediary. About this time, Satie made an exceptionally long statement on his views about composing ballets to the painter Moise Kisling (1952, 108–9), which is worth reproducing in full as it seems to be wholly genuine:

> The importance lies in beginning things where they ought to begin and not being troubled by what should be the final goal! Thus I maintain that one should first see the characters dance before writing the music that should illustrate their movements. The choreographer cares only for himself; the female dancer cares only for spectacular effects that will bring applause. And who cares about the composer – about his sensibility, indeed, about his message? No-one! People usurp it, or cast it aside, and in the end the only one who has something to say and who knows the reasons behind his works, finds himself again keeping them to himself, when he cannot tell a lie. What a drama! But we who know the music contained in each movement should be able to make our art like a machine – since it seems that no-one seeks more from it than that – and, all things being equal, I would prefer what I have imposed to what others try to impose upon me.

Whenever he talked about his art, Kisling says, Satie heated up, and on this occasion he felt so passionately about the subject that he left before he exploded into rage. But it seems to have been Massine and not the revered Picasso who annoyed him. From his hospital bed in 1925 he told Robert Caby (1952, 30) how Massine and Borlin had hurried him in *Mercure* and *Relâche*, threatening to 'demolish his plan. He was terribly constrained by this and maintained a secret and merciless grudge against them.' Though whether he agreed 'to certain repeats. . .against his will' in Act 2 of *Relâche* because 'he did not have time to bring other ideas to perfection' is doubtful, given the careful balancing we saw in chapter 8. Possibly the repeat of No. 12 as No. 17 and the transformation of No. 18 into No. 19 *within* Act 2 might substantiate this assertion, however. But it is certainly true that Satie, 'who "adored" commissions because they spurred him into the architectural crystallization' of his thoughts, liked 'to think about them and conceive them long in advance' (ibid.).

In the case of *Mercure*, the typed single-page scenario that Satie received from the Comte de Beaumont[63] was indeed a 'surprise', for in what must have been Picasso's original conception the tripartite ballet lasted only eight minutes. Satie must have discussed it with Picasso, for the finale of Tableau 3 (*Rapt de Proserpine*) has the word 'Cubisme' appended to it by Satie. Of all the sets designed by Picasso for *Mercure*, this bizarre collage comes closest to being Cubist in conception: Mercury strums a distorted stringed instrument (which might be a violin, guitar or lyre), whilst a collage of images of Proserpine appears above another such instrument that would not look out of place in an early Cubist creation.[64] Satie first annotated Picasso's plan in pencil, adding movement lengths and a key-scheme to correspond precisely with the timings proposed (see Fig. 10.6). But, either in later collaboration with Picasso, or during the

Movement title	In Universal Edition score		In BN 9596(2)	
	Key	No. of bars	Key	No. of bars
TABLEAU 1				
1. Ouverture	F	65	F	24
2. La Nuit	D min	24	D min	16
3. Danse de tendresse (=*Fugue-Valse, c.* 1906)	F	100	F	48
4. Signes du Zodiaque	D–C	30	C	12
5. Entrée et danse de Mercure (Final)	F / C–F	16] / 48]	A / F	16] / 32]
TABLEAU 2				
6. Danse des Grâces	D–Bb	64	Bb (orig. C)	32
7. Bain des Grâces	Eb	16	Eb	16
8. Fuite de Mercure	no key	12	C (orig. Bb)	16
9. Colère de Cerbère	C	16	(=8+9)	
TABLEAU 3				
10. Polka des lettres	F	24	F	16
11. Nouvelle Danse	A	32	A	16
12. Le Chaos (=10+11)	C	24	C	16
13. Final: Rapt de Proserpine	F	60	F	32
	(ends in F min)	531		292

10.6   Plan of *Mercure* (1924).

process of composition, Satie virtually doubled the length of *Mercure* to around fifteen minutes, and changed the key-scheme in the centre to give greater tonal variety. He also made Tableau 3 more substantial, and generally expanded the important numbers that framed each tableau. The only elements that remained unaltered were the key-scheme of Nos. 1–3 and 10–13 in Figure 10.6; the decision to centre the ballet in F major (though it ends in F minor); and the conception of the *Bain des Grâces* (No. 7) as a 16-bar movement in E♭ major. This suggests that the *Bain des Grâces* was intended as the central focus-point of *Mercure*, and Satie took the exceptional step of scoring it for strings alone – probably to make a stark contrast with the Graces themselves, who were actually men in drag. Figure 10.6 shows all these points more clearly, as well as demonstrating that there were far fewer repeated movements than in the interlocking scheme for *Relâche* (see Fig. 8.11). Satie kept repeated material to a minimum here, almost certainly because he wanted to match Picasso's series of different 'poses plastiques' with different music. Only Tableau 1 shows signs of having been conceived as a unified entity through recurring material. Indeed, the key scheme, the regular section lengths and the avoidance of popular themes make *Mercure* entirely different from *Relâche*. The only sign that Satie was pressed for time comes in the *Danse de tendresse*, which borrows an earlier *Fugue-Valse* from his Schola Cantorum period (BN 9635, 4–9, *c.* 1906) and expands it by twenty bars by repeating an internal section at different transposed pitches. But if we consider that its 100 bars make up almost one-fifth of *Mercure*, Satie's accusation of being hurried by Massine seems more relevant. As he told Massine on 7 April 1924: 'Don't worry. I'm finishing Part Two. . . I can't possibly go any faster. . .I can't hand over to you work which I couldn't defend. You who are conscience personified will understand me' (Vl, 170).

Whilst Satie knew well that Picasso was 'an egotist',[65] and whilst the Comte de Beaumont maintained (1925–6, 56) that 'in *Mercure* the musician and choreographer served purely as accompaniment to the painter', Satie nonetheless found the collaboration with Picasso extremely fulfilling and enjoyable. As Picasso knew far less about music than Satie knew about painting, he probably gave him the freedom to express himself as he wished. This view is borne out by Satie's interview with Pierre de Massot shortly before the première of *Mercure*. As Satie said (*Paris-Journal*, 30 May 1924, 2):

> Though it has a subject, this ballet has no plot. It is a purely decorative spectacle and you can imagine the marvellous contribution of Picasso which I have attempted to translate musically. My aim has been to make my music an integral part, so to speak, with the actions and gestures of the people who move about in this simple exercise. You can see poses like them in any fairground. The spectacle is related quite simply to the music-hall, without stylization, or any rapport with things artistic. In other respects, I always return to the sub-title 'Poses plastiques', which I find magnificent.

Whilst Picasso's contribution appears to give free rein to his fantasy and invention and to represent a new departure, there are still similarities with his earlier work. The Classical theme, for instance, had appealed to him since 1918, and as Douglas Cooper says (1968, 59), we can trace his use of free-flowing continuous line back to his drawings of 1917 and to a group of engravings done in 1922–3. He had also made use of the separation of line and colour in several paintings of the previous two years. In other words, Picasso took advantage of *Mercure* (as he had in *Parade*) to try out in the theatre a number of new techniques which he had found and explored in his paintings.

Mercure gave Picasso the chance to experiment with the projection of flat images into more palpable forms. While he often transferred painted images into sculpture, in *Mercure* he was able to go one stage further by projecting them into human form in the 'plastic poses' he created with Massine's help. This, of course, was at the opposite end of the spectrum from the flattened surfaces of Cubism, and was only attainable in the theatre. But the overriding image of the sets for *Mercure* is of the superposition of calligraphic designs on flat cut-out images, in which the minimum of painting is involved. As Gertrude Stein observed (cited in Vy, 79): 'In Europe, calligraphy has always been considered a minor art, but for the Spaniard Picasso, calligraphy is an art in itself. . . The scenery of *Mercure*. . .was written, quite simply written. There was no painting, it was pure calligraphy, something which lived inside him without the help of association with either ideas or emotions.' Given Satie's love of calligraphy and his avoidance of emotion or sentiment in his music, we can begin to understand why *Mercure* proved such an ideal collaboration for him.

Satie's links with the nihilistic Dada movement were understandably less productive, and involved writing and political intrigue rather than music. As Satie's career progressed, he moved further and further towards the left. As early as 1908 he was an active member of the Radical-Socialist Committee in Arcueil, and he joined the official Socialist Party on the day after the assassination of Jean Jaurès (31 July 1914), switching to the Communist Party after the Congress of Tours in December 1920. He loved to shock his society patrons with his Bolshevist sympathies, and whilst Templier (1969, 72) maintains that he 'knew absolutely nothing of Marxist doctrines', he was a fervent supporter of Lenin and was seen weeping in public on the day of his death (21 January 1924). In this respect Satie must have been at odds with Picabia, who thought that Lenin 'had succeeded in exploiting his ambition at the expense of his compatriots', and that one autocratic rule had merely replaced another after the 1917 Revolution.[66] Satie, as a poor composer with nothing to lose, was attracted to the concept of revolution in both art and life, and never considered (as his left-wing friend Koechlin did) that Communism could be detrimental to the future of art. Indeed, he found his Communist friends in the Arcueil 'Soviet' 'disconcertingly *Bourgeois*' in 1921 as far as art was concerned (BN 9670, 15). He found Bolshevist sympathisers among the Diaghilev ballet company in 1917, and undoubtedly supported Diaghilev in unfurling the Red Flag on stage at the opening of their season on 10 May, the week before the première of *Parade*. Thus his involvement in the Dada movement from 1919 onwards was predictable, and he supported its extremist founder Tristan Tzara throughout its short existence and is known to have collaborated with him on operatic plans in 1924.[67]

The Dada movement was renowned for its intrigues between rivalling factions, in which adherents like Picabia took delight in changing sides, often out of pure devilry. Indeed, a chronicle of the complex allegiances of the participants is far more interesting than any of their artistic products.[68] Cocteau's attempts to infiltrate Dada ranks and maintain his leadership of the avant-garde could alone fill a separate chapter, which would help to explain why Satie became so hostile towards him. In general, Satie supported the less doctrinaire and more talented Dadaists, like Picabia, Man Ray and Marcel Duchamp, and if his initial involvement was peripheral, it soon became less so. He is first mentioned by Picabia in February 1919 in his 'tableau-message' *Mouvement Dada*, when the Dada headquarters were still in Zurich. Satie's music was performed (with recitations) at a 'Dada-Soirée' in Zurich that year by Suzanne Perrottet.[69] Satie received Tzara's review *Dada* at this time, but when Tzara moved to Paris in January 1920, the poet André Breton temporarily turned him against Satie by warning him of his links with Cocteau. This Satie never forgave. After the failure of the Congrès de Paris (convened by Breton in February 1922 to establish a Dada constitution and himself as leader), Satie took great delight in assuming the presidency of Breton's public trial at the Closerie des Lilas on 17 February. Tzara, who had been under attack by Breton at the Congress, found a welcome ally in Satie, though at this stage Picabia supported the Breton camp, and even planned to found a new Salon with Breton as late as 1923. The Closerie des Lilas episode spelt the beginning of the end for Dadaism (which had always existed as an iconoclastic spirit rather than as an organized movement). Similarly, *Relâche* in 1924 marked the end of Picabia's short-lived extension of the spirit of Dadaism in Instantanéisme, as well as the downfall of Picabia's journal *391*, to which Satie contributed in 1921 and 1924.

In July 1923, Tzara had organized a 'happening' in which his 1922 supporters took part at the Théâtre Michel. This was known as *La Soirée du Cœur à barbe* after the journal *Le Cœur à barbe*, to whose sole issue of April 1922 Satie had also contributed, together with Rrose Sélavy (Marcel Duchamp) and Paul Eluard. The chaotic soirée on 6 July featured a pitched battle by Breton (in defence of Picasso) and Pierre de Massot, after which Breton was expelled by the police. Various works by members of Les Six were also performed; new films by Man Ray were shown; and Satie and Marcelle Meyer played the *Trois Morceaux en forme de poire*. The planned second performance predictably never took place, but Satie had declined to participate in a letter to Tzara on 7 July before he knew of this, adding: 'I like you a lot. . .but I don't like Breton and the others' (Vl, 186). He had relished the idea of Tzara's 'comic' soirée and the potential battle the day before, and on 9 July he told Jean Guérin how 'peculiar' the whole event had been, and how much it had 'delighted' Picasso. But once was enough, and he was probably disappointed by the lack of enthusiasm shown for his music amid the other distractions. The battle with Breton and Aragon, now the leaders of the new Surrealist movement, continued after the première of *Mercure* in 1924, when they were joined in their support of Picasso (at the expense of Satie) by Auric and Poulenc. Even if it had had other leaders, the Surrealists' concepts of automatic writing and the exploration of the subconscious mind were anathema to Satie, and as things were, both Aragon and

Breton were more actively opposed to music than most Dadaists were. Indeed, one wonders what Poulenc and Auric saw to support in them beyond the potential of their poetry for musical settings. According to Poulenc, 'Breton detested all music' (Vy, 58) – Satie's comic songs in particular – and Satie referred to the Surrealists in contempt as 'faux-Dadas'. The final battle over *Relâche* was lost as much by Satie's final illness as by any other factor, and it is encouraging to find later Surrealists – like E. L. T. Mesens, René Magritte and Joan Miró – taking a more mature view and paying posthumous homage to Satie's achievement in both words and painting.

It is fortunate for Satie that Picasso was above taking sides, and that Satie managed to persuade Picabia to work with him, otherwise *Mercure* and *Relâche* might never have taken place, and Satie might have carried the nihilistic stigma of Dadaism with him to the grave. As it was his reputation took a long time to re-establish itself after the uproar generated by his 1924 ballets, and there can be no doubt that the excitement of participation in Dadaism and writing articles for ephemeral associated journals like *Action*, *Le Mouvement accéléré* and *Création* diverted his energies from composition. So too did work on Cocteau and Radiguet's libretto for *Paul & Virginie*. This three-act opéra-comique[70] occupied Satie intermittently between August 1920 and 1923, and intensively between July 1921 and October 1922 (which largely accounts for the missing year in his composing career). An announcement in *Le Coq* in 1920[71] stated bluntly that 'On November 22 there took place the reading to Erik Satie of PAUL ET VIRGINIE [*chez* Cocteau]. . .PAUL ET VIRGINIE will be Satie's next work and his farewell to musical composition. Subsequently he intends to devote himself entirely to the cause of young musicians.' We know from Satie's letters and other accounts that he laboured hard on this now lost opera. In September 1921 (see Fig. 10.7) he told Cocteau that he was 'working on the second act – which is *progressing* very badly (much too heavy). As soon as I have the inspiration for it, I intend to write my score *very rapidly*. It's an experiment I want to undertake and *succeed* in – in the Rossini style, what!'[72] He even told Cocteau early in October 1921 that he wanted to write his score as swiftly as Rossini had written *The Barber of Seville* – in a single concentrated span (see Volta, *RIMF*, 1989, 57). Given Satie's track record, this experiment was doomed to failure, but he clearly wanted *Paul & Virginie* to be light, sparkling and spontaneous, and seemingly he was even prepared to change his compositional approach to achieve this.

Earlier that summer, Satie had worked on the scenery and costumes with André Derain, and in October he wanted Pierre Bertin to play the role of Paul, though Cocteau (as always) claimed he had a better idea. On 26 November 1921 Satie signed a contract with the impresario Jacques Hébertot, and *Paul & Virginie* was scheduled for performance at the Théâtre des Champs-Elysées in May 1922. But when this date drew near, the opera was still not finished and Diaghilev was now in dispute with Hébertot over who should produce it. In the summer of 1922 Hébertot was still pressing Satie to complete his opera for the coming Winter season, and Satie told Cocteau's mother on 21 July that 'I am working on it as much as I can – more even' (Vc). Composition was still advancing in August, but in October Rolf de Maré wanted a new work for

10.7   Letter to Jean Cocteau, 5 September 1921, describing work on the second Act of
Paul & Virginie (US-NYpm).

the Ballets Suédois, and Satie admitted to Paulette Darty that he was 'not very joyful'
about *Paul & Virginie*.[73] His interest seems to have petered out in 1923 and he told Jean
Guérin on 2 December that 'Cocteau continues to annoy me with his intrigues. I have
come to detest *Paul & Virginie*' (Vc).

On the other hand, Satie told Koechlin early in 1924 that the three acts of the opera
were 'nearly finished' (Koechlin, 1924, 207), and Milhaud in *Les Feuilles libres* (1924,
46) also speaks of it as if it had been completed before he began *Mercure*. As Satie
was not given to destroying his manuscripts, the opera will doubtless materialize one
day and change our perception of Satie the composer. But at present all that survives
are a few rudimentary sketches (see Appendix) and five pages of plans for dividing
Act 1 into eleven scenes, which include a short 'Danse de Virginie' and a 'Petite Marche
du Gouverneur (Huit mesures)' in scene 5. The start, with its Sailors' Chorus of basses
(*La 'Belle Cubaine'*) split up by recitatives for the female characters is given as Figure
10.8, with the complete cast list and their vocal ranges in Figure 10.9. There are,
however, some notable differences here with the 1973 published edition of the libretto.
Virginie's wicked aunt is listed as 'Mademoiselle de Charmillac' and referred to as
'La Marquise' in the edition, whereas in Figure 10.9 she is the 'Comtesse d'Herbeville'.

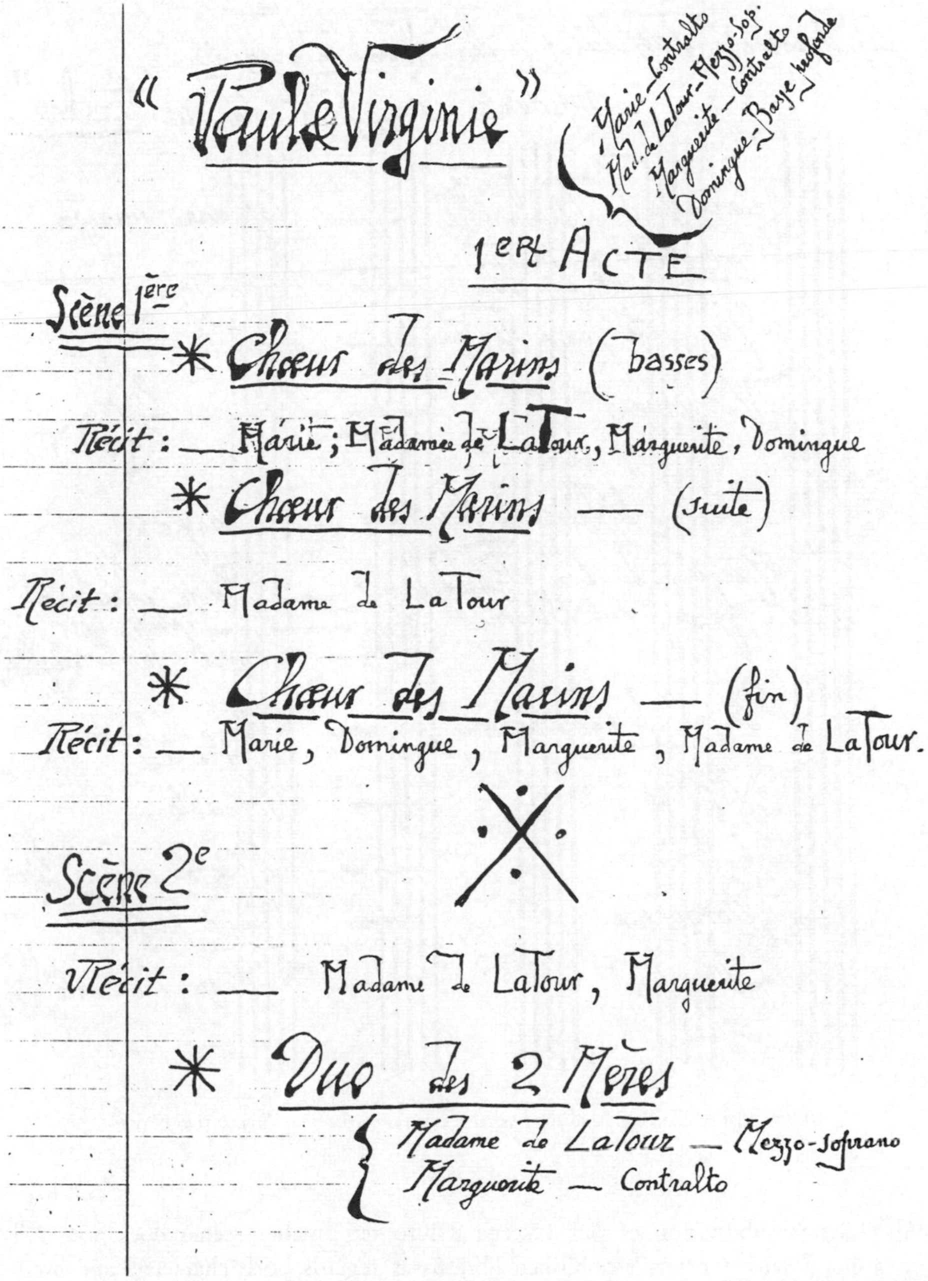

"Paul & Virginie"

Marie — Contralto
Mad.I LaTour — Mezzo-Sop.
Marguerite — Contralto
Dominique — Basse profonde

1er ACTE

Scène 1ère

※ Chœur des Marins (basses)

Récit : — Marie ; Madame de LaTour, Marguerite, Dominique
※ Chœur des Marins — (suite)

Récit : — Madame de LaTour

※ Chœur des Marins — (fin)
Récit : — Marie, Dominique, Marguerite, Madame de LaTour.

Scène 2e

Récit : — Madame de LaTour, Marguerite

※ Duo des 2 Mères
{ Madame de LaTour — Mezzo-Soprano
  Marguerite — Contralto

10.8   The first page of Satie's scenic plan for Act 1 of the opera *Paul & Virginie* (1920?).
The 'Chœur des Marins' is also known as *La 'Belle Cubaine'* (US-NYpm).

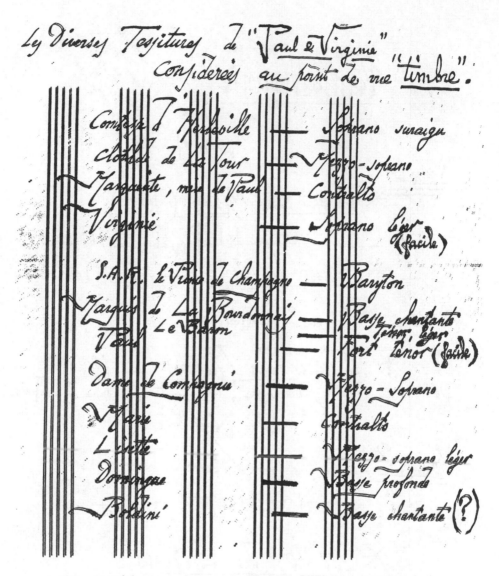

10.9   List of characters and their vocal tessituras for *Paul & Virginie* (US-NYpm).

Also, Satie's subdivision of Act 1 scene 2 into ten smaller scenes does not easily correspond with Cocteau's published libretto as regards both characters and events (especially in scenes 9–11). It therefore seems certain that Satie worked from an earlier version of the libretto which has since been lost. But, as always, Satie's planning was meticulous, and all we can surmise about his score is that it was compact, and that it bore some resemblance to the light neo-classical recitative style of *Le Médecin malgré lui*.

10.10   Satie, Jeanne Robert-Foster and Constantin Brancusi at the golf course at Saint-Cloud, 5 October 1923.

Besides being closely linked with painters, Satie also counted the Romanian sculptor Constantin Brancusi amongst his closest friends (see Fig. 10.10). Satie often wrote to him or visited him at his studio in the Impasse Ronsin, where everything was 'white and immobile', just as Satie had directed that *Le Fils des étoiles* should be in 1891. In the studio time stood still, and surrounded by sculptures whose honed simplicity paralleled Satie's music, Brancusi liked to photograph Satie with the camera purchased with Man Ray's advice in 1922. Figure 10.11 shows a later photo taken by Brancusi of the depressing entrance to Satie's lodgings in Arcueil.

Satie claimed he had found the key to composing *Paul & Virginie* in one of Brancusi's sculptures (Vy, 67), and in October 1921 he was so impressed by his bust of the Princesse Bibesco that he wanted to draw Derain a copy of it. For his part, Brancusi was greatly moved by the static beauty of *Socrate*, and under its influence sculpted a *Plato* and a *Socrate* himself. His bust of *Socrate*, polished to absolute smoothness like a Satie composition, can be seen at the centre of his studio (Vy, 66), whilst a preparatory sketch for this (bearing the words 'Dada brings us back to the matters of our time') can be seen on p. 67. Both Valentine Hugo and Satie described Brancusi as the 'brother of Socrates', and Shattuck (1952, 53) calls the *Messe des pauvres* sculptural music 'which gives the impression of turning on its pedestal like an object by Brancusi'. It is a great pity that Brancusi's designs for Satie's tomb were never carried through.

Satie's other, more practical, contact with sculpture came through Man Ray, who he met at an exhibition of his paintings in Paris on 3 December 1921. As Ray recalls (1963, 115), afterwards

> we passed a shop where various household utensils were spread out in front. I picked up a flat-iron, the kind used on coal stoves, asked Satie to come inside with me, where, with his help, I acquired a box of tacks and a tube of glue. Back at the gallery I glued a row of tacks to the smooth surface of the iron, titled it, The Gift, and added it to the exhibition. This was my first Dada object in France.

Thus, Man Ray's *Cadeau*, the first of his French 'Ready-Mades',[74] was in fact a collaboration with Satie, who Ray described as 'the only musician who had eyes' (Ve, 240). With only a few changes, Ray translated Satie's article 'Ce que je suis' (from his *Mémoires d'un amnésique*) and used it to introduce himself at his retrospective exhibition at the Institute of Contemporary Arts in London in 1959.[75]

The final aspect of composition as related to the other arts that I should like to consider is Satie's music for René Clair's film *Entr'acte*, his final score (entitled *Cinéma*). Although the film was shot at the Théâtre des Champs-Elysées (see Fig. 10.12) and at Luna Park in mid-June 1924, Satie had still not received details of its final cut version by 23 October. But he told Roger Désormière on the same day that 'There will be no delay: everything is arranged with the copyist. It is all much simpler to write than *Mercure*, you know' (Vc). In *Cinéma*, Satie discovered the ideal medium for his technique of composing in short juxtaposed contrasting motifs, to which eight appearances of the opening 8-bar motif[76] gave a sort of unity. Here it was the non-realistic musical equivalent of a film cutting from image to image that was revolutionary,

10.11   The staircase to Satie's room at 22 (now 34) rue Cauchy, Arcueil.

10.12   On the terrace of the Théâtre des Champs-Elysées during the filming of René Clair's *Entr'acte* in June 1924. From left to right: René Clair, Rolf de Maré, Jean Borlin, two unknowns, Jimmy Berliet (cameraman), Germaine Everling, Erik Satie.

rather than the musical content: 'furniture music' transferred to the cinema, as it were. As Satie predicted, the score emerged (through-composed) with relative ease,[77] and it is gratifying to realize that Satie, at the very end of his career, had at last found the perfect outlet for his idiosyncratic and objective approach to composition. Here development was redundant, virtuosity distracting, and the invention of ideas and textures paramount.

Ex. 89 *Cinéma* (1924), end of section 3 and start of section 4 (Salabert, pf solo version 4–5)

Just one example must suffice to show how this brilliant score, which seems to have no independent life of its own, is as inseparable from its film as Picabia maintained. At the start of Ex. 89 at the end of section 3, a paper boat drifts windborn across the roofs of Paris with a sudden change of texture into the treble to contrast with the rain of the previous subsection. This is the only time that Satie uses triplets in the score, and besides being poetic it serves to introduce section 4 in triple time, which begins in bar 9 of Ex. 89. This, incidentally, marks the appearance of the bearded *male* ballerina! The oscillating phrase at the start of Ex. 89 anticipates the coming melody of section 4, as well as relating to the main rondo theme, and it is perhaps not too fanciful to suggest a link with the Scottish 'Skye Boat Song' here. Further, the two ideas are interspersed by abrupt cadential chords (Ex. 89 bars 7–8) to mirror the cutting from image to image at this point. The boat is still heading towards the ballerina's studio, but its passage is interrupted by more dramatic shots, like water pouring onto the board on which Marcel Duchamp has just been playing chess with Man Ray, or the Place de la Concorde with moving traffic. Throughout Satie's score, cadences and sudden halts help emphasize the film's construction from 346 carefully enumerated images,[78] though as *Entr'acte* moves towards its climax on the roller-coaster in Luna Park, the pace of the music accelerates and the obvious cadences disappear. Many of the sections have to be repeated to fit the length of the film, and as Satie only specifies ten points of precise correlation (see Appendix), the synchronization has to be carefully worked out beforehand. But again, Satie must have realized that the film might not always be shown at the same speed, and so his aleatoric solution is more practical than it might appear.

Virgil Thomson (1951, 98) calls *Cinéma* 'the finest film score ever composed. . . it takes us back to the still innocent last days of Dada, before Surrealism had turned our fantasies sour, sexy and mean'. Satie would have been flattered, but I am sure he would have preferred the following summary by Picabia:[79] '*Entr'acte* does not believe in very much, in the pleasure of life perhaps; it believes in the pleasure of inventing, it respects nothing except the desire to burst out laughing, for laughing, thinking and working are of equal value and are indispensable to each other.' But it was Satie and René Clair who enjoyed the last laugh, for whilst Picabia's contribution is forgotten, *Entr'acte* lives on as the first true collaboration between music and the art of the cinema.

11

Satie on other composers

Satie had a wide knowledge of contemporary music, ranging from Lord Berners through Stravinsky to Malipiero. Even if he tended to see things in black and white, in terms of enemies versus friends, or 'pawns' versus poets, his perspective on current advances was quite remarkable given the confusion of those heady times. As he did not like being drawn into musical discussions, Satie refrained from stating chapter and verse, or from giving detailed criticism to other composers. But the young E. L. T. Mesens says (1952, 150) that Satie made original remarks with tact and discretion about his compositions, giving very curious advice, but without ever adopting the doctrinaire attitude so often found amongst musicians aware of their authority. He generally preferred to make comments through shrewd analogies, and the nearest Satie seems to have come to a precise observation was in the joke he made after the first performance of Debussy's *De l'aube à midi sur la mer* in October 1905. Hélène Jourdan-Morhange recalls (1945, 96) that Satie, 'overwhelming the admiring adjectives of the fervent Debussyists, cried out: "Ah! my old friend! There was especially a little moment between half-past ten and a quarter to eleven that I found amazing!"' As Satie was acutely aware of his role as an irreverent entertainer in both his letters and articles, he was never serious for long. But like Debussy he had a supreme talent for the apposite phrase and the serious word spoken in jest.

Where Satie acquired his knowledge remains something of a mystery. He preferred the company of anyone other than a professional musician. He generally disliked attending concerts of music other than his own, or that of his young protégés. There is no record of his analysing music other than a few rudimentary attempts at the Schola Cantorum, and when he went to libraries he read books rather than scores. Perhaps some of his views derived from opinions expressed by his friends Debussy or Dukas, or from the teaching of Roussel and d'Indy at the Schola Cantorum, but given his fierce independence even this is unlikely. Perhaps he studied scores in Debussy's library during his weekly visits, or borrowed scores to study in private in Arcueil, but there is no proof of this. Doubtless his excellent memory and his swift powers of perception of what was good or bad were his greatest assets, and for someone who preferred the art gallery to the concert hall, he must nonetheless have heard a great deal of music during his career. In any case, he could always cover himself with witty observations, like the one that opens Templier's study of Satie (1969, 1): 'Although our information is incorrect, we do not vouch for it.'

Satie's acquisition of relevant knowledge was made easier by his almost total rejection of the music of past generations. Most of what we know in this respect comes from his 1922 introduction to a concert by Marcelle Meyer (see Fig. 10.4), where all Satie did was to briefly look at her music and verify the dates of the composers concerned in Larousse. He only approaches fluency and safe ground when comparing the past to the present,[1] or when he comes to yet another ironical attack on music critics, whose ranks he resolutely refused to join.[2] Thus, all we know about Satie's views on Bach are that his 'style is grave, beautiful and tender' (Ve, 93) and that 'the idea of analysing' Fugue VII from *The Art of Fugue* 'terrified him exceedingly' at the Schola Cantorum.[3] Satie continued his plea to d'Indy as follows: 'I have not the necessary disposition; any more than the inclination, for I have always proceeded with words as I have with men – with sympathy or the opposite, not being any more of a physiognomist than I am an analyst.' And Satie proved his point by only getting as far as identifying the order of voices in the exposition and saying that the fugue in question was 'a vast stretto, more stretto than stretto. It's a stretto of great extent.'

But in his first 1922 article on Stravinsky (whose music he adored), we find that he admired Palestrina and Mozart for their 'transparency of sound', though 'the exquisite Mozart used it in such a way that it is impossible to tell how he achieved it' (W, 104). By comparison, Beethoven's craft was heavy, and Satie told Louis Lemonnier in 1897 that 'you are right to see in Beethoven a disturber of the public peace' (Vc). He admired Chopin as 'the definitive creator' of true piano music (Ve, 93), and his fondness for nineteenth-century French operettas can be seen in the number of themes he borrowed from this genre. His infinite preference for Offenbach[4] and Chabrier over Wagner or Florent Schmitt was a vote for lightness and Frenchness over complexity and Germanic heaviness. For patriotism played a large part in his instinctive (and subjective) taste. Most of the contemporary composers he wrote about were French, and the only other nations whose music he had time for were England and Italy. Above all, he hated fervent disciples: Wagnerites, Debussyists (and these came to include Ravel) and even Satieists – though he went to great lengths in 1920 to explain that 'there was no school of Satie' (Ve, 45) and that Les Six were independent personalities.

Although he considered that musical life revolved around Paris, Satie's background made him something of an anglophile.[5] He even planned an English tour in December 1916 in conjunction with Georges Jean-Aubry. 'War Emergency Concerts' were scheduled in London, Newcastle and Edinburgh before Satie's hatred of foreign travel and his need to work on *Parade* persuaded him to cancel them. Satie told his brother Conrad in 1914 that 'he had some regard' for Cyril Scott and Vaughan Williams as composers.[6] He had probably heard some of Scott's music *chez* Debussy, for Debussy wrote a perceptive certificate of appreciation for Scott in 1910, which said that 'This music unfolds – rather in the manner of these Japanese rhapsodies, which, instead of being confined to a traditional form, develop themselves according to the fantasy of countless arabesques.'[7] But Satie is more likely to have admired the way that Scott's 'rhythmic researches, technique, and even his way of writing might seem bizarre and disconcerting at first sight' (ibid.), for he naturally respected composers whose work resembled his own. In the case of Ralph Vaughan Williams, Satie probably met him while he was a pupil of Ravel in Paris in 1908, for the two composers were then on more friendly terms than they were after the War. In Vaughan Williams's career, his studies with Ravel came at a turning-point between his first and second periods, and Ravel's liberating influence can be seen in the sensuous sonorities of the song cycle *On Wenlock Edge* (especially in its addition of a string quartet). Whether Satie knew much of his music is doubtful, however. In the case of the eccentric Lord Berners, the similarities are so striking that Cecil Gray called him 'the English Satie'.[8] Berners was equally skilled in literature, painting and graphic design, and his aphoristic early experimental piano pieces all have French titles. The closest he comes to Satie's whimsical irony is in the *Dispute entre le papillon et le crapaud* (c. 1914–15) which has an accompanying watercolour cover and an illustrative story running through the music: just like the *Sports et divertissements*. But as even Berners's early copy of this (No. 12) was not put on sale until 1923, it is more likely that the influence came from Satie's humoristic piano pieces of 1913. *Le Poisson d'or* (with its poetic preface) and his *Trois Petites Marches funèbres*[9] of 1914 show Satiean influence in their conceptions, even if their musical content owes more to Stravinsky. Perhaps because of 'a misplaced desire to protect his own preserve' (Bryars, 1976, 309), but mainly, I suspect, because of Berners's inherited wealth, Satie was hostile towards him. He told E. L. T. Mesens (1952, 150) in 1921 that Lord Berners was 'a professional amateur. He hasn't understood.'

The Italian composer Satie most admired was Gian Francesco Malipiero. The turning-point in Malipiero's career came after hearing Stravinsky's *The Rite of Spring* in Paris in 1913, and it was probably the influence of Stravinsky and Debussy in powerful, imaginative compositions like the *Impressioni dal vero II* (1914–15) and *Pause del silenzio I* (1917) that led Satie to praise his 'great talent' in 1918.[10] At the opposite end of the Italian spectrum, Satie initially loathed the music of Alfredo Casella. As he told Henry Prunières on 3 April 1918:

> That's very true what you said about Casella. 'I don't like his music much because I find that in his music the form is generally lacking in sincerity and that he switches too easily from the style of Fauré to the style of Stravinsky.'
> You are severe but just – although very indulgent, because you could have added that he is *always* lacking in intelligence. Is it intelligent to depict Latin visions with Slavic means; to confuse the sky of Italy with the sky of Russia; to dress Romans as Cossacks?
> That's what our dear Casella does.
> So you are indulgent towards this poor man, who isn't a good man, fortunately.
> Before the war, he seemed to be a pianist; since then he proved that he never was. How will he play my music? Badly.								(Vl, 150–1)

This angry letter shows how closely Satie followed Casella's varied career, and he particularly disliked his eclectic assimilation of heterogeneous influences, and the absence of an authentic Italian voice in his early years. Thus within Casella's first period (before 1913), Satie, like Prunières, must have had in mind the Fauréan *Barcarola et scherzo* (Op. 4, 1903) in comparison with the Russian nationalist influence on the First Symphony (Op. 5, 1905–6). When Casella suddenly adopted an avant-garde manner in 1913–14 and began to assimilate the influences of Stravinsky, Bartók and late Debussy (as in the *Nove pezzi* (Op. 24, 1914)), Satie wrote him off as a jack-of-all-trades. He was not prepared to wait for an individual voice to emerge from the mish-mash of styles that confronted him, and probably because Casella had accepted an official position as professor of piano at the Licea di S. Cecilia in Rome in 1915, he dismissed him as a pianist too. Only after 1920, when Casella's style became more neo-classical and Italianate, did Satie begin to modify his earlier opinion. Casella's championship of young Italian composers helped, as no doubt did his friendship with Stravinsky (whose works he often conducted), and in May 1924 we find a much more benevolent Satie urging Casella to write to Rolf de Maré about a commission from the Ballets Suédois.[11] Satie's offer to support him paid off, for Casella's ballet *La Giara* (after Pirandello), with its Italian folk music influences, was performed at the Théâtre des Champs-Elysées on 19 November 1924, shortly before *Relâche*. Casella, who had conducted a performance of Satie's *Socrate* that September, was now on closer terms with him. On 14 September Satie told Casella how marvellous he anticipated that *La Giara* would be, on the basis of Rolf de Maré's description of the ballet.[12]

Such a volte-face was rare for the intransigent Satie, and one hopes that it was for purely musical reasons. Far more common was the move in the opposite direction, which often occurred after a personal slight, or from association with one of Satie's ever-increasing list of enemies. Such was the power of Satie's magnetic personality that this rejection seems to have assumed great importance for the composers concerned. But whereas Henri Sauguet was reinstated in Satie's good books in 1923, the break with Auric and Poulenc in 1924 was complete. Satie had met the precocious Auric in 1913, when as a youngster of only 13 he had published a complimentary article on Satie's music in the *Revue française de musique* that December. Thereafter their works regularly appeared together on the same programmes, and Satie's enthusiasm for his protégé reached its height in 1919. In a letter to the actor Pierre Bertin on 26 June, he classed Auric with his steadfast ally Darius Milhaud as 'two great artists for whom I have such a deep affection. . .These two artists are my consolation in the future and even in the present. I'm mightily glad to know they are there, strong and bold. I shall always march alongside these two men so full of steadfast courage' (Vl, 94). But that August, the first cracks began to appear in Satie's relations with Auric. As he told Valentine Hugo on 24 August, 'I'm not at all pleased with Auric. I know that he is *slandering* my *Furnishing Music*. That is his right; but it's mine to find it bad' (Vc). He became increasingly suspicious of Auric's growing attachment to the homosexual circle of Cocteau and Radiguet in 1922–3, and when the break came it was Auric rather than Poulenc who received the most cutting lashes from Satie's pen, for he had been the closest musically to Satie's ideals.

Satie regarded Poulenc as less mature[13] and more in need of help than Auric. Poulenc had drawn attention to himself in the Autumn of 1915 by writing to the most notable French composers for their opinions on César Franck. Satie's reply was wonderfully non-committal: 'Everything leads me to suppose that Franck was a huge musician. His work is astonishingly Franckist, in the best sense of the word' (Vl, 91). Then in September 1917, whilst awaiting the call-up for military service, Poulenc decided to study composition seriously. The pianist Ricardo Viñes suggested Paul Dukas as a teacher, who in turn sent him to Paul Vidal[14] at the Paris Conservatoire. When Vidal saw the dedication to Satie on Poulenc's *Rapsodie nègre*, he flew into a rage, saying: 'Your work is foul and inept. It's squalid *rubbish*. With these parallel fifths everywhere, you're just trying to mess me about; and where is this hole called Honolulu? Ah, I see you belong to the band of Stravinsky, Satie & Co.; so good night!'[15] Feeling confused and rejected, Poulenc confided the incident to Auric, who spoke to Satie about the problem. On 29 September, Satie sent Poulenc this advice (Poulenc, 1967, 14):

> I should like to see you. You seem to me to be lost, but easy to find. Fix a time and place to meet.
>
> Who is giving you such odd advice? It's funny.
>
> Never get mixed up with 'schools': there's been an explosion – quite natural, by the way.
>
> And then, in order to give you useful advice, I need to know what you are planning to do and are capable of doing.
>
> Your visit to Vidal was that of an *amateur pupil*, not of an *artist pupil*. He showed you that. He's one of the old school and he intimidated you.
>
> Laugh, my good friend.   (Vl, 93)

As Satie did not give technical criticism, Poulenc's *Rapsodie nègre* was performed as it stood at the Théâtre du Vieux-Colombier on 11 December 1917, and its success launched a career which far eclipsed that of Vidal. Both Satie and Stravinsky admired Poulenc's talent and facility, and in October 1923 Satie told Paul Collaer (Collaer, 1974, 14) that his recitatives for Gounod's *La Colombe* were 'staggering in their verve and exceedingly skilful. In short, the whole thing works.'

Milhaud was one of the few composers (with Dukas and Koechlin) who Satie stayed close to throughout his career. Satie obtained Diaghilev commissions for him – like writing the recitatives for Chabrier's opera *Une Education manquée* in 1923, which Milhaud repaid with the lucrative commission for 'furnishing music' from Mrs Eugène Meyer (Junior). Just as he had helped Debussy out of artistic crises, so Satie did the same for Milhaud when he thought his music was coming too close to Stravinsky's. If he did not attend all the premières of Milhaud's music,[16] he was always complimentary about it, and he referred to Milhaud affectionately as 'Dada'. From his lecture introducing Les Six to Brussels in April 1921 (Ve, 87–91), we can see that Satie divided the group into two halves. First, Auric, Poulenc and Milhaud, who were representative of the 'new spirit' and showed 'modern sensibility. . .spontaneity, fantasy and audacity'; and second, Durey, Honegger and Tailleferre, who were 'pure *impressionists*' and more conventional in their use of 'tried and tested formulae'. In February 1922 Satie deliberately excluded Honegger from Les Six in an article in *Les Feuilles libres* (Ve, 35), and for his part 'Honegger. . .never liked Satie's music', according to Poulenc (1978, 42). By 1924 the Six had dwindled to one (Milhaud) in Satie's view. Even in their heyday in 1921 they were never a homogeneous group, and what Satie had really intended to found in 1918 was a loose assemblage of Nouveaux Jeunes who met to give avant-garde concerts in the rue Huyghens. As this initial group included Satie himself, Milhaud, Koechlin and Roussel,[17] as well as Auric and Poulenc, the whole concept was flexibly based on youthfulness of spirit, as opposed to the 1923 Ecole d'Arcueil[18] where age was more of a criterion. The odd man out all through was Louis Durey, about whom Satie was extremely rude in private. He parodied his style in the first dance of *La Belle Excentrique* as early as 1920, telling Cocteau on 26 August that he was 'off to the Jardin des Plantes to see some fellow animals. They will give me some ideas. They aren't swine like Durey!' (Vc).

Otherwise Satie divided composers into poets and pawns. In the first category were Liszt, Chopin, Schubert and Mussorgsky: in the second, Satie placed only Rimsky-Korsakov,[19] but he might well have added other composers that he railed about at one time or another, like Florent Schmitt, Saint-Saëns and Ambroise Thomas. Whilst Debussy is listed as a 'poet-musician',[20] Satie is also careful to give Wagner due credit as a 'dramatic poet'. He also admired the audacity and novelty of the American George Antheil, but as far as Bartók was concerned, Satie was for once at a loss. When Poulenc invited both composers to a dinner in 1922, he recalled (1978, 24) that 'they looked at each other as a Martian would look at an inhabitant of the moon'.

In general, Satie was not given to shades of grey in his opinions, but his relations with Ravel were more complex than most. He met Ravel around 1893 at the café La Nouvelle Athènes in the Place Pigalle, which since the mid-1870s had been a rendezvous for Impressionist painters. Satie's friend Marcellin Desboutin was a frequent visitor there, and so was Ravel's father, Joseph. Ravel acknowledged Satie's influence on his music: notably in the *Ballade de la Reine morte d'aimer* (1893) and *Les Entretiens de la Belle et de la Bête* from the *Mother Goose* suite (1910), which Ravel called 'the fourth *Gymnopédie*'. Ravel gave Satie a copy of the suite, bearing a dedication 'to Erik Satie, grandfather of the *Entretiens* and other pieces, with the affectionate homage of a disciple' (Ve, 244). He also dedicated the third of his Mallarmé settings ('Surgi de la croupe et du bond') to Satie in 1913.

In January 1909 Ravel decided to found a new concert-giving organization devoted to contemporary music (the Société Musicale Indépendante) as he considered that the Société Nationale had become too reactionary in its choice of programmes. The first SMI concert on 20 April 1910 included the première of *Ma Mère l'Oye*, and in his search for original composers neglected by the Société Nationale, Ravel's sights quite naturally fell on Satie. Thus the early works of Satie were 'discovered' at an SMI concert in the Salle Gaveau on 16 January 1911, when Ravel insisted on playing the second *Sarabande* himself, perhaps because of its harmonic influence on Debussy, whom he had been accused of imitating. When the *Sarabande* was published later that year by

Rouart-Lerolle, Satie revoked its original dedication 'to my friend Arthur Dodement' and re-dedicated it in gratitude to Ravel.[21]

But even at this high-water mark, the relationship between the two composers was little more than one of formal courtesy. Satie seems to have distrusted Ravel's motives and considered him too much of an establishment figure who sought to shine at Debussy's expense. As he told his brother Conrad in 1911, Ravel is 'a Prix de Rome of great talent. . .a more showy version of Debussy!'[22] When his young Belgian protégé Roland-Manuel decided to study with Ravel rather than at the Schola Cantorum (as Satie had intended), Satie's antipathy towards Ravel increased. After Roland-Manuel had written a minuet in 1912 'on the blessed name of our great Ravel', Satie told him on 29 August that 'You ought to have written a solemn march rather than a minuet. Perhaps you will do so' (Vc). When Jean-Aubry asked him to write an article on Ravel after the War, Satie declined on 19 November 1919, saying that 'this article may not be very much to your taste. The fault lies entirely with the deplorable and outmoded aesthetic professed by our friend. It would be difficult for me to water down what my thinking dictates. I love Ravel deeply, but his art leaves me cold, alas!' (Vl, 89).

In 1920, egged on by Cocteau, Satie's views became more extreme. No doubt Ravel's dislike of *Socrate* came as a turning-point in their relations, as it had done with Roland-Manuel. As Milhaud recalled in 1957: 'He didn't understand it, that's all. And he told me that he could never agree with a work which for him was so poor – in invention, poor in everything.'[23] Satie's famous aphorism, that 'Ravel refuses the Légion d'Honneur but all his music accepts it', appeared in *Le Coq* in May 1920, and various other vitriolic attacks appear in his contemporary notebooks, like 'Ravel is the ring-leader of the sub-Debussyists.' Satie even told Milhaud that August that 'Ravel is a fool; he disgusts me by his superior manner' (Vc), and to Cocteau he observed that 'Ravel puts in the punctuation, but forgets to write anything underneath' (Ve, 245).

During 1921–2, Satie continued to belittle what he supposed had been Ravel's attempts to seek glory through his dangerous war work as a driver with the 13th Artillery Regiment, and his observations are uncharitable to say the least. But Ravel remained impervious to the attacks of the 'genial but clumsy precursor',[24] in public anyway. He explained this by saying that he did not 'retain the slightest malice against this big child. He was from Normandy, it's true, but he was a big child all the same.'[25] It was no doubt the dandified air of benevolent condescension that Satie most objected to, but Satie must have appeared childish at times to others as well.

The one composer, besides Debussy, for whom Satie showed unswerving admiration was Igor Stravinsky. They first met at Debussy's house in the Avenue du Bois de Boulogne in June 1911, at a luncheon shortly after the première of *Petrushka*,[26] when they photographed each other. As Stravinsky says of Satie (1979, 67): 'He was certainly the oddest person I ever met, but the most rare and consistently witty person too. I had a great liking for him and he appreciated my friendliness, I think, and liked me in return.' Stravinsky added the 'ice-cream wagon Valse' to his 'Three Easy Pieces' for piano duet in 1915 'in homage to Erik Satie', trying to 'portray something of his *esprit*' in it.[27] In return, Satie dedicated his song *Le Chapelier* to Stravinsky in 1916. The first variation in the central movement of his Sonata for two pianos (1943–4) is pure Satie too.

For his part, Satie eagerly anticipated a private performance of *Renard* in October 1918 at the home of its dedicatee, the Princesse Edmond de Polignac, telling her 'We shall have a fine show with *Renard*, for the work of Stravinsky is good, *very good*' (Vc). On 19 June 1923 he told Diaghilev that he was 'once again "licking his ears" over *Les Noces*' (Vc), and he had hoped to get his ballet *La Naissance de Vénus* performed in the same programme as Stravinsky's masterpiece, as we have seen. In 1918 Satie had tried in vain to prevent the publication of parts of *Le Coq et l'Arlequin* which he considered unjust to Stravinsky (Ve, 251), and when he wrote his first article on Stravinsky for *Vanity Fair* in July 1922, he carefully obtained his address from Poulenc and wrote to Stravinsky asking for detailed information about his life and works. This unprecedented piece of research shows how important this article was for Satie. As he stressed to Stravinsky during their ensuing correspondence that August: 'I do not presume to judge you: I admire you and I shall only speak of the beautiful "Light" that you are.'[28] What most impressed Satie was the clarity and transparency of sound Stravinsky achieved, even in his most complex works. 'If you listen to any work by Stravinsky', Satie enthused, 'you cannot fail to be struck by the extraordinary clearness with which you can perceive the "transparence" of vibration I have mentioned. *The Rite of Spring* is full of it; and it is perhaps in this work that it appears at its most forceful, at its most persuasive' (Ve, 63–4). Then Satie praises Stravinsky's conscientious pursuit of technical perfection, his skills as an orchestral conductor in rehearsal, and his power to 'shake the masses' through his

> dynamism. . .Where Stravinsky shows us all the richness of his musical power is in his use of 'dissonance'. Here he reveals himself and plunges us into a vast intellectual ecstasy. What a wonderful Magician!
>
> For him, 'dissonance' means 'pressure', and through it he 'leans' on the sensibility of the informed listener. His 'dissonance' is in no way harsh; it occurs 'in the wings', all glistening, always with a function.
>
> (Ve, 64)

Satie also praised Stravinsky as a 'liberator' for whom absolute Truth in art did not exist. He found in him a supporter in the battle against Wagner, and in his second article, for Marcel Raval's journal *Les Feuilles libres* (Ve, 38–41), he elevates Stravinsky to his zenith of musical esteem, as follows:

> For us wicked trouble-makers, Igor Stravinsky is one of the most remarkable geniuses who has ever existed in Music. The lucidity of his mind has liberated us; his fighting strength has granted us rights that we can never lose again. That is indisputable.
>
> His penetrating power is more incisive than Debussy's and cannot be blunted: it is too finely tempered. Stravinsky has such a variety of methods, such a sense of invention, that one can only remain amazed.

Recently, *Mavra* cast the musical world into a most instructive confusion. We have been able to read several admonishments from the Critics, each one more ludicrous than the other. Because they have understood nothing, it was much easier for these Gentlemen to 'run the thing down'. . .Soon they will understand it – too well, even – take it from me; and they will reveal *Mavra* to us, pointing out all its merits – agricultural and civic – and will take all the credit for it, without the slightest qualm.

Thus, Satie was one of the first to appreciate Stravinsky's *opera buffa*, as *Mavra* had only been performed at the Paris Opéra on 3 June 1922. He followed Stravinsky's career with interest as it unfolded, with admiration untinged by jealousy, and if there are conceptual links between *Petrushka* and *Parade*, these are entirely due to Cocteau. Their relationship was one of mutual respect, without any signs of imitation on Satie's part. He was never overawed by Stravinsky's rising dramatic genius, as Debussy was in his final years, and for his part Stravinsky rightly placed Satie in the forefront of French musical advance into the present century. As he exclaimed after hearing *Socrate* performed in Adrienne Monnier's bookshop in 1919: 'There is Bizet, Chabrier, and Satie' (Ve, 251).

12

Satie and the wider world

By the end of 1924, Satie's persistent iconoclasm had brought his reputation to a low
ebb. To critics at the time, the deliberate provocation of *Relâche* seemed like folly of the
worst order: Satie was deemed to have abandoned the serious vein of *Socrate* and the
Nocturnes, and even all thought for the future. The prior scandal surrounding *Mercure*
only made the instant gratification promised by the authors of *Relâche* look worse, but
to see the derogatory 1924 reviews in perspective we should remember that no
published scores of *Mercure* or *Relâche* were available at the time, and that to this day
Mercure is only available as a hire score (from Universal Edition). So the published
reviews reflect only the confused impression of the actual performances, tempered
adversely by Satie's past track record. Satie himself regarded the press with unequivocal
contempt, and made no effort to justify his scores in terms of formal balance or musical quality. We should also remember that there is no such thing as a *succès de scandale*
now, which is what Satie must have been aiming for. Even *The Rite of Spring* has
become domesticated. If, in retrospect we wonder what all the fuss was about, we
should remember that changing the perspectives of art was still relatively new in 1924,
and that it was still possible to 'amaze the bourgeoisie'; to shock and scandalize an
audience. Which is why Satie, with his usual foresight, considered *Relâche* as a new
beginning, rather than the nihilistic cul-de-sac his many critics saw. As he wrote in
1923: 'The future will prove me right. Haven't prophecies of mine already been
realized?'[1] More than any other contemporary artist, Satie combined the original
meaning of 'avant-garde' (as used by Baudelaire) – as someone out of step with society
– with its later acquired meaning of an artist as the 'advanced guard' of his time.
His underlying fear was not that *Relâche* was too advanced, but that it did not go
far enough.

As early as 1901, Satie had been concerned that he had been born into the wrong
period.[2] Various self-portraits he drew bear the legend 'I came into the world very
young in a very old time',[3] and his only concern about his reputation seems to have
been the fear that his music would not be thought of as essentially French in spirit.[4]
The one apparent oddity in all this is his references to *Relâche* as an 'obscene', and even
as a 'pornographic' ballet,[5] which suggests that the hyper-moral Satie had finally
burned his boats. But the obscenity lies in the dramatic action, such as the male
dancers undressing on stage (Act 2, No. 15), rather than in the music. Although he

applied these adjectives to his score, Satie knew that it was only pornographic by association, and had none of the overt sexuality he so loathed in the sensuous music of Richard Strauss. The continuity of his own moral stance can be seen in the fact that he was prepared to lose Poulenc and Auric as friends in 1924 when he disapproved of their activities.

But, in reality, Satie's loss of supporters was a gradual one engendered by his increasing intolerance after *Socrate*. If he never suffered the wholesale desertion that Debussy experienced after his elopement with Emma Bardac in 1904, Satie nonetheless had few real allies left after *Relâche*, and there were few recantations after his death. Even Cocteau, reminiscing in his journals (1957, 36), described Satie as 'egotistic, cruel and obsessive'. He 'never listened to anything that did not fit in with his dogma and flew into terrible rages with anyone who questioned it. He was egotistic because he thought of nothing except his music; cruel because he defended it[;] and obsessive because he continually re-polished it.' Only staunch advocates remained with him through thick and thin, like Koechlin, Milhaud and Paul Collaer, or his young friends Sauguet, Désormière and Robert Caby. If they might have been considered merely uncritical at the time, the post-war rehabilitation of Satie has vindicated their faith in his music, as he predicted.

The way critical opinion changed over the years is shown in the assessments of Georges Jean-Aubry, a writer who Satie always mistrusted. In the *Music Student* in December 1916 (p. 136), Jean-Aubry enthusiastically observed that:

> The attractive side of Satie's work is that, when one studies it at near-hand it reveals a perfect knowledge of musical resource. . .if his kingdom is a tiny one. . .at least he reigns there as sovereign, and exhibits there a nature of finesse, of raillery, and of clear-sightedness. . .Behind his apparent lack of respect for music, lurks a sincere love of it, such as one sometimes fails to find in the depths of the soul of certain master builders of works of large dimensions, for whom music is nothing more than scientific boredom.

But in 'The End of a Legend', his review of *Relâche* in *The Chesterian* (1924–5, 191–2), Jean-Aubry says that Satie's erstwhile supporters now realized that

> while listening to *Relâche*. . .they were, in fact, listening to nothing. It is possible to instil silence with imaginary harmonies or ingeneous [*sic*] melodies but one cannot make poor music sound rich or constant clumsiness appear simply naïve. . . The bubble burst. . .This master was nothing more than a shadow. Erik Satie is a shadow which has lost its substance, a fate that we had long since foreseen.

The epitome of the 'Emperor's new clothes' philosophy can be seen in Eric Blom's churlish obituary in the *Musical News and Herald* (1925, 52–3):

> Erik Satie's chief defect was that he did not know his place. He carried his musical fooling off with the air of fulfilling an artistic mission. Although he seemed so much a child of his time, he was in reality hopelessly out of it. . .The case was desperate. Lack of musicianship and discriminating invention, incapacity for clear and continu-

ous thinking, set Satie fumbling for some sort of originality until he hit upon the idea of letting his poverty-stricken creations face the world under high-sounding names. . .It was said of Satie by some manipulator of *clichés* that he was born before his time; all one can say now, with the sorrowful indulgence one owes to the departed, is that he unhappily died too late to leave a world of unwholesome flattery without bitterness.

Once everyone was safe from personal retribution, a flood of accumulated loathing of this sort was unleashed by Satie's death, much of it erroneous and unbalanced, and none of it based on a detailed knowledge of his music – a recurring problem in writings on Satie. Even Henry Prunières, with whom Satie had discussed musical matters in unusual detail, considered his volatile temperament had got the better of him in his last years as he grew jealous of the success of his younger protégés. 'His success killed him', he concluded.[6] One such protégé was Roland-Manuel, who Satie had considered as a potential member of Les Six and who had published perhaps the best of the appraisals of Satie in 1916.[7] Roland-Manuel broke with Satie in 1919 over his opinions of *Socrate*, and his 'Adieu à Satie' in the *Revue Pleyel*[8] was positively vitriolic in its condemnation of *Relâche*. The 'farewell' to Satie whilst he was still alive was a particularly unpleasant irony.

> *Relâche* marks an important date in the annals of French music [Roland-Manuel begins]. Let us thank it for proclaiming its true bankruptcy, for committing suicide so well, and for dying devoid of beauty, doubtless so as to deter its later converts from martyrdom. . .Dada waylaid Satie. Dada alone was capable of providing new nourishment for his incoercible appetite for hypocritical buffoonery, for his spirit of esoteric farce, in which the cunning of Normandy mixed so curiously with Scottish humour. . .*Relâche* is the most boring and most stupidly depressing thing in the world. . .Adieu *Relâche*. Adieu Satie. Hurry away to hell, together with the love of wrong spelling and the cult of false taste, this sham classicism which is nothing other than a lack of grace, and this abominable romanticism which is misjudged as sincerity.

As Roland-Manuel was known as an authority on Satie who was formerly close to the composer, these judgments have unfortunately stuck, especially with those who dislike his music and follow the far easier path of denigration. Together with the above dismissal, Roland-Manuel *praises* Satie's early works, the humorous piano pieces of 1912–15, and René Clair's cinema interlude in *Relâche*, giving the whole article the appearance of a balanced judgment, which lends it credibility and makes it attractive to those who like only his more accessible music. Roland-Manuel's entirely different tone in his *Revue musicale* retrospective of June 1952 (9–11) shows the influence of Satie's intervening rehabilitation, and confirms that Satie was again right to distrust him during his lifetime.

More surprising, but more creditable, are the generous posthumous tributes of Satie's enemies Auric, Laloy and Durey. Auric (1925, 98) talks of 'the profound significance of his art'; Laloy (1928, 225) speaks of his music as being tender and affectionate, 'like that of a child of the people, or a flower of the field'; whilst Durey (1930, 164–5) praises him 'for what he brought that was new to music: a clear judgment, a horror of hackneyed ways, love of discovery and of risk, the relief of good humour and systematic rejection of all that was heavy and tiresome'. Perhaps with Brancusi in mind, Durey compares Satie's art with 'a stone of small dimensions. . .but one of very pure whiteness and brilliance' (ibid.).

The gradual rehabilitation of Satie's reputation from the nadir of 1924–5 continued through the writings of Milhaud, Koechlin and Caby in the later 1920s to the deeper understanding of his art and life provided by Templier's 1932 biography (reissued in translation in 1969). At the end (1969, 113), Templier observed a distressing trait – first noted by Boris de Schloezer in 1924 – that '"the Satie case" belonged more properly to the realm of literary than to that of musical criticism'. Rollo Myers, in his 1948 study, attempted to deal with the crucial problem of 'how to disentangle the music and the musician from all the extraneous associations with which they are encrusted and overlaid',[9] though the situation is still that far more has been written about the events behind the music than about the music itself. And far less had been written about the techniques of Satie's art than about its precursive implications before Patrick Gowers began to set the record straight in his 1965–6 article and his 1966 dissertation.

In the interim the most powerful advocacy for Satie came from Wilfrid Mellers, Virgil Thomson, Roger Shattuck and John Cage. Mellers's 1942 article, 'Erik Satie and the "Problem" of Contemporary Music', followed Constant Lambert's lead in *Music Ho!* (1934) by actually saying something worthwhile about the music itself, and relating it successfully to the wider perspective of the other arts. As Mellers rightly says (1942, 211): 'I believe that no contemporary music has more to tell us about the position and predicament of the composer in the modern world than that of this slight and apparently unimportant composer.' Mellers stresses the way that Satie's 'technical veracity' depends on a childlike 'innocence of spirit' (ibid., 226), and one could not wish for a better description of the way the theme of isolation runs through Satie's career than the following (ibid., 222):

> The music of the early dances may be described as the revelation of spiritual solitude through a pure musical intelligence; the music of the period of *Parade* may be called the musical embodiment of the ironic contemplation of that isolation; finally in *Socrate* and the Nocturnes, the irony has again disappeared, and this music may be described as the musical incarnation of the pathos and suffering inherent in the negation which that isolation implies.

Shattuck, too, stresses the isolation and 'closet music' side of Satie, as he fruitfully places him alongside Jarry, Douanier Rousseau and Apollinaire in *The Banquet Years* (1968). Satie's *musique de placard* – meaning both closet music and poster music – implies both 'extreme intimacy and deliberate publicity', Shattuck says (1968, 176).

> Closet music is one degree more private than chamber music. Yet in thus restricting the dimensions of his work, Satie also made his reputation. The intimate works gained a special notoriety, like that of his private religious publication *Le Cartulaire*.

When he threw his little closet pieces in the face of traditional concert music, they assumed the proportions of manifestos: poster music. Thus intimacy becomes a public act. Satie's *musique de placard* conveys the same public privacy or private publicity as the drawings of Paul Klee and poems of e.e. cummings.

Virgil Thomson's contribution, if less subtle, was to place Satie firmly on the American musical map in a shower of superlatives.[10] In 1947 Thomson revived Milhaud's earlier verdict that there was a parallel between the three German B's – Bach, Beethoven and Brahms – and 'the three S's of modern music – in descending order of significance, Satie, Schoenberg, and Stravinsky' (1947, 118). 'The Satie musical aesthetic', Thomson proclaims (ibid., 119), 'is the only twentieth-century musical aesthetic in the Western world. Schoenberg and his school are Romantics. . .Of all the influential composers of our time. . .Satie is the only one whose works can be enjoyed and appreciated without any knowledge of the history of music.' This eulogistic attempt to redress the balance in Satie's favour, however excessive or dubious it may appear at first glance, certainly merits discussion, especially as its final sentence is often quoted by Satiean devotees. When compared with Schoenberg's technical revolution in Vienna (which does require a knowledge of Brahms at least to be fully understood), Satie's parallel revolution in aesthetics in Paris at first appears to be founded on a total rejection of past traditions. This does not make it any less significant, however, and neither should it be assumed that Satie made no positive contribution to replace the nineteenth-century traditions he rejected. Indeed, the problem with generalizations such as Thomson's is highlighted by the fact that, while Satie turned his back on Wagnerism, the traditional concept of thematic development, and all forms of expressive excess, he still favoured using widely-spaced piano textures with sonorous bass octaves along Brahmsian lines. Similarly, if he rejected variation form *per se*, the cellular concept of a movement like *Mort de Socrate* shows an intense awareness of the variation principle in the construction of its system of interlocking motifs based on perfect fourths and fifths (see Exx. 74–5). He created his own equivalents of Classical forms too out of a thorough questioning of what these forms implied, as we have seen. Given the number of innovations Satie made – which include an embryonic version of serialism in *Vexations* (1893: see Ex. 64) – it might arguably be said that Satie's 'minimalist' revolution was the more radical and consistently maintained, for only in Schoenberg's period of free atonality around 1910 did he totally turn his back on the past, in works like *Erwartung*. While Satie's technique was clearly inferior to Schoenberg's, and while he never got farther than experimenting with atonality (see Fig. 9.6), the apparently simple surface of his music should not be taken as an indication that the underlying aesthetic conception was in any way simplistic. He realized, long before anyone else, that the future lay with the small flexible ensemble rather than the full orchestra, and that a fundamental rethinking of what music was about was vital if it was to innovate rather than reiterate in the present century. In Satie the unimpressive surface is deliberate, the perfection in simplicity a means to an end, and the use of popular sources a way of making his aesthetic revolution accessible. Thus there is an underlying basis of truth in Thomson's argument, even if it requires considerable elaboration and qualification. It *does* require a knowledge of music history, both before and after Satie's career, to place his achievement in perspective, and to appreciate his music at more than its face value. If we can still *enjoy* his compositions without such knowledge, then we cannot fully appreciate a song like *Le Chapelier* without knowing about the sources from which it derives. Similarly, as we also discovered in chapter 3, we need to know something about Clementi before we can see what Satie was trying to achieve in the neo-classical *Sonatine bureaucratique* in 1917. But it cannot be denied that Thomson's staunch advocacy of Satie, together with his frequent performances of his music, have done much to stimulate interest in Satie's case and to keep his memory alive.

Even more important was John Cage's discovery of Satie's music after the Second World War. He began by giving Satie concerts at Black Mountain College in 1948,[11] and made a complete collection of his music. Cage's interest focused especially on *Vexations* and he mounted the first complete performance of it in New York in September 1963. When it was first published in America in *Art News Annual* (1958), Cage contributed an imaginary dialogue with Satie, which included the following among its more cogent observations:[12] 'To be interested in Satie one must be disinterested to begin with, accept that a sound is a sound and a man is a man, give up illusions about ideas of order, expressions of sentiment, and all the rest of our inherited claptrap. . . It's not a question of Satie's relevance. He's indispensable.' Satie's indispensability for Cage lay in six areas. First, in his being the only composer of note to be associated with the anarchistic 'happenings' of the Dada movement. In this, the concentration on the 'now-moment' in *Relâche* is all-important. Second, in his new attitudes to structure, which in works like *Cinéma* presents blocks of sound of predetermined length which may or may not be repeated (though this is as far as Satie goes in the direction of 'chance' elements). Third, in his incorporation of incongruous popular themes into his music. Fourth, in his exploration of the effects of boredom, and the replacement of traditional signposts like climaxes with stasis and experiments in the way we perceive time and space. Fifth, in his eschewal of development, and its substitution with repetition. And sixth, in his incorporation of the noises of the environment as an integral part of his 'furnishing music'. But, as Michael Nyman says in his article on 'Cage and Satie' (1973, 1229): 'For Satie, furniture music would be "part of the noises of the environment", whereas for Cage the noises of the environment are part of his music; for Satie "it would fill up those heavy silences that sometimes fall between friends dining together", while for Cage ambient music filled those empty silences that regularly fell between the notes of his music until about 1960.' The 'anti-art' concept is nonetheless there, and *4'33"* (1952) would not have been possible without *Vexations* and its initial period of specified contemplation. Where I believe that Cage misunderstood Satie is in his belief that 'Art when it is art as Satie lived it and made it is not separate from life. . .Satie never lived in an ivory tower. . .for there is nothing in life from which he separates himself.'[13] For Satie, as we have seen, the composition of self-contained, objective scores in hermetic isolation *was* an escape from life, however much he was aware of the reality beyond the walls of his 'ivory tower' in Arcueil.

Cage, in fact, began his acquaintance with Satie by making a two-piano arrangement of the *Portrait de Socrate* in 1945 for Merce Cunningham's ballet *Idyllic Song*. When he came to complete his arrangement of *Socrate* in October 1969, permission to use his new version was not forthcoming, so Cage set about making an imitation of the original using 'I Ching' chance methods. The result was *Cheap Imitation* for piano solo, which was used in Cunningham's dance *Second Hand* in 1970. Cage continued his connections with Satie in 'the gigantic *Song Books* [and] *Solos for Voice 3–92* (1970), which is a musical–theatrical exploration of a chance remark he made in the 1969 continuation of his *Diary: How to Improve the World (You will only make Matters Worse)*: 'We connect Satie with Thoreau" (Nyman, 1973, 1227). But Satie, whose scores were all prepared with immaculate precision, would surely have been as horrified by this aleatoric approach as he would have been by some of the arrangements of his music cited by Gillmor in his comprehensive discography (1988, 343–70).

As far as Satie's wide-reaching influence is concerned, we should be careful to distinguish between those composers, like Robert Caby, who have preserved the essential spirit of Satie's spare and predominantly harmonic style in their own music, and those, like John Cage, who have taken Satie's innovations as a basis for further exploration. Within the first category, the spirit of Satie is preserved in the earlier works of Auric, Poulenc and Milhaud, and the light-hearted compositions of Ibert, Françaix and Serge Lancen. The simpler music of Federico Mompou, with its occasional comments, bears Satie's imprint too. The appeal of his music, like that of Satie, 'has been disproportionate to his minimal means. He is a minimalist not in the currently fashionable sense, but simply because his few notes are preternaturally important, and thus in effect not minimal at all.'[14] There are also occasional echoes of Satie's timeless atmosphere, and early ametrical, self-contained phrases within the 'magical' sonorities of Maurice Ohana, who was similarly fascinated by medieval music. The jigsaw puzzle assembly of short motivic fragments can be found in compositions of Messiaen like *La Nativité du Seigneur* (1935), where the basis again lies in the genuine ametricality and religious ambience of Satie's Rose-Croix period. Indeed, the voluptuous sonorities of a recurring progression found in Acts 2 and 3 of *Uspud* (Ex. 90) even sound like Messiaen,

Ex. 90 *Uspud*, extract from Act 3 (BN 9631, 41–2)

though in Satie there is no complex underlying rhythmic organization, and the only colour he associated with his music was white. There are no Hindu rhythms or added values in Satie, and it is the dual purpose of Messiaen as 'compositeur et rythmicien' that most clearly separates him from Satie, and makes his organization of the 'techniques' of his 'musical language' the more comprehensive. But just as Satie arrives at total chromaticism in *Vexations*, so we find him using what amounts to a mode of limited transposition in Act 1 of *Uspud* (see Ex. 69): his concern to balance the vertical and horizontal, and his systematic approach to harmonic progressions in the Rose-Croix music show that the parallels with Messiaen are more than merely superficial.

As Peter Dickinson says (1967, 139): 'Almost every twentieth-century French composer has acknowledged some debt to Satie.' In some cases, this debt takes the form of imitation as a direct homage, as in the Ravel and Stravinsky pieces we saw in chapter 11, or in Charles Koechlin's *La Leçon de piano*, the fourth movement of his suite *L'Ancienne Maison de campagne* (1932–3). Here Koechlin takes the same Clementi Sonatina that Satie used in the *Sonatine bureaucratique* in 1917, but transforms it into 'real music' by the use of luminous bitonal harmonies and whole-tone scales. And Koechlin's *Danse lente* for Ginger Rogers (Op. 163 No. 2, 1937) has as much claim to be called the fifth *Gymnopédie* as Ravel's *Les Entretiens de la Belle et de la Bête* has to being the fourth.

In the second category of composers, for whom Satiean innovations have formed a basis for exploration and transformation, the work of minimalists like Terry Riley and Steve Reich immediately springs to mind. Reich's *Four Organs* (1970), which constructs a large-scale piece from a single chord, carries the repetition principle of the *Fête donnée par des Chevaliers Normands* (1892) to a logical extreme, whilst its involvement of four identical instruments recalls the four sopranos specified in *Socrate*. The difference, of course, lies in Reich's use of 'phasing processes' (wherein new patterns emerge from the phased superposition of short repeated fragments), and in the use of extra dimensions made available through modern technology. But as with Satie (and Cage in the early 1950s), Reich's art is essentially an impersonal one, though in its precision and absolute control it comes closer to the spirit of Satie than Cage does. One might also see parallels between Satie and Morton Feldman (a member of the Cage group in the 1950s) in his search for utter simplicity and restraint. Low density textures, slow speeds and soft dynamics pervade Feldman's compositions, as they did in Satie's Rose-Croix period, and his distinguishing of pieces by their 'weights' recalls Satie's experiments as a 'phonometrician' around 1912.

The parallels between Satie and British composers like Howard Skempton, John White, Christopher Hobbs and Gavin Bryars have been eloquently drawn by Bryars himself (1982, 9–12). His *Ponukelian Melody* (1975) is directly modelled in tempo and rhythm on *Les Pantins dansent* (1913), with the harmonic and melodic material derived from the Rose-Croix notebooks. Indeed, it is this early experimental period, with its absence of cabaret associations, that has most attracted post-war composers, and Edgard Varèse even refers to these works as pre-electronic music,[15] though this may seem far-fetched. Another close British link can be found in certain works of Harrison

Birtwistle in the late 1960s. His technique of laying contrasted blocks of sound end to end, virtually irrespective of context, in *Verses for Ensembles* (1969) recalls Satie's aims in *Parade* (as does the stridency of harmony and timbre). Birtwistle also made his own orchestration of Satie's *Mercure* in 1980, just as Douglas Young has recently made a modernistic scoring of the *Sports et divertissements*. If it might appear that virtually every avant-garde composer has some sort of embryonic links with Satie, this does not undermine the validity of such comparisons, and rather serves to stress the pervasiveness of his influence on the present century. Indeed, John Cage's argument that 'modern music will turn out to have been shaped to a greater extent by Webern and Satie than by Schoenberg and Stravinsky'[16] seems even truer than it did when he first made it nearly thirty years ago. Above all, it is Satie's capacity for constant renewal, for constantly re-evaluating music's position in relation to the other arts that has led to his being such a fruitful source of ideas for later generations. As Satie said in 1921 (Templier, 1969, 73): 'If anyone were to find something really new, I would start again at the beginning.'

Nor is music the only branch of the arts to feel Satie's influence. Just as Satie was closely associated with painters and scupltors during his lifetime, so we find posthumous homages to him by Surrealist artists such as Georges Malkine, René Magritte, Man Ray and Joan Miró (see Vy, 21, 57 and 59), as well as in the décors for *Socrate* by Alexander Calder (Vy, 61). As Ornella Volta points out, there is a parallel between Satie's 'pursuit. . .of the illusion of immobile music revolving in space' and Calder's introduction of 'the fourth dimension in sculpture' through his 'mobiles' (Vy, 21). Whilst Surrealism as a movement was only founded in December 1924 as Satie was forced to withdraw from composition, his titles and associations of ideas have provided a catalytic source of inspiration for artists since his death. From Miró's *Poèmes et chansons*,[17] inspired by such items as the texts for the third *Gnossienne* and the *Embryons desséchés*, it is only a short step to the work of the artists in Satie's Faction, formed in England in 1975 by John Furnival and Nick Cudworth (to mark the fiftieth anniversary of his death). In their aim to focus on Satie's entire contribution to art, the group published a limited edition folder in May 1976 comprising poems, graphics and drawings by fifteen different artists. The most notable of these are Cudworth's realizations of Satie's imaginary instruments – like the 'alto overcoat in C' and 'two side clarinets in G minor'. Other versions of the same instruments appear in *Satie's Cephalophones*, published later that year.[18]

It is hardly surprising that Satie has proved so fascinating to subsequent artists and musicians, for he was a unique composer of multiple paradoxes. In fact, he is the perfect embodiment of Socrates' observation that 'Life without paradox is not liveable.' To cite just a few: Satie's music and attitudes remained young as he grew old; he was a revolutionary who dressed in the bourgeois attire of the bureaucratic officials he waged war against; he was a sociable man at ease with all levels of society who constantly made enemies; and above all, for a *petit maître* whose technical expertise pales in comparison with that of Debussy or Ravel, he nonetheless exerted a wider and more liberating influence on the twentieth century than either of them, even though his style was rarely imitated. Satie had the capacity to generate paradox too. Virgil Thomson says (1947, 120) that 'the only thing really hermetic and difficult to understand about the music of Erik Satie is the fact that there is nothing hermetic about it at all', whereas most other writers stress how vital isolation was for Satie's Benedictine labours. Although he was very often miserable in Arcueil, he even refused to let his brother Conrad visit his squalid room in 1914. His reasons (which Conrad shared and understood) were not that the room was too pitiful to see, but that 'visits by friends break up my imaginary games and confuse my thoughts, which are hoarded up in its corners in an apparent disorder'.[19] There was, as we have seen, an occult and esoteric aspect to Satie's life which makes 'hermetic' the ideal word to apply to his process of creation.

Satie was without doubt a creature of extraordinarily curious habits, and while Cocteau and others maintained that everything he did had a logical reason, some of his antics defy all other explanations save paranoia. His attitude to the postal services is perhaps the oddest of all. Surprisingly, Satie detested modern technical innovations like the telephone, and would take the instrument off the hook when he visited the houses of friends, to avoid disturbances (Sauguet, 1952, 96).[20] By the same token, incidentally, he never showed any interest in recording his music, and it is thus ironical that he owes much of his recent popularity to discs and tapes. Satie would write countless letters and *pneumatiques*, sometimes six or more in a day. He arranged elaborate rendezvous; he sent birthday and New Year greetings to all his friends; he even sent Paulot Picasso a greeting on the day after his birth; and he also wrote to himself.[21] Hélène Hoppenot even saw him write a letter to her in the post office opposite her house, which was delivered soon afterwards.[22] But if Satie loved writing letters, he hated opening them. He used one of his grand pianos in Arcueil as a giant re-posting box. If he recognized the writing or was expecting a communication, he naturally read and answered letters, but many letters and parcels were found in his room after his death either in pristine condition, or with a small tear in one corner made to discern their importance. Undoubtedly the legal action of the Poueigh affair in 1917 increased his fear of receiving unpleasant news, but why he should have been afraid to open a Christmas parcel from Milhaud's mother remains a mystery. On 19 December 1922 he even asked Milhaud what it contained: 'I have received a package signed G. Milhaud and sent from Marseilles (Colonial Exhibition). This package has not yet been opened. What is it?' (Vc). It turned out to be a gift of chestnut fondants, for which Satie thanked her in his usual charming and individual style on 31 December. Anyone other than the long-suffering Milhaud would have thought that Satie was both paranoid and slightly crazy.

And so he must have appeared to both his friends and enemies. This aspect is thoroughly discussed in Bredel's thought-provoking biography, in which he observes that Satie's room in Arcueil looked like the abode of 'a deranged man' (1982, 77). Living alone encouraged the development of obsessions, hyper-moral attitudes, alcoholism, and the persecution complex that reached its height after *Socrate* and caused the loss of so many friends. Bredel compares his perversity with that of Diogenes the Cynic, who ended up living with great austerity in a barrel, censuring all intellectual pursuits. The comparison is by no means invalid, for Satie's letter to Conrad in 1911 – asking why Debussy cannot 'allow me a very small place in his shadow? I have no use for the sun' – is surely a reference to Diogenes' remark to Alexander the Great in Corinth. When Alexander asked Diogenes if he could oblige him in any way, Diogenes replied 'Yes, by standing out of my sunshine.' It is even more relevant that Alexander was so struck by Diogenes' independence that he said 'If I were not Alexander, I should wish to be Diogenes', which tells us much about how Satie viewed Debussy. Satie, who had been good at Latin and Greek in his youth, knew all about the Greek philosopher, for he told Pierre de Massot during a very hot spell in July 1923: 'So now I understand why Diogenes had a barrel and not a keg: he would fill it with water and keep himself cool inside' (Vc). Because of its deliberate provocation, Bredel calls *Relâche* 'Musique à Diogène' (1982, 112), and he suggests that to Satie's masochistic mind 'success was suspect if he did not scent scandal' too, the desire for this having probably originated in the uproar over Debussy's *Pelléas et Mélisande* in 1902. 'His life is his greatest work', Bredel concludes (1982, 115), but he is careful to point out how Satie kept his totally unparanoid music compartmentalized from the bizarre events that surrounded it, which is to my mind an even greater achievement.

Satie's career is capable of many interpretations, as we saw in chapter 1, and a further intriguing parallel can relate it almost entirely to the theatre, with its fusion of all the arts that interested him. While his associations with the cabaret run throughout his life, his active involvement with this medium exactly parallels the heyday of the shadow theatre, from its inception by Henri Rivière at Le Chat Noir in 1886 to the start of its decline around 1911. Satie's associations were all with establishments specializing in the *Théâtre d'Ombres*, especially La Lune Rousse, where its existence was prolonged under the creative directorship of Satie's collaborator Dominique Bonnaud after 1904. Then, after a short interregnum, Cocteau helped Satie transfer his cabaret interest to the theatre, and his subsequent theatrical career runs exactly parallel to Picasso's involvement in the medium, from its inception with *Parade* in 1916 to its close with *Mercure* in 1924. Another such thread is Satie's fascination with dance music, which stretches from the earliest *Valse-ballet* of 1885 to the ballet *Relâche*, via the *Gymnopédies*; *Danses Gothiques*; cabaret pieces like *Le Piccadilly* and *Poudre d'or*; the numerous minuets sketched between 1908 and 1920; *Parade*; *La Belle Excentrique* and *Mercure*.[23]

But however one views Satie's career, or the level of his technical achievement, the prevailing qualities of freedom of thought, independence of mind, tenacity and cunning awareness stand out. Perhaps the best comparison of all is the impersonal one made by Koechlin with Kipling's 'cat who walked by himself'. Like a 'free feline', Koechlin says (1924, 193), 'his music has in it the elegant suppleness, the sobriety of gesture, the precision of paw-play in mischievous games, the discreet sensibility that vulgar people persist in not understanding; finally, and above all, it has instinctive and absolute independence'. Satie was always aware of the dangers of compromise and the threat to artistic freedom inherent in patronage, as his analogy (recounted by his friend Fernand Léger) demonstrates (1952, 138):

> Let's take a hunter, for example. He likes the chase, he hunts the pheasant. He likes game, he comes to find you and asks you, as a colourist: 'Monsieur Léger, I know your work. I should very much like to have a very free painting for my dining room; that's settled, but I should like a pheasant in this painting, a handsome male pheasant with multi-coloured feathers.' You have this in your palette. But what would you reply?

So, rather than have conditions imposed upon him, Satie instigated his own projects. Even in his earlier theatrical collaborations he only wrote such music as seemed right to him at a particular time, whatever the play concerned. And as no composer has ever placed a greater responsibility on his audience than Satie, his true theatre might be said to be that of the imagination. The worst error lies in considering Satie as a negativistic composer hiding behind a veil of irony, lashing out irrationally at those who criticized his apparent frivolity, and developing his 'cult of restraint' and 'new spirit' of modernity as thin justifications for his own technical inadequacy. For Satie, musical integrity and the sheer joy of the creative act always came first. He went to great pains to achieve perfection in simplicity, and he always assumed full responsibility for his independent ideas and the way he used them in carefully structured, positive compositions. If, in the last analysis, these ideas prove to be more significant than the music that derives from them – as might be said to be the case with *Vexations* – then, as ever, Satie anticipated this. As he wrote in the credo that holds the key to understanding Satie the composer: 'Great Masters are brilliant through their ideas, their craft is a simple means to an end, nothing more. It is their ideas which endure. . .The Idea can do without Art.'

Chronological catalogue of Satie's compositions

In order to give as comprehensive a picture as possible of Satie the composer, the following catalogue includes projected, unfinished and lost compositions that were titled by Satie, as well as those that he completed. Satie's exercises at the Schola Cantorum are not included, unless they contributed to a titled composition. They are discussed in chapter 6 and can be found in BN 9577, 9579, 9591(1–3), 9601(1), 9613, 9617(1–2), 9620, 9634, 9636–59, 9661–5, 9667–8, 9670, 9675–6, 9677(2), 10033(1–12), and Ho 1, 3–7, 9, 24–5, 59–60 and 68. Subsequent arrangements by others are generally not included, for these (and a comprehensive discography) can be found in Gillmor, 1988, 325–70. Works with titles added by others, such as the Salabert publications of around 1968 by Robert Caby, are grouped together at the end. They mostly involve unfinished sketches or pieces from the Schola Cantorum period (1905–12). A particular problem arises with Satie's numerous cabaret songs in the period 1897–1909 because none of them are dated, few include a text, and many are arrangements of the works of other popular composers of the day. Only songs authenticated by Steven Moore Whiting in his dissertation (1984) are included here, and in some of these the dating is only approximate. Otherwise, the catalogue is arranged chronologically by the date on which Satie started each composition, and where the date is given in inverted commas in column 1 the information comes directly from a manuscript. The major manuscript sources in the Bibliothèque Nationale, Paris (BN) and the Houghton Library at Harvard University (Ho) are here amalgamated for the first time. The BN manuscripts are now in a fragile condition and are undergoing restoration. They can only be consulted by special permission. Where a distinction can usefully be made in this Appendix, details of the full scores and final printer's copies (in ink) are given first, followed by the locations of the sketches for each piece (usually in pencil). Satie's original capitalization is preserved in the titles (as elsewhere in this book). The other library sigla for manuscript sources follow the practice established in *The New Grove Dictionary of Music and Musicians* (London, Macmillan, 1980), as do the abbreviations for instruments (which are not repeated here).

The Appendix gives the following information: date of composition and orchestration in column 1. Then, in column 2: title; description and author of the text (if applicable); description of the music; dedication (if applicable); present location and details of the manuscripts; publication details of the music; details of the first performance of the music (where known). The place of first performance and publication is Paris, unless otherwise stated. Only a few early works have opus numbers, and these were probably added by Satie's father Alfred on publication to make his son appear more prolific and experienced than he really was. As many of Satie's compositions are modal or not in a specific key, information as to tonality is not given.

Abbreviations

arr.	arrangement, arranged by
cond.	conductor, conducted by
corr.	corrected
ded.	dedication, dedicated to
f., ff.,	folio, folios
facs.	facsimile
inc.	incomplete
incl.	includes, including
MS, MSS	manuscript, manuscripts
orch.	orchestrated, orchestrated by
orig.	originally
OS	orchestral score
perf.	performance, performed by
PLU	present location unknown
prem.	première
pubd	published, published by
pubn	publication
r	recto
red.	(piano) reduction
repr.	reprinted
rev.	revised
SACEM	Société d'Auteurs, Compositeurs et Editeurs de Musique
sc.	scene
SIM	Société Internationale de Musique
SMI	Société Musicale Indépendante
SN	Société Nationale (de Musique)
transcr.	transcribed, transcription by
unacc.	unaccompanied
unperf.	unperformed
unpubd	unpublished
v	verso
VS	vocal score

Library sigla

F:	France
BN	Département de la Musique, Bibliothèque Nationale, 2 rue de Louvois, Paris 2 (referred to as *F-Pn* in Grove)
Pbd	Paris, Bibliothèque Littéraire Jacques Doucet, 10 place du Panthéon, Paris 5
Pca	Paris, private collection of Robert Caby
Pfs	Paris, Archives of the Fondation Satie, 56 rue des Tournelles, Paris 3
Po	Paris, Bibliothèque de l'Opéra, 2 rue Auber, Paris 9
Ppc	Paris, private collection (not identified on the wishes of the owner)
Psa	Paris, private collection of Henri Sauguet
Psalabert	Paris, Archives of Salabert et Cie, 22 rue Chauchat, Paris 9
Ptb	Paris, private collection of Thierry Bodin
US:	United States of America
AUS	Austin, Texas, Harry Ransom Humanities Research Center
Ho	Houghton Library, University of Harvard, Cambridge, Massachusetts (referred to as *US-CA* in Grove)
Eu	Evanston, Illinois, Northwestern University Music Library
NYpm	New York, Pierpont Morgan Library

Other private collections outside Paris are described in full, when this is allowed by the owners of the manuscripts concerned.

'Honfleur. 9 Sept 1884'	**Allegro** music: 9 bars for pf MSS: BN 10050(2), 1f. pubn: facs. in Gillmor, 1972, plate 3. Bars 1–6 in W, 19 and Gillmor, 1988, 26 prem.: 12 April 1980 by Giancarlo Carlini (pf). Teatro di Porta Romana, Milan
1885	**Valse-ballet** music: salon piece for pf MSS: PLU pubn: musical supplement to *La Musique des familles*, 17 March 1887, by Alfred Satie (as 'Op. 62') As No. 1 of *Deux Œuvres de jeunesse*, Salabert, 1975 prem. (public): Opéra-Comique, 7 May 1979 by Anne-Marie Fontaine (pf)
1885	**Fantaisie-valse** music: salon piece for pf ded.: à mon ami J. P. Contamine de Latour MSS: PLU

pubn: musical supplement to *La Musique des familles*, 28
    July 1887
  As No. 2 of *Deux Œuvres de jeunesse*, Salabert, 1975
prem. (public): Opéra-Comique, 7 May 1979 by Anne-
    Marie Fontaine (pf)

1886   **Elégie**
music: setting for v, pf of unpubd poem by Contamine de
    Latour
ded.: à Mademoiselle Céleste Le Prédour
MSS: PLU
pubn: Alfred Satie, 1887 (as 'Op. 19')
  As No. 2 of *Trois Mélodies de 1886*, Salabert, 1968

1886   **Trois Mélodies**
music: 3 settings for v, pf of unpubd poems by Contamine
    de Latour
1 *Les Anges*
2 *Les Fleurs*
3 *Sylvie*
ded.: 1   à Charles Levadé
      2   à Comtesse Gérald de Marguenat
      3   à Mademoiselle Olga Satie
MSS: PLU
pubn: Alfred Satie, 1887 (as 'Op. 20')
  Nos. 1, 3 in *Trois Mélodies de 1886*, Salabert, 1968
  No. 2 in *Trois Autres Mélodies* (No. 3), Salabert, 1968

1886   **Ogives**
music: 4 pieces for pf inspired by the Gothic architecture of
    Notre Dame cathedral
ded.: 1   à J.P. Contamine de Latour
      2   à Charles Levadé
      3   à Madame Clément Le Breton
      4   à Conrad Satie
MSS: PLU
pubn: Imprimerie Dupré (private ed.), 1889; Le Chant du
    Monde/Sikorski (Hamburg), 1965

?1886   **1er Quatuor; 2d Quatuor**
music: 2 sketches for str quartet (unscored)
MSS: BN 10049, 1f.
unpubd

1887

Chanson

music: setting for v, pf of unpubd poem by Contamine de Latour

ded.: à Mademoiselle Valentine de Bret

MSS: PLU

pubn: Alfred Satie, 1888 (as 'Op. 52')

As No. 1 of *Trois Autres Mélodies*, Salabert, 1968

?1–'18 Sept 1887'

Trois Sarabandes

music: 3 dances for pf. The first is prefaced in the MS by an extract from Latour's *La Perdition*

ded.: 1 à Monsieur Conrad Satie (MS only)

2 à mon ami Arthur Dodement (MS; altered in another hand to 'à Mademoiselle Jeanne de Bret'). In 1911 ed. 'à Maurice Ravel'

3 No dedication

MSS: BN 14457(1–3). 3, 3, 2ff. No. 3 dated '18 Sept 1887', the others 'Sept 1887'

pubn: No. 1 in *Revue musicale SIM*, 7/3 (15 March 1911), 33–4. As in BN 14457 (without bars 53–5, 73–5 found in Rouart-Lerolle ed.)

No. 2 in supplement to *Musica* (*Album Musica*) No. 103 (April 1911), 89–90. A copy of No. 2 dated '1906' exists in *F-Ptb*, see Volta, 1982, 34, No. 51

All 3: Rouart-Lerolle, 1911 (No. 2 lacks the repeat of bars 82–6 as 87–91 found in the *Musica* edition, but Satie told Lerolle on 10 May 1911 that he preferred his shorter version)

prem.: No. 2 by Maurice Ravel (pf), SMI, Salle Gaveau, 16 Jan 1911

'Feb–2 April 1888'

Trois Gymnopédies

music: 3 dances for pf, inspired by an extract from *Les Antiques* by Contamine de Latour: 'Slicing obliquely through the shadows a raging torrent rushed in waves of gold over the polished flagstone, where atoms of amber, glistening in the firelight, joined their sarabande to the naked dance [gymnopédie]' (trans. Roger Nichols, Peters Edition, 1988)

Nos. 3, 1 orch. Debussy, 1896, for 2 fl, ob, 4 hn, str (No. 3), plus 2 hp, cymb (No. 1)

ded.: 1 à Mademoiselle Jeanne de Bret (1895 ed. onwards)

2 à Conrad Satie (1895 ed. onwards. Ded. in MS 'à mon ami Arthur Dodement')

3 à Charles Levadé

MSS: BN 8537(1–3), No. 1: 'Feb 1888' (3pp.); No. 2: 'March 1888' (3pp.); No. 3: '2 April 1888' (3pp.)

Humbacher coll., Basle. OS by Debussy, and copy by Satie with extra dynamics added by Debussy. Order: 1, 3

F-Psalabert. OS and parts copied by Satie. Order: 3, 1 (5, 9pp.)

BN 10046, str and ob parts (by professional copyist)

BN 9597(2), 1. Trial scoring of No. 3 by Satie (*c.* 1894) for ob, 2 cl, hps, str, voice (bars 1–3 only: see Ex. 16)

pubn: No. 1 as musical supplement to *La Musique des familles*, 18 Aug 1888 (with Latour's poem *Les Antiques*). Then by Imprimerie Dupré (private ed.), 1895

No. 2: Imprimerie Dupré (private ed.), 1895 (incl. bars 1–4 missing in BN 8537)

No. 3: Imprimerie Dupré (private ed.), 1888

All 3: Baudoux, 1898; Rouart-Lerolle, 1911; rev. ed. Salabert, 1969

Nos. 3, 1 orch. Debussy: Baudoux, 1898; rev. ed. by Peter Dickinson: Eulenburg, 1980

prem.: No. 3 by Maurice Ravel, SMI, Salle Gaveau, 16 Jan 1911

Nos. 3, 1 orch. Debussy: Salle Erard, cond. Gustave Doret, 20 Feb 1897

'8 July 1889'

Gnossienne [No. 5]
music: dance for pf
MSS: BN 10054(1), f. 1*r* and *v*, f. 2*r*
pubn: Salabert, 1968 (as 'No. 5')

?July 1889

Chanson Hongroise
music: 4 bars for pf inspired by Romanian folk music at the Exposition Universelle, 1889
MSS: BN 10054(1), f. 2*v*
pubn: in Wehmeyer, 1974, 32

'1890'
(1890–3?)

Trois Gnossiennes [Nos. 1–3]
music: 3 dances for pf
ded.: 1 à Roland-Manuel (1913 ed.)
      2 à Antoine de La Rochefoucauld (1893 facs.)
      3 No dedication
MSS: PLU. A facs. of No. 2 dated 'April 1893' appeared in *Le Cœur* in 1893 (see below), though this could be a later copy

BN 10053, f. 2*v*. Barred sketch for end of No. 2

BN Rés. Vma 163. First proofs (1912)

Ho 48. Start of No. 3 for small orch (2 bars only for ob, hp)

pubn: No. 1 in *Le Figaro musical*, 24 (Sept 1893) as 'No. 1'

No. 2 in *Le Cœur*, 6–7 (Sept–Oct 1893), 12 as '6e Gnossienne'. Facs. reproduced in Volta, 1987, 32

No. 3 in *Le Figaro musical*, 24 (Sept 1893) as 'No. 2'

All 3: Rouart-Lerolle, 1913. Here Nos. 2 and 3 are dated '1890' by Satie (in the 1912 proofs). No. 1 was dated '1890' between the first proof stage and publication

'5 Dec 1890'   **Danse**

music: Satie's first completed piece for small orchestra (2 fl, ob, 2 cl (B♭, A), bn, timp, hp). Used as No. 6: *En plus* in *Trois Morceaux en forme de poire* (1903)

MSS: Ho 48, 14pp. music

pubn: in Gowers, 1966, Ph.D. 5375, 32–40. Bars 1–10 in Gillmor, 1988, 128–9

'20 Jan 1891'   **[Première Pensée Rose + Croix]**

music: short march for pf. Possibly the *Marche antique pour la Rose-Croix* by Bihn Grallon (Satie) played at the 4th of Péladan's Rosicrucian soirées in late March 1892 (first suggested by Gillmor, 1988, 271 n. 12)

MSS: BN 10051(1), 1f.

pubn: Salabert, 1968 (ed. Robert Caby, who gave it the bracketed title above)

'22 Jan 1891'   **Gnossienne** [No. 4]

music: dance for pf

MSS: BN 10051(2), 2ff.

pubn: Salabert, 1968 (as 'No. 4')

?summer 1891   **Menuet de La Princesse Maleine**

music: ?Satie's first minuet for pf. A piece with this title (in Gothic calligraphy typical of Satie) appears in the painting *Marthe au piano* by Maurice Denis (*c*. Oct 1891). Satie is known to have considered setting Maeterlinck's play *La Princesse Maleine* (1889) about this time, and also suggested the idea to Debussy. Maeterlinck had, however, already granted the authorization to Vincent d'Indy, so neither Debussy nor Satie could proceed with the project

MSS: PLU

'28 Oct' 1891   **Leit-motiv du 'Panthée'**
music: Satie's only monodic composition (no forces specified)
ded.: au Sâr Joséphin Péladan
MSS: PLU
pubn: in Péladan: *Le Panthée. La Décadence latine, Ethopée, No. 10* (Paris, E. Dentu, 1892), at the start

?Nov 1891   **Prélude du 'Prince du Byzance'**
music: lost or never started. Announced in Péladan: *Le Panthée* (1892), 299–300, and intended as incidental music for his play *Le Prince du Byzance* (title as on first ed.)

'2 Nov 1891'   **Salut Drapeau!**
text: Giorgio Cavalcanti's speech in Act 2 sc. 9 of Péladan's 5-act 'romanesque drama' *Le Prince du Byzance* (Paris, Chamuel, 1896). Here (p. 54), Cavalcanti seizes the flag and proclaims Tonio to the people as the hereditary prince of the title
music: hymn for v (or voices in unison), pf (or org)
MSS: BN 10053 (5ff., recto only), plus 2pp. by Péladan converting the prose speech into 3 unequal verses
pubn: Salabert, 1968 (ed. Robert Caby as *Hymne. Pour le 'Salut Drapeau'*. The original MS has no bar lines and each vocal phrase should end with a minim and a crotchet rest. Publication as *Salut au Drapeau* was announced by Satie in the small *Uspud* brochure of 1895, but no copy has yet been found)

?Dec 1891   **Le Fils des étoiles**
music: incidental music for fls and hps for Joséphin Péladan's 3-act 'Pastorale Kaldéenne' *Le Fils des étoiles* (Beauvais, Imprimerie professionnelle, 1895). A *Gnossienne* in Act 1 (BN 10052(1), ff. 9v–12r) was reused as the *Manière de commencement* in the *Trois Morceaux en forme de poire* in 1903
MSS: BN 10052(1). Short score (24pp. music)
      BN 10052(2). Scenario by Péladan (5ff.)
pubn: 3 act-preludes only (Act 1: *La Vocation*; Act 2: *L'Initiation*; Act 3: *L'Incantation*), Baudoux, 1896 (in red ink, with 'Dédicatoire' by Satie, and the imprint of the Eglise Métropolitaine d'Art de Jésus Conducteur)
      Rouart-Lerolle, 1920; rev. ed., Salabert, 1972 (only these printed scores bear the misleading description 'Wagnérie Kaldéenne')

prem.: 3 act-preludes at public dress rehearsal for the first Soirée Rose + Croix, Galerie Durand-Ruel, 19 March 1892 (for fls and hps?)

Prelude to Act 1 by Maurice Ravel (pf), SMI, Salle Gaveau, 16 Jan 1911

?Feb 1892

Trois Sonneries de la Rose + Croix

music: 3 fanfares for tpts and hps (or orch?)

1 *Air de l'Ordre*

2 *Air du Grand Maître* (Le Sâr Joséphin Péladan)

3 *Air du Grand Prieur* (Le Comte Antoine de La Rochefoucauld)

MSS: BN 10040, 3ff., probably parts for tpts in F, as the MS contains only the passages in octaves in the 3 *Sonneries*, a perfect fourth lower

F-Pca, 1892 ed. corrected by Satie 'to conform with the orchestral parts'

pubn: Imprimerie Dupré, 1892 ('publié par les soins de la Rose + Croix')

Rouart-Lerolle, 1910; rev. ed., Salabert, 1971

prem.: at inauguration of the first Salon de la Rose-Croix, 10 March 1892, Galerie Durand-Ruel. Repeated at the first Rose + Croix Soirée on 22 March, when No. 3 appears as the *Sonnerie de l'Archonte*

1892

Danses Romaines; Danses Byzantines; Kharaseos

music: dances for orch, and a 1-act opera listed amongst Satie's compositions in his application for election to the Académie des Beaux-Arts in May 1892 (after the death of Ernest Guiraud). These works were probably never started

?1892

Fête donnée par des Chevaliers Normands en l'Honneur d'une jeune Demoiselle (XIe siècle)

music: prelude for pf based on Satie's first known compositional system, using interlocking chord progressions (see Fig. 9.1)

MSS: Ho 62, f. 2r and v (chordal cells), f. 3v (draft of central chordal passage on which prelude is based; see Ex. 79a). Earlier discarded versions using the same cells can be found in Ho 62, ff. 3r, 10v)

BN 10050(1), draft of prelude on verso of Sept 1884 Allegro. The style and calligraphy of the prelude both belong to the early 1890s, however, and other passages

using the same progressions can be found in *Uspud* and
the *Danses Gothiques* of 1892–3)

pubn: Rouart-Lerolle, 1929 (as the first of *4 Préludes*)

early June 1892   **[1er] Prélude du Nazaréen**

music: incidental music for *Le Nazaréen*, a 3-act esoteric play
by Henri Mazel (Paris, A. Savin, [1892]). Page 5 is
marked 'Décors à rêver. – Musique à faire.'

MSS: BN 10037(1), 4pp., adorned with Gothic castles and
other drawings (see Figs 4.1; 8.2)

pubn: Rouart-Lerolle, 1929 (as the third of *4 Préludes*)

'12 June 1892'   **[2e] Prélude du Nazaréen**

music: incidental music for *Le Nazaréen* by Henri Mazel

MSS: BN 10037bis, 3pp.

pubn: Rouart-Lerolle, 1929 (as the fourth of *4 Préludes*.
Chords 5–6 and 10–12 on p. 8 system 4 should be
repeated between chords 12 and 13: they were omitted
from the MS in this posthumous edition (see Fig. 8.3))

?July 1892   **Le Bâtard de Tristan**

music: announced as an opera in 3 Acts to a libretto by
Albert Tinchant in *Le Courrier du soir* on 22 July 1892,
to be performed at the Grand Théâtre in Bordeaux.
Satie's score was probably never started

?Sept–17 Dec 1892   **Uspud**

text: 'Ballet chrétien' in 3 Acts by Contamine de Latour and
Satie. First version (finished '17 Nov 1892') – with one
desert setting for all 3 Acts – in a private coll. in France
(see Volta, 1987, 71–9). All in Satie's hand, apart from
two interspersed letters by Latour.

Second version (recopied overnight on 16–17 Dec 1892 to
show to Eugène Bertrand at the Paris Opéra on 17th) in
BN 9631. This is all by Satie, and has different stage
settings for each Act. Pubd (all in lower case) in the
large *Uspud* brochure (with only minor changes) (Paris,
Imprimerie Artistique, [1893]). *Uspud* may well have
been intended for the shadow theatre as a genial parody
of Flaubert's *La Tentation de Saint Antoine*

music: short sections for fls, hps and str with text read in
between. The short score would, however, be more
practical on harmonium (see Fig. 2.2)

MSS: Private coll. in France, first version for fls and hps only (as in *Le Fils des étoiles*), carnet of 46pp. (incl. first version of text). Dated '17 Nov 1892'

BN 9631, second version for fls, hps, str ('quatuor'), 48pp. Music is the same, apart from the opening motif in octaves (missing in the first version). A few extra dynamics and pause bars are also added. Dated 'Novembre de 92' but actually recopied on 16–17 Dec 1892

pubn: extracts in small *Uspud* brochure (April 1895). Music as in BN 9631 (see W, 135)

Short score (as in BN 9631): Salabert, 1970

prem.: Opéra-Comique, 9 May 1979 by Michel Tranchant (pf), Hubert Camerlo (narrator), with slide projections by Robert Doisneau

Dec 1892   **Noël**

text: shadow play by Vincent Hyspa (lost)

music: lost, but score may have been compiled from existing pieces, like the *Gnossiennes*

MSS: PLU

prem.: ?25 Dec 1892, as first shadow play in cellars of the Auberge du Clou, 30 avenue Trudaine (together with *La Styliste* by Henri de Wendel). Scenery by Miguel Utrillo

?1893   **Eginhard. Prélude**

music: piece for pf, possibly incidental music for a play (author unknown)

MSS: BN 10038, 2ff.

pubn: Rouart-Lerolle, 1929 (as the second of *4 Préludes*)

'21–3 March 1893'   **Danses Gothiques** (*Cultifiements et Coadunations Choristiques. Neuvaine pour le plus grand calme et la forte tranquillité de mon âme*)

music: a continuous chunk of motivically interrelated music, split up into 9 dances by the insertion of titles (which sometimes appear in mid-motif). Composed in the midst of Satie's affair with the painter Suzanne Valadon

1   *A l'occasion d'une grande peine*

2   *Dans laquelle les Pères de la Très Véritable et Très Sainte Eglise sont invoqués*

3   *En faveur d'un malheureux*

4   *A propos de Saint Bernard et de Sainte Lucie*

    5 *Pour les pauvres trépassés*
    6 *Où il est question du pardon des injures reçues*
    7 *Par pitié pour les ivrognes, honteux, débauchés, imparfaits, désagréables, et faussaires en tous genres*
    8 *En le haut honneur du vénéré Saint Michel, le gracieux Archange*
    9 *Après avoir obtenu la remise de ses fautes*

ded.: à la Transcendante, Solennelle et Représentative Extase de Saint Benoît, Préparatoire et Méthodique du Très Puissant Ordre des Bénédictins. Le 21 Mars de 93 à Paris, le soleil étant sur la terre

MSS: BN 10048, 13ff. Dated at end '23 Mars de 93. Paris. 6, rue Cortot' and registered with SACEM on 24 March. 5 of the 10 motifs use cells found in the *Fête donnée* of ?1892 (see Fig. 9.1)

pubn: No. 1 in *Revue musicale SIM*, 7/3 (15 March 1911), 39–40

    All 9: Rouart-Lerolle, 1929

'2 April 1893'

Bonjour Biqui, Bonjour!

music: brief song for v, pf. Text (as title) by Satie, accompanied by his portrait of Valadon

ded.: à Suzanne Valadon [Biqui]

MSS: *F-Pfs*, 1f. (kept at 6 rue Cortot, Paris 18, as part of display in Satie museum)

pubn: facs. in Templier, 1969, plate 32; W, 136

1893

Ontrotance; Corcleru; Irnebizolle; Tumisrudebude

music: ballets in 1, 3, 2 and 3 Acts respectively, planned with Contamine de Latour as offshoots of *Uspud* starring members of the Uspud clan (see chapter 10 n. 11). Announced in the large *Uspud* brochure of April 1893, where *Ontrotance* is reported as being 'in preparation'. No trace of these ballets has survived

?mid-1893

Vexations

music: short self-repeating passage for pf, which is itself repeated 840 times, after a period of silent meditation

MSS: *F-Pfs*, 1f. (kept at 6 rue Cortot, Paris 18)

pubn: facs. in *Contrepoints*, 6 (1949), opposite p. 8; Eschig, 1969, as second of *Pages mystiques*

prem.: Richard David Hames (aged 13), Lewes Grammar School, Sussex, 1958 (inc. ?)

    Pocket Theatre, New York, 9 Sept 1963, organized by

John Cage (complete: 18 hours 40 minutes). Pianists: John Cage, David Tudor, Christian Wolff, Philip Corner, Viola Farber, Robert Wood, MacRae Cook, John Cale, David Del Tredici, James Tenney, Howard Klein (substitute), Joshua Rifkin (substitute)

?mid-1893   **Roxane**
music: setting for v, orch of poem by Contamine de Latour, listed in letter to Conrad Satie on 28 June 1893. Music and text lost

?Feb 1894   **Prélude de La Porte héroïque du ciel**
music: incidental music for esoteric drama in 1 Act by Jules Bois (Paris, Librairie de l'Art Indépendant, March 1894). Later orch. by Roland-Manuel
ded.: 'Je me dédie cette œuvre. E.S.'
MSS: PLU. BN Rés. Vma 170 (corr. proofs, 1912)
pubn: facs. in *Le Cœur*, 2/8 (March 1894), 4–5. Also pubd on pp. 20–1 of Bois's drama
Rouart-Lerolle, 1912; Salabert, 1968
prem.: ?With Bois's play, 29 May 1894 (play reviewed in *L'Observateur Français* on 30 May)
In orch. by Roland-Manuel, SMI, Salle Gaveau, 17 June 1912

c. 1894   **Messe de la foi**
music: mentioned in applications for election to the Académie des Beaux-Arts on 30 April 1894 and 14 April 1896. A drawing of an organ survives inscribed 'Messe de la foi de Erik Satie' (facs. in Vy, 100). Music lost or never started

1893–5   **Messe des pauvres** (*Grande Messe de l'Eglise Métropolitaine d'Art*)
music: Mass for org, with small choir of children and men (SB) specified in *Kyrie eleison*. In *Le Cœur*, 2/10 (June 1895), 3 Conrad Satie says that the work 'begins with a very characteristic prelude that forms the basis of the Mass'. This is the passage before the voices enter on p. 2 system 2 of the Salabert ed. Conrad also says that the *Prière des orgues* comes between 'the *Kyrie* and the *Gloria*', so the lost *Gloria* must have been the fifth movement (see list below). In p. 9 of the pubd ed., the *Chant Ecclésiastique* should end with the second system. It is followed by two harmonizations of the

Prière pour les voyageurs (systems 3–4 and 5–6). Satie intended the second, less chromatic (titled) version in contrary motion to be his final version, so p. 9 systems 3–4 can be dispensed with in performance. Satie almost certainly intended to write further movements for this Mass, but those he wrote were organized as follows:

1 *Prélude*
2 *Kyrie eleison* (?inc.)
3 *Dixit Dominus*
4 *Prière des Orgues*
5 *Gloria* (lost)
6 *Commune qui mundi nefas*
7 *Chant Ecclésiastique*
8 *Prière pour les voyageurs et les marins en danger de mort, à la très bonne et très auguste Vierge Marie, mère de Jésus*
9 *Prière pour le salut de mon âme*

Gowers (1965–6, 2) suggests a date of 1893 for No. 9, the other movements probably date from 1894–5

MSS: Nos. 1 and 2 (pubd ed. 1–2 system 1; 2 system 2–5 system 3): BN 9597(2), 11–25 (draft)

Sketches (in compositional order, as far as this can be discerned, with note-values half of those in the pubd ed.): Ho 62, f. 4r, v; BN 9597(1), 1; BN 9597(2), 40 (inverted); BN 9597(1), 5–6; BN 9597(1bis), f. 9; BN 9597(2), 7–9; BN 9597(2), 28–22 (inverted); BN 9597(1bis), ff. 6r–7r

No. 3: BN 9597(1bis), f. 10 (with 3 different versions of the text. This first verse of Psalm 109, set to the Primus Tonus chant in Gregorian notation, can be found in Ho 85, 1 (cf. *Paroissien Romain*, 218), though this melodic line was not preserved in any of the harmonized settings)

No. 4: Complete draft assembled from BN 9597(2), 6+BN 9597(1bis), f. 9v+BN 9597(2), 26–30. Earlier sketches: Ho 62, f. 5v; BN 9597(1bis), f. 9r

No. 5: PLU

No. 6: Ho 62, f. 5r, v (central part only)

No. 7: BN 9597(1bis), f. 1r

No. 8: First version (pubd ed., 9 systems 3–4): BN 9597(1bis), f. 5r. Second version (pubd ed., 9 systems 5–6): BN 9597(1bis), f. 3r

No. 9: BN 9597(1bis), f. 2r, v

Note: Lists of motifs for the Mass can be found in Ho 62, f. 6 (see Gowers, 1965–6, 14); BN 9597(1), 11–13; BN 9597(1bis), ff. 8r–10v. According to Steven Moore Whiting, Ho 62 includes several pages torn by Satie from BN 9597(1–2). It also contains other sketches which may have been intended for the Mass: *Spiritus sancte deus miserere nobis* (Ho 62, f. 11r); *Modéré* (for org?, dated '15 June 1893' in Ho 62, f. 7r, with a first version in Ho 51); *Harmonies de Saint-Jean* (Ho 62, f. 10r)

pubn: No. 3 (disguised in fake Gregorian notation, for org?) in brochure *Intende votis supplicum* (Paris, Librairie de l'Art Indépendant, March 1895); facs. in W, 42. Another setting of the same text can be found in a similar Gregorian fake in *La Revue musicale*, 214 (June 1952), facing 80

No. 4: facs. in *Le Cœur*, 2/10 (June 1895), 2

No. 6: extract in brochure *Commune qui mundi nefas* (private ed., January 1895), facs. in W, 38–9

Complete Mass (without *Gloria*): Rouart-Lerolle, 1920; Salabert. The text of the movement entitled 'Dixit domine' should read 'Dixit Dominus Domino meo/ Sede a dextris meis' (Psalm 109, verse 1)

1895	**Psaumes** music: announced as forthcoming in the small *Uspud* brochure (April 1895), 4. Music lost, or never started
'Jan 1897'	**Gnossienne** [No. 6] music: piece for pf MSS: BN 10054(2), ff. 1r and 2v pubn: Salabert, 1968 (as '6th Gnossienne')

March 1897	**Pièces froides**
	music: 6 pieces for pf in 2 sets. Satie began to orchestrate several of them, but never got beyond the first few bars
	1 *Airs à faire fuir* (3)
	2 *Danses de travers* (3)
	ded.: 1 à Ricardo Viñes
	      2 à Madame Jules Ecorcheville
	MSS: 1 BN 10047(1), 6pp., copy for printer; BN Rés. Vma 166, corr. proofs (1912)
	  Air No. 1: BN 9575(1), 27–9 (draft); Ho 55; BN 9575(2), 3–5, 25, 29, 30–1 (inc. scorings for various small orch formats); BN 9575(1), 24 (end, for pf)

Air No. 2: BN 9575(1), 29 (inc. draft); Ho 63, BN 9575(1), 24 (sketches); BN 9575(2), 6 (inc. scoring). The origins of No. 2 can be seen in Satie's harmonizations of *The Keel Row* in BN 10054(2), f. 2*v* (see Ex. 81)

Air No. 3: Ho 63, BN 9575(1), 23–4 (sketches)

2 BN 10047(2), 6pp., copy for printer; BN Rés. Vma 166, corr. proofs (1912; 2 sets); BN 9575(1), 9–12 (draft of all 3 dances)

Danse No. 1: Ho 64 (incl. sketches in 10 numbered cells, f. 7r, *v*)

Danse No. 2: BN 9575(1), 7, 9 (inc. scorings)

pubn: Rouart-Lerolle, 1912; Salabert, 1973. A complete, rejected version of the second *Danse de travers* was pubd by Salabert, 1970 (ed. Robert Caby). Its sources are BN 9575(2), 13 and Ho 64 (final version, ff. 5r, 6r, with sketches on f. 9r, *v*)

?1897
Je te veux

text: song by Henry Pacory. A more daring first version of the text can be found in BN 10057, and Satie may have assisted with the watered-down pubd version, as popularized by Paulette Darty

music: waltz song for v, pf with 2 verses and a repeated chorus. Satie also scored *Je te veux* for brasserie orch (fl, cl in A, bn, hn, 2 cornets in A, str), and for full orch (pic, fl, ob, 2 cl in B♭, bn or tuba, 2 hn, 2 cornets in B♭, 3 trbn, perc, str), adding a new Trio in the process. The 1897 dating comes from Roland-Manuel's lecture on Satie (1916, 11), though the song was not registered with SACEM until 20 Nov 1902

MSS: BN 10056, OS in D (brasserie orch), 4ff.

BN 10057, VS in C, 2pp.

BN 10058, OS in C (full orch, with added Trio), 8ff.

BN 10059, orch parts (vn 2, va, vc, cornet 2), mostly for BN 10058 above

F-Pca, pic part corr. by Satie

F-Psa, corr. proofs of VS

pubn: VS: Baudoux, 1902; Bellon Ponscarme, 1903; Rouart-Lerolle; Salabert

OS: Rouart-Lerolle, 1919; Salabert, 1978

June–July 1899
Jack-in-the-Box

text: pantomime in 2 acts by Jules Dépaquit

music: incidental music planned for a production at the Comédie Parisienne in Oct 1899 (letter to Conrad Satie, 15 June 1899). Satie also referred to his score as a 'suite anglaise', and described the project as 'more of a "clownerie" than a pantomime' to Conrad on 4 July 1899. Only a short score in 3 movements has survived, which was orch. by Milhaud:

1 *Prélude*
2 *Entr'acte*
3 *Final*

MSS: Ho 15 (short score, 15ff., versos only). Sketches in Ho 10, ff. 2*v*, 5*v*–6*v*, 8*r*, 11*r*; Ho 11, ff. 1–3*r*, 4*r*–11*r*; Ho 12, 30; Ho 33 (1p.: No. 1 titled *Gigue*); Ho 50 (5ff. No. 2 orig. titled *Marche sourde des Repasseurs de couteaux, des Tireurs de chenilles, et des Casseurs de briques* on f. 2*r*, and constructed from 16 numbered cells found on f. 1*r* – which also contains the theme of No. 1, bars 46–56, accompanied by a long heroic text by Satie)
        BN 17677(10), pf score by Milhaud, *c.* 1925, 5pp.

pubn: Universal Edition, 1929 (short score and OS by Milhaud)

prem.: 3 June 1926 (in Milhaud's orch.), Diaghilev's Ballets Russes, Théâtre Sarah Bernhardt. Sets and costumes by Derain, choreography by Balanchine
    In orig. version with Dépaquit's play, 29 Nov 1937, Salle d'Iéna, in soirée 'L'Humour d'Erik Satie'

?summer 1899

Un Dîner à l'Elysée

text: cabaret song by Vincent Hyspa
music: song for v, pf
MSS: Ho 12, 24–5; Ho 62, f. 1*v*; Ho 66. Titled *Peintres français*. Sketches in Ho 10, ff. 1–2*r*; Ho 11, ff. 12*v*–13*r*
pubn: in Vincent Hyspa: *Chansons d'humour* (Paris, Enoch, 1903), 107–13 (with drawings by Jules Dépaquit)

c. 1899

Le Veuf

text: humorous song by Vincent Hyspa ('Elle avait des cils noirs comme toutes les blondes')
music: cabaret song for v, pf. Exists in 2 versions: the first returns as the central section of No. 4 of the *Trois Morceaux en forme de poire* (1903)
MSS: First version: Ho 8, ff. 1*v*–2*r* (neat copy); Ho 10, ff. 9*v*–10*r*; Ho 11, ff. 15*v*–16*r* (drafts); Ho 10, f. 10*v*; Ho 11, ff. 14*v*–15*r* and 16*v*–17*r* (sketches)

Second version: Ho 11, ff. 11*v*–12*r* (neat copy); Ho 10,
ff. 8*v*–9*r* (draft); Ho 11, ff. 13*v*–14*r* (sketches)
pubn: facs. in Whiting, 1984, 150–1 and 153–4 (both versions); transcr. in Gowers, 1966, Ph.D. 5375, 169–72
(versions in reverse order)

c. 1899   **Sorcière**
text: song by Satie(?), written for Vincent Hyspa
music: cabaret song for v, pf
MSS: Ho 10, ff. 12*v*, 13*r*; Ho 73 (drafts)
Ho 10, ff. 11*r*, 13*r* (sketches)
unpubd

c. 1899   **Le Picador est mort**
text: ?song by Vincent Hyspa
music: cabaret song for v, pf
MSS: Ho 11, f. 18; Ho 73 (drafts)
Ho 10, f. 11*v* (sketch)
unpubd

c. 1899   **Enfant martyre**
text: ?song by Vincent Hyspa
music: cabaret song for v, pf
MSS: Ho 10, f. 12*r*; Ho 11, f. 19*v*; Ho 73 (drafts)
Ho 10, ff. 11*v*–12*r* (sketches)
unpubd

c. 1899   **Air fantôme** [*Petit Recueil des fêtes*]
text: song by Vincent Hyspa
music: cabaret song for v, pf
MSS: Ho 2, f. 13*v*; Ho 11, f. 17*v*; Ho 12, p. 13; Ho 73
(drafts)
Ho 10, f. 11*r*; Ho 12, f. 13*r* (sketches)
unpubd

c. 1899   **Aline-Polka** (Pacory arr. Satie)
music: short polka by Henry Pacory transcr. for pf by Satie
MSS: Ho 61 (1f., inc., 21 bars only)
unpubd

c. 1899–1900   **Geneviève de Brabant**
text: 3-act play in verse and prose by Lord Cheminot (Contamine de Latour), 32ff. MS in archives of Comte
Etienne de Beaumont (see Volta, 1987, 16–31)
music: short score for solo vv, chorus, pf (probably for

shadow theatre). Orch. by Roger Désormière in 1926
for fl, ob, 2 cl in B♭, bn, 2 hn, cornet, trbn, perc, str

  1 *Prélude*
ACT 1
  2 *Chœur*: 'Nous sommes la foule compacte'
  3 *Entrée des soldats*
ACT 2
  4 *Entr'acte*
  5 *Air de Geneviève* ('Innocente d'un crime que je n'ai pas
     commis')
  6 *Sonnerie de cor*
  7 *Entrée des soldats*
ACT 3
  8 *Entr'acte*
  9 *Chœur* (repeat of No. 2)
 10 *Air de Golo* ('Non, Sifroy n'est pas mort')
 11 *Entrée des soldats*
 12 *Cortège/Marche*
 13 *Entrée des soldats*
 14 *Petit air de Geneviève* ('Ah! Le ciel récompense ma vertu,
     ma constance')
 15 *Chœur final* ('L'affaire c'est bien passée')
Note: Nos. 1, 3, 4, 7, 8, 11 and 13 all use the same
     material, with slight variations
MSS: BN 15333, 8ff. (VS)
     Sketches: Ho 10, ff. 13*v*–16*v*; Ho 11, ff. 20–22; Ho 52
     (1f.); Ho 67, ff. 2*r*, 3*r*
pubn: Universal Edition, 1930 (VS and OS). New ed. of
     Satie's VS with Latour's libretto (ed. Ornella Volta),
     Universal Edition, 1989
prem.: 17 May 1926 (in Désormière's orch.), Théâtre des
     Champs-Elysées, produced by Manuel Ortiz in Satie
     Festival organized by Comte Etienne de Beaumont
     In version for marionettes, with Latour's libretto,
     13 April 1983, Compagnia Carlo Colla & Figli, Gran
     Teatro la Fenice, Venice

'18 April 1900'   **Prélude de 'La Mort de Monsieur Mouche'**
text: play in 3 Acts by Contamine de Latour (lost). Ho 10,
     f. 13*v* states that Acts 1 and 3 take place 'in a restau-
     rant', with Act 2 set 'chez Monsieur Mouche'
music: prelude for pf. Registered at SACEM on 18 April
     1900

MSS: BN 9600, ff. 1r, 2r (numbered 13, 15).

   Sketches in Ho 10, f. 13v

pubn: in *Carnets d'esquisses et de croquis*, 13–14 (ed. Robert
      Caby), Salabert, 1968

'5 Aug 1900'

Verset laïque & somptueux

music: piece for pf, last of the 'musique à genoux'

MSS: *F-Po* 1900 𝄞 XIV (255) (facs.)

pubn: facs. in *Autographes de Musiciens Contemporaines 1900*,
      vol. 8, 255 (pubd for Exposition Universelle), re-
      produced in Vy, 40

'March 1901'

The Dreamy Fish

text: tale by Lord Cheminot (Contamine de Latour).
   Lost

music: extended piece (187 bars) for pf to accompany above
      story. The theme in bars 17f. shows affinities with the
      prelude to *Jack-in-the-Box*. Bars 94–108 of the central
      section are taken from *Geneviève de Brabant*, No. 14

MSS: BN 9587, 14pp. (with many corrections). Sketches
      in BN 9600, ff. 2v, 3r (numbered 16–17); Ho 10,
      ff. 17r–18v; Ho 11, ff. 19r, 22–3 (also titled *Rêverie
      burlesque*); Ho 57 (4pp.)

pubn: Salabert, 1970 (ed. Robert Caby)

?1901

The Angora Ox (Le Bœuf Angora)

text: tale by Lord Cheminot (Contamine de Latour).
   Lost

music: inc. score for large orch (pic, 2fl, ob, eng hn, 2 cl in
      A, 2 bn, 2 hn in F, 2 tpt in C, 3 trbn, tuba, timp, perc,
      str). Bars 66–73 recur in *Redite* in the *Trois Morceaux en
      forme de poire* (1903)

MSS: BN 10062, 9pp., inc. OS with some corr. (?by
      Charles Koechlin); BN 9598, 7–8 (inc. short score)

   Sketches in BN 9598, 4, 6–8, 10–11; BN 9629, 6–7,
      16, 19

unpubd. Transcr. in Gowers, 1966, Ph.D. 5376, 173–90
      (Exx. 57 (short score), 58 (OS))

?1901

Chanson barbare

music: inc. piece for pf

MSS: BN 9598, 4

unpubd

?1901

Tendrement [formerly *Illusion*]

text: song by Vincent Hyspa

music: orig. waltz in B♭, titled *Illusion*. Scored for pic, fl, ob, 2 cl in B♭, bn or tuba, 2 hn, 2 cornets in B♭, 3 trbn, perc, str. Registered at SACEM on 13 Jan 1902. Reappears as waltz song *Tendrement* (in A♭), with 2 verses and recurring chorus, as popularized by Hyspa and Paulette Darty. Registered at SACEM on 29 March 1902. Also exists as pf solo

MSS: As *Illusion*: Ho 35 (OS, 7pp., and pf solo version, 1p.)

As *Tendrement*: BN 10073 and Ho 69 (pf solo version). Ho 10, ff. 19*v*–20*v*; Ho 58, f. 3*v*; BN 9629, 2–3, 9 (sketches and melodic drafts)

F-Psa, corr. proofs

F-Ptb, corr. proofs

pubn: *Illusion* (OS), Salabert, 1979

Tendrement (VS), Baudoux, 1902; Bellon Ponscarme, 1903; Rouart-Lerolle; Salabert

?1901

Poudre d'or

music: waltz for pf or orch (pic, fl, ob, 2 cl in A, bn or tuba, 2 hn, 2 cornets in A, 3 trbn, perc, str)

ded.: à Mademoiselle Stéphanie Nantas

MSS: BN 10061, OS (final version, 8ff., when BN 10060, ff. 7–8 are added)

BN 10060, draft OS. Registered with SACEM on 11 March 1902: ff. 7–8 (coda) belong with BN 10061

F-Psalabert, pf solo (MS for printer, 2pp.)

F-Psa, orch parts

Ho 58, part for trbn 2

BN 9614, 1–5 (sketches, orig. title *Pluie d'or*)

BN Rés. Vma 169, corr. proofs

pubn: Pf solo: Baudoux, 1902; Rouart-Lerolle; Salabert
OS: Salabert, 1978

Aug–Nov 1903
(using material written
in 1890–1; ?1899–1903)

Trois Morceaux en forme de poire

music: 7 pieces for pf duet

1　*Manière de commencement* (a *Gnossienne* from Act 1 of *Le Fils des étoiles*, 1891)

2　*Prolongation du même* (uses inc. *Café-concert* song *Le Roi soleil de plomb*, c. 1900)

3　*Morceau I*: Lentement (1903)

4　*Morceau II*: Enlevé (uses cabaret songs *Impérial-Napoléon*, c. 1901, with first version of *Le Veuf*, c. 1899, in the centre)

5   *Morceau III*: Brutal (1903)
6   *En plus* (uses *Danse* for orch, 5 Dec 1890)
7   *Redite* (based on bars 66–73 of *The Angora Ox*, *c.* 1901;
    see Gillmor, 1988, 131–2 for a comparison)
MSS: *F-Po* Nouveaux Fonds Rés. 218 (final copy of all 7,
    incl. letter of intent of '6 Nov 1903')
  No. 1: BN 10052(1), ff. 9*v*–12*r* (1891); BN 10045, ff. 2*r*, 3,
      4*v* (sketches, 1903)
  No. 2: BN 9600, f. 7*v* (*Le Roi soleil de plomb*); BN 9600,
      ff. 8, 9*r*, 11*v*, 12*r*; BN 9614, 29, 22, 31 [in order]
      (sketches and drafts)
  No. 3: BN 9599, 19–21 (draft)
  No. 4: BN 9598, 5 (*Impérial-Napoléon*, *c.* 1899: listed
      as the 'Romanian song "Impérial César"' in the MS).
      First version of *Le Veuf*, see 1899 above. Arr. of *Le
      Veuf* for pf duet: BN 9598, 14–15, 20; BN 9599, 14–15,
      17; BN 10045, ff. 1*v*, 5*r*, 6*r*; plus BN 9629, 17–19
      (draft, 1903)
  No. 5: BN 9614, 27 (bars 5–20); Ho 53 (central section
      before letter C. This also appears earlier in Ho 64, f. 6*r*
      as part of the piece titled *Danse de travers II*, a rejected
      version pubd by Salabert in 1970); BN 10044 (draft,
      5pp., with 2pp. sketches)
  No. 6: Ho 48 (14pp., 1890); BN 10045, f. 4*r* (sketches,
      1903)
  No. 7: BN 10062 (?1901); BN 9629, 6–7; BN 9614, 33–4
      (drafts, 1903)
  Corr. proofs: BN Rés. Vma 164 (1911)
pubn: Nos. 3 and 4 (bars 1–32) in *Revue musicale SIM*, 7/3
    (15 March 1911), 35–8
  All 7: Rouart-Lerolle, 1911
prem.: (public) ?18 April 1916, Société Lyre et Palette, 6 rue
    Huyghens by Satie and Ricardo Viñes

?June 1904   **La Diva de l'‘Empire’**
text: cabaret song by Dominique Bonnaud and Numa Blès
music: 'Intermezzo Américaine' or 'Marche chantée' with
    2 verses and recurring chorus for v, pf. Also exists as
    pf solo (referred to by Satie as the *Stand-Walk Marche*
    or the *Little Girl* March), and in a version for brasserie
    orch (pic, fl, cl in A, bn, hn, cornet in A, trbn, perc,
    str)
ded.: à Paulette Darty

MSS: BN 10064, VS in G for printers, 1904, 1f.

BN 10065, OS in G, 4ff., no voice part

BN 10066, pf solo in D, 2pp., titled *Stand-Walk Marche*

BN 10067, vocal part only, in D, 2pp.

BN 10068, orch parts for fl, bn, cornet in A, trbn (from BN 10065)

pubn: VS: Bellon Ponscarme, 1904; in journal *Paris qui chante*, 4/155 (7 Jan 1906), 12ff.; Rouart-Lerolle, 1919; Salabert, 1976

OS: Rouart-Lerolle, 1919; Salabert, 1978

prem.: in revue *Dévidons la bobine* by Bonnaud and Blès at Berck (Pas-de-Calais) on 26 July 1904, sung by Paulette Darty

In concert: 8 April 1905 by Paulette Darty and Satie, Théâtre des Bouffes-Parisiens (45e Samedi Populaire, featuring 'Les Danses d'Erik Satie' pubd by Bellon Ponscarme, organized by Louis Payen and Emile Vuillermoz)

1904   **Le Piccadilly. Marche**

music: March for pf (orig. titled *La Transatlantique*). Also arr. for str orch. See chapter 9, p. 202

MSS: BN 9629, 30–3; BN 10070 (versions for pf solo, the latter titled *La Transatlantique*)

BN 10071 (OS for str, printer's copy)

pubn: Pf solo and OS: Alexis Rouart, 1907; Salabert, 1975

Aug 1904–6   **Pousse l'amour** (?later revived as *Coco chéri*)

text: operetta (or fantaisie) in 1 Act by Maurice de Féraudy (of Comédie-Française) and Jean Kolb. Libretto lost, though Satie described it as 'killing' in a letter to Paulette Darty (who arranged the commission) on 16 Aug 1904

music: only sketches of 4 numbers survive, as far as is known. Ho 3 may be a rehearsal score

MSS: Ho 2, ff. 16v–17, 19v–20; Ho 3, ff. 1v, 2r (*De Féraudy. Valse*)

Ho 8, f. 7r (*Valse du Champagne*)

Ho 8, f. 15v (draft); Ho 3, f. 5v (neat copy of *Le Champagne. Valse* – different from *Valse du Champagne* above)

Ho 3, ff. 2v–5r (*Chanson Andalouse*, possibly for *Pousse l'amour*)

unpubd (though Satie signed a contract with A. Ponscarme et Cie. on 26 April 1906, and received 100 francs for 'deux manuscrits de musique intercalée dans *Pousse l'amour*', which was then destined for the Théâtre des Capucines)

prem.: Comédie Royale, Paris, 22 Nov 1907

?Revived as *Coco chéri*, Théâtre des Beaux-Arts, Monte Carlo, 28 Feb 1913

c. 1905   **Chez le docteur**

text: humorous song by Vincent Hyspa (11 verses)

music: cabaret song for v, pf

MSS: BN 10074, neat copy, 1p. No text

Ho 2, ff. 15*v*–16*r*; Ho 71 (drafts)

Ho 8, ff. 10*v*–11*r* (sketches)

pubn: in *L'Album musical*, 33 (Paris, Enoch, March 1906); Salabert, 1976

c. 1905   **L'Omnibus automobile**

text: humorous song by Vincent Hyspa (6 verses)

music: cabaret song for v, pf

MSS: Ho 8, f. 9 (draft)

pubn: in *L'Album musical*, 33 (Enoch, March 1906); Salabert, 1976

c. 1905   **Impérial-Oxford**

text: song by Contamine de Latour (lost)

music: cabaret song for v, pf. Registered at SACEM on 18 Aug 1905 as 'chanson sans paroles'

MSS: Coll. Oliver Neighbour, London (neat copy)

Ho 8, ff. 2*v*–3*v* (sketches)

pubn: extract in W, 153

c. 1905   **Légende Californienne**

text: song by Contamine de Latour (lost)

music: cabaret song for v, pf. Registered at SACEM on 18 Aug 1905 as 'chanson sans paroles'. Later orch. as the *Grande Ritournelle* in *La Belle Excentrique* (1920)

MSS: Ho 34 (short score with orch indications)

BN 9629, 26–7 (sketches)

pubn: extract in W, 155. As part of *La Belle Excentrique*: Editions de La Sirène, 1922; Eschig, 1950; rev. ed. by Ornella Volta, Eschig, 1987

1905   **Allons-y Chochotte**

text: song by D. Durante (5 verses)

music: cabaret song for v, pf written for Paulette Darty. Registered with SACEM on 11 Jan 1906

MSS: Ho 39 (neat copy with text, 2pp.)
　　BN 9617(2), 20–1 (neat copy in A major)
　　Ho 2, ff. 17v–19r, 20v–21r (sketches)
pubn: Salabert, 1978; extract in W, 154

c. 1905　**Rambouillet**
text: author unknown
music: song (?without words) for v, pf
MSS: Ho 40, 1p.
pubn: Salabert, 1978 (as first of *Trois Mélodies sans paroles*)

c. 1905　**Les Oiseaux**
text: author unknown
music: song (?without words) for v, pf
MSS: Ho 41, 1p.
pubn: Salabert, 1978 (as second of *Trois Mélodies sans paroles*)

c. 1905　**Marienbad**
text: author unknown
music: song (?without words) for v, pf
MSS: Ho 42, 1p.
pubn: Salabert, 1978 (as third of *Trois Mélodies sans paroles*)

c. 1905–6　**Psitt! Psitt!**
text: author unknown ('Les homm'se donn'nt vraiment trop
　　　d'mal pour apprend'un tas d'langues')
music: humorous cabaret song for v, pf
MSS: Ho 9, ff. 9v–12, 14 (drafts)
　　Ho 9, ff. 13, 15 (sketches)
unpubd

c. 1905–6　**Padacale**
music: inc. sketch for pf
MSS: BN 9642, 46
unpubd

c. 1905–6　**Aim-Chéri**
music: inc. waltz for pf
MSS: BN 9642, 49
unpubd

c. 1906　**Fugue-Valse**
music: extended piece for pf, later adapted as the *Danse de
　　　tendresse* in *Mercure*
MSS: BN 9635, 4–9 (draft); BN 9635, 2–3 (sketches)
pubn: see *Mercure* (1924)

1906   **Chanson médiévale**
text: chivalric poem by Catulle Mendès
music: song for v, pf. Written as an exercise at the Schola
     Cantorum
MSS: BN 9617(1), 3–5 (draft); Ho 46 (melody only, 1f.,
     with comments by Vincent d'Indy)
pubn: Salabert, 1968 (as second of *Trois Autres Mélodies*).
     Facs. of Ho 46 in W, 124

'July 1906'   **Passacaille**
music: piece for pf
MSS: BN 10039 (copy for printer, 2pp.); Ho 8, ff. 17*v*–19*v*
     (sketches)
pubn: Rouart-Lerolle, 1929; Salabert

'21 Oct 1906'   **Prélude en tapisserie**
music: piece for pf
MSS: BN 9617(1), 12–15 (neat copy, dated 'Arcueil, le
     21 octobre 1906')
     BN 9617(2), 26–30 (sketches, numbered cells)
pubn: Rouart-Lerolle, 1929; Salabert (dated '12 Oct 1906'
     at end, probably in error)

summer 1907   **Nouvelles 'Pièces froides'**
music: 3 pieces for pf. According to a letter to Florent
     Schmitt, Nos. 1–2 were completed by 22 Aug 1907
1 *Sur un mur*
2 *Sur un arbre*
3 *Sur un pont*
MSS: BN 9613, 14–25 (neat copies of all 3)
     Ho 70, 2ff., *r* only (first version of No. 1 titled *Sérénade
     Sépulcrale – Prélude*. This shows bars 3–21 of No. 1 as a
     complete piece in C major, with the recurring melody
     outlined like a 'chant donné' in red ink. Sketches for
     the remaining bars (1–2, 22–4) can be found on f. 2*v*,
     also in C, together with a transposition of bar 19 as it
     appears in No. 1 above. A melodic draft (also in C)
     appears in Ho 7, f. 10*r*)
     BN 9653, 4–5 (first version of No. 2); 6–8 (sketches
     for No. 2 entitled *'Suite pour un chien'* – cf. *Préludes
     flasques*, 1912)
pubn: Salabert, 1968

'29 Jan 1908'   **Fâcheux exemple**
                            music: inc. Schola Cantorum counterpoint exercise in
                                3 parts
                            MSS: BN 9641, 4–5
                            pubn: Salabert, 1968 (as third of *Musiques intimes et secrètes*.
                                The last 5 bars are completed by the editor, Robert
                                Caby)

'12 Feb 1908'   **Désespoir agréable**
                            music: Schola Cantorum exercise in 3 parts
                            MSS: BN 9641, 8–9
                            pubn: Salabert, 1968 (as first of *Six pièces de la période
                                1906–13*, ed. Robert Caby)

late Aug 1908–Oct 1912   **Aperçus désagréables**
                            music: 3 pieces for pf duet
                            1 *Pastorale* (Oct 1912)
                            2 *Choral* (Sept 1908)
                            3 *Fugue* (late Aug/Sept 1908)
                               The *Fugue*, with its dialogue between the 2 performers,
                                was designed for Satie to play with Debussy. They
                                first did this early in Sept 1908, as a description of the
                                piece has survived in a letter from Debussy to Lacerda
                                on 5 Sept (Nichols, *Debussy Letters*, 1987, 196). The
                                other two pieces may have been similarly conceived.
                                Satie also planned a set of 4 *Impressions Parisiennes*
                                about this time (BN 9579, 1), whose titles were *Le
                                Réveil de Paris*; *L'Autobus*; *L'Avenue du Bois* [*chez
                                Debussy*]; *Les Courses* (cf. *Sports et divertissements*,
                                No. 13)
                            MSS: BN 10041 (neat copies for the printer, Nos. 1–3)
                                BN 9577, 12–13 (first version, No. 1, inc.)
                                BN 9577, 2–5 (arr. of No. 2 for str quartet, made on the
                                advice of the composer Robert Montfort in Aug 1912.
                                Satie intended to arr. the *Fugue* too, but never did)
                            pubn: Demets, 1913; Eschig, 1967

1908–9   **Petite Sonate**
                            music: 82-bar movement written in the class of Vincent
                                d'Indy at the Schola Cantorum (part of the 'IIIe
                                Cours'). A possible second movement can be found in
                                Ho 4
                            MSS: BN 10033(11) (neat copy, 5pp.)
                                BN 9643, 22–3, 34–6, 44–6; BN 9649, 4–6, 14, 20–2;
                                BN 9650, 4–9 (sketches)

Ho 4, ff. 1*v*–3*v* (a complete 71-bar movement in C
marked 'Lent' may well be the slow movement of this
Sonata, though it has no title)

pubn: Bars 1–10 as 'Choral No. 12' in *Douze petits chorals*
(ed. Robert Caby), Salabert, 1968

1908–9 **Chœur d'adolescents**

music: inc. piece for ?vv, pf, perhaps for use in Arcueil
(marked 'Salvazet' in the top right-hand corner)

MSS: Ho 5, ff. 14*v*–15*r*

unpubd

1908–9 **Dieu Credo rouge**

music: inc. piece for ?vv, pf, perhaps for use with Parti
Radical-Socialiste in Arcueil

MSS: Ho 5, ff. 15*v*–16*r*

unpubd

c. 1908–9 **'Il portait un gilet'**

music: cabaret song for v, pf

MSS: BN 9579, 18–21 (2 settings)

unpubd

c. 1909 **Deux Choses**

music: 2 pieces for pf

1 *Effronterie*

2 *Poésie*

MSS: No. 1: BN 9589(1), 14–15, 18–19, 22–3, 26–7 (draft);
BN 9589(2), 4–11, 24–5, 27 (sketches). Also titled
Elégie commerciale on p. 24

No. 2: BN 9589(2), 16–17. Titled *Deux Choses: Poésie*

A third inc. *Chose* for pf, titled *Tohu-bohu* can be found in
BN 9589(2), 26. Later in this notebook there are
sketches for a set of ?3 *Pensées mécaniques*

pubn: Salabert, 1968 (as Nos. 2–3 of *Six pièces de la période
1906–13*, ed. Robert Caby)

c. 1909 **Profondeur**

music: piece for pf, one of many minuets written during
the Schola Cantorum years. Other untitled minuets
can be found in BN 9658, 9662 and Ho 5

MSS: BN 9621, 8–9, 12–13 (neat copy, as *Profondeur*)

BN 9658, 12–15 (sketches, incl. other titles for this piece:
Bévue indiscrète (p. 12); *Le Vizir autrichien* (p. 13))

pubn: Salabert, 1968 (as No. 5 of *Six pièces de la période
1906–13*, ed. Robert Caby)

c. 1909   **Menuet basque**
music: inc. minuet for pf
MSS: BN 9658, 8–9
unpubd

c. 1909   **Le Conteur magique**
music: inc. minuet for pf
MSS: BN 9662, 4
unpubd

c. 1909   **Songe-creux**
music: minuet for pf, with numerous acciaccaturas, arpeg-
    giations, anticipations, and other melodic decorations
    typical of this period
MSS: BN 9655, 26–7 (draft: the sketches for *Songe-creux* on
    pp. 28–9 are crossed out)
pubn: Salabert, 1968 (as the last of *Six pièces de la période
    1906–13*, ed. Robert Caby)

c. 1909   **Le Prisonnier maussade**
music: minuet for pf
MSS: BN 9620, 10–11
pubn: Salabert, 1968 (in *Carnet d'esquisses et de croquis*, 4, ed.
    Robert Caby)

c. 1909   **Le Grand Singe**
music: minuet for pf
MSS: BN 9658, 6
pubn: Salabert, 1968 (in *Carnet d'esquisses et de croquis*, 4, ed.
    Robert Caby)

?Sept 1909   **Le Dîner de Pierrot**
music: probably a coll. of cabaret songs arr. around a
    'fantasy' by Jules Dépaquit
MSS: PLU or lost
unpubd
prem.: by pupils of the Patronage Laïque, Ecole Maternelle
    d'Arcueil-Cachan, 17 Sept 1909

?Oct 1909   **La Chemise**
text: fantasy by Jules Dépaquit (lost)
music: coll. of cabaret songs arr. into an entertainment
MSS: Drafts: Ho 4, ff. 17*v*–18*r* (song in B♭ with orch indi-
    cations for pic, fl, ob, cl, bn, cornet, trbn, str – quoted
    in Whiting, 1984, 195–7); Ho 4, ff. 18*v*–19*r* (song in
    B♭); Ho 4, ff. 20*v*–21*r* (song in G, incl. 'Rose est per-

mise chemise'); Ho 5, ff.13v–14r (song with orch indications); BN 9651, 12–13 (arr. of the accomp. of the
verse and chorus of an untitled song in C)

Sketches: Ho 4, ff. 14v–16r, 20r; Ho 5, f. 12v

unpubd

prem.: ?24 Oct 1909 by Paulette Darty, Vincent Hyspa,
Jules Dépaquit and Satie (pf) at annual Matinée Artis-
tique, Salle du Gymnase Municipal, 1 rue des Ecoles,
Arcueil-Cachan (?as a dress-rehearsal for Paulette
Darty's performance at La Scala, Paris on 21 Nov
1909)

June–6 Sept 1911
(orch. Sept–Oct 1911,
parts copied Nov 1911–
early 1912)

En Habit de cheval (orig. title *Divertissement*)

music: 4 pieces for pf duet, later orch. for 2fl, ob, eng hn,
2 cl in Bb, 2 bn, sarrusophone, 2 hn, 2 tpt in C,
3 trbn, tuba, contrabass tuba, str. See chapter 7, n. 18

1 *Choral*
2 *Fugue litanique*
3 *Autre choral*
4 *Fugue de papier*

MSS: F-Psalabert (OS, 32pp.)

BN 10043, pf duet (copy for printer, 16ff.)

BN Rés. Vma 162 (proofs of duet version, with numerous corrections)

BN 9591(4), 2–37, pf duet (neat copies)

BN 9591(5), 12–13, pf solo or short score version of
No. 1 ('June 1911')

BN 9591(5), 16–29, pf solo or short score version of
No. 2 ('July 1911': the difficulty of these early solo
versions probably led Satie to decide on an arr. for pf
duet)

Sketches: No. 1: Ho 31 (orch draft)

No. 2: BN 9656, 12–23; BN 9661, 2, 6, 8–10, 12–18,
20–1; BN 9665, 20–3; Ho 32 (orch draft)

No. 3: BN 9591(3), 20–1; Ho 32 (orch draft)

No. 4: BN 9591(1), 4–11; BN 9591(2), 2–13; BN 9592,
13–24; Ho 32 (inc. orch draft)

pubn: Pf duet: Rouart-Lerolle, 1911; Salabert

OS: Rouart-Lerolle, 1912; Salabert

prem.: orch version: SMI, Salle Gaveau, 17 June 1912

1912

Deux Préludes pour un chien

music: 2 pieces for pf

MSS: BN 9619, 4 (No. 1, inc.); BN 9619, 6–7 (No. 2)

pubn: No. 2 as *Prélude canin*, No. 4 of *Six pièces de la période*
1906–13, ed. Robert Caby, Salabert, 1968

July 1912

Préludes flasques (pour un chien)
music: 4 pieces for pf. The 4th was added later, and was
orig. called *Sous la futaille*. Debussy was so annoyed by
this title that Satie changed it to *Avec camaraderie*
1 *Voix d'intérieur* ('11 July')
2 *Idylle cynique* ('21 July')
3 *Chanson canine* ('23 July')
4 *Avec camaraderie* (n.d.)
MSS: BN 10035 (printer's copies of all 4. At one stage
No. 4 was intended as No. 2)
Sketches: No. 1: BN 9673, 4–5
No. 2: BN 9674, 6, 8–9
No. 3: BN 9610, 1–20; BN 9660, 2–3. (The final
version, with its distinctive notation, emerges on
BN 9610, 17–20)
No. 4: BN 9632, 2–3 (as *Sous la futaille*, but almost
identical to *Avec camaraderie*. Together with this
draft appear the words 'Trop gratter, cuit/ Remue
désagréable')
pubn: Eschig, 1967
Note: BN 9674, the notebook labelled *Préludes flasques pour*
un chien, contains 2 further complete preludes on
pp. 2–5, 12–13. These were pubd as the *Deux Rêveries*
nocturnes by Salabert, 1968 (ed. Robert Caby). Satie
also wrote the titles for another set of pieces, the
Répliques hivernales in BN 9674, 21. The second of
these, *La Lanterne*, may have been carried forward to
the *Descriptions automatiques* in 1913

'12–23 Aug 1912'

Véritables Préludes flasques (pour un chien)
music: 3 preludes for pf
1 *Sévère réprimande* ('12 Aug')
2 *Seul à la maison* ('17 Aug')
3 *On joue* ('23 Aug')
ded.: the preludes carry the preface: 'Très "neuf heures du
matin" – Ricardo Viñes'
MSS: *F-Ptb* (neat copies for printer in a separate notebook)
Sketches: No. 1: BN 9618, 4–5
No. 2: BN 9618, 7–11 (with a rejected first version on
p. 6)
No. 3: BN 9618, 12–16

pubn: Demets, 1912; Eschig

prem.: 5 April 1913 by Ricardo Viñes, SN concert at Salle Pleyel

Note: An extra *Véritable Prélude flasque* appears on BN 9618, 17, entitled *Arrière-propos*. This was pubd in *Carnet d'esquisses et de croquis*, 16 (ed. Robert Caby), Salabert, 1968

Feb–28 March 1913 (play)
By late June 1913 (7 little dances for pf)
? early 1921 (7 dances orch. by Satie)

Le Piège de Méduse

text: 'lyric comedy in 1 Act by M. Erik Satie with dance music by the same gentleman'. This surrealistic play in 9 scenes was pubd in a de luxe limited ed. (100 copies) with 3 Cubist woodcut engravings by Georges Braque in June 1921 (Paris, Editions de la Galerie Simon). An Eng. trans. can be found in W, 138–47. This play may owe something to a lost collaborative venture for a 5-Act play with Jules Dépaquit in 1898 (see Satie, ed. Volta, 1988, 62). It is also prefigured in Satie's bizarre theatrical vision which appeared in the *Revue musicale SIM* on 15 Jan 1913 as part of his surrealistic *Mémoires d'un amnésique*

music: 7 'toutes petites dances' for Jonah [Jonas] the monkey following sc. 1, 2, 4, 6–9. For pf solo (1913) or small orch (cl, tpt, trbn, perc, vn, vc, cb, probably orch. for the public première in 1921)

1 *Quadrille*
2 *Valse*
3 *Pas vite*
4 *Mazurka*
5 *Un peu vif*
6 *Polka*
7 *Quadrille*

MSS: Text: *F-Pfs* (complete text)

BN 9586(2), cover gives Satie's orig. plan in 7 scenes

Music: BN 10036, pf solo (copy for printer, as *Toutes petites danses pour le Piège de Méduse*), 7ff. (rectos only))

Ho, unnumbered MS (OS, 8pp.)

pubn: Pf solo: Chester, 1929; Salabert, 1954

OS: Salabert, 1968. See also the complete package of text, music and recording, presented by Ornella Volta (Paris, Le Castor astral, 1988)

prem.: private: salon of M. et Mme Fernand Dreyfus (parents of Roland-Manuel), 1 rue de Chazelles, late 1913 or early 1914. The cast (Volta, 1988, 67) was:

Baron Medusa — Roland-Manuel
Polycarpe (his butler) — Marcel Ormoy
Jonah the monkey — Jean Dreyfus
Astolfo (Frisette's suitor) — André Biguet
Frisette (Medusa's foster-daughter) — Suzanne Roux
Visitors at end of play — M. et Mme
Dreyfus, M.
Roux

Jonah's dances perf. at the pf by Satie (who 'prepared' the pf by sliding sheets of paper between the strings and the dampers to give a muted, mechanistic effect)

public: 24 May 1921, Théâtre Michel, 38 rue des Mathurins, produced by Pierre Bertin. The cast (from the Théâtre de l'Odéon) was:

Baron Medusa — Pierre Bertin
Polycarpe — André Berley
Jonah the monkey — M. Blancard
Astolfo — M. Vinck
Frisette — Mlle Martal
Orch cond. Darius Milhaud

'21–6 April 1913'   **Descriptions automatiques** (also referred to as *Vocations électriques* in June 1913)
music: 3 pieces for pf
1 *Sur un vaisseau* ('21 April')
2 *Sur une lanterne* ('22 April')
3 *Sur un casque* ('26 April')
ded.: 1 à Madame Fernand Dreyfus
      2 à Madame Joseph Ravel
      3 à Madame Paulette Darty
MSS: BN 9586(1), 10–15, 20–3; BN 9630, 4–7 (neat drafts of Nos. 1–3)
  Sketches: No. 1: BN 9586(2), 4–5; Ho 24 (which shows that the orig. title of the set was *Descriptions hypocrites*, and that No. 1 was titled *Sur un loup*, then *Sur un thon*, before Satie decided on *Sur un vaisseau*)
  No. 2: BN 9586(1), 24; Ho 24
  No. 3: BN 9586(1), 1–8, 16–19; BN 9586(2), 6–7; Ho 24
pubn: Demets, 1913; Eschig
prem.: 5 June 1913 by Ricardo Viñes, SMI concert at Salle Erard

'2 June–25 Aug 1913'   **Croquis et agaceries d'un gros bonhomme en bois**
music: 3 pieces for pf

1 *Tyrolienne Turque* ('28 July')
2 *Danse maigre (à la manière de ces messieurs)* ('2 June')
3 *Españaña* ('25 Aug')
ded.: 1 à Mademoiselle Elvira Viñes Soto
       2 à Monsieur Hernando Viñes Soto
       3 à Mademoiselle Claude Emma Debussy [Chou-
          chou]
MSS: Neat copies of Nos. 1–2, PLU
   BN 9582, 16–21 (neat copy of No. 3)
   Sketches: No. 1: BN 9619, 22–5
   No. 2: PLU
   No. 3: BN 9580, 2–9; BN 9619, 16–21; BN 9619, 26–30
      (rejected sketches for another version of No. 3)
pubn: Demets, 1913; Eschig
prem.: 28 March 1914 by Ricardo Viñes, SN concert at Salle
   Pleyel

'30 June–4 July 1913' **Embryons desséchés**
music: 3 pieces for pf
1 *d'Holothurie* ('30 June')
2 *d'Edriophthalma* ('1 July')
3 *de Podophthalma* ('4 July')
ded.: 1 à Mademoiselle Suzanne Roux
       2 à Monsieur Edouard Dreyfus
       3 à Madame Jane Mortier
MSS: Neat copies, PLU
   BN Rés. Vma 161 (corr. proofs)
   Sketches: No. 1: BN 9590, 1–7
   No. 2: BN 9590, 8–10
   No. 3: BN 9590, 12–21. (The cover of this sketchbook
      contains 2 versions of a preface for this set, which were
      never used. The text of the second version is printed in
      Wilkins, 1975, 292)
pubn: Demets, 1913; Eschig
prem.: ?19 Jan 1914, Georges Auric. (Satie says in a letter to
   Jacques-Paul Viardot on 8 May 1915 that the première
   was given by Jane Mortier, but the date of this has yet
   to be discovered)

'2 Aug 1913' **San Bernardo**
music: inc. piece for pf, possibly an alternative for *Españaña*
   (*Croquis* No. 3). Also cf. *Danses Gothiques* No. 4
MSS: PLU (sold in Paris on 17–18 Nov 1975 – Catalogue

Marc Loliée, No. 20. Consists of 5 lines of music on a single folio)

unpubd

'23 Aug–5 Sept 1913'   **Chapitres tournés en tous sens**
music: 3 pieces for pf
1   *Celle qui parle trop* ('23 Aug')
2   *Le Porteur de grosses pierres* ('25 Aug')
3   *Regrets des Enfermés (Jonas et Latude)* ('5 Sept')
ded.:   1   à Robert Manuel
         2   à Monsieur Fernand Dreyfus
         3   à Madame Claude Debussy
MSS: BN 9580, 10–15, 16–19; BN 9583, 2–5 (neat drafts of Nos. 1–3)
   Sketches: No. 1: BN 9580, 2
   No. 2: PLU
   No. 3: BN 9580, 20–3; BN 9582, 22–9
pubn: Demets, 1913; Eschig
prem.: 14 Jan 1914 by Ricardo Viñes, Salle Erard

'9–17 Sept 1913'   **Vieux sequins et vieilles cuirasses**
music: 3 pieces for pf
1   *Chez le Marchand d'Or (Venise XIIIe siècle)* ('9 Sept')
2   *Danse cuirassée (Période grecque)* ('17 Sept')
3   *La Défaite des Cimbres (Cauchemar)* ('14 Sept')
ded.:   1   à Ricardo Viñes
         2   à M.-D. Calvocoressi
         3   à Emile Vuillermoz
MSS: BN 9583, 8–11; BN 9633, 16–17; BN 9583, 18–21 (neat drafts of Nos. 1–3)
   Sketches: No. 1: BN 9582, 32; BN 9583; 6–7
   No. 2: BN 9605(3), 13 (sketch of melody *As-tu vu la casquette?* in D)
   No. 3: BN 9633, 1–15
pubn: Demets, 1913; Eschig

early Oct 1913   **[Trois Nouvelles Enfantines]**
music: 3 easy 2-part pieces for pf
1   *Le Vilain petit Vaurien*
2   *[Berceuse]*
3   *La Gentille toute petite fille*
MSS: BN 9612, 1, 2–3, 6–7 (neat copies of Nos. 1–3. Other unpubd *Enfantines* appear on pp. 4–5, 8–9)
pubn: Eschig, 1972 (ed. Nigel Wilkins)

'10 Oct 1913'   **Menus propos enfantins** (*Enfantines I*)
music: 3 beginners' pieces for pf, all using the same 5-finger
     scale
1   *Le chant guerrier du Roi des Haricots*
2   *Ce qui dit la petite Princesse de Tulipes*
3   *Valse du Chocolat aux Amandes*
ded.: à Mademoiselle Valentine Gross
MSS: Draft of No. 1: PLU; BN 9612, 10–11, 16–18 (drafts of
     Nos. 2–3) (Other rejected *Menus* appear in BN 9612,
     12–13, 14–15, 19. A list of composition dates for all the
     Enfantines occurs in BN 9593(1), 24, and other rejected
     pieces in this style can be found in BN 9576, 1–4.
     Fingering trials (possibly for the *Enfantines*) appear in
     BN 9578(2), 16; BN 9592, 2–5; BN 9674, 22)
pubn: Demets, 1914; Eschig

'22 Oct 1913'   **Enfantillages pittoresques** (*Enfantines II*)
music: 3 beginners' pieces for pf, using 3 different 5-finger
     scales
1   *Petit Prélude à la journée*
2   *Berceuse*
3   *Marche du Grand Escalier*
ded.: à Madame Léon Verneuil
MSS: PLU
pubn: Demets, 1914; Eschig

'26 Oct 1913'   **Peccadilles importunes** (*Enfantines III*)
music: 3 beginners' pieces for pf, using 3 different 5-finger
     scales
1   *Etre jaloux de son camarade qui a une grosse tête*
2   *Lui manger sa tartine*
3   *Profiter de ce qu'il a des cors aux pieds lui prendre son cerceau*
ded.: à Madame Marguerite Long
MSS: PLU
pubn: Demets, 1914; Eschig

early Nov–'16 Nov 1913'   **Les Pantins dansent**
text: poem in 6 verses *Les Pantins dansent* by Valentine de
     Saint-Point, the second of her *Poèmes ironiques* (pubd in
     a small volume of *Poèmes drames idéistes du premier
     Festival de la Métachorie*, New York, 3 April 1917 –
     information kindly supplied from *F-Pfs* by Ornella
     Volta; see chapter 7, n. 25)
music: 'poème dansé' for pf or small orch (fl, ob, cl in B♭, bn,

hn, tpt, str) to accompany the reading of the poem and a dance arr. by Valentine de Saint-Point. 2 versions exist. The first rejected version of early Nov. 1913 (see Ex. 54) is scored for 2 fl, cl in Bb, bn, hn, 2 tpt, hp, str

MSS: First version: BN 9604, 18–23 (pf score with orch indications)

Second version: BN 9588, 6–9 (pf score with orch indications). Sketches: BN 9588, 2–5

OS: PLU (copy at *F-Psalabert*)

pubn: Version 2 for pf in *Montjoie!* (Jan 1914); Rouart-Lerolle, 1929; Salabert

OS: bars 31–8 (facs.) in *Montjoie!* (Nov–Dec 1913), 12; Salabert, 1967

Version 1: unpubd

prem.: Version 2: 18 Dec 1913, Festival de la Métachorie, Salle Léon-Poirier. Orch cond. Maurice Droeghmans, poems read by Edouard de Max. Dance by Valentine de Saint-Point

c. 1914

Un Acte

text: inc. scenario for a 1-Act ballet or opera with 11 numbers, set in a village. No characters are named by Satie

MSS: BN 9593(3), 10

unpubd

'17–30 Jan 1914'

Choses vues à droite et à gauche (sans lunettes)

music: 3 pieces for vn, pf

1   *Choral hypocrite* ('17 Jan')
2   *Fugue à tâtons* ('21 Jan')
3   *Fantaisie musculaire* ('30 Jan')

MSS: *F-Po* Nouveaux Fonds Rés. 219 (copies for printer of Nos. 1–3, 14pp. music)

Sketches: No. 1: BN 9573(1), 19; BN 9573(2), 14–15

No. 2: BN 9573(1), 6–15, 19–24; BN 9573(2), 4–11. The draft of a first version occurs in BN 9573(2), 1–3, with sketches for it in BN 9573(1), 1–5 and BN 9573(2), 24 (see Ex. 41). Another (untitled) early draft (in G) running to 32 bars can be found in Ho 18, 2–5, with other early episodic sketches in 2 parts on 6–7. The cover of Ho 18 lists the original order as 3, 1, 2 (in terms of the printed version)

No. 3: BN 9573(2), 12–13, 16–23

An extra unused movement, another chorale (perhaps

intended to come between Nos. 2 and 3) exists complete in BN 9573(1), 16–18 (see Ex. 42)

pubn: Rouart-Lerolle, 1916; Salabert

prem.: 2 April 1916 by Marcel Chailley (vn) and Ricardo
Viñes. Ecole Lucien de Flagny, 25 rue de la Tour
(during '14ème Examen Musical de quelques élèves du
Professeur Lucien de Flagny, sous la Présidence de M.
Ricardo Viñes')

Unused extra chorale: 29 May 1987 by Helen Sanderson
(vn) and Robert Orledge. Northcott Theatre, Exeter
University

'14 March–20 May 1914'   **Sports et divertissements**

music: 21 pieces for pf written to illustrate a set of drawings
made by Charles Martin in 1914 (or vice versa?). Satie
provided humorous texts in the form of prose poems to
accompany each piece, turning it into a complete artistic experience for the performer. The available printed
scores show a second (more Cubist) set of 20 drawings
made by Martin in 1922, which are therefore not connected to the music other than by their titles. The pubd
order of 1923, chosen by their editor Lucien Vogel, is as
follows:

1   *Choral inappétissant* ('15 May')
2   *La Balançoire* ('31 March')
3   *La Chasse* ('7 April')
4   *La Comédie italienne* ('29 April')
5   *Le Réveil de la Mariée* ('16 May')
6   *Colin-Maillard* ('27 April')
7   *La Pêche* ('14 March')
8   *Le Yachting* ('22 March')
9   *Le Bain de mer* ('11 April')
10 *Le Carnaval* ('3 April')
11 *Le Golf* ('20 May')
12 *La Pieuvre* ('17 March')
13 *Les Courses* ('26 March')
14 *Les Quatre-coins* ('24 April')
15 *Le Pique-nique* ('19 April')
16 *Le Water-chute* ('14 April')
17 *Le Tango – perpétuel* ('5 May')
18 *Le Traîneau* ('2 May')
19 *Le Flirt* ('29 March')

20   *Le Feu d'Artifice* ('6 April')

21   *Le Tennis* ('21 April')

Satie's chosen order in 1914 (MS in *F-Psa*) was (in terms of the above list): 1, 8, 18, 17, 10, 5, 11, 7, 12, 21, 15, 13, 9, 3, 2, 16, 6, 14, 4, 20, 19

To complicate matters further, Satie also authorized Marcelle Meyer to give the première of the *Sports et divertissements* on 31 Jan 1922 in the following order: 1, 9, 16, 12, 6, 11, 19, 10, 21, 17, 5, 8, 18, 3, 13, 14, 15, 7, 20, 2, 4

Thus, apart from the opening chorale, there is nothing consistent or final as regards the ordering of the 21 pieces. But the second and third orders (chosen by Satie) are preferable to the usual order (chosen by his publisher)

MSS: Apart from a trial draft of No. 1 (*F-Psa*), the orig. 21 plates prepared by Satie for Lucien Vogel in 1914 are now lost. The drafts and sketches in the BN notebooks are listed below in chronological order of composition. All drafts are accompanied by their texts, and most have regular bar lines:

14 March, No. 7: *La Pêche*: BN 9627(2), 4–5 (draft); BN 9627(1), 2–3; BN 9604, 12–13 (sketches)

17 March, No. 12: *La Pieuvre*: BN 9627(2), 8–9 (draft); BN 9627(1), 4–7; BN 9604, 12–13 (sketches)

22 March, No. 8: *Le Yachting*: BN 9627(1), 8–9 (draft); BN 9627(2), 12 (sketch of text)

26 March, No. 13: *Les Courses*: BN 9627(3), 8–9 (draft)

29 March, No. 19: *Le Flirt*: BN 9627(3), 4–5 (draft)

31 March, No. 2: *La Balançoire*: BN 9627(3), 2–3 (draft)

3 April, No. 10: *Le Carnaval*: BN 9627(4), 2–3 (draft)

6 April, No. 20: *Le Feu d'Artifice*: BN 9627(4), 4–5 (draft)

7 April, No. 3: *La Chasse*: BN 9627(4), 6–7 (draft); BN 9627(4), 1 (sketches)

11 April, No. 9: *Le Bain de mer*: BN 9627(5), 2–3 (draft); BN 9627(5), 9 (revised ending)

14 April, No. 16: *Le Water-chute*: BN 9627(5), 4–5 (draft, with 5 versions of the semiquaver descent of the water-chute, see Orledge, 1984–5, 166–8)

19 April, No. 15: *Le Pique-nique*: BN 9627(6), 1–2 (draft, orig. titled *Le pick-nick*, with a longer first version of the text (which preceded the music) on p. 1)

21 April, No. 21: *Le Tennis*: BN 9627(6), 6–7 (draft, plus a complete rejected first version on p. 3)

24 April, No. 14: *Les Quatre-coins*: BN 9627(7), 1 (draft)

27 April, No. 6: *Colin-Maillard*: BN 9627(7), 2–3 (draft)

29 April, No. 4: *La Comédie italienne*: BN 9627(7), 4–5 (draft)

2 May, No. 18: *Le Traîneau*: BN 9627(8), 6–7 (draft, with the start of a rejected version on p. 1)

5 May, No. 17: *Le Tango*: BN 9627(8), 16–17 (draft); BN 9627(8), 8–15 (sketches for 4 earlier versions)

15 May, No. 1: *Choral inappétissant*: BN 9627(9), 9 (draft, with draft of *Préface* on p. 8)

16 May, No. 5: *Le Réveil de la Mariée*: BN 9627(9), 6–7 (draft, titled *Le Réveil de la Mariée – Sérénade*); BN 9627(8), 2–4; BN 9627(9), 1–5 (sketches. Those on BN 9627(9), 1 are titled *Sérénade matinale à la mariée*)

20 May, No. 11: *Le Golf*: BN 9627(10), 4–5, 8–9 (draft of 9th (final) version); BN 9627(6), 4–5; BN 9627(9), 10–11 (sketches of text, 3 complete versions); BN 9627(9), 12–21 (sketches of music, 6 starts – one leading to a complete first version on pp. 16–17 (see Ex. 87)); BN 9627(10), 1–2 (sketches for starts 7–8)

pubn: With both sets of drawings by Charles Martin (1914 and 1922), Editions Lucien Vogel, 1923 (10 copies only, reserved for the Librairie Maynial, numbered 1–10)

With the 20 drawings of 1922 only, coloured by Jules Saudé, Vogel, 1923 (215 copies, numbered 11–225)

With one 1922 drawing only, Vogel, 1923 (675 copies, numbered 226–900)

With Satie's music only (in facs., plus the cameos by Martin preceding each piece), Rouart-Lerolle, 1926; Salabert, 1964

Reproduction of music and 20 drawings of 1922 (with Eng. trans. of texts by Stanley Applebaum), Dover Publications, 1982 (in this ed. Martin's cameos are missing)

prem.: private: 14 Dec 1919 by Satie?, *chez* Mme Vogel, 18 rue Bonaparte, Paris 6

public: 31 Jan 1922 by Marcelle Meyer, Salle de La Ville l'Evéque, 18 rue de La Ville l'Evéque

'25 June'–early July 1914

Heures séculaires et instantanées

music: 3 pieces for pf, with surrealistic accompanying

stories which Satie forbade to be read aloud during performance

1 *Obstacles venimeux* ('25 June')
2 *Crépuscule matinale (de midi)* ('3 July')
3 *Affolements granitiques* (n.d.)

ded.: 'A sir William Grant-Plumot, je dédie agréablement ce recueil. Jusqu'ici, deux figures m'ont surpris: Louis XI & sir William: le premier, par l'étrangeté de sa bonhomie; le second, par sa continuelle immobilité. Ce m'est un honneur de prononcer, ici, les noms de Louis XI & de sir William Grant-Plumot.' Sir William was almost certainly a figment of Satie's imagination, perhaps his nickname for Shakespeare?

MSS: BN 9593(3), 2–3, 6–7; BN 9593(1), 5, 4, 6–7; Ho 26, 2–5 (drafts of Nos. 1–3. In No. 3, the complex enharmonic notation of simple chords and scales (printed ed. p. 8) was added later, when the bar lines were removed)

BN 9593(1), 1; BN 9593(3), 1 (drafts of accompanying texts. Plans for the titles can be found on the cover of BN 9588, and BN 9593(1), 4 above is headed *Suite Indo-Montmartroise*)

Sketches: No. 1: BN 9593(3), 1

No. 2: BN 9593(3), 8

No. 3: BN 9593(1), 8–11, 14, 20, with pencil draft of start on 18–19. The sketches in Ho 26 show that No. 3 orig. had a different text (beginning 'Il a une taille de guêpe &, en même temps, de taureau'). This may have given Satie the idea for his next set of pieces, the *Trois Valses*, sketches for which are incl. in the same notebook

pubn: Demets, 1916; Eschig

prem.: 11 March 1917 by Ricardo Viñes. Galerie Barbazanges, Faubourg St. Honoré

?late June 1914   **Obstacles venimeux**

music: inc. set of 3 pieces for pf, probably replaced by the first of the *Heures séculaires et instantanées*. Mostly simple 2-part music, similar to the 1913 *Enfantines*

MSS: BN 9604, 5–8 (sketches for all 3 pieces: 'No. 1: Le Résident Général sommeille doucement, étendu sur un paquet de hamac. 1er obstacle: un scorpion/ 2me

obstacle: un boa/ 3me obstacle: son concierge.' No. 2: untitled. No. 3: marked 'La chaleur est diluvienne')
unpubd

Note: Satie planned several sets of pf pieces with humorous titles in 1914, but none proceeded even as far as the *Obstacles venimeux*. They are as follows (in chronological order, as far as can be ascertained):

[May–Nov 1914]

1 *Les Globules ennuyeux* (May 1914)
   1 *Regard*
   2 *Superficie*
   3 *Canalisation*
MSS: BN 9627(10), cover (with texts for Nos. 1, 3 on p. 3. No music)

2 *Les Etapes monotones* (May 1914)
   1 *Curiosité visqueuse*
   2 *Frisson impoli*
   3 *Tentacules chevalines*
MSS: BN 9627(10), cover (no texts or music)

3 *La Chimère désolée* (?May 1914)
   1 *Kiosque*
   2 *Moisissures*
   3 *Estafilade*
MSS: Ho 22, cover (no texts or music)

4 *Obstacles ennuyeuses* (June 1914)
   1 *Les Catafalques endormis*
   2 *Les Poussières peureuses*
   3 *Vasques chancelantes*
MSS: BN 9588, cover (no texts or music)

5 *Sous les catalpas (Trois belles Mazourkas)* (July 1914)
   1 *Ce qui dit le hibou*
   2 *Après le bon déjeuner*
   3 *Le joli bal de coton*
MSS: BN 9626, cover (no texts or music)

6 *Le Cheval est un animal hippique, équestre & domestique* (July 1914)
   1 *Equestre – Un général sur le dos*
   2 *Domestique – Une charrue derrière lui*
   3 *Hippique – Un rival à vaincre*
MSS: BN 9626, cover (no texts or music)

7 *Soupirs fanés* (Nov 1914)
MSS: BN 9615(3), 6–7, brief musical sketches marked 'Grand

Sommeil nocturne; Familial désespoir' [No. 1?], with more sketches on p. 12 (no specific titles or texts)

8   *Souvenirs fadasses* (Nov 1914)

    1   *Barbouillage*

    2   *Poil*

    3   *Recrudescence*

MSS: BN 9615(3), 8, 7 (texts for Nos. 1, 2. No identifiable music)

'21–3 July 1914'

Les Trois Valses distinguées du précieux dégoûté

music: 3 waltzes for pf, prefaced with quotations from La Bruyère (1688), Cicero and Cato

1   *Sa taille* ('21 July')

2   *Son binocle* ('22 July')

3   *Ses jambes* ('23 July')

ded.: 1   à Roland-Manuel

      2   à Mademoiselle Linette Chalupt

      3   à René Chalupt

MSS: BN 9628(1), 2–7, 8–11, 14–19 (neat copies for printer, with texts, of Nos. 1–3)

    BN Rés. Vma 173 (corr. proofs, 1916)

    Sketches: No. 1: BN 9628(2), 2–5, 6–9

    No. 2: BN 9626, 2–5; BN 9628(2), 2–5; Ho 26, 9–13 (first version)

    No. 3: BN 9628(2), 2–5, 10–11; Ho 26, 16–19, 21–2 (emergence of final version, minus p. 7, systems 1–2 of printed ed. With different text); Ho 26, 14–15 (first version, melody only)

pubn: Rouart-Lerolle, 1916; Salabert

prem.: 19 Nov 1916 by Satie. Société Lyre et Palette, 6 rue Huyghens, with first exhibition of negro sculptures in Paris and an exhibition of modern art (35 paintings by Kisling, Matisse, Ortiz de Zarate, Modigliani and Picasso)

'20 Nov–2 Dec 1914'

Trois Poèmes d'amour

text: 3 short poems by Satie; modern equivalents of 13th-century French troubadour poetry

music: 3 songs for v, pf – 'Musique de M. Erik Satie (sur des paroles magiques de lui-même)'

1   *Ne suis que grain de sable* ('20 Nov')

2   *Suis chauve de naissance* ('25 Nov')

3   *Ta parure est secrète* ('2 Dec')

ded.: à Henri Fabert

MSS: BN 9615(1), 4–7, 10–13, 16–19 (neat copies of Nos. 1–3
with humorous texts. The preface (BN 9615(1), 1), the
commentary for the performers, and an introductory
'ritournelle' to No. 1 (p. 3) were all removed before
publication. Satie also deliberately numbered the songs
'1–3–2' at this stage, but thought better of it before
publication. See Orledge, 1984–5, 158–63 for further
details of the compositional process)
BN 9615(2), 12–14, 18–20, 24–6 (transpositions for tenor,
pf of Nos. 1–3, made for M. Fabert of the Paris Opéra)
BN 9615(5) (copy for printer of Nos. 1–3 in elaborate
Gothic calligraphy. As printed, the decorative anacruses
in No. 3 were added at this stage)
BN 20314(1–3) (neat copies made for Jane Bathori, as in
printed ed.)
BN Rés. Vma 168 (corrected proofs)
Sketches: No. 1: BN 9593(2), 1–7 (with draft on 4–7)
No. 2: BN 9593(2), 8–9, 12–13, 16–17; BN 9615(3), 2–3
No. 3: BN 9593(2), 8–10, 14–15, 18–23; BN 9615(4), 1–9
pubn: in *Gazette du Bon Ton* (Dec 1914); Rouart-Lerolle,
1916; Salabert
prem.: 2 April 1916 by Henri Fabert and Satie. Ecole Lucien
de Flagny, 25 rue de la Tour

?1915
Rêverie sur un plat
music: inc. piece for pf
MSS: BN 9625(1), 6–7
unpubd

?1915
La Mer est pleine d'eau: c'est à n'y rien comprendre
music: inc. piece for orch (2 cl, eng hn, str)
MSS: BN 9625(2), 6–8
unpubd. Extract in Orledge, 1990

?March–Nov 1915
Cinq Grimaces pour 'Le Songe d'une nuit d'été'
music: incidental music for Jean Cocteau's unrealized production of Shakespeare's *A Midsummer Night's Dream*
(adapted text lost). Planned for the Cirque Médrano
with scenery and costumes by the Cubist painter Albert
Gleizes. Rehearsals (involving the 'clowns Fratellini')
were terminated during Nov 1915. The idea for the
production came from Edgard Varèse, who planned a
'pot-pourri de musiques françaises' by Florent Schmitt,
Ravel, Stravinsky and Satie (Vy, 51). Only Satie's

5 pieces for orch (pic, fl, ob, eng hn, cl, bn, dbn, hn, 2 tpt, 2 trbn, tuba, timp, perc, str) were composed (with some assistance from Milhaud):

1 *Préambule*
2 *Coquecigrue*
3 *Chasse*
4 *Fanfaronnade*
5 *Pour sortir* [*Retraite*]

MSS: Ho 30 (OS, 24pp. No. 5 completed by Milhaud (1 Nov 1925) from Satie's inc. draft dated '2 April 1915')

Ho 27, 6 (orig. plans for the *Grimaces*: 'Prologue.

1 Fanfare de cirque burlesque: 20 mesures ignoblement bêtes.
2 Chants de coqs et cocassesseries diverses: 16 mesures.
3 Stupide fanfare de chasse. Cuivres, puis bois: deux reprises de 8 mesures.
4 Sonnerie abjecte jouée par tout l'orchestre: Polka militaire et grossière, fortement idiote: 16 mesures.
5 Retraite ridicule et saugrenue rendue par tout l'orchestre: 12 mesures, reprises 200 fois.'

(Ho 27, 16–19 may well be Satie's first sketches for the *Grimaces*))

BN 9625(1), 3 (plans for titles, as in printed version, but with whole project described as *Grimaces, Pataqués & Interstices pour le 'Songe d'une Nuit d'Eté'*)

Sketches and orch preparations (based on the pf red. made by Milhaud in 1915):

No. 1: BN 9625(2), 16–19; BN 9625(4), 2–3
No. 2: BN 9625(2), 14; BN 9625(4), 10–14
No. 3: BN 9625(3), 2–3, 6–7
No. 4: BN 9625(4), 6–7
No. 5: Ho 72 ('Thème de la retraite'); BN 9625(1), 2–3; BN 9625(3), 8–9; BN 9625(5), 1–9, with complete short score on 12–13

pubn: Pf red. by Milhaud: Universal Edition, 1929

OS by Satie (No. 5 completed by Milhaud), Universal Edition, 1929

'23 Aug–6 Oct 1915'   **Avant-dernières pensées**
music: 3 pieces for pf
1 *Idylle* ('23 Aug')
2 *Aubade* ('3 Oct')
3 *Méditation* ('6 Oct')
ded.:   1   à Debussy

2   à Paul Dukas

3   à Albert Roussel

MSS: BN 9578(1), 2–5, 8–11, 14–19 (copies for printer of Nos. 1–3)

BN Rés. Vma 158 (corr. proofs)

Sketches: No. 1: *F-Ppc*

No. 2: BN 9578(2), 3–11 (orig. title *Etrange rumeurs*)

No. 3: BN 9578(2), 12–15

pubn: Rouart-Lerolle, 1916; Salabert

prem.: 30 May 1916 by Satie *chez* Mme Germaine Bongard, 5 rue de Penthièvre in a Satie/Granados concert (in conjunction with an exhibition of modern painting). (The programme in *F-Pfs* states that this was the première, though a performance of the *Avant-dernières pensées* by Satie is listed during the concert at the Société Lyre et Palette on 18 April 1916)

Jan–6 Feb 1916   **L'Aurore aux doigts de rose** (Verley arr. Satie)

music: the second of 2 *Pastels sonores* for pf by Satie's pupil Albert Verley, which Satie orchestrated and then arr. for pf duet. Scored for pic, 2 fl, ob, eng hn, 2 cl in Bb, 2 bn, 2 hn, 2 tpt in C, 2 trbn, tuba, timp, perc, hp, str

MSS: BN 10034 (OS by copyist, 11pp.)

pubn: Satie's arr. for pf duet pubd privately by Verley, 1916 (copy in BN Fol. Vm.[12] a. 471)

'14 April–26 May 1916'   **Trois Mélodies**

music: 3 songs for v, pf

1   *La Statue de bronze* (Léon-Paul Fargue) ('26 May')

2   *Daphénéo* (Mimi Godebska) ('14 April')

3   *Le Chapelier* (René Chalupt, based on chapter 7: 'A Mad Tea-Party' in Lewis Carroll's *Alice in Wonderland*. The music is based on the 'Chanson de Magali' from Act 2 sc. 3 of Gounod's opera *Mireille*, 1864) ('14 April')

ded.:   1   à Madame Jane Bathori

2   à Emile Engel

3   à Igor Strawinsky

MSS: Ho 43–4 (neat drafts of vocal parts of Nos. 3, 1)

BN Rés. Vma. 172, 159, 160 (corr. proofs of Nos. 1–3)

Sketches: No. 1: BN 9585, 8–15 (incl. rejected first version of vocal line on 10)

No. 2: BN 9584, 2–13 (3 different versions; final version on 10–13)

No. 3: BN 9581, 16–18 (first version); BN 9581, 18–21 (final version) pubn: Rouart-Lerolle, 1917; Salabert

prem.: Nos. 2, 3: 18 April 1916 by Jane Bathori and ?Ricardo
Viñes. Société Lyre et Palette, 6 rue Huyghens

All 3 (order 2-1-3): 30 May 1916 by Jane Bathori and
?Satie in 'Audition Erik Satie – Granados' *chez* Mme
Germaine Bongard, 5 rue de Penthièvre, in conjunction
with an exhibition of modern painting (the programme
was illustrated by Matisse and Picasso)

July 1916

Fables de La Fontaine

text: scenario by René Chalupt for ballet (planned for
Diaghilev's Ballets Russes), with designs by Charles
Stern

music: lost or never started. Satie told his patroness Misia
Edwards on 9 July 1916 that it was to be 'very modern'
and absolutely 'without pastiche'

MSS: PLU

May 1916–May 1917
(orch completed 8 May
1917; opening *Choral*
and *Final* added
April–5 May 1919 for
Diaghilev's revival at
the Salle Gaveau on
18 May)

Parade

music: 'Ballet réaliste sur un thème de Jean Cocteau'. Satie
only began to make headway on his score after Picasso
joined the team on 24 Aug 1916. He introduced the
Cubist Managers, designed the sets and costumes, and
opposed Cocteau's ideas for choral and spoken effects.
Scored for large orch (pic, 2 fl, ob, eng hn, cl in E♭,
2 cl in B♭, 2 bn, 2 hn, cornet in B♭, 2 tpt in C, 3 trbn,
tuba, timp, hp, perc (and other 'noise-making' instruments), str)

Introduction: *Choral* [April–May 1919]; *Prélude du
Rideau rouge* [by 12 Dec 1916]

Part 1: *Le Prestidigitateur Chinois* [May–1 Sept 1916]

Part 2: *Petite Fille Américaine* [Oct 1916; Ragtime and
Titanic sections by 19 Oct]

Part 3: *Acrobates* [early Nov 1916]

Part 4: *Final* [April–May 1919], and *Suite au 'Prélude du
Rideau rouge'* [Dec 1916]

Note: The pf duet score as pubd in 1917 (completed on 9
Jan) lacks the *Choral* and *Final* above

ded.: on pf duet version: à Madame Edwards (née M.
Godebska)

MSS: *F-Psalabert* (OS, 93pp.)

BN 17677(5), *Choral* and *Final* (7pp. for pf duet, copy for
printer. These pages were never added to the pubd duet

score, and they show that the *Suite au 'Prélude du Rideau rouge'* is to be used in concert performances only, and not in the theatre. This is almost certainly the MS of the 'three minutes' of music Satie added in 1919)

BN Rés. Vma 165 (corr. 2nd proofs for pf duet)

Orchestral drafts: BN 9602(1), 2–20 (Part 1 complete: printed OS 9–36)

BN 9602(2), 2–20 (Part 2 to the sinking of the Titanic: OS 37–63 bar 4)

BN 9602(3), 4–15 (rest of Part 2–middle of Part 3: OS 63 bar 5–82 bar 7. The rest of Part 3 is missing)

Short scores with orch indications (for rest of ballet): BN 9602(4), 18–21 (opening *Choral*: OS 2–4. Bars 1–8 were added last)

BN 9603(1), 2–4 (*Prélude du Rideau rouge*: OS 5–8)

BN 9602(4), 10–17 (Part 4: *Final*: OS 98–end of 114)

BN 9603(1), 5 (*Suite au 'Prélude du Rideau rouge'*: OS 115)

Preliminary sketches: Introduction and Part 1: BN 9603(2), 11 (first version of *Prélude du Rideau rouge*)

BN 9585, 2–3 (orch layouts for Part 1)

BN 9585, 6–7 (unused theme for Managers)

BN 9603(3), 1–15 (sketches for repetitive Managers' theme found in OS 9–16 [?May 1916])

BN 9603(5), 11 (unused theme for 'Roue de la lotérie': OS 17)

BN 9603(5), 18 (sketches for OS 32 bar 3–33 bar 3, with cl/cornet line set to words: 'Il lui crevèrent les yeux, lui arrachèrent la langue')

Part 2: BN 9603(5), 19 (sketches for start: OS 37–38 bar 2)

BN 9672, 1–5, 14–15 (sketches for OS 40 bar 4–end of 45)

BN 9603(4), 4–5 (sketches for OS 48 bar 3–49 bar 4)

BN 9603(4), 8–10 ('Ragtime' theme [modelled on *That Mysterious Rag* by Irving Berlin and Ted Snyder (Ted Snyder & Co., New York and Canada, 1911)])

BN 9603(2), 1–7 ('Ragtime' section: OS 49 bar 5–57 bar 2)

BN 9672, 6–12 (6 versions of music for giant wave that engulfs the Titanic; leading to BN 9603(4), 2 – the 7th version, still in triplet quavers – and BN 9602(2), 18–19, the final version as in OS 61–2; see Fig. 7.2)

BN 9603(4), 1–3, 7 ('Titanic' section: OS 59 bar 3–end of 66, with pic/fl theme (OS 64–6) set to words: 'Tic! Tic! Tic! le "Titanic" s'enfonce, allumé dans la mer')

Part 3: BN 9603(4), 16–21 (sketches for start: OS 69–end of 80)

BN 9603(1), 6–15 (sketches for OS 73–88)

BN 9603(1), 18–19 (sketches for OS 93 bar 3–end of 95 [*Suprême effort et chûte des Managers*])

Part 4: BN 9602(4), 5–7, 22–4 (return of 'Ragtime' section: OS 101–2)

BN 9602(4), 8 (return of Managers' theme: OS 111 bars 5ff.)

Also: BN 9677(5) (list of instruments and 'noise-makers' for *Parade*, with ranges of xylophone and bouteillophone, 2pp.)

pubn: extract (in facs.) of 'Entrée des Managers (pour le bon vieux Kisling. Erik Satie. 31 Mai 1917 [actually 1916]' on p. 3 of programme for an *Instant musical d'Erik Satie*, Société Lyre et Palette, 19 Nov 1916 (this theme (OS 9 bar 1–10 bar 1) was probably the initial idea for *Parade*)

Pf duet score (without *Choral* and *Final*): Rouart-Lerolle, 1917 (with preface by Auric and scenario by Cocteau); Salabert

OS: Rouart-Lerolle, 1917; Salabert, 1960; miniature score: Salabert, 1979

prem.: For pf duet: 19 Nov 1916 (inc.) by Satie and Mlle Juliette Meerovitch, Société Lyre et Palette, 6 rue Huyghens

As ballet: 18 May 1917 by Diaghilev's Ballets Russes, Théâtre du Châtelet, orch cond. Ernest Ansermet. Choreography by Léonide Massine. Performed at end of programme after *Les Sylphides*, *Le Soleil de nuit* and *Petrushka*. Cast:

Le Prestidigitateur Chinois	Léonide Massine
La Petite Fille Américaine	Mlle Maria Shabelska
Les Acrobates	Mlle Lopokova, M. Zverew
Le Manager en frac	M. Wozikovski
Le Manager de New-York	M. Statkevitch
Le Manager à cheval	MM. Oumanski and Nova

March 1917   **L''Embarquement pour Cythère'**
music: inc. piece for vn, pf inspired by Watteau's painting.

This work is mentioned in letters to the violinist Hélène Jourdan-Morhange on 23–4 March 1917 (*F-Pfs*), and may have been intended as a companion piece to the *Choses vues à droite et à gauche* (1914)

ded.: à Hélène Jourdan-Morhange

MSS: BN 9623(1), 22–31 (sketches for a piece for vn, pf in G major, in 12/8 time, contemporary with *Mort de Socrate* (1917))

unpubd. Extracts in Orledge, 1990

1917   **Conte pour un ballet**

music and scenario: lost. Planned with Louise Faure-Favier (see Volta, 1987, 97)

July 1917   **Sonatine bureaucratique**

music: neo-classical Sonatine for pf, modelled on Clementi's Sonatina in C (the first of his 6 Progressive Pianoforte Sonatinas, Op. 36 (1797, rev. ed., *c.* 1820))

1   Allegro
2   Andante
3   Vivace

ded.: à Juliette Meerovitch, amicalement

MSS: BN 9624, 16–21, 22–5, 28–31 (drafts for movements 1–3. 1 has different text to pubd ed.; 2 is inc., again with a different text; 3 is also inc.)

     Sketches: 1 BN 9624, 5, 10–13
                2 BN 9624, 7, 22–3, 32–3
                3 BN 9624, 6, 8–9, 25, 40

pubn: Stéphane Chapelier, 1917; Philippo, 1954; Editions Combres, 1975; Salabert, 1976

1917   **Musique d'ameublement**

music: 2 'furnishing' pieces for small ensemble

1   *Tapisserie en fer forgé*
     4 bars for fl, cl, tpt, str 'pour l'arrivée des invités (grande reception). A jouer dans un vestibule. Mouvement: Très riche.'

2   *Carrelage phonique*
     4 bars for fl, cl, str. 'Peut se jouer à un lunch où à un contrat de mariage. Mouvement: Ordinaire.'

MSS: *US-Eu* (neat copies, Nos. 1–2)

     BN 9623, 36–7 (plans and sketches)

pubn: No. 2 in facs. in John Cage: *Notations* (New York, Something Else Press, 1969)

     Nos. 1–2 in *Musique d'ameublement*, Salabert, 1975, 4

?1917   **La Veille du combat**
music: inc. song for v, pf
MSS: BN 9623(4), 2–4 (pf part inc.)
unpubd

6 Jan 1917–Spring 1918   **Socrate** (referred to in 1917 as *Vie de Socrate*)
(orch. rev. Oct 1918;   text: extracts from the *Dialogues de Platon* (trans. Victor
work commissioned in   Cousin). Satie chose this in preference to the more
Oct 1916)   modern trans. of Mario Meunier for its clarity, simplicity and beauty, and he found Plato to be 'a perfect
collaborator'. From the 39 chapters of *Le Banquet*,
Satie set 4 passages from chapter 32, and 1 passage
from each of chapters 33 and 35 as Part 1. From the
64 chapters of *Phèdre*, he set 2 passages from chapter 4,
and 1 from chapter 5 as Part 2. From the 67 chapters
of *Phédon*, he set 4 passages from chapter 3, 1 from
chapter 33, 2 from chapter 35, 3 from chapter 38, 2
from chapter 65, and 1 from chapter 67 as Part 3. Satie
made no additions or changes of order to the 20 paragraphs he selected (information from Volta, 1987,
59–60, n. 19)
music: 'Symphonic drama in 3 parts' for 4 sopranos (2 high;
2 mezzo) and small orch (fl, ob, eng hn, cl, bn, hn, tpt,
hp, timp, str)
1   *Portrait de Socrate* (Alcibiade, Socrate)
2   *Bords de l'Ilissus* (Socrate, Phèdre)
3   *Mort de Socrate* (Phédon)
ded.: à Madame la Princesse Edmond de Polignac
MSS: Archives of Prince Louis de Polignac, Paris (OS)
BN Rés. Vma 171 (corr. proofs of VS)
Orchestral drafts: BN 9623(5), 1–17 (Part 1)
BN 9623(5), 18–24; BN 9623(6), 13–17 (Part 2, material
found in VS 15–20 bar 3 and 20 bar 4–23 bar 5. The rest
of the orchestral draft is missing)
Sketches and drafts for v, pf: Part 1:
BN 9623(1), 21–2, 32–40 (VS 4 bar 8–11 bar 1)
BN 9623(4), 5–6, 8–10, 12–17 (VS 1–6 bar 10; 15–17 are
a neat copy of BN 9623(1), 32–5)
BN 9623(2), 1–7 (VS 11 bar 2–14 bar 9; the last 2 bars of
Part 1 are missing)
Part 2: BN 9623(2), 8–31 (VS 15–34)
Part 3: BN 9623(1), 1–20 (VS 35–55 bar 8; earliest draft)
BN 9611, 4–24 (VS 35–end 61; second draft)

BN 9623(3), 4–19, 2–3, 20 (VS 62 bar 1–end; though the end is different from VS 71)

pubn: VS (with preface by René Chalupt): Editions de La Sirène, 1919 (1920 on cover: Satie hoped that this would appear by mid-Dec 1918, but there were long delays); Eschig, 1973

OS: Eschig, 1950 (for hire only); rev. ed. in accordance with Polignac MS in preparation by Eschig, 1990

prem.: 3 April 1918, private performance of extracts by Jane Bathori and Satie *chez* la Princesse de Polignac, 57 avenue Henri-Martin

24 June 1918, extracts (incl. Part 3) *chez* Jane Bathori

21 March 1919, Part 1 by Suzanne Balguerie and Satie at Adrienne Monnier's bookshop (La Maison des Amis des Livres), 7 rue de l'Odéon

25 May 1919, ?complete performance by Balguerie and Satie *chez* Mme Berchut, 3 rue Edward Fournier, Paris 16

Public première with pf: 14 Feb 1920 by Jane Bathori and Suzanne Balguerie, with André Salomon (pf), SN, Salle de l'Ancien Conservatoire

Public première with orch: 7 June 1920 by Marya Freund, orch cond. Félix Delgrange. Festival Erik Satie, Salle Erard, 13 rue du Mail

'Aug–Nov 1919'   **Nocturnes** (5)

music: a set of 3 Nocturnes in D major for pf, to which a further 2 were added (in F♯ minor and F major). Satie planned to publish 7 Nocturnes and it seems likely from the 'Harmonies pour les 5e–6e & 7e Nocturnes' (see Fig. 9.5) that these were meant to form another set of 3 centred on F major, with the 4th Nocturne as a sort of interlude between the 2 groups. However, only No. 5 materialized before Satie passed on to other projects

Première Nocturne ('Aug 1919')

Deuxième Nocturne ('Sept 1919')

Troisième Nocturne ('Oct 1919')

Quatrième Nocturne ('Oct 1919')

Cinquième Nocturne ('Nov 1919')

ded.: 1   à Madame Marcelle Meyer

     2   à André Salomon

     3   à Madame Jean Hugo

4 à Madame la Comtesse Etienne de Beaumont
5 à Madame Georges Cocteau

MSS: 1 BN 9609(2), 2–6 (draft, with descriptive commentary about an 'old Will-o'-the-wisp' that was withdrawn before publication. Orig. title: *Faux Nocturne*)
2 BN 9666, 6–9 (rough draft)
3 BN 9609(1), 2–5 (rough draft)
4 BN 9609(1), 10–11 (draft. A neat copy of bars 13–16 can be found on BN 9666, 10)
5 PLU

Sketches: 1 BN 9609(2), 1
2 BN 9666, 5 (intervallic plan)
3 BN 9609(1), 1
4 BN 9609(1), 6–8 (unused sketches); 9 (first version of start)
5 BN 9609(1), 12–13 (unused sketches)

Note: Numerous sketches for the starts of other Nocturnes exist in BN 9609(2), 7–14; BN 9609(3), 4–15; BN 9609(4), 1–13; BN 9673, 1–3, 18–20. As these are mostly in D major, it is likely that they were rejected trials for Nocturnes 1–3. However, Satie did advertise a '6ème Nocturne' with Demets in 1920, and he told Robert Caby in 1925 that it was virtually complete and might one day be published. The only contender for this title is the draft found in BN 9609(2), 15–18, which only lacks a left-hand part in bars 6–7. Although it is cast in D major, its modulatory range is far wider than that of Nocturnes 1–3, and as Satie's plan for three nocturnes in F (5–7) was never carried through, it seems likely that this could be the lost '6ème Nocturne'. I have completed the missing part in accordance with Satie's instructions as to key, and in the style of the rest of the piece, and I plan to publish it in the near future

pubn: 1–3: Rouart-Lerolle, 1919; Salabert
4–5: Demets, 1920; Eschig

prem.: 1: 18 March 1920 by Jane Mortier, Salle Pleyel
1–3: 7 June 1920 by Ricardo Viñes. Festival Erik Satie, Salle Erard, 13 rue du Mail
(6: 29 May 1987 by Robert Orledge, Northcott Theatre, Exeter University)

'Nov 1919'

Marche de Cocagne

music: march for 2 tpt in C, later used as the outer sections
of the 2nd of the *Trois Petites Pièces montées* (bars 1–8,
repeated as 17–24)

MSS: PLU

pubn: in facs. (dated 'Nov 1919') in *Almanach de Cocagne
pour l'An 1920* (Editions de La Sirène, 1920) with woodcut illustrations by Raoul Dufy (reproduced in Vy, 75)

Nov–Dec 1919
(orch. Jan 1920)

Trois Petites Pièces montées

music: 3 short pieces for pf duet or orch (fl, ob, cl in Bb, bn,
hn, 2 tpt in C, trbn, perc, str) inspired by the stories
of *Pantagruel* and his father *Gargantua* (1532–4) by
François Rabelais. No. 1 also exists as pf solo

1 *De l'enfance de Pantagruel* (*Rêverie*)

2 *Marche de Cocagne* (*Démarche*)

3 *Jeux de Gargantua* (*Coin de Polka*)

MSS: PLU. Facs. of No. 1 for pf solo in Hôtel Drouot Catalogue, 1979, No. 165

BN Rés. Vma 167 (corr. proofs for pf duet)

pubn: No. 1 for pf solo: Editions de La Sirène, 1920; Eschig
1968

Pf duet: Editions de La Sirène, 1921; Eschig, 1977

OS: Editions de La Sirène, 1921; Eschig, 1977

prem.: 23 Feb 1920, Comédie des Champs-Elysées, orch
cond. Vladimir Golschmann

Feb–March 1920

Musique d'ameublement (Sons industriels)

music: 2 short 'entr'actes' for pf duet, 3 cl (in Eb, Bb, A),
trbn. No. 1 may be Satie's version of the student song
'Gaudeamus igitur' which ends Brahms's *Academic
Festival Overture* (1880). No. 2 contains extracts from
Mignon's Act 1 Romance ('Connais-tu le pays, où
fleurit l'oranger?') in Ambroise Thomas's *Mignon*
(1866), and a version of the second theme of Saint-
Saëns's *Danse macabre* (bars 50–7, 1874)

1 *1er Entr'acte* (*Chez un 'bistrot'*)

2 *2d Entr'acte* (*Un salon*)

MSS: *F-Ppc* (score, 12pp.)

BN 9601(1), 1–9; BN 9601(2), 3–5, 26–30 (sketches)

pubn: unpubd, except for a facs. of p. 1 of the score in
Volta, 1988, 28 which explains the intentions of this
'furnishing divertissement organized by the group of

musicians known as the "Nouveaux Jeunes". . .
Furnishing music replaces "waltzes" and "operatic
fantasias" etc. Don't be confused! *It's something else!!!*
No more "false music". . .Furnishing music completes
one's property;. . .it's *new*; it doesn't upset customs;
it isn't tiring; it's French; it won't wear out; it *isn't
boring.*'

prem.: 8 March 1920, Galerie Barbazanges, Faubourg
St-Honoré, by Satie and Milhaud (pf duet), other
instrumentalists not known. Performed between the
3 Acts of Max Jacob's comedy (now lost): *Ruffian
toujours, truand jamais.* An exhibition of children's
drawings (*Les Belles Promesses*) also ran simultaneously
at the gallery, and the whole event was organized
by Pierre Bertin (who played the role of Lucien in
Jacob's play)

'June 1920'

Premier Menuet
music: piece for pf. Satie probably planned a set of 3 minuets,
but only 1 was pubd
ded.: à Claude Dubosq
MSS: BN 10042 (copy for printer, 4pp., 'June 1920')
  BN 9605(2), 2–5 (draft)
  BN 9605(1), 1–3; BN 9605(2), 8 (sketches)
pubn: Editions de La Sirène, 1922; Eschig
prem.: 17 Jan 1922 by Marcelle Meyer. Salle de La Ville
l'Evêque, 18 rue de La Ville l'Evêque

July–Oct 1920

La Belle Excentrique
music: 3 dances and an interlude (to cover costume changes,
where necessary). Written for the dancer Caryathis
(*née* Elisabeth Toulemon; later Mme Elise Jouhandeau)
as a 'fantaisie sérieuse' for small orch (pic, ob, cl, hn,
tpt, trbn, perc, str) or pf duet (or pf solo?)
– *Grande Ritournelle*
1 *Marche Franco-Lunaire* (completed 26 Aug)
2 *Valse du 'Mystérieux baiser dans l'œil'* (completed 23 Sept)
3 *Cancan Grand-Mondain* (Sept–Oct)
Note: The *Grande Ritournelle* reuses the *Légende Californienne* of *c.* 1905. In Satie's contract with Editions de La
Sirène of 22 July 1921 (facs. in Volta, 1987, 38) the
order is as above, and the total duration (12 minutes)
implies that the *Grande Ritournelle* was played twice,
probably between each of the dances. But as Satie him-

self chose a single costume (by Cocteau) for all 3 dances (rejecting designs by Jean Hugo, Marie Laurencin, Kees van Dongen and Paul Poiret!) there was no practical need for a repeat of the interlude. Thus it seems likely that Satie's order given on the cover of BN 9605(1) – with the *Grande Ritournelle (milieu)* coming only once between dances 2 and 3 – is the most sensible solution for future performances (see the preface to the rev. 1987 Eschig ed. by Ornella Volta)

MSS: OS: PLU (sold at Hôtel Drouot, 18 March 1933)

F-Pbd (Nos. 1, 2 in pf solo version)

Pf duet version: PLU

F-Pca (formal plan. An early plan for *La Belle Excentrique* also exists inside the front cover of Ho 21 which describes it as 'Très Parisien', and shows that Satie intended it as a musical tour through 'three periods' of Parisian popular entertainment, titled as follows:

1 '1900: Marche pour une Grande Cocotte'
2 '1910: Elégance du Cirque (Ecuyère)'
3 '1920: Cancan Moderne')

Sketches and drafts: *Grande Ritournelle*: BN 9629, 26–7; Ho 34 (as *Légende Californienne*, c. 1905); BN 9669, 1; Ho 27, 14–15 (both 1920)

No. 1: BN 9605(1), 7–8 (first draft); BN 9605(2), 6–19 (sketches for final version, see Ex. 25)

No. 2: BN 9605(3), 5–11

No. 3: BN 9605(3), 4 (rejected version); BN 9605(4), 1–17 (sketches for final version)

pubn: Pf duet: Editions de La Sirène, 1922; Eschig 1950; rev. ed. by Ornella Volta, Eschig, 1987

OS: Editions de La Sirène, 1922; Eschig, 1950

prem.: Private: 8 Jan 1921 *chez* Pierre Bertin, 120 boulevard du Montparnasse

Public: 14 June 1921, Théâtre du Colisée, 38 avenue des Champs-Elysées, danced by Caryathis. Orch cond. Vladimir Golschmann

Sept–'Dec 1920'   **Quatre Petites Mélodies**

music: 4 miniature songs for v, pf

1 *Elégie* (Lamartine; stanza 7 of 'L'Isolement' (April 1818), pubd in *Premières Méditations* (1820)) ('27 Sept')
2 *Danseuse* (Cocteau) ('8 Oct')
3 *Chanson* (anon., 18th century) ('25 Nov')

4   *Adieu* (Radiguet: orig. title 'Mouchoir', pubd in *Les Joues en feu* ('Lettres d'un Alphabet') (Paris, François Bernouard)) (Nov–'Dec 1920')

ded.: No. 1: à la Mémoire de Claude Debussy (En souvenir d'une admirative et douce amitié de trente ans)

MSS: Drafts: No. 1: BN 9576, 10–11

No. 2: BN 9616, 6–7

No. 3: BN 9616, 11 ('25 Nov'); Ho 45 final copy 'Dec 1920')

No. 4: BN 9574, 6–7 ('Dec 1920')

Sketches: No. 1: BN 9576, 8–9

No. 2: PLU

No. 3: BN 9616, 10 (first version)

No. 4: BN 9574, 1–4

pubn: No. 1: in *La Revue musicale*, 1/2 (Dec 1920): Musical supplement: *Le Tombeau de Debussy*, No. X, p. 32

No. 3: facs. as *Chanson à boire* in the *Almanach de Cocagne pour l'An 1921* (Editions de La Sirène)

All 4: Editions de La Sirène, 1922; Eschig

prem.: No. 1: 19 Dec 1920 by Jane Bathori and André Salomon (pf), Galerie La Boétie

All 4: 12 April 1921 by Pierre Bertin and ?Satie, Galerie Georges Giroux, Brussels

?April 1920–Dec 1923
(mostly July 1921–
Oct 1922)

Paul & Virginie

text: opéra-comique in 3 Acts based on the story by Bernardin de Saint-Pierre. Dialogue by Jean Cocteau, lyrics by Raymond Radiguet and ?Cocteau (see Volta, *RIMF*, 1989 for a full account of this opera). The orig. libretto (from which Satie worked) has disappeared since its sale in 1970, though it was all in Cocteau's hand (90pp.) and was dated 'Bassin d'Arcachon, le 16 septembre 1920'. Only a later revision by Cocteau is now known to exist (in the Cocteau Archives at Milly-la-Forêt) and it was from this that the recent editions were prepared: in Raymond Radiguet: *Gli inediti* (ed. Liliana Garuti Delli Ponti) (Parma, Ugo Guanda editore, 1967), 58–159; and in *Paul et Virginie* (Paris, J.C. Lattès, Edition Spéciale, 1973), 119pp. Here the Acts are as follows:

Act 1: Le paradis perdu [on the Ile Saint-Louis, now Mauritius]

Act 2: Chez les sauvages [in Paris]

Act 3: Le vrai paradis [as Act 1]

(The plot is outlined in chapter 10 n. 70).

Satie's letter to Cocteau on 20 April 1920 suggests that he was part of the project from its inception. The sketches in BN 9576 even suggest that an operatic trilogy was planned in the summer of 1920 comprising *Paul & Virginie*, *Robinson Crusoé* and *Don Quichotte*. So the oft-quoted passage about *Paul & Virginie* being 'read' to Satie for the *first time* on '22 Nov' 1920 was probably a piece of publicity for the project by Cocteau, like his observation (also in *Le Coq*, No. 4 (Nov 1920)) that '*Paul et Virginie* will be Satie's next work and his farewell to musical composition.'

music: inc. opéra-comique in 3 Acts. Only a few sketches survive, plus Satie's plans for Act 1 and a list of the characters and their vocal ranges. However, André Derain was brought in to design sets and costumes (surely on Satie's recommendation) in the summer of 1921 and Satie is known to have reached Act 2 (in the 'genre Rossini') in September 1921 (see Fig. 10.7). He wanted Pierre Bertin to play Paul in Oct 1921 and signed a production contract with Jacques Hébertot for the Théâtre des Champs-Elysées on 26 Nov. In May 1922, however, Cocteau turned his sights towards Diaghilev's Ballets Russes, and Satie (who was not overkeen on Hébertot) accepted this change in early Nov. Diaghilev planned to include the work in his 'Second French Festival of Opéras-Comiques 1924–5', but before this (in Dec 1923) Satie had eventually abandoned the opera, due to Cocteau's incessant 'intrigues', and perhaps due to his lack of progress in writing the sort of score he thought appropriate.

As Satie never destroyed his scores, it is possible that a good deal more of *Paul & Virginie* will eventually come to light, and lead to a re-evaluation of Satie's later career. But it seems likely that the music was light and neo-classical, probably similar to that found in Satie's recitatives for Gounod's *Le Médecin malgré lui*, a Diaghilev commission which helped to divert his attention from his own opera in the latter half of 1923.

After Satie broke with Cocteau in Jan 1924, Cocteau approached other composers to complete *Paul & Virginie*, incl. Poulenc (Aug 1924), Henri Sauguet (1931) and Nicolas Nabokov. Only Sauguet began work on it (1931–3), using Satie's annotated libretto (containing 'musical intentions rather than musical notes'). But all that emerged was a setting of the *Chanson de Marins [La 'Belle Cubaine']* from Act 1, and Cocteau's opera is likely to remain an interesting curiosity that never reached the stage

MSS: *F-Ppc* (notebook containing 9pp. of sketches in pencil, inked over in black (1–7, 9–10) with the start of the *Chœur des Marins [La 'Belle Cubaine']* (p. 18) and verse 1 of its text on the cover (beginning: 'Ils étaient tous jeunes & beaux/ Sur la "Belle Cubaine" oh! ho!'). On p. 1 are the words: 'La Mélodie et son accompagnement feront corps/ Légère, très levée & pétillante comme du champagne, telle doit être la musique de *Paul & Virginie*' (cited in Volta, *RIMF*, 1989, 70))

BN 9671, 7–13 (*La 'Belle Cubaine*', complete text from Act 1 (5 verses) and musical sketches in G minor for verse 1, ?1922). Extracts pubd in Orledge, 1990

F-Ppc (notebook containing 3pp. of sketches for *La 'Belle Cubaine*' and the text of verse 1, summer 1922)

BN 9576, 5 (sketch in 1913 *Enfantines* style, with humorous text, relating to a dance by Paul, and a song by Virginie that 'made the monkeys weep'. Written in Sept 1920. On pp. 6–8 are sketches in similar style for *Robinson Crusoé* and *Don Quichotte* (see Volta, 1988, 17–19))

BN 9607, 2–3 (brief sketches, *c.* 1923)

US-NYpm, Frederick R. Koch Foundation Collection, No. 1180, box 121 (plans for the division of Act 1 into 11 scenes, on pp. 1, 3, 5, 7, 9 of a 96-page lined notebook ('Le Fénelon') (see Fig. 10.8, which shows the *Chœur des Marins [La 'Belle Cubaine']* at the start. Satie abandoned these plans with the start of Act 2 on p. 11. Also ½-sheet of MS paper containing 'Diverses Tessitures de "Paul & Virginie" considerées au point de vue "timbre"' (see Fig. 10.9). Here, La Marquise (Virginie's wicked aunt in the 1973 ed. of the libretto) is cast as the 'Comtesse d'Herbeville' (coloratura soprano) and her side-kick 'Le Comte' is cast as 'Le Baron' (light tenor). This, and the subdivision of the pubd libretto of Act 1 into only 2 scenes confirms that Satie worked from an earlier libretto, even if the events outlined are broadly synonymous)

June–Aug 1921   **Alice au Pays de Merveilles** (*Alice in Wonderland*)
text: scenario (lost) for a ballet based on Lewis Carroll's classic story compiled by Louise Norton (later Mrs Edgard Varèse) at Satie's request (source: Varèse, 1972, 161). Henri-Pierre Roché also briefly worked on the scenario in Aug 1921, but found it boring and too complicated (according to his diaries in *US-AUS*)
music: lost or never started

summer 1921   **La Naissance de Vénus**
(Aug 1921–Dec 1922)   text: scenario (lost) for a ballet, inspired by Botticelli's painting, by Satie and André Derain, intended for Diaghilev's Ballets Russes. Satie mentions the project in letters to Derain, and in Sept 1921 the ballet was scheduled to appear at the Paris Opéra in conjunction with Stravinsky's *Les Noces*
music: lost or never started

summer 1921   **Supercinéma**
(Aug–Sept 1921)   text: scenario (lost) for a ballet by Satie and André Derain for Rolf de Maré's Ballets Suédois. Mentioned in letters from Satie to Derain as being postponed till the 1922 season (5 Sept 1921)
music: lost or never started

'30 Aug 1921'   **Sonnerie pour réveiller le bon gros Roi des Singes (lequel ne dort toujours que d'un œil)**
music: fanfare for 2 tpt in C
MSS: *US-NYpm*, Frederick R. Koch Foundation Collection, No. 379, box 65 (score, 1p., '30 Aug 1921', see Fig. 6.4)
BN 9615(4), 18–19 (draft)
BN 9670, 6 (sketch, see Fig. 6.3)
pubn: facs. in *Fanfare* No. 1 (1 Oct 1921), 11
Editions BIM (Bulle, Switzerland), 1981
prem.: 7 May 1979, Opéra-Comique, by Jacques Lecointre, Hákan Hardenberger (tpts)

Feb–May 1923   **Divertissement (La Statue retrouvée)**
(Dec 1922–30   text: scenario (lost) by Jean Cocteau commissioned by
May 1923)   Comtesse Edith de Beaumont in Dec 1922 for a Masked Ball at her Paris Hôtel in May 1923. The *Divertissement* was to be performed by guests at the Ball and was to centre on the newly-restored 18th-century organ in the Beaumont's music-room. For this brief

part of the entertainment, the production team of *Parade* was reassembled: Picasso being brought in to design the sets and costumes in Feb 1923, and Massine to regulate the choreography in April

music: 53 bars for org, with tpt at the end (see Ex. 88):

1 *Entrée (Mouvement de Marche)* (after 24 May)
2 *1ère Recherche*
3 *2ème Recherche*
4 *A deux (vers la statue)*
5 [*Retraite*] with tpt (17–24 May)

MSS: BN 9608, 2–9 (neat org score)
   BN 9607, 5–11 (sketches)

unpubd

prem.: 30 May 1923 during Masked Ball (*L'Antiquité sous Louis XIV*) at the Hôtel of Comte Etienne de Beaumont, 2 rue Duroc. Dancers incl. Mme Olga Picasso, the Marquise de Médicis, Léonide Massine, Comte and Comtesse de Beaumont, Mme Daisy Fellowes (who, as an inspired last-minute replacement for Mme René Jacquemaire, inspired Satie to add the opening *Entrée*). Erik Satie (org); see also *Ludions* (1923)

'28 March 1923'

Tenture de Cabinet préfectoral

music: 12 bars of 'furnishing music' for small orch (pic, cl in B♭, bn, hn, tpt in C, perc, str) commissioned (via Milhaud) by Mrs Eugène Meyer (Junior) for her home at 2201 Connecticut Avenue, Washington D.C.

ded.: à Madame Eugène Meyer

MSS: *F-Ppc* (score, 1p.)
   F-Pbd (sketch, 1p., facs. in Rey, 1974, 124)

pubn: Salabert, 1975 (OS in *Musique d'ameublement*, 2–3)

finished May 1923

Ludions

music: 5 short songs for v, pf (or org) to humorous poems by Léon-Paul Fargue

1 *Air du Rat*
2 *Spleen*
3 *La Grenouille américaine*
4 *Air du Poète (Papouasie)* ('May 1923')
5 *Chanson du chat*

MSS: Ho 29 (neat copies of Nos. 1–5, labelled 'Chant & Piano: Madame Jacquemaire' on the cover
   F-Pca (neat copy of No. 2, made to send to USA)
   F-Pfs, on deposit from a private coll. (complete sketch of

all 5 songs on pp. 1–19 of a separate notebook, dated '15 Mai 1923' at end. At this stage the songs were ready to copy into Ho 29)

BN 9606, 2–9 (arr. of pf part for org for private première, with 'Orgue: Mme Jacquemaire' on cover (see below))

BN 9594, 5 (plans for ordering cycle and its tonality)

Sketches: No. 1: BN 9594, 4 (v part), 6–7 (rejected 1st version), 11–13 (rejected 2nd version), 14–15 (final version), 18–20 (other harmonic sketches)

No. 2: BN 9594, 2–3 (rhythmic sketch), 8–9 (rejected 1st version in invertible counterpoint, see Ex. 43a)

Nos. 3–4: PLU

No. 5: BN 9594, 4–5 (v part), 22

pubn: No. 4 in facs. in *Les Feuilles libres*, No. 35 (Jan–Feb 1924), 332–3; and in *The Transatlantic Review*, No. 1 (May 1924)

All 5: Rouart-Lerolle, 1926; Salabert

prem.: private: 30 May 1923 during Masked Ball (*L'Antiquité sous Louis XIV*) *chez* Comte Etienne de Beaumont, 2 rue Duroc. By Mme René Jacquemaire (later the Comtesse Marie-Blanche de Polignac) and Satie (org). (It was at this première that Satie forgot to name Fargue as the author of the poems, after which the two became enemies. Information supplied by Ornella Volta. See also *Divertissement* above)

public: 21 Dec 1923 by Jane Bathori and Satie (pf), Salle des Agriculteurs

?July 1923

Le Roi de la grande Ile

text: poem by ?Satie ('Le Roi de la grande Ile un grand repas donnait') intended for the *Almanach de Cocagne pour l'An 1924* and annotated for printing by the editor Bertrand Guégan in July 1923

music: song for v, pf

MSS: PLU. Listed in Catalogue autographe Berès (Hôtel Drouot, 20 June 1977, No. 74), 1p.

unpubd

?summer 1923

Concurrence

text: scenario (lost) for a ballet planned by Satie and André Derain. (Note: A ballet titled *La Concurrence* with scenery and costumes by Derain and music by Auric was performed by the Ballets de Monte Carlo at the Théâtre des Champs-Elysées, Paris in 1932, but it is not known whether this drew on ideas from the 1923 project)

music: lost or never started

?summer 1923

Couleurs

text: scenario (lost) for a ballet with André Derain

music: lost or never started

July–15 Dec 1923
(Act 1 completed
25 Aug; Act 2
completed 11 Sept;
Act 3 completed
6 Oct; orch.
Oct–15 Dec)

Recitatives for Gounod's opera 'Le Médecin malgré lui'

text: libretto by Jules Barbier and Michel Carré first performed (with spoken dialogue) at the Théâtre-Lyrique,
Paris on 15 Jan 1858

music: recitatives for vv and orch (forces unknown) for
Diaghilev's Monte Carlo production of Gounod's
3-Act opéra-comique in Jan 1924

MSS: OS, PLU

F-Ppc (VS with some orch indications – fl, str – in 8 notebooks of 'scènes nouvelles' (137pp.). Copies in F-Pfs)

Sketches and preparatory material:

BN 9595(1) (typed libretto annotated by Satie of passages
to be set, 15pp.)

BN 9595(2) (rhythmic plans for recitatives on left-hand
pp., running parallel to copied texts on right-hand
pp., 73pp.)

BN 9595(3) (ranges of the singers concerned: Martine
(mezzo-soprano); Sganarelle (baritone); Valère (bass);
Lucas (tenor), plus guides to preparing OS, notebook
of 20pp. marked 'Pour Derain')

BN 9595(3bis) (3 postcards giving bar-lengths of the
recitatives with key-signatures, in preparation for writing OS)

BN 9595(4), 1–13 (sketches for Act 2 sc. 2)

BN 9595(5), 3–11 (sketches for rest of Act 2)

BN 9595(5), 12–19 (sketches for Act 3, as far as 'Quin-
tette' in E major)

BN 9595(6), 1–13 (sketches for rest of Act 3, up to final
'Octuor')

unpubd

prem.: 5 Jan 1924 by Diaghilev's Ballets Russes at Casino de
Monte Carlo. Sets and costumes by Alexandre Benois,
choreography by Bronislava Nijinska. Cast incl. Serge
Lifar. Satie's name was (?deliberately) omitted from
the programme prepared by Louis Laloy. Further per-

formances took place in Monte Carlo on 13, 19 and 22 Jan 1924

Feb 1924

[2 short ?operas]
text: 'deux petites choses' by Tristan Tzara (lost)
music: lost or never started

1924

Quadrille
text: scenario (lost) for ballet by Satie and Georges Braque for Diaghilev's Ballets Russes (Satie received an advance for this on 6 April 1924)
music: lost or never started. The ballet was to be based on Chabrier's *Souvenirs de Munich* (1885–6, a set of quadrilles for pf duet based on themes from Wagner's *Tristan und Isolde*)

late Feb–16 May 1924
(Tableau 1 completed during March; Tableau 2 completed 9 April; Tableau 3 completed 17 April: orch. mid-April–16 May)

Mercure [*Les Aventures de Mercure*]
text: 'Poses plastiques' in 3 tableaux by Picasso
music: ballet score for orch (pic, fl, ob, 2 cl in B♭, bn, 2 hn, 2 tpt in C, trbn, tuba, perc, str), commissioned by Comte Etienne de Beaumont for his Soirées de Paris
  1 *Ouverture: Mouvement de Marche*
TABLEAU 1
  2 *La Nuit*
  3 *Danse de tendresse* (a transposed and expanded version of the *Fugue-Valse, c.* 1906)
  4 *Signes du Zodiaque*
  5 *Entrée et danse de Mercure*
TABLEAU 2
  6 *Danse des Grâces*
  7 *Bain des Grâces*
  8 *Fuite de Mercure*
  9 *Colère de Cerbère*
TABLEAU 3
  10 *Polka des Lettres*
  11 *Nouvelle Danse*
  12 *Le Chaos* [*Apparition du Chaos*] (Nos. 10 and 11 combined, in the Polka tempo of No. 10)
  13 *Final: Rapt de Proserpine*
ded.: A Madame la Comtesse Etienne de Beaumont
MSS: *F-Pfs* (coll. Henri de Beaumont) (OS, 79pp., titled *Les Aventures de Mercure*; pf red., 19pp., titled *Mercure*)
Ho 80 (9 postcards showing page plan for OS of 79pp. with section lengths, keys and titles. Overall title:

Les Aventures de Mercure. No. 12 titled *Apparition du Chaos*)

BN 9596(2) (typed plan for ballet, 1p., by Picasso or Comte de Beaumont, with pencil annotations by Satie giving orig. plan of tonalities, section lengths and timings (which were expanded during composition, see Fig. 10.6). No. 13 is marked 'Cubisme' by Satie)

Sketches and drafts:

No. 1: BN 9596(2), 3, 18, 14–16 (final version)

No. 2: BN 9596(2), 4–5 (4 marked 'Apollon & Vénus' from orig. plan)

No. 3: BN 9635, 4–9 (draft of *Fugue-Valse*, see movement list above)

No. 4: BN 9596(2), 5 (rejected version), 6–9, 12–13 (final version)

No. 5: BN 9596(1), 3–5

No. 6: BN 9596(1), 8–12

No. 7: BN 9596(1), 11, 13

No. 8: BN 9596(1), 14–15

No. 9: BN 9596(1), 16–17

No. 10: BN 9596(1), 18–19

No. 11: BN 9596(1), 20–1

No. 12: BN 9596(1), 22–4

No. 13: BN 9622(2), 1–3

pubn: OS: Universal Edition, 1929; 1977; rev. ed. by Robert Caby, 1980 (for hire only).

(Rescored version by Harrison Birtwistle, Universal Edition, 1980)

prem.: 15 June 1924 at Théâtre de la Cigale, Montmartre (as part of a Soirée de Paris organized by Comte Etienne de Beaumont, which also incl. Milhaud's ballet *Salade*). Sets and costumes by Picasso, choreography by Léonide Massine (who danced the role of Mercure), lighting by Loïe Fuller. Orch cond. Roger Désormière (who was forbidden by Satie to repeat any of the movements during the scenery changes)

late May–20 Oct 1924 (Act 1 completed 27 July; Act 2 completed 27 Aug; orch. late Aug–20 Oct) (With 1st version as

Relâche

text: As ballet *Après-dîner* in 1 Act (9 scenes) by Blaise Cendrars (Nov 1923). Scenario pubd in Sanouillet, 1966, 255–6. No music composed

As 'Ballet instantanéiste' *Relâche* in 2 Acts by Francis Picabia (Feb 1924), using some ideas from *Après-dîner.*

Après-dîner and *Cinéma* interlude: Nov 1923–10 Nov 1924, the work being interrupted for *Mercure* in Feb–mid-May 1924)

Scenario pubd in Sanouillet, 1966, 256–7 (incl. orig. plan for filmed interlude between Acts)

music: ballet score for orch (fl, ob, cl in A, bn, 2 hn, 2 tpt in C, trbn, perc, str). Uses popular songs (like *Cadet Rousselle*, *Savez-vous planter des choux*) and was referred to as an 'obscene' or 'pornographic' ballet by Satie. The movement titles below come from the OS:

ACT 1
1 *Ouverturette* [*Ouverture*]
2 *Projectionette* [*Projection*]
3 *Rideau*
4 *Entrée de la Femme*
5 *'Musique' entre l'entrée de la Femme et sa 'Danse sans musique'*
6 *Entrée de l'Homme*
7 *Danse de la Porte tournante (l'Homme et la Femme)*
8 *Entrée des Hommes*
9 *Danse des Hommes*
10 *Danse de la Femme*
11 *Final*

ACT 2
12 *Musique de Rentrée*
13 *Rentrée des Hommes*
14 *Rentrée de la Femme*
15 *Les Hommes se dévêtissent (La Femme se rhabille)*
16 *Danse de Borlin et de la Femme* [*Danse de l'Homme et de la Femme*]
17 *Les Hommes regagnent leur place et retrouvent leurs pardessus*
18 *Danse de la Brouette (La Femme et le Danseur)*
19 *Danse de la Couronne (La Femme seule)*
20 *Le Danseur dépose la Couronne sur la tête d'une spectatrice*
21 *La Femme rejoint son fauteuil*
22 *La 'Queue' du Chien (Chanson Mimée)* [*Petite Danse finale*]

MSS: *F-Psalabert* (OS, 134pp., 'Oct 1924')
  F-Psalabert (pf red., 71pp.)
  BN 9622(1), 12 (tonal plan and first draft of movement lengths for Act 1, see Fig. 8.11)
  BN 9622(4), 1 (ibid. for Act 2)
  BN 9678 (plans for pagination of OS, with keys and section lengths, Acts 1–2, 8pp.)

Ho 82 (plan for pagination of movements in OS 69–134 (Act 2) on postcard from Georges Braque (No. 17 titled: *Les Hommes regagnent leur place et se dévêtissent*))

Ho 83 (21 fragments showing Satie's attempts to bisect *Relâche* into 2 mirrored and proportionally subdivided Acts during the orchestration (Aug–Sept 1924, see Figs. 8.13–16))

Sketches and drafts: ACT 1 (BN 9622(1–3)):

No. 1: BN 9622(1), 4, 6–7 (draft of *Marche*), 8 (Largo introduction), 17 (unused)

No. 2: BN 9622(1), 9–10

No. 3: BN 9622(1), 11

No. 4: BN 9622(2), 14–17

No. 5: BN 9622(3), 1–3

No. 6: BN 9622(3), 4–7

No. 7: BN 9622(3), 8–9

No. 8: BN 9622(1), 1 (first version); BN 9622(2), 10–11 (final melody); BN 9622(3), 10, 12–13 (draft)

No. 9: BN 9622(3), 10–11

No. 10: BN 9622(3), 14–17

No. 11: BN 9622(1), 2–3

ACT 2 (BN 9622(4–5), with recurring material from Act 1 not written out in full. Satie indicates the sections to be used, with their transpositions in Act 2):

No. 12: BN 9622(4), 2–5

No. 13: BN 9622(4), 6–9

No. 14: BN 9622(4), 10–13

No. 15: BN 9622(4), 14–15

No. 16: BN 9622(4), 16–20; BN 9622(5), 1–3 (revision of bars 21–37)

No. 17: BN 9622(5), 4–7

No. 18: BN 9622(5), 8–11 (with calculation as to how 5/4 bars fit in with overall scheme of 2/4 bars in units of 8); Ho 74 (5 bars, noteheads only, miscopied page)

No. 19: BN 9622(5), 12–15

No. 20: BN 9622(5), 16–18

No. 21: No draft, as this is a literal transposition of No. 4 up a semitone

No. 22: BN 9622(1), 13; BN 9622(5), 20–1 (only first 4 and last 4 bars written out. The rest derives from No. 2, from letter A, down a minor 3rd)

pubn: OS: Rouart-Lerolle, 1926; Salabert (for hire only)

Pf red.: Rouart-Lerolle, 1926; Salabert

prem.: 4 Dec 1924 by Rolf de Maré's Ballets Suédois, Théâtre des Champs-Elysées. Scenery and costumes by Picabia, choreography by Jean Borlin. With Borlin as 'L'Homme' and Edith Bonsdorff as 'La Femme'. Orch cond. Roger Désormière. 12 performances were given in 1924–5, though the orig. première planned for 27 Nov had to be cancelled at the last minute due to the illness of Borlin

26 Oct–10 Nov 1924   **Cinéma. Entr'acte symphonique de 'Relâche'**

music: score for small orch (fl, ob, cl in A, bn, 2 hn, 2 tpt in C, trbn, perc, str) to accompany film interlude by René Clair between the Acts of *Relâche*. The opening section, with Satie and Clair firing a cannon on the roof of the Théâtre des Champs-Elysées, was shown with No. 2 of *Relâche* (*Projectionette*) before the curtain rose for Act 1 (No. 3: *Rideau*). Clair's film was shot, entirely on location in Paris, in June 1924 (see Fig. 10.12). Although Picabia was shown the finished film on 3 July, Satie had to write to Clair to ask him for the final details of the scenes involved on 23 Oct. Clair's analysis of the film in 346 sequences can be found in Clair, 1970, 115–40. Satie's revolutionary score, in which self-contained segments are to be repeated ad lib. to fit the film, is divided into 10 titled sections:

1   *Cheminées, ballons qui explosent*
2   *Gants de boxe et allumettes*
3   *Prises d'air; jeux d'échecs et bateaux sur les toits*
4   *La Danseuse; et figures dans l'eau*
5   *Chasseur; et début de l'enterrement*
6   *Marche funèbre*
7   *Cortège au ralenti*
8   *La Poursuite*
9   *Chûte du cerceuil et sortie de Borlin* (score Fig. XXIV)
10   *Final (écran crevé et fin)*

MSS: *US-AUS* (OS, 56pp., 'Nov 1924')

Ho 84 (tonal plan and section lengths, 1p.)

BN 9678 (plan for pagination of OS with key scheme and section lengths, 4pp. lettered A–D, see Fig. 8.12)

BN 9677(9) (timings for film, 1p. (15 mins film, plus 1'10" for opening projection sequence). Not by Satie)

BN 9622(6), 6–21 (continuous draft with orch indications; with material found on OS 39–41 coming first on 3–5 (these are the 21 bars between Figs. XVIII and XX of the pf red.))

pubn: OS: Rouart-Lerolle, 1926; Salabert (for hire only)
Pf red.: Salabert, 1972

Pf duet arr. (by Milhaud): Rouart-Lerolle, 1926; Salabert

prem.: 4 Dec 1924 at Théâtre des Champs-Elysées (with *Relâche*), orch cond. Roger Désormière. Photography by Jimmy Berliet. Assistant Director: Georges Lacombe. Producer: Rolf de Maré (see Fig. 10.12). Cast included: Jean Borlin, Francis Picabia, Erik Satie, Man Ray, Marcel Duchamp, Marcel Achard, Pierre Scize, Louis Touchagues, Rolf de Maré, Roger LeBon, Mamy, Georges Charensol, Mlle Friis

Untitled compositions for piano, edited for publication by Robert Caby
(pubd by Salabert, 1968, unless otherwise indicated)

[*Prière*] (c. 1893) — pubn: in *Pages Mystiques* (Eschig, 1969: with *Vexations* and some *Harmonies* (see BN 9674, 20))

[*Petite ouverture à danser*] (c. 1897) — MSS: BN 10054(3) (piece in Gnossienne style, without dynamics, phrasing or barlines)

[*Caresse*] (March 1897) — MSS: BN 9575(1) (with sketches for the *Pièces froides*)

[*Rêverie du pauvre*] (1900) — MSS: BN 9600, ff. 4v–5r (numbered 20–1) (with sketches for *The Dreamy Fish* and *La Mort de Monsieur Mouche*)

[*Petite musique de clown triste*] (c. 1900) — MSS: BN 9600, ff. 3v–4r (numbered 18–19)
pubn: Eschig, 1980

[*Douze petits chorals*] (c. 1906–9) — MSS: BN 10033(11), 1 (Choral No. 12 is the introduction to the *Petite Sonate* of 1908–9. The others are exercises from the Schola Cantorum period)

[*Nostalgie/Froide Songerie*] (c. 1906–8) — pubn: as Nos. 1–2 of *Musiques intimes et secrètes*

[*Air/Essais/Notes* (×3)/ *Exercices* (×5)/ *Harmonies/Songerie vers Jack'/Bribes/Choral/ Gambades/Petite Danse*] (1897–1919) — MSS: BN 10054(2), ff. 2v, 1v ([*Songerie vers 'Jack'*]) and other fragments (pubd ed., 6). These are the result of a chromatic adaptation of the folksong melody *The Keel Row* in Jan 1897 (cf. Ex. 81)

Ho 3, ff. 7r–8v ([*Exercices*] on p. 12, c. 1905)

BN 9615(4), 14 ([*Air*], ?1914)

BN 9577, 9–11 ([*Gambades*], 1912)

BN 9673, 12 ([*Petite Danse*], found among unused sketches for the *Nocturnes*, 1919)

pubn: in *Carnet d'esquisses et de croquis*

Note: The other pieces edited by Robert Caby can be found under the entries for 1908–9 and 1912 in the main body of the Appendix. M. Caby has also orchestrated many of Satie's piano pieces, and scores and parts are available from Editions Salabert. He has arranged sixteen of the pieces edited for Salabert in 1968 as a *Quatuor intime et secret* (Salabert, 1979), which gives them a whole new dimension. It was one of Satie's regrets in 1925 that he had never written a string quartet, and Caby's sincere compilation goes some way towards filling this gap. For details of the movements involved, see Gillmor, 1988, 341–2. Gillmor also gives details of Caby's imaginative orchestrations in his Catalog of Musical Works (1988, 325ff.).

For Satie's own arrangements see *Aline-Polka* (1899) and *L'Aurore aux doigts de rose* (1916). Satie also made many arrangements of popular songs by other composers for his own use as cabaret accompanist to Vincent Hyspa and others between 1898 and 1909. The other composers include Paul Delmet, Laurent du Rillé, Georges Tiercy, Emile Debraux, and even Bizet and Offenbach – whose 'Ronde' from *Le Brésilien* turns up in Hyspa's song *Le Président aux Concours des animaux gras* in 1899 (Ho 12, 20–1). Alternatively, Hyspa often had a popular tune in mind when he wrote his humorous poems, which he then passed on to Satie to arrange – as in *Les Complots* (1898–9; Ho 10, f. 4 and Ho 16, f. 1), *Félix à Lens* (1899; Ho 12, 7) or *Le Zèbre à Félix Faure* (1898; Ho 12, 8). These cabaret arrangements occur mainly in Ho 2–12 and 16, and full details are given in Steven Moore Whiting's dissertation (University of Illinois, 1984). As nearly 100 songs are involved, and the sources are extremely complicated, this peripheral aspect of Satie's composing career has not been fully documented here.

Notes

1 Satie's career as a composer: some interpretations

1 From 'L'Esprit musical' in *Sélection*, 3/6 (April 1924), published in Ve, 99–101; W, 111–13. The dots in the text are not omissions, but the breathing points that Satie inserted into any text that he had to deliver in person, in this case in Brussels and Antwerp on 15 and 21 March 1924. Earlier in the lecture, Satie admitted that 'I am abandoning. . . just for today, my habitual irony.'

2 It also forms the principal hypothesis of the 1976 thesis of Charles Blickhan.

3 See Shattuck, rev. ed., 1968, 113, 145. This viewpoint is also shared by Alan Gillmor (1983, 110), who adds that 'there was no violent break in his stylistic development, no fundamental change of direction. His ideas were manifested early and he served them throughout his entire life with undeviating loyalty.'

4 Information kindly communicated to me during an interview in Paris on 23 September 1987.

5 With whom he had recently become reconciled after a quarrel several years before.

2 Why and where Satie composed

1 Vc, original letter in the collection of Thierry Bodin.

2 Satie sent the little *Marche de Cocagne* for two trumpets instead for the first (1920) edition of Guégan's *Almanach de Cocagne*, where it appeared as the frontispiece.

3 OS in *US-AUS*, 56, bar 4, dated '[10] Novembre 1924'.

4 As musical supplements to Alfred Satie's *La Musique des familles* on 17 March and 28 July 1887 respectively. At that time the administrator of this revue was Edmond Bailly, who later founded the celebrated Librairie de l'Art Indépendant, under whose auspices the esoteric journal *Le Cœur* was published (to which both Erik and Conrad Satie contributed in the 1890s).

5 A Spanish-born poet, whose full name was José-Maria Vincente Ferrer, Francisco de Paula, Patricio Manuel Contamine (1867–1926). He was known to his friends as Patrice Contamine, but signed himself Contamine de Latour or Lord Cheminot (around 1900). Satie was closest to him in the years 1886–92 and 1900–5, when they collaborated on numerous songs and theatrical projects.

6 In *La Musique des familles*, 18 Aug 1888. The origin of the title *Gymnopédie* may have come from a line in Latour's poem *Les Antiques*, published in the same issue.

7 I am indebted to Steven Whiting for this information, which comes from the journal *Le Chat Noir*.

8 Such as Mlle Berka, whose name and address Satie noted on the cover of Ho 9, probably in 1907, together with the time of her lesson (4 pm). In 1911 he told his brother Conrad that 'While I was studying I gave lessons and earned a royal living' (Vl, 28).

9 'One of the most beautiful', as Satie described it in *La Lanterne japonaise*, 1/6 (1 Dec 1888), 3.

10 His amusing advertisement in *Le Chat Noir* of 9 Feb 1889 ran as follows: 'The indefatigable Erik Satie, the male sphinx, the composer with the wooden head, announces the appearance of a new work which, henceforth, he holds in the highest esteem.

It is a suite of melodies conceived in the mystico-liturgical vein that the author idolizes, with the suggestive title *The Ogives*.'

11 Whenever he played duets he preferred to be partnered by women. As he told Henri-Pierre Roché in 1918 (document in *US-AUS*), they were 'decidedly more intelligent than men'. He also requested '*one* female virtuoso of enormous malice' to play his piano pieces in America when trying to arrange a tour there in 1919, and he confided many of his later premières to Marcelle Meyer. There may, however, have been other, less artistic, reasons behind his preference for lady pianists.

12 See Jullien, 1977, 168. La Purée is slang for poverty. Herbert (1962, 2; 1967, 279) says that he was a grocer from Lyon, a virtually illiterate hanger-on, who nonetheless wrote some poetry. Vl, 70 says his portrait was also painted by Steinlen.

13 See Caby, 1950, 6. 'The other lodgers pardoned him' for this unusual disturbance, however. Satie's derelict pianos were bought by Derain and Braque after his death. Neither had been tuned in twenty-five years, and Satie's repairs consisted of tying on the pedals with string. How much use they were to him in composing *Relâche* is a moot point. The scores of *Jack-in-the-Box* and *Geneviève de Brabant* (which Satie thought he had lost on a bus) were found behind these pianos in October 1925.

14 He was so worried about a tiny grease-mark on a letter to Roché in 1919 (*US-AUS*) that he wrote a special postscript laying the blame on the postman who delivered it! Even so, there is no visible blemish on the *pneumatique* in question, and Satie was probably more concerned about the way the ink had run on his signature.

15 In Conrad Satie's record of a conversation with his brother on 21 October 1914 (*US-AUS*), he noted Satie's remark that he 'didn't like the sun [which] was his personal enemy. Brutal. He spoke ill of it.' In many ways Conrad's protective relationship with his eccentric and talented brother can be compared to that of Theo for Vincent van Gogh.

16 Cited in Ve, 262. The other deadly sins were clubs, newspapers, gambling, sports, brothels and the café-concert, from which the moralistic Satie only indulged in the second and the last (as far as is known).

3 Parody, pastiche, quotation and the question of influences

1 A duet (with chorus) sung by Mireille and her lover Vincent in Act 2 scene 3 of Gounod's

5-Act 'opéra dialogué' of 1864. Here the libretto by Michel Carré is based on Frédéric Mistral's Provençal poem *Mirèio*, which had been published in 1859.

2 This comes from chapter 7: 'A Mad Tea-Party'. In Chalupt's adaptation the Hatter's watch is running three days slow, even though he has always taken care to grease it only with the *best* butter. Unfortunately, breadcrumbs have also got into the works in the process, and even dipping it in tea will not make it go any faster.

In Carroll's original text, however, the Hatter's watch is only 'two days wrong', which may seem insignificant until we realize that on 4 May 1862 (when Carroll told Alice Liddell the story on her tenth birthday) there was exactly two days' difference between the lunar and calendar months (see *The Annotated Alice*, ed. Martin Gardner, Harmondsworth, Penguin Books, rev. ed. 1970, 96). The concept of a watch running on lunar time would surely have appealed to Satie, though he does not seem to have checked Chalupt's poem for accuracy in this instance. But his fascination with Carroll's topsy-turvy world controlled by logic grew in subsequent years, and in 1921 he planned to convert *Alice in Wonderland* into a ballet with the help of Louise Norton (see Varèse, 1972, 161).

3 That is, he began with the vocal entry on a fresh page (BN 9581, 19), complete with introductory clefs and time-signature, then later wrote the introductory bar on top of bars 33–5 of the first version (vocal line) on p. 18.

4 From a letter of 9 July 1916 (VI, 116). This project for Diaghilev was Satie's idea and runs parallel to his initial sketches for *Parade*. No trace of it has survived.

5 Libretto by Jules Barbier and Michel Carré, after Molière, first performed at the Théâtre-Lyrique, Paris on 15 January 1858.

6 Typical pages from this sketchbook are reproduced in Shattuck, 1958, 72–3 and Rey, 130.

7 These were Martine (mezzo-soprano), Sganarelle (baritone), Valère (bass) and Lucas (tenor). This sketchbook is marked 'Pour Derain' and may have been intended for one of their collaborative ballets of 1923, either *Concurrence* or *Couleurs*.

8 The first of his 'Six Progressive Pianoforte Sonatinas' of 1797. A revised sixth edition appeared around 1820, and this was probably the text Satie used.

9 Whether the two had a common ancestry in Vincenzo Tommasini's arrangement of Domenico Scarlatti's sonatas in *Les Femmes de bonne humeur* is open to question. This ballet was produced by Diaghilev in Rome in the spring of 1917 and conducted by Ernest Ansermet (who also rehearsed *Parade* there). Satie remained in Paris, but he would almost certainly have known about Tommasini's ballet, and Stravinsky would have heard it in Rome.

10 As in OS 20–8, figs. 9–13.

11 The third movement of his Sonata in B♭ minor (Op. 35), composed in 1837. Satie also uses the rhythm of the start of this in the 'Marche funèbre' section of *Cinéma* in 1924.

12 The finale of his A major Sonata (K 331; 1781–3). Satie transposes the third (A major) strain as his central section, with typically unlikely chromatic harmonies and Mozart's complete theme converted from 2/4 to 3/4 time.

13 It begins in Seville with 'La belle Carmen et le peluquero', then moves to the 'Puerta [Porte] Maillot', the 'Plaza Clichy' and the 'Rue de Madrid' – to which the Paris Conservatoire had also moved early in 1911 (to no. 14).

14 Op. 58 No. 5. Both Debussy and Satie knew Scott's music and showed a limited admiration for it. This is explored further in chapter 11.

15 See Myers: *Emmanuel Chabrier and His Circle* (London, Dent, 1969), 72–3; Myers, 1968, 68;
   Gillmor, 1988, 20–1.
16 In Ex. 12b I have adopted Satie's notation and text from BN 14457 of early September 1887,
   which also appears in the edition printed in the *Revue musicale SIM*, 7/3 (15 March 1911)
   33–4. The more familiar Rouart-Lerolle edition of 1911 represents a second, revised version
   (which is also six bars longer).
17 Satie's admiration for Viollet-le-Duc undoubtedly sprang from his bold use of polychrome
   colour and intricate design, as in the choir chapels of Notre-Dame which he decorated
   in 1866–7. Here he put his theories of the harmony between colours into practice,
   juxtaposing striking matt colours in unexpected combinations (often emphasized by
   threads of black) to give an impression of depth and weight. His *trompe l'œil* use of colour
   to achieve the spatial effects created by natural light may well have influenced Satie's *trompe
   l'oreille* experiments with space and time in the 1890s. The principle of bold juxtaposition
   finds Satiean parallels too.

4 Satie and Debussy

1 Stanza 7 of *L'Isolement* (April 1818), the first of Lamartine's *Premières Méditations*, published
   in 1820 (*chez* Nicolle, rue de Seine, Paris) exactly a century before Satie's setting.
2 These were meant to represent Satie's enemies Poulenc, Auric and Laloy, according to Paul
   Collaer (1974, 20).
3 As is evident from the following letter to Milhaud of 4 February 1921:

> I shall go *chez* Caryathis in the evening (*tomorrow*) – Last Saturday was '*perfect*',
> it appears.
>   They had a fine session: . . .spewing, urinating on the staircase, etc. . . .One
> of them even left his underpants! Odd.
>   I hope that tomorrow evening will be even more 'merry'. That's what I'm
> going for again – and for myself. . .
>   P.S. I think it would be better not to have any more '*parties*' chez Caryathis,
> at least for a while. I shall go tomorrow 'just to see'.   (Vc)

4 See Ve, 31, from *Le Coq Parisien*, No. 4 (November 1920), 10: '*A Contradiction*: Cocteau
   adores me. I know it (*only too well*). . .But why does he kick me under the table?!'
5 The composer Robert Caby, in a letter to the author of 28 July 1988, states unequivocally
   that 'Satie was never a homosexual, only a *Platonist* completely divorced from sexual
   activity, as all the homosexuals who knew him have testified, beginning with those in
   Cocteau's circle.'
6 Dedication by Debussy (in red ink) in a presentation copy (No. 45) of his *Cinq Poèmes de
   Baudelaire*, 27 October 1892, now in the collection of Margaret Cobb, New York.
7 No. 2 (June 1920), 8, in an article entitled *Pas de Casernes* (No Barracks).
8 As Satie says in his 1922 article (Ve, 69). His memory here may not have been altogether
   reliable. He may have chosen *Le Fils des étoiles* because it fitted in with his argument
   about his being the cause of Debussy's move away from Wagnerian influences towards
   Impressionism.

9 Michelet, 1937, 73. The frequent references to Villiers de l'Isle-Adam within this section (pp. 67–70) mean that Satie and Debussy must have met before 1889, for this was the year the poet died.

10 Ibid., 75. This refers to the literature on astrology, magic, alchemy and mysticism attributed to Hermes Trismegistus, reputedly dating back to the Egyptian god Thoth.

11 These are mostly recent publications by Léon Vanier (19 quai St-Michel) and include two books of which no trace remains: *Rose-Croix* by Albert Jounet [Alber Jhouney] and *Le Chemin de la Croix* by Charles Morice. See Debussy's letters to Emile Baron in Francis Ambrière: 'La vie romaine de Claude Debussy', *La Revue musicale*, 15/142 (Jan 1934), 25.

12 See Léo R. Schidlof (actually Comte Henri de Lénoncourt): *Dossiers secrets d'Henri Lobineau* (Paris, Philippe Toscan du Plantier, 1967). This movement, dating back to the Knights Templar and concerned with the Holy Grail and the re-establishment of the Merovingian dynasty as the true kings of France (descended from Christ and Mary Magdalene), remains a highly secret Masonic organization. (See Orledge, 1982, 46, 124–7, 356n.44; also Michael Baigent, Richard Leigh and Henry Lincoln: *The Holy Blood and the Holy Grail* (London, Jonathan Cape, 1982). Debussy, incidentally, would have been the Thirty-third Grand Master of the Prieuré de Sion for thirty-three years, the perfect number and the zenith of Freemasonry. In their numerology, 33 symbolizes the union of Isis and Osiris; while the number of the Prieuré de Sion was 58 (= Set, Isis, Osiris and Nephthys: 7+8+15+28). Perhaps Debussy chose 58 rue Cardinet for this reason in 1898?

   The main proof we have of Debussy's connection with the Prieuré de Sion lies in the inscription in BN 17726, p. 2r: 'Le Scorpion oblique et le Sagittaire rétrograde ont paru sur le ciel nocturne.' In the circle of the zodiac, Scorpion and Sagittarius are adjacent, and if the first is slanting and the second faces backwards, this indicates the point where they intersect. Here was situated the thirteenth sign of the zodiac – Ophiuchus, The Serpent Holder – which was unique to the Prieuré de Sion. As the astronomical name of this constellation 'in the night sky' is Aesculapius (the Greek God of Medicine), it is an overwhelming coincidence that the music over which Debussy's direction appears is that which accompanies the first entry of the evil doctor in his unfinished Poe opera *The Fall of the House of Usher*. Edgar Allan Poe's own life was ruled by the dark planets Jupiter and Mars (associated with Scorpio and Sagittarius), and a further coincidence arises from Satie's description of Debussy as 'Jupiter' in conversation with his brother Conrad in 1914. Lastly, Debussy must have known about the much-discussed secrets of Rennes-le-Château, whose solving had made the painter Poussin, and latterly the priest Bérenger Saunière, wealthy men, for Saunière was entertained at Debussy's home (at 42 rue de Londres) when he came to Paris in 1893 to study Poussin's *Les Bergers d'Arcadie*, a vital clue in unravelling the mystery of Rennes-le-Château. (See Gérard de Sède: *Signé: Rose+Croix* (Paris, Librairie Plon, 1977), 28, and David Wood: *GENISIS: The First Book of Revelations* (Tunbridge Wells, Baton Press, 1985) for further information.) Péladan, incidentally, would permit no other landscapes than those of Poussin to be hung in his Salons de la Rose-Croix in the 1890s.

13 Paris, La Colombe, 1960, 23. Lévi's real name was Alphonse-Louis Constant (1810–75).

14 According to Léon Vallas: *Claude Debussy et son temps* (Paris, Albin Michel, 1958), 140. The manuscript has unfortunately since disappeared.

15 Published in Joséphin Péladan: *Le Panthée*, vol. X of *La Décadence latine, Ethopée* (Paris, E. Dentu, 1892).

16 In March 1892. Grallon is listed as the conductor of Palestrina's *Missa Papae Marcelli* and as 'our chapelmaster' (BN Rés. Vma 174(7–8)). Bihn Grallon is also mentioned as the composer of a *Marche antique pour la Rose-Croix* at the fourth soirée, which may well be the piece published as the *Première Pensée Rose+Croix* by Robert Caby in 1968. This possibility was first suggested in Gillmor, 1988, 271 n.12.

17 See Howat, 1983, 134–5.

18 See Gillmor, 1988, 87–8, who first analysed it thus.

19 In tableau 3 of a manuscript formerly in the collection of André Meyer, Paris.

20 Such as his alchemical vision about a 'magic nut. . .in a casket of alpaca bone studded with seven diamonds' in the *Revue musicale SIM*, 9/1 (15 Jan 1913), trans. in W, 61–2, or his account of Nicolas Flamel in *Catalogue*, No. 4 (30 June 1922), trans. in W, 120–1. The symbolic alchemy in Satie's ballet *Mercure* is also convincingly discussed in Vy, 81.

21 *Le Nazaréen*, a drama in three acts (Paris, A. Savin, ?1892). See Yves-Alain Favre, 'Henri Mazel ou Le Symbolisme élargi' in *Revue à rebours*, numéro spécial Nos. 15–16 (1981) for further details (a source kindly supplied to me by Ornella Volta). The final title of the play in Mazel's complete works (Mercure de France, 1933, vol. I) was *Le Chevalier Nazaréen*, in which Favre says (p. 8) that 'Mazel evokes an incident in medieval Macedonian history, which remains Christian beneath its Oriental and Islamic influences.' At the start (play, p. 5) *Le Nazaréen* simply states: 'Décors à rêver. – Musique à faire.' But either of Satie's two preludes might have been intended for the start of Act 2 where, as Baudouin's daughter Hermosina languishes in silken luxury on an ivory litter in the ducal palace (p. 86), 'fragrant perfumes burn in incense-burners in the corners. A soft music floats in the distance.' Given Satie's other Rose-Croix fanfares, it seems strange that he did not supply any of those required elsewhere in Mazel's play. But, as far as I know, this was never performed in public during Satie's lifetime.

22 Mazel's equivalent of the Knights Templar.

23 Note that Satie called his Rose-Croix and other mystic compositions 'musique à genoux'. The last of these is the *Verset laïque & somptueux* of 1900.

24 *The Holy Blood and the Holy Grail* (London, Jonathan Cape, 1982), 51.

25 For fuller details see Léon Guichard's article in *Cahiers Debussy*, No. 1 (1974), 10–14, and Orledge, 1982, 46–7. Bois's one-act play in verse was first published in *La Revue indépendante* in April–June 1890.

26 A 'drame romanesque' in five acts (Paris, Chamuel, 1896). Usually referred to as *Le Prince de Byzance*, but not so titled on the first edition.

27 Péladan cites these rejections unashamedly at the back of the 1896 edition of *Le Prince du Byzance*, perhaps as examples of the stupidity and philistinism of those who dared to criticize his masterpieces.

28 In 'Fragments d'une conférence sur Eric [*sic*] Satie (1920)', here as trans. by Leigh Henry in *Fanfare*, 1/2 (15 Oct 1921), 23.

29 His opera *Rodrigue et Chimène* (1890–2) to a libretto by Mendès (now lost) after Guillén de Castro and Corneille. See Orledge, 1982, 17–35.

30 Ve, 69; W, 110.

31 As recorded by Maurice Emmanuel and published in his *'Pelléas et Mélisande': Etude historique et critique. Analyse musicale* (Paris, Mellottée, 1926), 35–6. Emmanuel later confirmed the October 1889 date and the accuracy of his music examples in a letter to Charles Koechlin of 4 March 1927 (see Orledge, 1982, 49).

32 See Volta: *Erik Satie à Montmartre* (Catalogue of the 1982–3 Exhibition at the Musée de Montmartre), 23.

33 An orchestral song, now lost, with words by Contamine de Latour. Satie tended to exaggerate his achievements in this period. For example, when he applied to fill the vacant seat of Debussy's teacher Ernest Guiraud at the Académie des Beaux-Arts in June 1892, he listed his individual *Gymnopédies*, *Sarabandes* and *Gnossiennes* as thirteen orchestral suites, as well as inventing an opera (*Kharaseos*) and various Roman, Gothic and Byzantine dances for orchestra. Word of all this had probably reached Chausson by 1893. Needless to say, Satie's application failed, as it did in 1894 and 1896.

34 In 'Mémoires d'un Amnésique: Mes trois candidatures' in *Revue musicale SIM*, 8/11 (Nov 1912), 70. He later used the music of Saint-Saëns and Ambroise Thomas as wallpaper in his Furniture Music (1920).

35 See Koechlin, 1924, 194. Koechlin admits he 'did not in the least understand the harmonies of *Le Fils des étoiles* (which were so new then)'. But soon Koechlin became one of Satie's staunchest admirers, thanks to Debussy's advocacy (see Orledge, 1987).

36 Letter from Koechlin to the late Rollo Myers, 27 December 1948.

37 Compare bars 17–18 in both *The Dreamy Fish* and *Jack-in-the-Box*.

38 The central section of *The Dreamy Fish* reuses the 'Petit air de Geneviève' from Act 3 of *Geneviève de Brabant* as follows: bars 89–90 and 111 reuse its introduction; bars 94–101 reuse verse 1; and bars 102–8 (second beat) reuse verse 2 as far as bar 7.

39 Recalled in Cocteau, 1924, 221.

40 Satie must have played it to Debussy, for he mentions it in the same paragraph as the *Morceaux en forme de poire* in his letter to Debussy on 17 August 1903. See Satie, ed. Borgeaud, 1962, 73, or Vl, 146.

41 Written while Debussy was on holiday with Lilly at Bichain in the summer of 1903. They corresponded rarely because Satie saw Debussy so often. Satie's attitude is one of exaggerated respect mixed with high-spirited entertainment. Satie still addresses Debussy as 'vous', but being a gentleman he usually did so in letters, even to close friends.

42 Nos. 3 and 5 in the printed score of 1911.

43 The *Prolongation du même* (No. 2) is based on an unfinished cabaret song *Le Roi soleil de plomb* of c. 1900 (see Gillmor, 1988, 127), and the *Redite* (No. 7) is based on bars 66–73 of *The Angora Ox*, music for a short story by Latour of around 1901.

44 According to Satie's letter to Roland-Manuel of 9 September 1911.

45 Cited in Steegmuller, 1970, 146. Cocteau mistakenly gives the date as April 1915 in his retrospective account.

46 Catalogue of the Satie Exhibition (ed. F. Lesure) at the Bibliothèque Nationale, 1966, No. 62, p. 21.

47 Albert Roussel: 'A propos d'un récent festival', *Le Gaulois*, 12 June 1926, 3.

48 BN Rés. Vma 174 (17).

49 Trans. by Roger Nichols in *Debussy Letters* (London, Faber, 1987), 196 (letter 168). The 'aforementioned establishment' was, of course, the Schola Cantorum.

50 The pagination of BN 10041 shows that the Fugue was the first of the *Aperçus* to be written, probably in late August–early September 1908. Satie then added the Chorale in September 1908, but only decided to publish them after he had added the opening Pastorale in October 1912.

51 The production at the Théâtre du Châtelet, conducted by André Caplet, with Ida Rubinstein as the Saint, had been a rushed and ill-organized affair, with much of the music for Acts 2–4 orchestrated by Caplet. The première on 22 May 1911 lasted nearly five hours, and substantial cuts were made to Act 2 ('La Chambre magique') before Satie saw it (see Orledge, 1982, 217–36 for fuller details).

52 On the cover of BN 9647. Satie also planned to write a piece called 'Avenue du Bois [de Boulogne]' as the third of a series of *Impressions Parisiennes* around 1908–9 (BN 9579, 1).

53 As reported by Conrad Satie after a talk with Satie on 30 September 1914 (coll. Robert Caby). Satie here referred to Debussy as 'Jupiter', as we have seen. Photographs of Satie playing with Dolly Bardac and the young Sheridan Russell *chez* Debussy around 1905 can be found in Templier, 1969 (plate 19) and in Tinan, 1973 (plates 2–5).

54 In this case the 'Soldiers' Chorus' from Gounod's *Faust* (tableau 2: September 1913) and Mendelssohn's 'Wedding March' (end of tableau 3: October 1913).

55 Like the folksong 'Il était un' bergère' (tableau 3) and the French air 'En avant Fanfan-la-Tulipe' (tableau 4: final dance). 'Il était un' bergère' had also been used earlier by Satie in the trio section of *de Podophthalma* from the *Embryons desséchés*, as we saw in chapter 3. See Orledge, 1982, 177–85 for further details on *La Boîte à joujoux*.

56 *Españaña* is dedicated to Mlle Claude Emma Debussy [Chouchou], and the *Idylle* (*Avant-dernières pensées*) to Debussy himself. Satie's *Elégie* of 1920 is dedicated to the memory of Debussy.

57 François Lesure (ed.): *Monsieur Croche et autres écrits. Edition complète de son œuvre critique* (Paris, Gallimard, 1971), 237.

58 Ibid., 236–7, 15 May 1913.

59 *Debussy Letters*, trans. Roger Nichols (London, Faber, 1987), 291. What Debussy had been doing was recomposing his incidental music for the *Chansons de Bilitis* (1900–1) as the *Six Epigraphes antiques* of July 1914. His only original work of 1914 was the little *Berceuse héroïque* in November, written as a tribute to Albert I of Belgium, whose cause both he and Satie supported.

60 From a letter from Satie to Dukas of 22 November 1915 (Vc).

61 According to a letter from Satie to Mme Fernand Dreyfus (Vc).

62 From the draft of a letter (to Jean Poueigh?) in BN 9623(2), 38.

5 Satie's compositional aesthetic

1 The original French text is published in Ve, 48–9 and part of it appears in translation in Shattuck, 1968, 167. The ordering comes from a transcription made by Pierre-Daniel Templier around 1930 from a (badly) typed copy by Satie. This was lent to Templier by Conrad Satie, but is now lost. According to Volta (Ve, 258), Léon Guichard examined the autograph when it was in better condition some years ago, and maintained that the original title was 'La Matière (Idée) et la Main d'Œuvre (Ecriture)', rather than 'Main d'Œuvre (Couture)' – that is 'Writing' rather than 'Craftsmanship'. Volta adopts this revision in

her 1981 edition. But when I studied BN 9611 recently, it seemed like 'Couture' to me, and because both of the first two paragraphs discuss craftsmanship I have preserved this title here. The last sentence about Impressionism appears only in BN 9611, and when the article was first published by Robert Caby (1928, 8) it also lacked the first sentence.

2 For full details of Satie's Conservatoire career see Gowers, 1966, Ph.D. 5374, 1–31. Also Gillmor, 1988, 9–13. Satie's lack of progress in the piano classes of Emile Descombes (1879–82) led to his temporary dismissal in June 1882, and he fared little better in those of Georges Mathias between November 1885 and November 1886. No professor, it seems, was ever eager to have Satie in his class. Taudou told him to devote his time to the piano, whereas Mathias tried to persuade him that he was really a composer! Mathias, had he known it, was right, but for the wrong reasons.

3 The manuscript is in a private collection in France (46pp.) and is discussed in Volta, 1987, 70–9. See also Orledge, 1987, 40–1.

4 Vincent d'Indy: *Cours de composition musicale,* '1er livre, rédigé avec la collaboration de Auguste Sérieyx, d'après les notes prises aux Classes de Composition de la Schola Cantorum en 1897–98' (4th edition, Paris, Durand, 1912), chapter VI, 91 and 94.

5 Ornella Volta has shown (1987, 37–40; preface to the 1987 Eschig edition) that Satie composed three dances for Caryathis to perform at the Théâtre du Colisée in June 1921. Their order was *Marche Franco-Lunaire, Valse du 'Mystérieux baiser dans l'œil'* and *Cancan Grand-Mondain,* with the *Grande Ritournelle* interspersed to cover her envisaged costume changes between the dances. The ordering in BN 9605(3) shows the *Grande Ritournelle* occuring only once in the 'middle' between the *Valse* and the *Cancan,* but Volta has argued (from Satie's timing of *La Belle Excentrique* as '12 minutes' on his 1921 contract) that the *Ritournelle* was repeated between each dance. One certainty is that the *Ritournelle* was not meant to introduce the dances, as it appears to do in the printed edition (which Satie sanctioned). His intention here was probably to keep it as a separate, floating item for use when required in performance as an interlude. According to Caryathis's memoirs (Elise Jouhandeau: *Joies et douleurs d'une Belle Excentrique* (Paris, Flammarion, 1960)), she and Satie turned down various costume designs by renowned figures such as Marie Laurencin, Kees van Dongen and Paul Poiret in favour of a single mask-like creation designed by Cocteau. As the music was already composed by then, Satie did not choose to alter it and let the *Grande Ritournelle* stand as an interlude, whose exact placing in the première remains unknown.

6 Satie invariably worked across double pages in his small oblong pocket books. Thus Ex. 25a is spread across pp. 8–9 of BN 9605(2) and Ex. 25b across pp. 10–11, with his first trial harmonizations (Exx. 25c–f) fitted in around his second draft of the melody. The order I have established here (from a thorough study of his notebooks and working practices) is, of course, open to question. But in this case it seems reasonable to assume that Satie filled up pp. 10–15 with consecutive attempts to find an acceptable start for his March. Ex. 25c has been taken as his first draft because it goes as far as bar 8, and Satie at the outset would have had greater confidence before he realized fully what he wanted to achieve. In this case he intended to match his final draft of the melody (Ex. 25b) with a complete harmonization on p. 11. He then began to have doubts, and I believe it is again reasonable to suppose that his next trial drafts (Exx. 25d–f) were fitted in on the remaining space on the facing p. 10. When he found these unsatisfactory, he turned over the page and continued on pp. 12–15

(Exx. 25g–z), finally squeezing the version he approved of (Ex. 25aa) into the top right hand corner of p. 15 (as was often the case). As these sketches were only of short fragments, they do not cross from one page to another, as the melodic drafts did. Sometimes Satie wrote one draft on top of another, and much deciphering can be necessary to establish a viable order. The final version of bars 3–4 (in Ex. 25q), for instance, was inked in over the top of Ex. 25g (in pencil) on p. 12, but such is the clarity and precision of Satie's writing at all stages that both versions are easily discernible here.

7 See Orledge, 1984–5, 158–63.

8 Though consonance was used by the later troubadours. Diminutive endings such as these were popular at the time, though not 'cigarette', of course! The following poem by Colin Muset (who lived in eastern France in the first half of the thirteenth century) offers a useful comparison:

> Sopris sui d'une amorette.
> D'une jone pucelette
> Bel est et blonde et blanchette
> Plus que n'est une erminette
> Sa la color vermeillette
> Ensi com une rosette.

> (From Arthur Guirdham: *The Cathars and Reincarnation*
> (Wellingborough, Turnstone Press Ltd, 1982), 188.)

9 From an article written in August 1922 and published in (unknown) English translation in *Vanity Fair*, 10/6 (Feb 1923), 38 and 88. It appears in full in Ve, 61–5, and in W, 102–6.

6 Satie, counterpoint and the Schola Cantorum

1 Kindly communicated to the author by Robert Caby on 23 September 1987.

2 His proudly labelled 'Cahier de Contrepoint No. 1' (BN 9638) is dated '1905 (Novembre)'.

3 Roussel (1869–1937) had been appointed professor of counterpoint at the Schola Cantorum in 1902, a post he held till 1914. He did not finish d'Indy's ten-year composition course himself till 1908 – the same year that Satie graduated in counterpoint. Satie's other teacher, besides d'Indy, was Auguste Sérieyx (1865–1949), who was involved in the foundation of the Schola and co-wrote the vast four-volume *Cours de composition musicale* with Vincent d'Indy, which is a résumé of the course Sérieyx took himself between 1897 and 1907.

4 See BN 9634–68 and 10033 in particular, which include various original pieces Satie wrote during his Schola years, like the *Nouvelles 'Pièces froides'* of 1907 (BN 9653) and *En Habit de cheval* (see Appendix). Schola work can also be found, mixed with cabaret songs, in Ho 1, 3–7 and 9.

5 Noted down by Satie on BN 9639, 4 on 29 October 1906, presumably from a verbal comment by Roussel.

6 Such as composing his First Violin Sonata in D minor (Op. 11) and his incidental music for *Le Marchand du sable qui passe* (Op. 13), for a play by Georges Jean-Aubry.

7 These pieces were edited by Robert Caby for publication by Salabert in 1968 (see Appendix). Satie left the last 5 (of 16) bars unfinished when he submitted *Fâcheux exemple* (BN 9641, 4–5), and *Désespoir agréable* bears the indication 'avec une ironie contagieuse' in bar 10.

8 As might well be the case with the deliberately abstruse enharmonic notation in the *Affole-ments granitiques* (the last of the *Heures séculaires et instantanées*) in 1914. Here, Satie origi-nally wrote the final cadence as C and F major chords (Ho 26), adding the enharmonic notation in sharps and double sharps later. The rising scale preceding the cadence was also first written in F major. Mixed-clef pieces like Ex. 35 can also be found in BN 9645, 9647 and 9652.

9 D'Indy's inaugural discourse delivered on 2 November 1900 (*Une Ecole de Musique répondant aux besoins modernes* (Vienna, Ligugé, 1900)), shows on pp. 5–7 that the course for com-posers was divided into two separate stages. Probably after discussion with d'Indy, Satie took only the counterpoint course from the first stage, ignoring the foundation courses in harmony, Gregorian chant and choral writing. For a full-time student this whole stage was meant to last two years, with the second stage taking a further eight years. I am grateful to Roger Nichols for sending me a copy of d'Indy's discourse.

10 Another complete 71-bar movement in C marked 'Lent' has survived as Ho 4, ff. 1*v*–3*v*. Although untitled, this may well be a slow movement for the *Petite Sonate*, though no trace of a Finale remains.

11 Published as *Douze petits chorals* (revised by Robert Caby) by Editions Salabert, 1968. No. 12 is none other than the slow introduction to the *Petite Sonate* of 1908.

12 With another unfinished fugue in B minor in BN 10033(1), probably in 1908.

13 Sketches and drafts for the *Fugue litanique* appear in BN 9591(2, 4), 9592, 9656, 9661, and Ho 32.

14 Satie also wrote a 32-bar outline for a loose 2-part fugue in G (also in 2/4 time) in Ho 18, 2–5. It is very possible that this is another rejected start for the *Fugue à tâtons*, though it remains untitled and is therefore omitted from Ex. 41. The cover of this notebook shows that the original order of the *Choses vues* was: 'I. *Fantaisie musculaire*/II. *Choral hypocrite*/III. *Fuge* [*sic*] *à tâtons*'.

15 As he says in his 1913 autobiographical sketch for E. Demets (Ve, 142).

16 In 'Mémoires d'un amnésique' in *Revue musicale SIM*, 9/2 (15 Feb 1913), 69.

17 In 'Eloge des critiques', *Action*, 2/8 (Aug 1921), 8.

18 From a letter to Mme G. M. Tuttle, president of the Comité Franco-Américain du Conser-vatoire, on 5 November 1918 (Vc).

19 This manuscript in *US-NYpm* has in pencil at the bottom (subsequently erased): 'for Leigh Henry – this is an introduction to the ballet JACK-IN-THE-BOX, first produced in England this year'. The writing, however, is not Satie's; nor did he ever intend the *Sonnerie* to assume this function.

7 Orchestration versus instrumentation

Some small parts of this chapter (and chapter 8) first appeared in *Proceedings of the Royal Musical Association*, cxi (1984–5), 155–79.

1 Ed. Stanley Sadie (London, Macmillan, 1980), vol. XIII, 691.

2 From BN 9677(7). As these come alongside notes about 'Truth in Art' written for *Fanfare*, No. 7 (1 Jan 1922), 129, they may date from the same period. As Ornella Volta has discovered (Ve, 309), two suites of orchestral music by Schmitt had been performed

at the Concerts Lamoureux in October 1921, part of his incidental music for Gide's *Antoine et Cléopatre* (after Shakespeare), and it may have been these which provoked Satie's condemnation.

3 The only instance I know of when Satie modified his orchestral forces comes in *La Belle Excentrique*. On 25 August 1920 he wrote a letter, probably to the designer Irène Lagut, asking her to tell Georges Auric that his orchestra had grown by a bassoon and an oboe. But that was before he had even finished composing the first of his dances for Caryathis – the *Marche Franco-Lunaire*, and it also shows that he was thinking of his orchestration as he composed.

4 BN 10052(1). This includes music to be played during the three acts of *Le Fils des étoiles*, which was not performed at the soirée. As Satie's score was in no way synchronized with Péladan's drama, and seems to have been conceived independently in three precisely balanced sections, it must have been omitted for purely practical reasons.

5 Consisting of five superposed fourths, the fourth of which (counting upwards from the bass) is always augmented. The others are always perfect. The whole score of *Le Fils des étoiles* is constructed from only ten identifiable motifs and, as Patrick Gowers has shown (1965–6, 15–16), these can be traced back to Ex. 44 as variations, retrograde versions, or rudimentary developments of it. In BN 10052(1) the only performance indications are 'Modéré', plus the crescendo markings in Ex. 44. There is no sign of the levels the crescendos begin or end at. They were removed from the Baudoux red ink edition of 1896, when the 'mp' and 'En blanc et immobile' markings were added – producing an even less expressive effect than was Satie's original intention. The bar lines appear only in Satie's manuscript short score.

6 BN 9631, dated 'Novembre 1892'. No full score was made since *Uspud* was turned down for performance by the Paris Opéra on 17 December that year.

7 Ho 48, 14pp. In its piano duet version, as No. 6 of the *Trois Morceaux en forme de poire*, the harp part becomes the Seconda part (see Gillmor, 1988, 128–30). The same notebook also contains two bars of what was published in 1913 as *Gnossienne No. 3* (scored for the same combination as the *Danse*, but beginning as an oboe melody over harp chords).

8 BN 9572(2), 30–1, the first *Air à faire fuir* scored for 2 flutes, 2 clarinets in A, 2 horns in F, timpani, harp, first violins, cellos and double-bass.

9 This information was kindly communicated to the author in a letter of 11 April 1989.

10 Originally called the 'Little Girl' March, in a letter to Paulette Darty on 16 August 1904, when Satie had just sold it for 200 francs 'to my good old editor friends' Bellon, Ponscarme et Cie. This 'Intermezzo Américaine' (its other sub-title) had words by Dominique Bonnaud and Numa Blès, founders of La Lune Rousse, where Satie often performed. By the time of its sale Satie was working with Jean Kolb and Maurice de Féraudy on a 1-Act operetta *Pousse l'amour*, whose libretto Satie found 'killing'. Little music survives, and it is doubtful if the piece entitled *Coco chéri* (performed in Monte Carlo on 28 February 1913) is one and the same, as is sometimes maintained. Indeed, *Pousse l'amour* nearly floundered when Féraudy lost his temper with the director of the Théâtre des Capucines in Paris during a rehearsal early in January 1907. As Satie told Paulette Darty on 6 January: 'Our little play, you might say, is at the bottom of a canal, and will stay there for a long while, since no-one is going to look for it. Poor me! And people will say I'm lucky!

It's enough to make you die laughing. Nothing like it ever happened before, not even in the comics' (Vl, 81). *Pousse l'amour* did, however, somehow reach the stage of the Comédie Royale, Paris on 22 November 1907.

11 Satie's cabaret and other pre-Schola orchestrations very rarely exceed the ranges found in Ho 65, whereas those from 1913 onwards frequently do so (see Ex. 54a – flutes bars 45–6; Ex. 55a – clarinet bars 1–4; Ex. 59 – first violins bar 4; and *Parade* generally). It is of course possible that Ho 65 is a master-list collated from the varying information Satie was given at the Schola Cantorum in 1909, but having seen the notes he took during this period, I doubt it (see Ex. 50).

12 Whose real name Satie wrote out on BN 10062, 1, but crossed out heavily in black ink, for reasons unknown.

13 In No. 7: *Redite*. Gillmor (1988, 131–2) shows how Satie used bars 3–4 before 1–2 in his 1903 duet version. The original version comes as f. 5r in BN 10062, where the plaintive theme is doubled at the unison on first bassoon and second (muted) trumpet. This piece of imaginative scoring is purely Satie's own. An edited reproduction of the score of *The Angora Ox* appears in Gowers, Ph.D. 5376 (1966), 180–90 (as Ex. 58).

14 See Orledge: *Charles Koechlin. His Life and Works* (London, Harwood Academic Publishers, 1989), chapter 9 for further details on Koechlin as an orchestrator.

15 All page numbers come from the Salabert orchestral score of *Parade* (E.A.S. 16425; 115pp.). Here the horns sound a perfect fourth higher in the bass clef.

16 As, for instance, in *Istar: Variations symphoniques* (1896), or his symphonic triptych *Jour d'été à la montagne* (1905). Satie noted on BN 9651, 31 that 'one can do anything with three trumpets'.

17 Though copying out the parts took longer than the orchestration itself, and Satie was still preoccupied with this task a few days before the première at the Salle Gaveau on 17 June 1912.

18 The complete orchestral lists are as follows:

> 1 *Choral*: 2 flutes, 2 clarinets in Bb, 2 bassoons, sarrusophone, 2 horns in F, 2 trumpets in C, 3 trombones, tuba, contrabass tuba, strings.
>
> 2 *Fugue litanique*: 2 flutes, cor anglais, 2 clarinets in Bb, 2 bassoons, 2 horns in F, 2 trumpets in C, 3 trombones, tuba, contrabass tuba, strings.
>
> 3 *Autre choral*: flute, cor anglais, clarinet in Bb, bassoon, horn in F, strings.
>
> 4 *Fugue de papier*: 2 flutes, oboe, cor anglais, 2 clarinets in Bb, 2 bassoons, 2 horns in F, 2 trumpets in C, strings.

These are confirmed by the final orchestral score (32pp.) in the archives of Editions Salabert.

19 It appears under the subtitle 'What I am' in the *Revue musicale SIM*, 8/4 (15 April 1912), 69, where Satie talks humorously about 'a common-or-garden F♯ which registered 93 kilos on my phono-scales' and 'came out of a fat tenor whom I also weighed'.

20 In a letter to Ricardo Viñes on 30 March 1912 (which also stresses that his current work is phonometric rather than musical). Satie's clumsy and much-corrected arrangement of the *Choral* from the *Aperçus désagréables* for string quartet confirms this remark. It was made on the advice of his fellow-composer Robert Montfort in August 1912 (BN 9677). Satie intended to arrange the *Fugue* as well, but never did so.

21 No. 3 of the *Préludes flasques*, completed on 23 July 1912. Many sketches and drafts for this appear in BN 9610 and 9660.

22 At the Théâtre Michel, rue des Mathurins, Paris 9 on 24 May 1921. Satie tried (unsuccessfully) to insist that the play was taken off, threatening Bertin with legal action on 19 May. His other reason was that his dances were to be played on the piano rather than in his instrumental version (which was eventually conducted by Milhaud).

23 At the home of Roland-Manuel's parents at 1 rue de Chazelles, Paris 17. It is not known exactly when Satie orchestrated his dances for *Le Piège de Méduse*. It is possible that he only did so at the time of the stage première in 1921.

24 *Revue musicale SIM*, 10/1 (1 January 1914), 71. The tautologous Valentine de Saint-Point was a niece of the poet Lamartine, and had close links with the Futurist movement at the time.

25 The text (which Ornella Volta has discovered and kindly communicated to me) was printed as the second of Valentine de Saint-Point's *Poèmes ironiques* in a booklet entitled *Poèmes drames idéistes* in conjunction with the first Metachoric Festival in New York on 3 April 1917 (*F-Pfs*). It runs as follows:

> Je mourrai, un jour de fête,
> Alors que les pantins dansent.
> Je n'entre pas dans leur danse,
> Je ne fête pas leurs fêtes.
> Je mourrai, un jour de fête,
> Alors que les pantins dansent.
>
> Alors qu'ils crient et qu'ils hurlent
> Tous, une gaieté prescrite,
> Rien je ne crie ni ne hurle,
> Même une vertu prescrite.
>
> Et leur vacarme est si faux
> Que je ne puis m'écouter.
> Dans un factice, si faux,
> Vie ne se peut écouter.
>
> Mon silence, mort au bruit,
> Silence pour quoi je vis,
> Cela seul par quoi je vis,
> Mon silence, mort au bruit.
>
> Ma solitude est si lourde,
> Amertume inguérissable;
> Solitude riche et lourde,
> Solitude inguérissable!

> Je mourrai, un jour de fête,
> Alors que les pantins dansent.
> Je n'entre pas dans leur danse,
> Je ne fête pas leurs fêtes.
> Je mourrai, un jour de fête,
> Alors que les pantins dansent.

(Prose translation: 'I shall die on a fête day when the puppets are dancing. I do not join in their dance, I do not celebrate their festivities. I shall die on a fête day when the puppets are dancing. When they all shout and scream with prescribed gaiety, I shout and scream nothing, not even a banished virtue. And their uproar is so false that I cannot listen. In so false and artificial a situation, life cannot hear itself. My silence, dead to the noise, the silence which is my goal; the only thing I seek is my silence, dead to the noise. My solitude is so oppressive, an incurable bitterness; a solitude precious and oppressive, an incurable solitude!

I shall die on a fête day when the puppets are dancing. I do not join in their dance, I do not celebrate their festivities. I shall die on a fête day when the puppets are dancing.')

26 BN 9604, 18–23. The scoring of both versions is given in the Appendix. Both sketchbooks involved (BN 9604 and 9588) also include lists of pieces planned for 1914, and refer to the *Obstacles vénimeux* (which became the first of the *Heures séculaires et instantanées*). In BN 9604, Satie began to sketch the *Obstacles vénimeux* as a set of pieces in their own right. On BN 9588, 2–5 Satie also sketched two orchestral starts for *Les Pantins de Valentine de Saint-Point* showing his concern to find exactly the right sounds with which to begin his piece. The second (published) version is dated '26 Novembre 1913', and the first version probably dates from earlier that month.

27 Taken from the extract published in Schmitt, 1913, 12, a facsimile of the manuscript score, which has since disappeared.

28 The first of the *Pastels sonores* (in which Satie played no part) bears the Ravelian title *Cloches dans la vallée*. Both were published Chez L'Auteur, 86bis boulevard Victor-Hugo, Neuilly in 1916.

29 The score Satie sent (BN 10034: 12pp.) was prepared by a professional copyist at Verley's expense, so presumably it was Verley who encouraged Satie to explore the possibilities of an American performance. Satie was by no means averse to this, and between 1916 and 1919 he made several attempts to get his music played in America, even proposing to go there himself on a lecture and concert tour (in a letter to Henri-Pierre Roché of 1 December 1918 (*US-AUS*)). There is, however, more to the saga of *L'Aurore* than meets the eye. Varèse had been the instigator of a project to produce a French version of *A Midsummer Night's Dream* to rival that of Max Reinhardt in Berlin (1910). The score was to be a 'pot-pourri of French music' by Florent Schmitt, Ravel, Satie, Stravinsky and Varèse himself, but only Satie's *Cinq Grimaces* were written (in 1915) for the impending circus-style production by Cocteau (Volta, 1987, 86–7). According to Volta (VI, 105), 'Varèse later claimed to have contributed to the orchestration' of the *Cinq Grimaces*, and Satie was understandably annoyed by this as he was sensitive about his skills as an orchestrator. Thus when Varèse asked his permission to perform the *Cinq Grimaces* in America in 1916, Satie sent him *L'Aurore* 'in exchange', partly because the *Grimaces* were not yet ready to play in their orchestral version, and partly out of revenge – for a work by an unknown pupil of Satie was hardly what Varèse had in

mind, even though Satie might have orchestrated it. Needless to say, Varèse never conducted *L'Aurore* in America, and the score found its way back to the Bibliothèque Nationale, Paris through Darius Milhaud, to whom Varèse had sent it in April 1928. Satie's original manuscript has not yet been located.

30 The forces are listed in the Appendix. Given the key-signature, the Bb clarinets would be better in A. The tuba plays only two notes during the 40 bars of BN 10034, and the piccolo's three notes occur during the first 4 bars of Ex. 55a.

31 Satie's score originally began (as in the 1917 duet reduction) with the *Prélude du Rideau rouge*. He added the Chorale (OS 2–4) and the Finale (OS 98–114) in 1919.

32 A new corrected edition of the orchestral score of *Socrate* is being prepared by Editions Eschig. This is based on the manuscript score in the Polignac archives, which has at last been made available for this purpose. I had to rely on the existing Eschig hire score (109pp.) whilst writing this book.

33 OS 50 bar 2 – 52 bar 1 (VS 29 bar 3 – 30 bar 2). In the repetitive passage between VS 29 bar 3 and 31 bar 9 (OS 50 bar 2 – 54 bar 6) the winds play only 16 notes in 29 bars, an exceptional event in Satie's ubiquitous mixed scoring.

34 In the first page of his orchestral draft for *Socrate* (BN 9623(5)), Satie originally marked the repeated timpani quaver F#s *forte*, with the other parts *piano* – a dramatic conception he quickly abandoned. His only addition to the music during orchestration was the final bar of Part 1 (BN 9623(5), 17; VS 14, last bar), which suggests that he might have intended Parts 1 and 2 to be continuous in the initial stages of composition.

8 Questions of form, logic and the mirror image

1 Now in *F-Pfs*: it previously belonged to Mme Claude Rostand (Geneva). John Cage's post-war Satie revival was spurred on by the discovery of *Vexations*, which Henri Sauguet made available to him shortly after his first Satie concerts at Black Mountain College in 1948 (see Bryars, 1983, 13).

2 Three in the second *Ogive*, one in the third, and one (repeated) in the fourth.

3 The two penultimate chords change from G major (A1) to E minor in A2 and the reprise of A1.

4 The last of the *Heures séculaires et instantanées* of 1914.

5 *Cours de composition musicale* (Paris, Durand, 1912), I, 23.

6 The rest of this article, a landmark in Satie scholarship, is thoroughly recommended to anyone seeking a fuller account of Satie's Rose-Croix music. It includes an invaluable guide to the harmonic characteristics of the various compositions on p. 2.

7 Otherwise the only chords used are root position major and minor chords (5–3s), first inversions of the same (6–3s), and three VIIb chords (spelt as 6–3–2s) – all of which occur in the latter part of section 2, to distinguish it from the rest.

8 See the end of system 1 and the start of system 4 in Figure 8.2.

9 From the letter printed on p. IV of the final section of Péladan's play *Le Prince du Byzance* (Paris, Chamuel, 1896).

10 Bars 82–6 should be repeated as 87–91, making 101 bars in all. They are present in BN 14457 and in the first printing in the supplement to *Musica*, No. 103 (April 1911),

89–90, but not in the Rouart-Lerolle edition of 1911 (which Satie told Lerolle he preferred, in a letter of 10 May 1911). Satie also cut 6 bars out of the first *Sarabande* in the *SIM* edition of March 1911 (bars 53–5 and 73–5 of the Rouart-Lerolle edition), and he may have been trying to make all three *Sarabandes* approximately the same length (98–96–100 bars).

11 This again shows that Satie copied out the hands separately, from an earlier draft that has unfortunately not survived. In this case, the right hand was definitely copied ahead of the left and Satie got right through the five-chord phrase before realizing his error.

12 In the play this read: 'Symbole généreux de la noble Apulie.' Apulia, on the heel of Italy, was the region in which the play was set, during the Renaissance. Act 2 was set in the palace at Taranto. Perhaps Péladan changed the text of *Salut Drapeau!* to enable it to be used as an independent concert item? Its compositional process was first analysed by Patrick Gowers (1965–6, 20–22).

13 The recurring chain in *Salut Drapeau!* uses only major, minor and diminished triads, again notated as first inversions (6–3s). The barring in the published edition (Salabert, 1968) is the work of Robert Caby, as are the dynamic gradations and phrasing. *Salut Drapeau!* as Satie intended it is shown in Ex. 70.

14 There is evidence of proportional planning in the third *Sonnerie* and in the *Prière des orgues* from the *Messe des pauvres* too (see Gillmor, 1988, 88 and 105). In fact, the third *Sonnerie* is a mirror image of the first in proportional terms, with the shorter portion of the Golden Section division appearing before the longer (as Gillmor has shown).

15 Page 2 system 4 ('Il faut bon vivre') to p. 3 system 2 (pause), and p. 3 system 2 to the start of system 5.

16 Despite numerous drafts in BN 9597(1–2) and Ho 62, Satie never seems to have completed the opening *Kyrie* to his satisfaction, and in BN 9597 (1bis) he describes the work as the *Grande Messe de l'Eglise Métropolitaine d'Art*. The *Prélude* mentioned by Conrad Satie in *Le Cœur* (June 1895) is almost certainly the section in the printed score before the Basses enter on p. 2, but the fourth movement (*Gloria*) cited by Conrad has since disappeared. In the published version, the *Chant ecclésiastique* should end on p. 9 system 2, followed by two different harmonizations of the *Prière pour les voyageurs*. Satie's list of motifs for the Mass (Ho 62, f. 6r) includes three labelled 'le ㉝–㉟', and although 'le ㉟' actually appears in the *Kyrie*, it does suggest that Satie had a more extensive collection of movements in mind than has survived. The six motifs of the opening movement were all inspired by the words 'Kyrie eleison'.

17 The order of composition in BN 9617(2), 26–30, as far as it can be discerned, is: bars 72–5, 65–71, 7–10, 27–30, 1–2 (=5–6, 12–13, 25–6), ‾11, 20, 55‾, 47–8, 21–2, 76–81, 45–6, ‾40–1‾, 14–15‾, 60–1, ‾62–4, 42–4‾, 3–4, 51–4, 56–9. The gaps were then filled by the various ideas in different transpositions. There were plenty of unused ideas too amongst Satie's 1906 sketches, though in this case it is as impossible to establish the criteria for selection and rejection, as it is for their ordering into the draft in BN 9617(1), 12–15.

18 Ho 64, f. 7r and *v* shows that Satie's final order was: 1, part of 1, 4 transposed, 5 transposed (plus a short chromatic extension), 4 transposed, part of 1, 4, 5 (with the earlier extension transposed), 7 varied chromatically, 9, 9 minus its last two crotchets, 7 varied, plus a coda repeating the last two beats of 7 twice as the dance fades into the distance. The unused numbered cells for the first dance were not used in the second and third *Danses de travers*.

19 Bars 110–45 of the vocal score published by Max Eschig (E.D.2.L.S., 71pp.). This is a reproduction (minus the preface by René Chalupt) of the 1919 score published by Editions de La Sirène. Satie disliked its spacious format (devised by Blaise Cendrars) as it involved him in too many page turns when he accompanied *Socrate* in public. He fell out with Henri Sauguet in June 1923 after one such performance when he accused him of turning in the wrong places.

20 Using the Fibonacci series (1, 3, 5, 8, 13, 21 etc.) which is often found in Golden Section ratios. Here, 78–13=65 and 65–5=60.

21 Compare bars 6 and 41, and 10 and 45. Bars 19–21 in the first half originally continued as in bars 54–6 of the second half.

22 Especially in his favourite rondo structures, best exemplified in the three dances of *La Belle Excentrique* and in the film score *Cinéma*.

23 As his fellow humorist Alphonse Allais called him.

24 Some were added in the final manuscript for the printer (BN 10047(1)), but the majority of these unusually expressive directions (to No. 1 only) were added at the proof stage (BN Rés. Vma 166). Why the dynamics were not transferred to the parallel third dance is another mystery, and we can only assume that *Airs* Nos. 2 and 3 were meant to be quiet and monotone in comparison with No. 1.

25 The refrain, for instance, originally began thus: 'Ange d'or, fruit d'ivresse,/ Charme des yeux,/ Donne-toi, je te veux,/ Tu seras ma maîtresse.' It was to these words that Satie composed his celebrated melody.

26 The manuscript of the *Sérénade Sépulcrale – Prélude* in Ho 70 makes this 'chant donné' origination even clearer. It represents a first version of *Sur un mur* in C, but without the introduction (bars 1–2) and coda (bars 22–4). The melody was written out separately first in Ho 7, f. 10r, also in C, and it is perfectly possible that this may alternatively derive from a contemporary Schola dictation exercise, although it is not marked as such.

27 Which Satie added later after he had played the first two *Nouvelles 'Pièces froides'* as a pair to Florent Schmitt on 22 August 1907 (see BN Satie letter 18) – just as he added a fourth *Prélude flasque* to the three he had composed as a group in July 1912. The central part of *Sur un pont* is, however, quite close in mood and texture to *Sur un mur*, and the prominent falling fourths at the start of its four 8-bar repeated phrases are linked to the falling fourths which start the other two pieces.

28 Notably in the theses of Earl Rosenbaum (1974), Charles Blickhan (1976) and Jacinthe Harbec (1987). Harbec also subjects *Parade* to a rigorous Schenkerian analysis and discovers a pyramidal structure in Satie's shorter first version of the ballet (1987, 109).

29 This is based on the Salabert printed OS, which unfortunately lacks bar numbers. In this, p. 9 should read 'Premier Manager', with 'Prestidigitateur Chinois' coming on p. 17, as in the 1917 piano duet reduction. The music of OS bars 45–56 was titled 'Entrée des Managers' in the extract copied for Moise Kisling by Satie on '31 May 1917' (actually 1916: see Vy, 54–5).

30 With Mlle Juliette Meerovitch, for the Société Lyre et Palette.

31 Just as Debussy had modified *Jeux* for him in 1912. Satie's revision occupied him for at least a week (27 April–5 May) and Diaghilev's revival, planned for 11 May at the Salle Gaveau, had to be postponed till 18 May.

32 BN 17677(5) was hitherto assumed to date from the Spring of 1917. From the Henri-Pierre Roché correspondence in *US-AUS*, we know that Satie was 'not displeased' with the 'three minutes of music' he had added for Diaghilev, though he found returning to his 1917 style difficult, as so much had happened in the interim. But he approved of Diaghilev's idea and considered that *Parade* would be improved by his 1919 addition of the *Choral* and *Final*.

33 This command also appears at the end of the manuscript OS (Salabert, 91). This score also shows that the Chorale and Finale were added after the rest of *Parade* was orchestrated. The last three bars of the Chorale (p. 3) were pasted over Satie's original title page, and he left the pages of the Finale unnumbered (although two separate numberings were added later in another hand). The greater number of corrections in the Finale suggests that Satie was pressed for time.

34 In BN 9615(1), 1 in Satie's elaborate, but later suppressed preface, and in the fair copies on pp. 10–19. The songs appear with the correct numbering, but in the same order in the printed edition of 1916.

35 OS 20 bars 4–5; OS 54 bars 3–4; OS 107 bar 7–108 bar 1.

36 Though Louise Varèse took Satie's remark to refer to the verbal 'nonsense that enlivened every page' in his humorous piano music of 1913–15, and so missed the deeper significance of his revelation.

37 Satie's fascination with mirrors and the world beyond them was also shared by Cocteau, and can be seen in such later films as *Le Sang d'un poète* (1930) and *Orphée* (1949).

38 Such as the back cover of BN 9579, which probably dates from 1908–9.

39 The poets Aragon and Breton, and former friends like Auric, Poulenc and Cocteau.

40 370 car headlights, whose intensity apparently varied with the rhythm of the music (see Sanouillet, 1966, 170).

41 The first performance announced for 27 November had had to be cancelled due to the indisposition of Jean Borlin. He was confined to bed with a fever and a high temperature and was unable even to walk, let alone dance. The fashionable Parisian audience for *Relâche* (*Closed*), however, suspected another of Picabia's hoaxes and hung around the closed theatre till 11 p.m. An unsigned report in *Le Journal littéraire* ('Nos échos', 6 Dec 1924, 4) says that a group of them then repaired to a nearby café (Chez Weber), whose manager found on closing that all his ashtrays had vanished! The culprits included 'a musician whose name figures on the programme of the Théâtre des Champs-Elysées', which suggests that the high-spirited Satie was still up to his old tricks.

42 André Messager, in his hostile criticism in *Le Figaro* (9 Dec 1924, 5), says that the car refused to start and had to be pushed onto the proscenium!

43 Although Dadaism had been a dead duck since the fiasco of Breton's Congress of Paris in February 1922, Satie's previous associations with the movement had been literary and political rather than musical.

44 The Ballets Suédois programme at the Théâtre des Champs-Elysées on 25 October 1923 also included Satie's *Gymnopédies* (in Debussy's orchestration), the *Trois Petites Pièces montées*, and the dances from *Le Piège de Méduse*, as well as Cole Porter's ballet *Within the Quota* (orchestrated by Koechlin), and works by Koechlin's pupils known as L'Ecole d'Arcueil (Maxime Jacob, Henri Cliquet-Pleyel, Roger Désormière and Henri Sauguet). Prior to this concert, in an open letter to *L'Echo des Champs-Elysées* (12 Oct 1923), Satie had

dissociated himself from Les Six, 'of which several members have irretrievably entered into the realms of "La Gloire"'. This attack caused considerable consternation.

45 The scenarios for both *Après-dîner* and *Relâche* are reproduced in full by Sanouillet (1966, 255–7).

46 Picabia specified 6 minutes 50 seconds of music in Act 1, but only 3 minutes 10 seconds in Act 2. The title *Relâche* came as an afterthought, for Picabia's scenario was originally titled *Après-dîner* too (Sanouillet, 1966, 256–7).

47 This is paralleled by the ingenious reuse of 2/4 material from letter D in the Overture as the sweeping waltz theme of the *Danse de la Porte tournante* (No. 7).

48 Ho 80 (*Mercure*), on 9 separate cards, and BN 9678 (*Relâche*), on 8 pp. The 4 pages of plans for *Cinéma* are marked A–D as part of the same manuscript. Page A is given as Figure 8.12.

49 The division into sevenths involves *Relâche* as a whole, of course, and takes no account of the bisection into two Acts.

9 Compositional systems and other sources of inspiration

1 Although three times was a gross underestimate on Satie's part, the choice of number is likely. In the case of tripartite groups like the *Gymnopédies* or *Embryons desséchés*, the Bellman's lines from Lewis Carroll's *The Hunting of the Snark* always spring to mind:

> Just the place for a Snark! I have said it thrice:
> What I tell you three times is true. (From Fit the First: *The Landing*, verse 2, first published in 1876.)

2 The complete piece is found in BN 10050(1) on the same sheet of paper as Satie's earliest known composition, a brief Allegro for piano written in Honfleur in 1884. This should not, however, be taken as an indication that the *Fête donnée* was composed in 1884, for the calligraphy is different. Only the Allegro has the diagonal ledger lines also found in the *Gymnopédies* in 1888. By the early 1890s, Satie was writing ledger lines horizontally, as in the *Fête donnée* manuscript.

3 Another less strict (and much corrected) example using only cells 2, 4, 6–8 and 13 was also rejected at the same time (Ho 62, f. 10*v*, cited in Gowers 1965–6, 12). Gowers was the first to explore this early compositional system, and my own research owes much to his pioneering work.

4 The first version of this piece, together with some other linked fragments based on *The Keel Row*, were published by Robert Caby in 1968 as part of his *Carnet d'esquisses et de croquis* (p. 6). The title *Songerie vers 'Jack'* is Caby's own.

5 Published in 1972 by Eschig in a transcription by Nigel Wilkins from BN 9612, 1–7. The titles *Le Vilain petit Vaurien* and *La Gentille toute petite fille* are by Satie, as are the charming little stories which show how Satie was able to appeal to children at their own level, without any degree of adult condescension or studied cleverness.

6 Although the *Third Nocturne* is dated October 1919, and the second one September 1919, Satie seems to have had a clear conception of all three by August, and may well have sketched most of their material by then. This suggests that the compositional system for the *Second Nocturne* dates from July or early August 1919. Statements like this about his

compositions, especially self-satisfied ones, are extremely rare. As a result of the *Nocturnes*, Satie told Paulette Darty on 22 November 1919: 'I have changed a lot during these last months. I am becoming very serious. . .Too serious even' (Vc).

7 Satie probably improved this before he delivered it to its dedicatee, the pianist Marcelle Meyer, on 29 August, and he certainly removed its text about an 'old Will-o'-the-wisp' before then (BN 9609(2), 2–6), and suppressed its title of *Faux Nocturne*. He also cut four bars from the *Third Nocturne* in BN 9609(1), 5. This revision made the two halves of the B section (bars 17–22 and 23–8) balance each other exactly. The four bars were removed between bars 24 and 25 in the printed edition. After the three *Nocturnes* had appeared in print, Satie told Valentine Hugo on 6 February 1920 (*US-AUS*) that the *First Nocturne* gained from being placed alongside the two others. He was delighted by the extent to which Cocteau, Milhaud, and even Durey liked them.

8 BN 9602(2), 15–18, which I have recently edited for publication. Although it is in D major, like Nos. 1–3, its intensity and chromaticism set it apart from this initial group.

9 The sixth *Nocturne*, mentioned earlier, also specifies the keys through which it passes in the manuscript, and shows similarities with Ex. 85.

10 There are even starts of two whole-tone scale nocturnes in BN 9673, 1 and 20, but neither proceeded beyond the usual four bars. Both abandon whole-tone harmonies during their third bars. Like Fauré, Satie experimented with this Debussyan scale more than is generally realized, and we find a plan for organizing whole-tone harmonies in BN 9586(2), 10 around 1913 (labelled 'Harmonies délectables').

11 Even the 12/8 metre is not common to all the nocturnes, for BN 9609(1), 12 contains a sketch for the '5e Nocturne' in 4/4 time, which could have been influenced by Poulenc's *Trois Mouvements perpétuels* from the previous year (see Orledge, 1984–5, 174, Ex. 9).

12 This operetta is also referred to in the text of *La Défaite des Cimbres* (*Vieux sequins*, No. 3) three weeks later (p. 10 system 2).

13 The source for this may well have been Le Carpentier's *Méthode de piano pour les enfants*, which Messager says (1926, 3) was among Satie's effects found in Arcueil after his death – though his claim that the score of *Jack-in-the-Box* was 'inserted between two of its pages' is wrong. Satie would probably have possessed the 54th edition published by Mackar and Noël in Paris in 1894, in which 'Mon Rocher de Saint-Malo' appears as the 'Vingt-deuxième récréation' on p. 33. Besides using Le Carpentier's *Méthode* for his own piano pupils, its simple, largely two-part pieces may have served as a model for the *Enfantines* later in 1913.

14 In *de Podophthalma* (BN 9590, 12–21) Satie decided on the trio theme first, adding the main idea from *La Mascotte* second. Then came the linking *scherzo* passages, and finally the Beethovenesque coda.

15 Ornella Volta has discovered (1988, 28) that the *Mysterious Rag* was sung and danced in 1913 at the Moulin Rouge by Manzano and La Mora in the review *Tais-toi, tu m'affoles*, and published that year by Salabert, in the form of an arrangement by Francis Salabert 'en nouveau pas de l'ours'. This first use of Ragtime music in a European orchestral work was thus not dependent on early records imported from America by such as Ernest Ansermet, Gabrielle Buffet-Picabia or Yves Nat, as is often maintained. Rather the example was provided by Debussy's *Golliwogg's cake walk* and *The Little Nigar* of 1908–9. However,

Satie was impressed by the jazz records imported in 1916–17 and he considered that 'jazz tells us of its suffering and one doesn't care a damn. That is why it is *beautiful, real*' (Ve, 166). According to Gabriel Fournier (1952, 130) Satie played the jazz compositions of 'Jelly Roll' Morton at the Salle Huyghens around 1917, but again this cannot have been based on records, as Morton only started making these in Chicago in 1923. Morton is, however, known to have toured England and France in 1914, and Satie may have met him then (under his real name of Ferdinand La Menthe) and obtained copies of his latest pieces direct from their author. (This information was kindly supplied by Dr John Reade.)

16 In a letter to Valentine Gross on 25 October 1916 (*US-AUS*), Satie describes this piece as '*Canevas-Rag*', that is the outline draft of a Rag, or one based on an existing tune.

17 According to Mayr (1924, 11), *Relâche* also uses 'Le Père Dupanloup', 'As-tu vu la cantinière?' and 'R'tire tes pieds, tu n'vois pas que tu m'ennuies', to which Bredel (1982, 163) adds 'Y'a une pie dans la poirier'. However, even in the more explicit cases listed in section 4, Satie largely fashions his own melodies using the popular songs as a basis, with only occasional direct quotation (see Wehmeyer, 1974, 273). On this subject, Satie wrote in the 1924 programme for *Relâche* (Camfield, 1979, illustration 253) that its music 'depicts characters "*on the razzle*". For that, I made use of popular themes. These themes are strongly "*evocative*". . .Yes, very "*evocative*". Even "*peculiar*". . .The "*timorous*" – and other "*moralists*" – will reproach me for using these themes. I don't bother with the opinions of such people. . .Reactionary "*mutton-heads*" will hurl their thunderbolts. Bah!. . . I only permit one judge: the public. They will recognize these themes and will not be in the least bit offended in hearing them.'

18 See Yann le Pichon: *The World of Henri Rousseau* (New York, Viking Press, 1982), which also shows (p. 80) that the model for the curtain in *Parade* came from Rousseau's *Portrait of a Woman* in Picasso's own collection at 23 rue La Boétie, Paris 8.

10 Composition and the other arts

1 Satie's friend, the artist Augustin Grass-Mick, confirms his expert knowledge in 1897 and his fondness for discussions about painting (1950, 7).

2 Vl, 152. Satie was immensely proud of his achievement in *Socrate*, which he intended to be the highlight of the American tour he proposed to Henri-Pierre Roché in December 1918 (*US-AUS*). In his plan for this he stressed how un-boring his artist friends had found it in the readings he had arranged, and how it had the potential to make him famous, and even wealthy. 'I regard it as my lucky star', he wrote. 'Your old friend has scored a bull's-eye here.'

3 Satie had been introduced to these painters by Miguel Utrillo, the Catalan art critic and owner of the Auberge du Clou, at a New Year's Eve Ball at the Moulin de la Galette on 31 December 1890. This information comes from *Erik Satie à Montmartre* by Ornella Volta (1982, 22), to whose painstaking research I am indebted in this chapter.

4 Cited in Volta, 1982, 8–9. This shows that Satie's views on simplicity in art were consistently adhered to throughout his career.

5 In an elaborately calligraphed carnet (46pp.) in red and black ink (see Volta, 1987, 70–9; Orledge, 1987, 35–41 for fuller details). The first version, dated 17 November 1892, is

interspersed with letters, high-flown religious statements and letters by Latour and Satie referring to its creation. At the end of Act 3 Satie writes: 'This work has been finished to our great joy, the "72me des Travaux de Consolation Hermétique", the evening about to begin', rather as Flaubert gave the precise time and weather when he finished the 1849 version of *La Tentation de Saint Antoine*. If by this Satie meant that it took 72 meetings with Latour to produce *Uspud*, at most a 30-minute work, progress must have been slow indeed. If it means they had been working on it for 72 days, they would have begun on 7 September 1892, shortly after Satie's break with Péladan. The revised second version (BN 9631), on the other hand, was hastily compiled overnight on 16–17 December to show to Eugène Bertrand at the Paris Opéra the following day. Perhaps with an eye on public performance, the text is now shorter, less extravagant, and without occult symbolism or interspersed letters. There is now a different stage setting for each Act, though the music is still the same.

6 Satie's open letter to *Gil Blas* on 14 August 1892 asserted his independence as follows (trans. in W, 150), in typical archaic prose and ordered layout:

> Truly it doth amaze me that I,
> a poor man with thought for nothing
> but my Art, should be continually
> pursued and hailed as Initiator
> in music among the disciples of Master
> Joseph Péladan.
> This grieves me sorely and offends,
> For inasmuch as I am the pupil of anyone,
> Methinks this anyone can but be
> myself; the more so since methinks
> Master Péladan, learned man
> as he may be, could never have
> disciples, no more in music than
> in painting or aught else besides.
> Whereas good Master Joséphin Péladan,
> Whom I greatly respect and hold in deference,
> has in no wise exercised authority on
> my aesthetic independence; his
> relationship with me is not that of my
> master, but of my collaborator, just as
> in like wise my old friends
> Masters J-P. Contamine de Latour
> and Albert Tinchant.

7 The 1893 version of *Uspud* is the same as that found in BN 9631, and is not a third version. The musical extracts in the small *Uspud* brochure of 1895 are also the same as in BN 9631.

8 Latour's poetry found more appropriate settings with Charles Levadé, another member of Satie's circle, on whom Massenet exerted a marked influence in such Latour songs as *Sonnet* and *Dernier Reproche*. *Sonnet* was published by Alfred Satie in 1888.

9 *Impérial-Oxford*, in the manuscript owned by Oliver Neighbour, is a good example. All we know is that the poem was by Contamine de Latour, but as little of the poetry Satie set in his cabaret songs was ever published, they are likely to remain incomplete entities. The setting of Catulle Mendès' *Chanson médiévale* in 1906 was a Schola Cantorum exercise.

10 See Volta, 1987, 16–31, and Volta, 1988, 13–17 for fuller details. Volta has recently discovered the original scenario of this 'pièce en vers et en prose en trois actes par Lord Cheminot [Latour]', and has edited it for publication by Universal Edition (1989).

11 These plans were announced in the large *Uspud* brochure of April 1893 and derive from the genealogical table found at the start of the first version of the ballet (cited in Volta, 1987, 71). The subjects Satie chose were *Irnebizolle* (sister of Uspud) for a 2-Act ballet; *Corcleru* (great-great-uncle of Uspud) for a 3-Act ballet; *Ontrotance* (great-uncle of Uspud) for a 1-Act ballet; and *Tumisrudebude* (mother of Uspud) for a 3-Act ballet. There is even incest afoot in the Uspud clan, for Saint Plan, the father of Uspud and Irnebizolle, is given as both the brother and the husband of Tumisrudebude, and thus marries his sister!

12 See Kington, 1976, 7–8. Allais' stories, in which fiction masquerades as truth, are full of such inventions. His 'Negroes Fighting in a Cave at Night' was simply a black rectangular canvas, exhibited in 1882 at the Exposition des Arts Incohérents – an exhibition held in Paris by 'people who didn't know how to draw' (mostly writers). Allais' only contribution to music was a *Funeral March* for a deaf man, made up of 24 blank bars with the tempo marking *Lento rigolando*. This and his seven single-colour 'abstract' canvases (exhibited 1882–5) are reproduced in Alphonse Allais (ed. François Caradec and Pascal Pia): *Œuvres posthumes*, vol. II (Paris, La Table Ronde, 1966), 376–81. It would be interesting to know if John Cage or Mark Rothko had heard of these creations.

13 See Ve, 102–13. The pseudonym may have been a joke at the expense of Narcisse Lebeau (real name, Vital-Hoquet) – a plumber turned poet who had introduced both Satie and Latour to the Chat Noir in 1887.

14 Some of his pronouncements from the Eglise Métropolitaine d'Art are signed 'François de Paule (Sire des Marches de Savoie)' in 1895. Satie was fond of puns and playful nicknames too. Some of his letters to Roché in 1919 (*US-AUS*) are signed 'Titie', and Roché was christened 'Chéché' by Satie.

15 In the section 'Echos: Ça et là', 10/2 (15 February 1914), 19.

16 Vc, and partially cited in Ve, 293 n. 146.

17 The *Commandements* are given in full in Ve, 139 and trans. in W, 81.

18 From Santiago Rusiñol: *Obras completes* (Barcelona, Editorial Selecta, 3/1976), II, 740, cited in Volta, 1987, 82. The El Greco paintings are identified in Vl, 50.

19 From the privately printed *Cartulaire No. 2–63* of June 1895 (trans. in W, 52).

20 Published in facsimile in *La Revue musicale*, 214 (June 1952), facing p. 80. The full text of this movement should read: 'Dixit Domina Mea, Sede a dextris meis', which is the first verse of Psalm 109. A plainsong setting of it also appears in Ho 85.

21 Maurice Utrillo was born in 1883, but Miguel Utrillo (later Satie's employer at the Auberge du Clou) did not acknowledge paternity until 27 January 1891.

22 This has a frontispiece and engravings by La Rochefoucauld, and was published by the Librairie de l'Art Indépendant in March 1894.

23 In his article 'Les Indépendants' in *Essais d'art libre* (June–July 1894), 125. La Rochefoucauld's portrait of Satie was exhibited at the Salon des Indépendants in 1894.

24 Letter of 18 May 1917 (coll. Edouard Dermit) cited from a copy in *F-Pfs*.

25 In *The Quest for Proust* (trans. Gerald Hopkins) (London, Jonathan Cape, 1950), 168.

26 From Richard Dorment: 'The travels and travails of Gauguin' in *The Daily Telegraph* (24 January 1989), 14.

27 Cited in Ve, 38. Satie's battle was against professional establishment figures, and this remark should not be taken as implying that he regarded himself as anything other than a professional (but independent) composer.

28 His contributions have been carefully collected and translated in W, 158–70. They cover the period from 17 October 1909 to 29 November 1910, though his philanthropic work for local children must have started earlier for Satie was awarded the 'palmes académiques' for his services at a ceremony in the Town Hall on 4 July 1909.

29 These included compilations of cabaret songs arranged into 'fantaisies' in collaboration with Jules Dépaquit, like *Le Dîner de Pierrot* (17 September 1909) and *La Chemise* (performed by Darty at La Scala, Paris on 21 November 1909, and probably tried out beforehand in Arcueil on 24 October: see Appendix). Satie complained to Paulette Darty that receipts for his annual 'matinée artistique' for the Patronage Laïque had dropped from 200 francs on 24 October 1909 to a mere 11 francs 45 centimes in October 1910, which hardly encouraged him to continue in this direction. Satie's withdrawal from the Patronage Laïque in March 1910 (because of his dissatisfaction with the way it ran its affairs) probably had something to do with the decline in support for Satie's final concert in Arcueil.

30 Montfort's cycle of six songs by Carco entitled *Pendant qu'il pleut* was published by B. Roudanez in 1914, and his *Aquarelles* for piano (1913) were written as a 'subtle consolation to Erick [*sic*] Satie in his prison' (Remy-Bicqué, trans. Andrews, 1927, 9). I am indebted to Ornella Volta for providing me with this information.

31 The Rouart-Lerolle reprint (1926) and that of Salabert (1964) only reproduce Satie's music together with the little designs Martin made in 1914 to preface each piece (transferred from the title pages to each piece, where they appear in the first edition). The 1982 Dover edition omits these, but includes the 1922 Martin plates – which in the 1923 edition were illuminated in colour by Jules Saudé.

32 This occurred in 1916 on the death of Vogel's associate Emile Lévy. In 1922 Vogel bought back the rights to *Sports et divertissements* from M. Maynial, hence his 1923 edition. The whole complex history can be found in Volta, 1987, 41–53, which also gives other examples of the 1914 and 1922 Martin designs, and lists the different orders of performance that Satie approved at one time or another (see Appendix).

33 The first merely explains the various golfing items in the picture. The second mostly describes the old Colonel who is 'fat as a barrel' and suffers from 'rheumatism', and the third is a revision of this. All three (BN 9627(9), 10–11) are much too long for Satie's vignette, and are more like a preface to it. They are associated with Satie's first six attempts at the music using the *Jack-in-the-Box* rhythm (BN 9627(9), 12–21), whereas the final versions of the text are associated with Satie's last three attempts along the lines of Figure 10.3 in a fresh start in BN 9627(10), 1–9.

34 In BN 9627(10), 3.

35 Published in 1918, but dating from 1913–16. The best-known example is *Il pleut*, which is printed with the letters trickling like water down the page.

36 At the Salle de La Ville l'Evêque on 17 January. Here Marcelle Meyer accompanied the Belgian singer Berthe Albert in a lightning tour of the music of Bach, Gluck, Monteverdi, Mozart, Rameau, Byrd, Couperin, Domenico Scarlatti and Pergolesi (some of whose dates Satie provided). During the long concert, Meyer also gave the first performance of Satie's *Premier Menuet* of 1920, hence Satie's inclusion of his own date of birth later in the list. The full text and layout can be found in Ve, 91–5.

37 Poulenc had set six poems from *Le Bestiaire* in 1918–19, and Honegger set six of the *Alcools* in 1916–17. Durey also set extracts from *Le Bestiaire* in 1918.

38 For instance, he admired the poetry of Suzanne Kra (who approached him in July 1917) and Max Jacob (who sent him poems in October 1919), but he did not attempt to set the work of either of them.

39 Over his friendship with Satie's arch-enemy, the critic Louis Laloy, with whom Cocteau indulged in opium-smoking sessions (following the lonely death of his beloved Radiguet in December 1923). Satie never forgave Auric and Poulenc for their open friendship with Cocteau during this trip and the loss of such former allies made him more intransigent during his final creative year.

40 Letter of 6 September 1922 from Vc. The original is in *US-NYpm* and is cited by permission of the Frederick R. Koch Foundation.

41 M. Lafosse-Satie, Satie's heir, has unfortunately refused me permission to cite an extract from this letter of 6 June 1923 (amongst others) because it was not already published.

42 Fargue's poem ends with the words: 'Un petit Potasson/ C'est mon goret, c'est mon pourçon, mon petit potasson.' Fargue does not seem to have prevented the use of this song by his circle, despite his enmity with Satie.

43 The full texts are printed in Ve, 52–9; trans. in W, 118–23.

44 Which began in the first section of this chapter with *Le Fils des étoiles*.

45 At 5 rue de Penthièvre, Paris 8. Germaine Bongard was the sister of the couturier Paul Poiret and ran her own fashion house at her Hôtel. Satie's *Avant-dernières pensées* were also listed as a première at this concert, though it is possible that Satie played them himself on 18 April that year for the Société Lyre et Palette in the rue Huyghens. Two of the *Trois Mélodies* (*Le Chapelier* and *Daphénéo*) also received their first performances by Jane Bathori at this concert, but *La Statue de bronze* was not finished until 26 May, so the performance *chez* Mme Bongard four days later must have been the first.

46 The programme began with a 'Hommage à Satie' by Cocteau, and ended with verses dedicated to Satie by Blaise Cendrars, entitled *Le Music-kiss-me*. I am grateful to Ornella Volta for providing me with programmes for these events (from *F-Pfs*).

47 Entitled 'Les Belles Promesses'. A comedy by Max Jacob (*Ruffian toujours, truand jamais*) was also performed on the same occasion.

48 The first song, Satie's *Elégie* in memory of Debussy, had been performed separately at the Galerie La Boétie by Jane Bathori and André Salomon on 19 December 1920.

49 'Quelque chose d'analogue à un bon fauteuil'. Cited in Myers, 1968, 60, who translates this as 'an easy-chair'. Matisse (who admired Satie) is also credited by Cocteau with the invention of the term Cubism. '"Too much Cubism", he exclaimed when he saw the canvases brought back from the south of France by Georges Braque. They represented groups of homes in the form of cubes' (Cocteau, 1926, 224).

50 Satie related these incidents to Robert Caby from his hospital bed in 1925. He kindly passed them on to me in an interview in September 1987.

51 Written for the violinist Hélène Jourdan-Morhange and dedicated to her in March 1917. *L'Embarquement pour Cythère*, designed as a companion piece for the *Choses vues à droite et à gauche* of 1914, never progressed beyond the sketches found in BN 9623(1), 22–31, as far as I know.

52 Letter of 23 March 1922 in Vl, 161. It is quite possible that Satie is referring to *La Naissance de Vénus* here.

53 Satie also planned a ballet *Quadrille* with Braque in 1924 for Diaghilev (see Appendix).

54 Called *Le Music-Hall* in the French version.

55 Such as BN 9603(1), 16–17 with its settings of 'a-é, o-a, é-u, a-é, o-é-i-é' etc. Like the 'Tic! Tic! Tic!' which opens the song of the sinking Titanic, the music remained in the orchestral score with the words removed. The 'a-é' section can be found in the oboe and cor anglais parts of *Acrobates* (OS 88) and the Titanic song on piccolo and flute in OS 64–6.

56 Vc, the original of this letter is in *F-Po* (Fonds Kochno). Nonetheless, Satie hurried through a performance of *Socrate* at the Salle Gaveau the following evening in order to get to his box at the Théâtre Sarah-Bernhardt in time for *Parade*. As he did so he vented his spleen on poor Henri Sauguet, who was turning the pages for him as he accompanied Suzanne Balguerie.

   A publicity flyer of mid-May 1917 for the première of Apollinaire's 'moralité en deux actes' *Les Mamelles de Tiresias* (on 10 June) states that the music will be by Germaine Albert-Birot, with 'bruits reglés par Eric [*sic*] Satie' (document in *US-AUS* kindly communicated to me by Dr David Mateer). Satie had earlier turned down Apollinaire's request to write the music for this production, but he may have been persuaded to improvise some sort of *musique concrète* on the night. Thus it may have been Cocteau rather than his 'noises' that Satie most objected to in *Parade*.

57 Satie had had trouble with Cocteau's unbounded egotism before the 1920 revival. On 13 December he told Valentine Hugo (cited in Steegmuller, 1970, 261) that 'Cocteau is repeating his tiresome "antics" of 1917. He is being such a nuisance to Picasso and me that I feel bruised all over. It's a mania with him. *Parade* is his alone. That's all right with me. But why didn't he do the sets and costumes and write the music of this poor ballet?'

58 Cited in Howe, 1948, Part II, 25.

59 See the rest of this article (1976, 314–18) for a full discussion of Satie as an artist.

60 These identifying details come from BN 9608, a neat score marked 'Orgue: Mme Fellowes'. This score was hitherto thought lost and references to a *Divertissement* in Satie's correspondence of this period are usually explained as preliminary sketches for *Mercure* (as in Cooper, 1968, 57). It is more likely that Daisy Fellowes was one of the dancers than the organist, however, for Satie would surely have played this part himself at the Ball.

61 Formerly Olga Koklova, a ballerina with the Ballets Russes.

62 Later Marie-Blanche de Polignac, as Ornella Volta has recently discovered. She was more talented as a singer than as a dancer.

63 BN 9596(2), which is reproduced in facsimile in Wehmeyer, 1974, 270. Cocteau invariably went to masked balls dressed as Mercury, so it is possible that the whole ballet originated as a joke at his expense (see Vl, 168).

64 This set is reproduced in Vy, 81, along with a selection from Picasso's other sets for *Mercure* on pp. 78 and 80–1.

65 As he told Robert Caby in 1925. Satie said he did not expect Picasso to visit him in hospital as he was so bound up in his own affairs. This information was communicated to me in an interview with Caby on 23 September 1987.

66 In Francis Picabia: 'Souvenirs sur Lenine', *L'Eclair* (23 August 1922), 1.

67 No details are known about these other than the letter to the conductor Roger Désormière of 16 February 1924, in which Satie says that 'I count on writing two little pieces in collaboration with Tzara' (Vc). Satie met Tzara for dinner on 14 February and again at the Dôme (a café) on 20 February, presumably to discuss these plans.

68 For a full history of the Dada movement see Sanouillet, 1964, which focuses on Picabia's involvement with it.

69 Cited in Vy, 56. Later, in 1923, we find the Ragtime from *Parade* being performed in Holland under the title 'Ragtime Dada' at a Dada exhibition organized by the painters Theo van Doesburg, Kurt Schwitters and Vilmos Huszár. 'Dada' means 'hobby-horse' in French, and 'Yes, yes' in Romanian (from whence Tzara originated). This last meaning perhaps explains the frequency of the word 'Oui' in Satie's letters of the 1920s.

70 Published in *Gli inediti* (Parma, 1967), 58–159, and by J. C. Lattès (Paris, 1973). Cocteau wrote the dialogue and Radiguet at least some of the light, rhythmic lyrics. Their aim was to turn Bernardin de Saint-Pierre's story of tragic love partly into a contemporary social satire, and partly into a 'game of death and life', which in Radiguet's case turned out to be uncannily prophetic. In Act 1 ('Paradise lost') the fatal letter from Virginie's aunt (La Marquise) in Paris arrives (via the Governor of the Ile St Louis – now Mauritius – M. de La Bourdonnais) to shatter the primitive bliss of island life. Virginie is summoned to Paris to be educated in a convent and married as befits her station as a Countess.

In Act 2 Cocteau and Radiguet indulge in a satire of Parisian intrigue and false values. The title 'Chez les sauvages' tells us that the real savages are here, not on the desert island. Virginie's aunt is shown in her true colours, promising the dowry left to Virginie by her grandfather to a Count ('Le Baron' in Fig. 10.9) if he will persuade her to marry the wealthy Prince Adalbert de Champagne. The marriage will also help to restore Virginie's aunt to favour at Court. Virginie's faithful negro companion, Marie (who accompanied her from the island), warns her of the plot, and as the Prince arrives at the end of Act 2, they escape to Le Hâvre to catch a ship back to the island and her fiancée Paul.

In Act 3 ('The true paradise') we are back on Mauritius, where there has just been a hurricane. The Governor tells the islanders that Virginie's ship, the Saint-Géran, has been wrecked off the Gold Coast. Only Marie has survived. But when Virginie's body is brought back for burial, she 'appears' to her beloved Paul, to her mother, and to all her faithful friends who are pure in heart. Virginie tells them that they are now dead too; that all their troubles are over. Death is the true paradise, in which all the best aspects of the simple life are preserved for eternity. They will 'live' happily ever after in the place they love best, unseen by those (like the Governor) who have sought to disrupt their primitive bliss.

See Ornella Volta's article in the *Revue internationale de musique française* (June 1989) for full details on *Paul & Virginie*.

71 Issue No. 4 (November 1920), trans. in Wilkins, 1980, 422.

72 Ve, the original is now in *US-NYpm*. According to Henri-Pierre Roché's diaries (*US-AUS*), Satie told him (after a dinner *chez* Brancusi) on 22 February 1922 that he was not prepared

to 'redo the whole first act of *Paul & Virginie*', and it was Cocteau's changes of plan regarding the opera, as much as anything, that led to Satie never completing it (see Appendix: *Paul & Virginie* (text)).

73 Letter to Paulette Darty of 28 October 1922 from Vc.

74 The finished article is illustrated in Ray, 1964, 116. One might well describe Satie's *Danse cuirassée* (1913) as a musical 'ready-made', because it consists entirely of a borrowed popular song. As such it anticipates the first sculptural 'ready-made' (by Marcel Duchamp) by a year.

75 Satie's text and Ray's adapted translation are given in full in Vy, 70–1.

76 This motif is itself simply constructed from bar 1 and seven repetitions of bar 2.

77 In BN 9622(6). The neat full score is now in *US-AUS* (see Appendix). Much of it had been pre-planned, of course.

78 See René Clair, 1970, 115–40 for full details of these images, and Marks, 1983, 245–77 for an excellent article on *Entr'acte*.

79 Cited in Clair, 1970, 112. Prokofiev would have preferred this too.

11 Satie on other composers

1 As, for instance, when he says that there is only 'a minimal difference in instrumental technique' between Mozart and Pergolesi, who wrote 'piano music for the harpsichord'; whilst 'today impressionist musicians write their orchestral music for the piano' (Ve, 92–3).

2 This accounts for his refusal to enter into detailed musical discussions, however capable he might have been of doing so. One of his most violent attacks on critics comes in BN 9627(6), 24:

> There are three categories of critics: those who know; those who appear to know; those who know nothing. The last category is the most widely prevalent. It spreads out immodestly, like a goitre. It shows outward signs of infirmity, with all its unpleasantness.
>
> The critic of this category – almost always – is a by-product either of literature or the arts. A reject. The total ignorance he parades, despite himself, relegates him to the lowest rank of intellectual society. He is a sort of pariah who gives himself the affectations of a judge. Nothing more.

3 From Ho 39, cited in Wilkins, 1975, 298.

4 Satie used a 'Ronde' from Offenbach's operetta *Le Brésilien* in his cabaret song *Loubet Assassin* (Ho 12, 20–1), otherwise known as *Le Président aux Concours*. He also admired the operas of Rossini.

5 See Bryars, 1982, 4–14 for full details on Satie's English and Scottish connections. His parents were married in St Mary's Church, Barnes in 1865 and christened him Eric. He is known to have had a rudimentary command of English because a bizarre letter to his brother Conrad exists from August 1897 which is half in French and half in rough English translation. Satie spoke in English to Man Ray when he met him in December 1921 too. While Satie only went to England once (on holiday to Brighton as a toddler), he had several English friends, including Leigh Henry. See Jean-Aubry, 1916, 135.

6 In notes taken down by Conrad Satie on 30 September 1914 (coll. Robert Caby).

7 Cited in *Cahiers Debussy*, No. 3 (1976), 9. The certificate is dated 'Paris, 18 September 1910'.

8 In *A Survey of Contemporary Music*, cited in Bryars, 1982, 6.

9 Respectively 'Pour un homme d'état', 'Pour un canari' and 'Pour une tante à héritage'. Berners sketched a watercolour cover for 'Pour un canari' (see Bryars, 1976, 309).

10 In a letter to Henry Prunières on 9 March 1918 (Vc). Malipiero's use of block-like constructions and bold contrasted 'panels' of sound in *Pause del silenzio I* would undoubtedly have appealed to the composer of *Parade*.

11 This was one of the main ways Satie tried to help younger composers. He also introduced Koechlin and Sauguet to Diaghilev with a similar end in view, in 1917 and 1923 respectively. This letter to Casella of 15 May 1924 was supplied from *F-Pfs*.

12 I was unfortunately not permitted by Satie's heir to quote directly from this letter.

13 'He's an urchin' ('C'est un gamin'), he told Robert Caby in 1925.

14 Paul Vidal (1863–1931), the conductor and composer, had won the Prix de Rome in 1883 with his cantata *Le Gladiateur* (in competition with Debussy), and Satie would have automatically been hostile towards him for this reason. Vidal was chief conductor of the Paris Opéra from 1906, and a professor of composition at the Paris Conservatoire after 1909, where his pupils included André Caplet.

15 Cited in Henri Hell: *Francis Poulenc* (Paris, Librairie Arthème Fayard, 1978), 61–2. See also Poulenc, 1978, 39–40.

16 Satie missed *Les Choéphores* on 15 June 1919, the Sonatina for flute and piano in January 1923, and the opera *La Brebis égarée* at the Opéra-Comique on 10 December 1923. See Wilkins, 1980, 418–25 for extracts from Satie's 41 letters to Milhaud.

17 According to Koechlin's letter to Rollo Myers of 27 December 1948 (now in *US-NYpm*). See Orledge, 1987, 30.

18 This was organized by Milhaud and Satie around Henri Sauguet (newly arrived from Bordeaux), by the addition of Henri Cliquet-Pleyel, Satie's favourite conductor Roger Désormière, Baron Jacques Bénoist-Méchin (who soon left), and Maxime-Benjamin Jacob. All but Bénoist-Méchin were pupils of Charles Koechlin. Milhaud's role in organizing both Les Six and the Ecole d'Arcueil as viable groups seems to have been greater than Satie's. His main object, which Satie supported as a sort of godfather, was to publicize the music of rising young composers. The other catalyst behind Les Six was Cocteau who, as Mme Milhaud said (in an interview with Roger Nichols on 4 June 1987) 'couldn't do anything if he didn't have the impression he was doing everything!' Both groups were short-lived and there was no real inter-influence either within or between them.

19 He made the distinction in 'Ne confondons pas' in 1920 (Ve, 45), being careful to point out that Vincent d'Indy was no pawn.

20 The relationship between Satie and Debussy was discussed in chapter 4 and is therefore omitted here.

21 The other dedication in BN 14457 'to Mlle Jeanne de Bret' is not in Satie's hand.

22 Cited in Ve, 245. Even though Ravel never won the Prix de Rome, he had entered for it five times in 1900–5. The scandal of the *affaire Ravel* in 1905 cut no ice with Satie, who considered that aspiring to the Prix de Rome was as bad as achieving it. He even considered Debussy's work for the Conservatoire to be a sign of 'weakness. . .He certainly was a

victim of his place of learning, though he put right the wrong things about it as much as he could, and energetically' (W, 93).

23 In a BBC interview on 24 October 1957, cited in Nichols, 1987, 114.

24 Cited in Jourdan-Morhange, 1945, 95. By April 1922, Satie classed Ravel with Florent Schmitt as 'two monkeys'-droppings without talent' in a letter to Henry Prunières (Vc).

25 Cited in the Catalogue of the Maurice Ravel Exhibition at the Bibliothèque Nationale, 1975. Item 296, p. 62.

26 See Igor Stravinsky and Robert Craft: *Expositions and Developments* (London, Faber, 1962), 138.

27 From Igor Stravinsky and Robert Craft: *Dialogues* (London, Faber, 1982), 41.

28 The 8 letters from Satie to Stravinsky between 14 June 1913 and 15 September 1923 are printed in *Avec Stravinsky* (Monaco, Editions du Rocher, 1958), 206–10. This letter is dated 9 August 1922, and the last one ends with the words: 'I adore you; are you not the Great Stravinsky?'

12 Satie and the wider world

1 Cited in Ve, 43 from 'Out of Date' in *Les Feuilles libres*, 5/31 (March–April 1923), 42.

2 In a letter to his brother Conrad of 4 February 1901: 'Je vois bien que je ne suis né à mon époque' (Vc).

3 See Ve, 217 for reproductions of some of these Socratean busts. The legend 'Je suis venu au monde très jeune dans un temps très vieux' is probably an adaptation of Alfred de Musset's saying 'Je suis venu trop tard dans un monde très vieux', as Volta suggests. Another bust drawn for Henri-Pierre Roché around 1919 (which incorporates piano keys into his beard) bears the depressing legend: 'Life is a flower, an old flower' (*US-AUS*).

4 As, for instance, when he thanked the Comtesse de Beaumont for sponsoring a Satie festival on 7 June 1920, which had helped to restore the balance against the accusations of 'Bochisme' which arose from the première of *Parade* in 1917. As Satie said on 11 June: 'Thanks to you, people finally see me as a bit more *French* than they did before. My *Bochisme* is now more Parisian, and has become legendary' (Vc).

5 See Vy, 85; Wilkins, 1980, 416 and Mayr, 1924, 11.

6 'The Failure of Success' in *The Musical Digest*, 8 (28 July 1925), 5, cited in Gillmor, 1983, 109.

7 *Erik Satie. Causerie faite à la Société Lyre et Palette le 18 Avril 1916* (Paris, H. Roberge, 1916). Satie was closely associated with this Society, which had been founded in 1914 by the ex-patriot Swiss painter Emile Lejeune. They met at his studio at 6 rue Huyghens in Montparnasse, where Satie's works were frequently performed. It was from these concerts that Les Nouveaux Jeunes and Les Six emerged in 1917–18.

8 No. 15 (15 December 1924), 21–2.

9 From p. 127 of the 1969 Dover reprint of Myers's *Erik Satie*.

10 Satie's influence on Thomson's own work can be seen in the opera *Four Saints in Three Acts*, a hermetic creation with no real plot, written to a libretto by Gertrude Stein in 1927–8.

11 With a 25-concert Satie Festival 'which included a star-studded performance of *Le Piège de Méduse* with Buckminster Fuller as the Baron and sets by de Kooning' (Nyman, 1973,

1227). See the rest of Nyman's article for a fuller discussion of Satie's influence on Cage. Also Dickinson, 1967, 145–6.

12 This is reprinted in *Silence* (London, Calder and Boyars, 1968), 82.

13 From John Cage: 'More Satie', *Musical America*, 71 (1 April 1951), 26.

14 From Wilfrid Mellers's article on Mompou ('A new everlasting feeling') in *The Guardian* (7 March 1989).

15 In an interview with Gunther Schuller reported in *Perspectives of New Music* (Spring–Summer 1965). Satie also referred to his *Descriptions automatiques* as '*Vocations électriques*' in a letter to Ricardo Viñes of 6 June 1913 (Vc).

16 Cited in Bryars, 1982, 8.

17 Conceived at the request of Louis Broder, and published by Editions Aimé Maeght (Paris, n.d., 74 pp.). Cited in Vy, 114.

18 See Volta, 1988, 29 for an illustration of the 'alto overcoat in C', and Bryars, 1982, 12. Other drawings by Cudworth and Furnival inspired by Satie can be found in Vy, 44 and 46.

19 From notes taken by Conrad after a discussion with his brother on 30 September 1914 (coll. Robert Caby).

20 In fact, he only used it for urgent messages to the very rich. As, for instance, when he rang the Comtesse de Beaumont on 22 March 1922 to discuss the collaboration of Massine and Derain in a theatre project.

21 There is a particularly elaborate example in the Fondation Satie, addressed in Gothic script to 'Messire Erik Satie, Parcier & Maître de Chapelle de l'Eglise Métropolitaine d'Art de Jésus Conducteur' at 6 rue Cortot. It is in red and black ink, decorated with the logo of the Church in both an ogive and a circle (reproduced in Vy, 94–5). The letter, dated 'le 24 du mois de juillet de 96' and posted the following day, contains only the following message: 'Ce sera pour demain, Messire. Humblement.' ('Tomorrow will be the day, Messire. Humbly', and Satie signs himself with the familiar double cross in red). This may well refer to his move to the tiny 'placard' within 6 rue Cortot, as Volta suggests (Vl, 69).

22 Cited in Volta: *Erik Satie* (Seghers, 1979), 53.

23 This theme is explored fully in Ornella Volta's book *Satie and the Dance* (due to be published by Peregrine Smith Books, Layton, Utah in 1990).

Select bibliography

In this bibliography articles, books and dissertations are co-ordinated into a single list. The most important items are marked with an asterisk. Satie's own writings can be found in Satie (ed. Volta), 1981 (Ve), and selected writings are translated in Wilkins, 1980 (W).

Allais, Alphonse (ed. François Caradec and Pascal Pia): *Œuvres posthumes* (8 vols., Paris, La Table Ronde, 1966)

Antheil, George: *Bad Boy of Music* (New York, Doubleday, Doran, 1945)

Apollinaire, Guillaume: '"Parade" et L'Esprit Nouveau', *Excelsior* (11 May 1917), 5

Arnaud, Noël: 'Rétrobiographie ombilicale d'Erik Satie', *Cahiers dada surréalisme*, 2 (1968), 40–54

Aschengreen, Erik (trans. Patricia McAndrew and Per Avsum): *Jean Cocteau and the Dance* (Copenhagen, Gyldendal, 1986)

Auric, Georges: 'Erik Satie: musicien humoriste', *Revue française de musique*, 12 (10 Dec 1913), 138–42

'Relâche, les Ballets Suédois', *Les Nouvelles littéraires* (13 Dec 1924), 7

'La Leçon d'Erik Satie', *Revue musicale*, 6 (Aug 1925), 98–9

'Découverte de Satie', *Revue musicale*, 214 (June 1952), 119–24; repr. in *Revue musicale*, 386–7 (1985), 77–82

Auriol, George: 'Erik Satie: The Velvet Gentleman', *Revue musicale*, 5 (March 1924), 208–16; repr. in *Revue musicale*, 386–7 (1985), 23–31

Austin, William: 'Satie Before and After Cocteau', *Musical Quarterly*, 48/2 (April 1962), 216–33

*Axsom, Richard Hayden: *Parade: Cubism as Theater* (New York and London, Garland Publishing, 1979) (printing of D.Phil. diss., University of Michigan, 1974)

*Bancroft, David: 'Two Pleas for a French, French Music', *Music and Letters*, 48/2 (April 1967), 109–19; 48/3 (July 1967), 251–8

Barbier, Jean-Joël: *Au piano avec Erik Satie* (Paris, Garamont-Archimbaud, 1986)

Bathille, Pierre: 'Aspect littéraire d'Erik Satie', *La Nouvelle Revue critique*, 17 (Feb 1933), 73–80

Bathori, Jane (trans. Felix Aprahamian): 'Les Musiciens que j'ai connu: III Eric [*sic*] Satie, L'Ecole d'Arcueil (Henri Sauguet, Maxime Jacob, Cliquet-Pleyel, Roger Désormière)', *Recorded Sound*, 15 (1964), 238–45

Beach, Sylvia: *Shakespeare and Company* (London, Faber, 1960)

Beaumont, Comte Etienne de: 'The Soirées de Paris', *The Little Review*, 11 (1925–6), 55–7

Béhar, Henri: *Etude sur le théâtre dada et surréaliste* (Paris, Gallimard, 1967), see 101–5

Bélicha, Roland: 'Chronologie Satiste ou Photocopies d'un original', *Revue musicale*, 312 (1978), 7–63

Berthe, Mireille: *Parade, ballet cubiste* (Mémoire de Maîtrise, Université de Strasbourg II, 1979)

*Bertin, Pierre: 'Erik Satie et le Groupe des Six', *Les Annales*, 58/4 (Feb 1951), 49–60

'Comment j'ai connu Erik Satie', *Revue musicale*, 214 (June 1952), 73–5

Le Théâtre et (est) ma vie (Paris, Le Bélier, 1971)

Billy, André: *Stanislas de Guaita* (Paris, Mercure de France, 1971)

Blickhan, Charles: *Erik Satie: Musique d'ameublement* (DMA diss., University of Illinois, 1976)

Blom, Eric: 'Erik Satie (1866–1925): an original but ineffectual musician', *Musical News and Herald*, 69 (18 July 1925), 52–3

Bois, Jules: *Les petites religions de Paris* (Paris, Léon Chailley, 1894)

Boulez, Pierre: 'Chien flasque', *Revue musicale*, 214 (June 1952), 153–4; repr. in *Revue musicale*, 386–7 (1985), 118–19

*Bredel, Marc: *Erik Satie* (Paris, Editions Mazarine, 1982)

Bruyère, André: 'A Honfleur, au dernier siècle, Erik Satie', *Bulletin des Amis du Musée de Honfleur* (1970), 15–26

*Bryars, Gavin: 'Berners, Rousseau, Satie', *Studio International*, 192/984 (Nov/Dec 1976), 308–18

'Satie and the British', *Contact*, 25 (Autumn 1982), 4–14

*'"Vexations" and its Performers', *Contact*, 26 (Spring 1983), 12–20

Busser, Henri: *De Pelléas aux Indes Galantes* (Paris, Arthème Fayard, 1955)

Caby, Robert: 'Erik Satie: "Le plus grand musicien du monde"', *Le Monde* (1 Dec 1928), 8

'Quelques émouvantes aspects de la musique d'Erik Satie', *Montparnasse*, 22 (Jan 1929), 4–5

'La commémoration de la mort d'Erik Satie aujourd'hui à Arcueil-Cachan', *L'Humanité* (30 June 1929), 4

'Erik Satie', *Orbes*, 1/3 (Spring 1932), 31–4

'Il y a vingt-cinq ans mourait Erik Satie, "musicien médiéval" aux prises avec les hommes, les rêves et le démon', *Le Figaro littéraire* (24 June 1950), 6

*'Erik Satie à sa vraie place', *Revue musicale*, 214 (June 1952), 27–32

'Une grande musicien dans l'air léger de la butte Montmartre', in *Erik Satie à Montmartre* (Catalogue, ed. Ornella Volta) (Paris, Musée de Montmartre, 1982), 15–19

Cage, John: 'Satie Controversy?', *Musical America*, 70 (15 Dec 1950), 12

'More Satie', *Musical America*, 71 (1 April 1951), 26

*'On Erik Satie', *Art News Annual*, 27 (1958), 74–81; repr. in *Silence* (London, Calder and Boyars, 1968), 76–82

Cage, John (with Roger Shattuck and Alan Gillmor): 'Erik Satie: a Conversation', *Contact*, 25 (Autumn 1982), 21–6

Cailleux, Françoise: *Erik Satie et l'aphorisme* (Mémoire de Maîtrise, Université de Paris-Sorbonne, 1985)

Calvocoressi, Michel-Dimitri: 'M. Erik Satie', *Musica*, 10 (April 1911), 65–6

'The Origin of Today's Musical Idiom', *Musical Times*, 53 (Dec 1911), 776–8

'More about Satie', *Musical Times*, 65 (May 1924), 423

'Erik Satie: A few recollections and remarks', *Monthly Musical Record*, 55 (1 Jan 1925), 6–7

'Milhaud on Satie', *The Dominant*, 2/1 (Feb 1929), 23–6

'Concerning Erik Satie', *Musical Mirror and Fanfare* (April 1933), 208–9

'A point for Satie's biographers', *Musical Times*, 78 (July 1937), 622

Camfield, William: *Francis Picabia: His Art, Life and Times* (Princeton, Princeton University Press, 1979)

Campiotti, Giuseppina: *Erik Satie nella cultura del suo tempo* (diss., Università Cattolica del Sacro Cuore, Milan, 1973)

*Carroll, Noël: 'Entr'acte, Paris and Dada', *Millennium Film Journal* (New York), 1/1 (Winter 1977), 5–11

Cendrars, Blaise: *Blaise Cendrars vous parle. . .* (Paris, Denoël, 1952)

    Œuvres complètes, vol. VIII (Paris, Denoël, 1965)

*Chalupt, René: 'Quelques souvenirs sur Erik Satie', *Revue musicale*, 214 (June 1952), 39–46

Chennevière, Rudhyar: 'Erik Satie and the Music of Irony', *Musical Quarterly*, 5/4 (Oct 1919), 469–78

Clair, René: 'Picabia, Satie et la première d'Entr'acte', *L'Avant-scène*, 86 (Nov 1968), 5–7

    *(trans. Richard Jacques and Nicola Hayden): *A Nous La Liberté and Entr'acte* (London, Lorrimer Publishing, 1970)

    (trans. Stanley Appelbaum): *Cinema Yesterday and Today* (New York, Dover, 1972)

Clanet, Bernard: *Essai sur une personnalité particulière: Erik Satie* (diss., Université de Caen, Faculté de Médecine, 1985)

Clough, Rosa: *Futurism: The Story of a Modern Art Movement* (New York, Philosophical Library Inc., 1961)

Clouzot, Marie-René: *Souvenirs à deux voix, De Maxime Jacob à Dom Clément Jacob* (Paris, Edition Privat, 1969)

Cocteau, Jean: 'Avant "Parade"', *Excelsior* (18 May 1917), 5

    'La Collaboration de "Parade"', *Nord-Sud*, 4–5 (June-July 1917), 29–31

    'Parade: Ballet Réaliste', *Vanity Fair*, 5 (Sept 1917), 37, 106

    Le Coq et l'Arlequin: Notes autour de la musique (Paris, 1918); repr. in *Œuvres complètes*, vol. IX (Lausanne, Marguerat, 1950); trans. Rollo Myers in *A Call to Order* (London, Faber and Gwyer, 1926), 3–77

    'Parade', *Comoedia* (21 Dec 1920), 1

    'La reprise de Parade', *Paris-Midi* (21 Dec 1920)

    'Erik Satie', *Fanfare*, 1/2 (15 Oct 1921), 21–5

    'Picasso', *Les Feuilles libres*, 5/34 (Nov-Dec 1923), 217–32

    *'Fragments d'une conférence sur Eric [sic] Satie (1920)', *Revue musicale*, 5 (March 1924), 217–23; repr. in *Erik Satie* (Liège, Editions Dynamo, 1957), and in *Revue musicale*, 386–7 (1985), 32–8

    'L'exemple d'Erik Satie', *Revue musicale*, 6 (Aug 1925), 97–8

    Rappel à l'ordre (Paris, 1926); trans. Rollo Myers as *A Call to Order* (London, Faber and Gwyer, 1926)

    'Satie', *Revue musicale*, 214 (June 1952), 17–18

    (ed. Wallace Fowlie): *The Journals of Jean Cocteau* (London, Museum Press, 1957), 36–8; repr. in *My Contemporaries* (ed. Margaret Crosland) (London, Peter Owen, 1967), 47–50

    (ed. André Fermigier): *Jean Cocteau entre Picasso et Radiguet* (Paris, Hermann, 1967)

Cœuroy, André: 'La Musique et les lettres: Hommages littéraires à Erik Satie', *Revue musicale*, 5 (March 1924), 283–4

'Les Revues et la Presse: La double visage d'Erik Satie', *Revue musicale*, 5 (March 1924), 284–5

'The Esthetics of Contemporary Music', *Musical Quarterly*, 15/2 (April 1929), 246–67

'Further Aspects of Contemporary Music', *Musical Quarterly*, 15/4 (Oct 1929), 547–73

*Collaer, Paul: 'Erik Satie', *Arts et Lettres d'Aujourd'hui*, 2/11 (16 March 1924), 251–7 (with Catalogue of Works)

'L'Influence d'Erik Satie', *Séléction*, 3/6 (April 1924), 82–5

'Erik Satie: "Mercure". "Relâche".', *Séléction*, 4/4 (Jan 1925), 304–6

La Musique moderne (Brussels, Editions Meddens, 1955; 3/1963); trans. Sally Abeles as *A History of Modern Music* (Cleveland, World Publishing Company, 1961)

*'La fin des Six et de Satie', *La Revue générale: perspectives européennes des sciences humaines*, 6–7 (June–July 1974), 1–25

Collart, Marie-Isabelle: *Biblio-discographie descriptive d'Erik Satie*, (diss., Liège, Institut Provincial d'Etudes et de Recherches Bibliothéconomiques, 1982)

Collet, Henri: 'Un livre de Rimsky et un livre de Cocteau – les cinq russes, les six français et Erik Satie', *Comoedia* (16 and 23 Jan 1920)

'Erik Satie', *L'Esprit nouveau*, 2 (Nov 1920), 145–58

*Contamine de Latour, P[atrice]: 'Erik Satie intime', *Comoedia* (3, 5 and 6 Aug 1925)

Cooper, Douglas: *Picasso Theatre* (London, Weidenfeld and Nicolson, 1968)

Cooper, Martin: *French Music: From the Death of Berlioz to the Death of Fauré* (London, Oxford University Press, 1951)

Cortot, Alfred: 'Le cas Erik Satie', *Revue musicale*, 19/183 (April–May 1938), 248–72; repr. in *Revue musicale*, 386–7 (1985), 51–76

Cotte, Roger: *La Musique maçonnique et ses musiciens* (Braine-le-Comte, Editions de Baucens, 1975)

Cox, David: 'Erik Satie: Inspired Eccentric', *The Listener*, 64/1646 (13 Oct 1960), 657

Crespelle, Jean-Paul: *La Folle époque, des Ballets Russes au Surréalisme*, (Paris, Hachette, 1968)

Crosland, Margaret: *Jean Cocteau* (London, Peter Nevill, 1955)

Raymond Radiguet (London, Peter Owen, 1976)

Dalhaus, Carl (ed.): *Studien zur Trivialmusik des 19. Jahrhunderts* (Regensburg, Gustav Bosse Verlag, 1967)

Dautun, Yves: 'Figures de Musiciens: Le Solitaire d'Arcueil', *Le Petit Parisien* (28 July 1928), 5

'Un Grand Musicien Méconnu: Erik Satie', *Le Petit Parisien* (20 Aug 1929), 6

*Debold, Conrad: *'Parade' and 'Le Spectacle Intérieur': The Role of Jean Cocteau in an Avant-Garde Ballet* (Ph.D. diss., Emory University, 1982)

*Dickinson, Peter: 'Erik Satie (1866–1925)', *Music Review*, 28 (1967), 139–46

Donnay, Maurice: *Autour du Chat Noir* (Paris, Bernard Grasset, 1926)

Des Souvenirs (Paris, Arthème Fayard, 1933)

Doret, Gustave: *Temps et contretemps: Souvenirs d'un musicien* (Fribourg, Editions de la Librairie de l'Université, 1942)

Downes, Olin: 'Passing of Satie and His Cult – An Aged Plotter of Revolution', *New York Times* (6 Sept 1925), section 7, p. 7

Drew, David: 'Modern French Music' in *European Music in the Twentieth Century* (ed. Hartog) (New York, Praeger, 1957), 232–95

*Dumesnil, Maurice: 'Erik Satie: The Mischievous Man of French Music', *The Etude* (Philadelphia), 60 (Dec 1942), 816, 849, 855

*Durey, Louis: 'Erik Satie', *Arts* (Brooklyn), 17 (1930), 162–5

*Ecorcheville, Jules: 'Erik Satie', *Revue musicale SIM*, 7/3 (15 March 1911), 29–40

Emié, Louis: 'Eloge d'Erik Satie', *Les Feuilles libres*, 3/5 (Oct 1921), 267–71

Faure, Michel: *Musique et Société du Second Empire aux Années Vingt* (Paris, Flammarion, 1985)

Fields, Armond: *Henri Rivière* (Salt Lake City, Gibbs M. Smith, 1983)

Fisher, Fred: 'Erik Satie's Piano Music: A Centenary Survey', *Clavier*, 5/5 (Oct 1966), 14–19
    'Weightless Atmosphere Disclosures in the Shape of a Musical Rack – A lesson on Satie's Dessicated [sic] Embryo No. 2', *Clavier*, 5/5 (Oct 1966), 25–7

Flament, Albert: 'Jack in the Box: La pierre de Satie', *L'Intransigeant* (17 May 1926), 1

Fleuriel, Marie-Claude: *L'Œuvre de piano d'Erik Satie* (Mémoire de Maîtrise, Université de Paris-Sorbonne, 1978)

*Fournier, Gabriel: 'Erik Satie et son époque', *Revue musicale*, 214 (June 1952), 129–35; repr. in *Revue musicale*, 386–7 (1985), 83–9

Freud, Sigmund (trans. A. A. Brill): *Psychopathology of Everyday Life* (New York, Modern Library, 1938)
    (trans. Joan Rivière): *The Ego and the Id* (London, Hogarth Press, 1957)

Fry, Roger: *Cubism* (New York, McGraw-Hill, 1966)

Fumet, Stanislas: 'Eironeia', *Revue musicale*, 214 (June 1952), 19–22; repr. in *La Poésie à travers les arts* (Paris, Alsatia, 1954), 127–31

Fursy, Henri: *Mon Petit Bonhomme de Chemin: Souvenirs de Montmartre et d'Ailleurs* (Paris, Louis Querelle, 1928)

Gallez, Douglas: 'Satie's *Entr'acte*: A Model of Film Music', *Cinema Journal*, 16/1 (Fall 1976), 36–50

Gandrey-Rety, Jean: 'Au Théâtre des Champs-Elysées: *Relâche*', *Comoedia* (6 Dec 1924), 2

Gérard, Yves: *Introduction à l'œuvre d'Erik Satie* (diss., Paris Conservatoire, 1958)

*Gillmor, Alan: *Erik Satie and the Concept of the Avant-Garde* (Ph.D. diss., University of Toronto, 1972)
    *'Satie, Cage, and the New Asceticism', *Journal of the Canadian Association of University Schools of Music*, 5/2 (Fall 1975), 47–66; rev. version in *Contact*, 25 (Autumn, 1982), 15–20
    *'Erik Satie and the Concept of the Avant-Garde', *Musical Quarterly*, 69/1 (Winter 1983), 104–19
    Erik Satie (Boston, Twayne Publishers, 1988)

Gilman, Lawrence: 'Monsieur Satie and Mr Carpenter', *North American Review*, 215 (May 1922), 692–7

Godebska, Maria: 'A "Spectacle-Concert" in Paris [the *Petites Pièces montées*]', *The Chesterian*, 1 (1919–20), 165–7

Golding, John: *Cubism: A History and Analysis, 1907–14* (New York, Harper and Row, 1959)

Golschmann, Vladimir: 'Golschmann Remembers Erik Satie', *Musical America*, 22 (Aug 1972), 11–12, 32

Gosling, Nigel: *Paris 1900–1914: The Miraculous Years* (London, Weidenfeld and Nicolson, 1978)

*Gowers, Patrick: 'Satie's Rose Croix Music (1891–1895)', *Proceedings of the Royal Musical Association*, 92 (1965–6), 1–25
    Erik Satie: His Studies, Notebooks and Critics, (Ph.D. diss., 3 vols., Nos. 5374–6, University of Cambridge, 1966)

(with Nigel Wilkins): 'Erik Satie' in *The New Grove Dictionary of Music and Musicians* (ed. Stanley Sadie) (London, Macmillan, 1980), vol. XVI, 515–20; rev. ed. in *The New Grove Twentieth-Century French Masters* (London, Macmillan, 1986), 129–48

*Grass-Mick, Augustin: 'Pour commémorer – Le Souvenir d'Erik Satie', *Arts* (4 Aug 1950), 1, 7

Greer, Thomas Henry: *Music and its relation to Futurism, Cubism, Dadism and Surrealism* (Ph.D. diss., North Texas State University, 1969)

Guarnieri-Corazzol, Adriana: *Erik Satie tra ricerca e provocazione* (Venice, Marsilio, 1979)

Guichard, Léon: 'Erik Satie et la musique grégorienne', *Revue musicale*, 17 (Nov 1936), 334–5

  *'A propos d'Erik Satie. Notules incohérentes', *Université de Grenoble. U.E.R. de Lettres. Recherches et Travaux*, Bulletin No. 7 (March 1973), 63–80

Hahn, Reynaldo: 'L'Humour d'Erik Satie', *Le Figaro* (19 Dec 1937), 3

*Harbec, Jacinthe: *'Parade': Les influences cubistes sur la composition musicale d'Erik Satie* (MA diss., McGill University, 1987)

Harding, James: *The Ox on the Roof: Scenes from Musical Life in Paris in the Twenties* (London, Macdonald, 1972)

  Erik Satie (London, Secker and Warburg, 1975)

Harrison, Max: 'Satie: Disquiet and Dislocation', *Composer*, 38 (Winter 1970–1), 27–8

Helm, Everett: 'Satie. Still a Fascinating Enigma', *Musical America*, 48 (Feb 1948), 27–8, 166

Henry, Leigh: 'Erik Satie and the Ironic Spirit', *The Egoist*, 1 (1 July 1914), 252–4

  'Erik Satie and "L'Esprit Gaulois" in Music', *Musical Standard*, 14 (2 Aug 1919), 28–9; (9 Aug 1919), 31–2; (16 Aug 1919), 45–6

  'Contemporaries: Erik Satie', *Musical Opinion*, 43 (March 1920), 459–60

Herbert, Michel: *La Chanson à Montmartre* (Paris, Editions de La Table Ronde, 1962; 2nd 1967)

Herrand, Marcel: 'L'Humour d'Erik Satie', *Le Figaro* (23 Nov 1937), 5

Hesford, Bryan: 'Towards Understanding Erik Satie's "Messe des Pauvres"', *Musical Opinion*, 105 (March 1982), 201–7

Hill, Barbara Ferrell: *Characteristics of the Music of Erik Satie that suggest the Id* (DMA diss., University of Colorado, 1966)

Howat, Roy: *Debussy in proportion. A musical analysis* (Cambridge, Cambridge University Press, 1983)

*Howe, Martin: 'Erik Satie and his Ballets', *Ballet*, 5/8 (Aug–Sept 1948), 25–32, 37–9, 53–4; 6/1 (Oct 1948), 25–30

Hugnet, Georges: *L'Aventure Dada (1916–22)* (Paris, Galerie de l'Institut, 1957); rev. ed. (Paris, Seghers, 1971)

Hugo, Valentine: 'Le Socrate que j'ai connu', *Revue musicale*, 214 (June 1952), 139–45; repr. in *Revue musicale*, 386–7 (1985), 111–17

Hurard-Viltard, Eveline: *Le Groupe des Six ou le matin d'un jour de fête* (Paris, Méridiens Klinck-sieck, 1987)

Hyspa, Vincent: *Chansons d'humour* (Paris, Enoch, 1903)

Jacob, Dom Clément: 'Erik Satie et le chant grégorien', *Revue musicale*, 214 (June 1952), 85–94; repr. in *Revue musicale*, 386–7 (1985), 90–9

Jacob, Max: *Correspondance* (Paris, Editions de Paris, 1953)

Jacob, Maxime: 'L'Exemple d'Erik Satie', *Vigile*, 2 (1930), 123–35

Jankélévitch, Vladimir: *Le Nocturne: Fauré/ Chopin et la nuit/ Satie et le matin* (Paris, Albin Michel, 1957), 123–216

Jean-Aubry, Georges: 'Erik Satie – A Musical Humorist', *Music Student*, 9 (Dec 1916), 135–6
  La Musique française d'aujourd'hui (Paris, Perrin, 1916); trans. Edwin Evans (London, K. Paul, Trench and Trubner, 1919)
  'The End of a Legend', *The Chesterian*, 6 (1924–5), 191–3
Jeanne, Paul: *Les Théâtres d'ombres à Montmartre de 1887 à 1923: Chat Noir, Quat'z'Arts, Lune Rousse* (Paris, Les Presses modernes au Palais-Royal, 1937)
Jeanne, René: 'Le Cinéma aux Ballets Suédois', *Les Nouvelles littéraires* (13 Dec 1924), 7
Jeanneret, Albert: 'Parade', *L'Esprit nouveau*, 4 (1921), 449–52
  'Socrate', *L'Esprit nouveau*, 9 (1923), 989–95
Jourdain, Francis: *Né en 76* (Paris, Les Editions du Pavillon, 1951), see 244–7
Jourdan-Morhange, Hélène: *Ravel et nous* (Paris, Editions du Milieu du Monde, 1945)
  Mes amis musiciens (Paris, Les Editeurs Français Réunis, 1955)
Jullien, Philippe (trans. Anne Carter): *Montmartre* (Oxford, Phaidon, 1977)
Kerdyk, René: 'Quand Erik Satie écrivait à Vincent Hyspa', *Paris-Midi* (17 May 1937), 2
Kington, Miles (ed.): *The World of Alphonse Allais* (London, Chatto and Windus, 1976)
Kisling, Moïse: 'Souvenir de Satie', *Revue musicale*, 214 (June 1952), 107–10
*Koechlin, Charles: 'Erik Satie', *Revue musicale*, 5/2 (March 1924), 193–207; repr. in *Revue musicale*, 386–7 (1985), 8–22
  'Erik Satie', *Journal des débats* (16 May 1926)
  'Conférence sur Satie et l'Ecole d'Arcueil', 40pp., Dec 1927 (Unpubd. MS in coll. of Madeleine Li-Koechlin, L'Hay-les-Roses, France)
La Grange, Henri-Louis de: 'Satie revisité', *Contrepoints*, 6 (1949), 171–2
*Lajoinie, Vincent: *Erik Satie* (Paris, L'Age d'Homme, 1985)
Laloy, Louis: 'Au Théâtre des Champs-Elysées – Reprises de "Parade"', *Comoedia* (23 Dec 1920), 1
  '"Mercure" aux Ballets Russes', *Comoedia* (2 June 1927), 1
  La Musique retrouvée: 1902–27 (Paris, Librairie Plon, 1928)
*Lambert, Constant: *Music Ho! A Study of Music in Decline* (London, Faber, 1934), see 115–25; extracts (trans. Marcelle Jossua) appear in 'Erik Satie et la musique abstraite', *Revue musicale*, 214 (June 1952), 101–6
Lannes, Roger: 'Souvenirs d'une croisade – Darius Milhaud a évoqué hier Erik Satie', *L'Intransigeant* (12 Dec 1938), 2
Lanser, René: 'Notes et souvenirs', *Le Matin à Anvers* (9 July 1925)
Latour: see Contamine de Latour
Léger, Fernand: 'Satie inconnu', *Revue musicale*, 214 (June 1952), 137–8; repr. in *Revue musicale*, 386–7 (1985), 100–1
Leiris, Michel: 'L'Humour d'Erik Satie', *La Nouvelle Revue Française*, 26/1 (1938), 163–4
Lesure, François (ed.): *Erik Satie* (Catalogue of the exhibition held at the Bibliothèque Nationale between 26 May and June 1966) (Paris, Imprimérie Senlis, 1966)
Lockspeiser, Edward: *The Literary Clef: An Anthology of Letters and Writings by French Composers* (London, John Calder, 1958), see 160–6
Lyle, Wilson: 'Erik Satie and Rosicrucianism', *Music Review*, 42 (1981), 238–42
Mann, Michael: 'Reaction and Continuity in Musical Composition', *Music Review*, 15 (1954), 39–46

Maré, Rolf de: 'A propos de Relâche', *Comoedia* (27 Nov 1924), 2

'The Swedish Ballet and the modern aesthetic', *The Little Review*, 11 (1925–6), 24–8

Les Ballets Suédois (Paris, Editions du Trianon, 1931)

*Marks, Martin: 'The Well-Furnished Film: Satie's Score for *Entr'acte*', *Canadian University Music Review*, 4 (1983), 245–77

*Martin, Marianne: 'The Ballet *Parade*: A Dialogue Between Cubism and Futurism', *The Art Quarterly*, new series 1/2 (Spring 1978), 85–111

Marval, Louis de: 'A propos d'Erik Satie', *Schweizerische Musikzeitung*, 107/6 (Nov–Dec 1967), 340–2

Massine, Léonide: *My Life in Ballet* (London, Macmillan, 1968)

Massot, Pierre de: 'Vingt-cinq minutes avec: Erik Satie', *Paris-Journal* (30 May 1924), 2

'Hommes d'aujourd'hui: Erik Satie', *L'Ere nouvelle* (14 Sept 1924), 2

'Quelques propos et souvenirs sur Erik Satie', *Revue musicale*, 214 (June 1952), 125–8

Francis Picabia (Paris, Seghers, 1966)

Mauclair, Camille: 'Le Souvenir de Péladan', *Les Nouvelles littéraires*, 4/125 (7 March 1925), 1

*Mayr, W.: 'Entretien avec Erik Satie', *Le Journal littéraire*, 24 (4 Oct 1924), 11

Mellers, Wilfrid: 'The Classicism of Erik Satie', *The Listener*, 18 (11 Aug 1937), 318

**'Erik Satie and the "Problem" of Contemporary Music', *Music and Letters*, 23/3 (July 1942), 210–27; repr. in Mellers: *Studies in Contemporary Music* (London, Dennis Dobson, 1947), 16–42

(trans. Marcelle Jossua): 'Erik Satie et la musique fonctionelle', *Revue musicale*, 214 (June 1952), 33–7 (extracts from previous entry)

'Film Music: The Musical Problem' in *Grove's Dictionary of Music and Musicians* (5th ed., London, 1954), vol. III, 103–4

Caliban Reborn: Renewal in Twentieth-Century Music (New York, Harper and Row, 1967; London, Gollancz, 1968)

Mesens, E. L. T.: 'Hommage à Erik Satie', *Sélection*, 3/10 (Aug 1924), 535–8

**'Le Souvenir d'Erik Satie', *Revue musicale*, 214 (June 1952), 147–51

Messager, André: 'Les Premières – Théâtre des Champs-Elysées – *Relâche*', *Le Figaro* (9 Dec 1924), 5

'Les Premières. Ballets Russes – *Jack-in-the-Box* d'Eric [*sic*] Satie', *Le Figaro* (7 June 1926), 3

Metzger, Heinz-Klaus and Rainer Riehn (eds.): *Musik-Konzepte*, No. 11 (special Satie edition) (Munich, Jan 1980)

Michelet, Victor-Emile: *Les Compagnons de la hiérophanie: Souvenirs du mouvement hermétiste à la fin du 19e siècle* (Paris, Dorbon-Ainé, 1937)

Milhaud, Darius: 'Les dernières œuvres d'Erik Satie et les premières œuvres d'Henri Sauguet', *Les Feuilles libres*, 5/37 (Sept–Oct 1924), 46–8

Etudes (Paris, Claude Aveline, 1927)

**'Les derniers jours d'Erik Satie', *Le Figaro littéraire* (23 April 1949), 5

Notes sans musique (Paris, Julliard, 1949); trans. Donald Evans (London, Dennis Dobson, 1952/ repr. Calder and Boyars, 1967)

'Lettre de Darius Milhaud', *Revue musicale*, 214 (June 1952), 153

Ma Vie heureuse (Paris, Belfond, 1974)

Monnier, Adrienne (trans. Richard McDougall): *The Very Rich Hours of Adrienne Monnier* (New York, Charles Scribner's Sons, 1976)

Motherwell, Robert: *The Dada Painters and Poets – An Anthology* (New York, Wittenborn, Schulz Inc., 1951)

Myers, Rollo: 'The Strange Case of Erik Satie', *Musical Times*, 86/1229 (July 1945), 201–3

'Quelques Réflexions sur le Rôle de la Musique dans le Ballet contemporain', *Polyphonie*, 1 (1947–8), 66–70

Erik Satie (London, Dennis Dobson, 1948); repr. (New York, Dover, 1968)

'Importance de Satie dans la musique contemporaine', *Revue musicale*, 214 (June 1952), 77–81

'Notes sur *Socrate*', *Revue musicale*, 214 (June 1952), 81–4

'The Significance of Satie: a centenary tribute', *Music and Musicians*, 14 (May 1966), 16–17, 41

'A Music Critic in Paris in the Nineteen-Twenties: Some Personal Recollections', *Musical Quarterly*, 63/4 (Oct 1977), 524–44

'esoterik Satie', *Music and Musicians*, 27 (July 1979), 74–5

Nichols, Roger (trans. and ed.) and François Lesure (ed.): *Debussy Letters* (London, Faber, 1987)

Ravel Remembered (London, Faber, 1987)

[Nos Echos] (No author given): 'Nos Echos – *Relâche*', *Le Journal littéraire*, 33 (6 Dec 1924), 4

Nyman, Michael: 'Cage and Satie', *Musical Times*, 114/1570 (Dec 1973), 1227–9

Oberthur, Mariel: *Les Cabarets artistiques au pied de la colline de Montmartre* (diss., 3e cycle, Université de Paris IV, 1979)

'Erik Satie et les cafés de Montmartre', in *Erik Satie à Montmartre* (Catalogue, ed. Ornella Volta) (Paris, Musée de Montmartre, 1982), 10–14

(trans. Sheila Azoulai): *Cafés and Cabarets of Montmartre* (Layton, Utah, Gibbs M. Smith, 1984)

*Orledge, Robert: *Debussy and the Theatre* (Cambridge, Cambridge University Press, 1982)

*Satie's Approach to Composition in His Later Years (1913–24)', *Proceedings of the Royal Musical Association*, 111 (1984–5), 155–79

*'Satie, Koechlin and the Ballet *Uspud*', *Music and Letters*, 68/1 (1987), 26–41

*'Satie at Sea, and the Mystery of La 'Belle Cubaine'', *Music and Letters*, 71/3 (1990)

Oxenhandler, Neal: *Scandal and Parade: The Theater of Jean Cocteau* (New Brunswick, New Jersey, Rutgers University Press, 1957)

Paris, Alain: 'A la recherche d'Erik Satie', *Le Courrier musical de France*, 52 (1975), 130–1

Pearsall, Ronald: 'The Sophistication of the Graceful', *Music Review*, 23 (1962), 205–7

Penrose, Roland: *Picasso: His Life and Work* (New York, Harper Brothers, 1958)

*Perloff, Nancy: *Art and the everyday: the impact of Parisian popular entertainment on Satie, Milhaud, Poulenc and Auric* (Ph.D. diss., University of Michigan, 1986)

Pernoud, Georges: 'Erik Satie à cinquante ans', *A la page: L'Hebdomadaire des jeunes*, 24 (June 1966), 898–907

Peter, René: *Claude Debussy* (Paris, Gallimard, 1931; rev. ed. 1944), see 69–72

Peterkin, Norman: 'Erik Satie's "Parade"', *Musical Times*, 60/918 (Aug 1919), 426–7

Picabia, Francis: 'Erik Satie', *Paris-Journal* (27 June 1924), 1

'Instantanéisme', *Comoedia* (21 Nov 1924), 4

*'Pourquoi j'ai écrit "Relâche"', *Le Siècle* (27 Nov 1924), 4

'Pourquoi "Relâche" a fait relâche', *Comoedia* (2 Dec 1924), 1

'Erik Satie', *L'Ere nouvelle* (8 July 1925), 3

(ed. Olivier Revault d'Allones): *Ecrits, Vol. 1: 1913–20* (Paris, Pierre Belfond, 1975) (ed. Olivier Revault d'Allones and Dominique Bouissou): *Ecrits, Vol. 2: 1921–53 et posthumes* (Paris, Pierre Belfond, 1978)

Vive Erik Satie/ Francis Picabia (Liège, Editions Dynamo, 1957)

391. Revue publiée de 1917 à 1924 par Francis Picabia (Réédition intégrale presentée par Michel Sanouillet) (Paris, Le Terrain Vague, 1960)

Picard, Gaston: 'L'Ecrivain chez Erik Satie', *Le Figaro: Supplément littéraire* (11 July 1925), 2

Polignac, Princesse Edmond de: 'Memoirs', *Horizon*, 12/68 (Aug 1945), 110–41

Politis, Hélène: 'Sermons humoristiques: les Ecrits d'Erik Satie', in *Ecrit pour Vladimir Jankélévitch* (Paris, Flammarion, 1978)

Porter, David: 'Recurrent Motifs in Erik Satie's *Sports et divertissements*', *Music Review*, 39 (1978), 227–30

Poulenc, Francis: 'La Musique de piano d'Erik Satie', *Revue musicale*, 214 (June 1952), 23–6; repr. in *Revue musicale*, 386–7 (1985), 102–5

    Moi et mes amis (Paris, Editions La Palatine, 1963); trans. James Harding as *My Friends and Myself* (London, Dennis Dobson, 1978)

    (ed. Hélène de Wendel): *Correspondance 1915–63* (Paris, Editions du Seuil, 1967)

Prieberg, Fred: 'Erik Satie', *Musica* (Kassel), 9 (1955), 366–9

Privitera, Massimo: *Erik Satie: Produzione & Riproduzione* (diss., University of Bologna, 1981)

Proust, Marcel: *Les Plaisirs et les jours* (Paris, Calmann-Lévy, 1896)

Prunières, Henry: 'Socrate d'Erik Satie', *Revue musicale*, 386–7 (1985), 6–7

Radiguet, Raymond: 'Parade', *Le Gaulois* (25 Dec 1920), 4

Rašín, Vera: '"Les Six" and Jean Cocteau', *Music and Letters*, 38/2 (April 1957), 164–9

Raval, Marcel: 'Cariathys [*sic*] à l'Olympia', *Les Feuilles libres*, 25 (Feb 1922), 64–5

Ravel, Maurice: *Contemporary Music* (Houston, Rice Institute Pamphlets, 1928), vol. 15, 131–45

Ray, Man: *Self Portrait* (London, Andre Deutsch, 1963; repr. Bloomsbury Press, 1988)

Remy-Bicqué, Jean (with trans. by William Andrews): *Robert Montfort* (Paris, Sacre du Printemps, Carrefour de la Croix-Rouge, [1927])

*Renshaw, Rosette: 'Erik Satie (1866–1925)', *La Nouvelle Revue Canadienne*, 1/2 (1951), 76–80

Rey, Anne: *Dada et le pré-surréalisme dans l'œuvre d'Erik Satie* (diss., Université de Paris, 1967)

    Erik Satie (Paris, Editions du Seuil, 1974: coll. Solfèges No. 35)

Richard, Marius: 'Une Controverse Musicale: Claude Debussy et Erik Satie', *La Liberté* (13 Jan 1932), 2

Ries, Frank: *The Dance Theater of Jean Cocteau* (Ann Arbor, Michigan, UMI Research Press, 1986)

Roberts, W. Wright: 'The Problem of Satie', *Music and Letters*, 4 (1923), 313–20

Rogers, M. Robert: 'Jazz Influence on French Music', *Musical Quarterly*, 21/1 (Jan 1935), 53–68

*Roland-Manuel, Alexis: *Erik Satie. Causerie faite à la Société Lyre et Palette, le 18 Avril 1916* (Paris, H. Roberge Imprimeur, 1916), with valuable list of works

    'Adieu à Satie', *Revue Pleyel*, 15 (Dec 1924), 21–2

    'Satie tel que je l'ai vu', *Revue musicale*, 214 (June 1952), 9–11

Rorem, Ned: 'Notes on "Parade"', *Opera News*, 45 (28 Feb 1981), 8–18

*Rosenbaum, Earl: *Erik Satie: Parade* (MA diss., California State University, 1974)

Roussel, Albert: 'A propos d'un récent festival', *Le Gaulois* (12 June 1926), 3

Roy, Jean: 'Satie poète', *Revue musicale*, 214 (June 1952), 55–7

   'Erik Satie' in *Présences contemporaines, musique française* (Paris, Nouvelles Editions Debresse, 1962), see 15–55

   'L'Original Erik Satie', *Musica*, 138 (Sept 1965), 13–15

   'Erik Satie: Le mythe et la réalité', *Panorama de la musique*, 29 (May–June 1979), 6–9

Ruppel, K. H.: 'Monsieur le Pauvre', *Melos*, 33 (1966), 205–9

Sandro, Paul: 'Parodic Narration in "Entr'acte"', *Film Criticism*, 4/1 (Fall 1979), 44–55

*Sanouillet, Michel: *Picabia* (Paris, Editions du Temps, 1964)

   Dada à Paris (Paris, Jean-Jacques Pauvert, 1965)

   *Francis Picabia et '391': vol. I (Paris, Le Terrain Vague, 1960); vol. II (Paris, Eric Losfeld, 1966)

   **'Erik Satie et son "violon d'encre"', *Travaux de linguistique et de littérature publiés par le centre de philologie et de littératures romanes de l'Université de Strasbourg*, 7/2 (1969), 167–80

Santi, P.: 'Il "point de départ" di Satie', *Chigiana*, 23 (1966), 183–99

*Sasser, William Gray: *Erik Satie: A Study of Mutations in His Style* (MA diss., University of North Carolina, Chapel Hill, 1949)

   'Le développement du style d'Erik Satie', *Revue musicale*, 214 (June 1952), 111–17

*Satie, Conrad: 'Erik Satie', *Le Cœur*, 2/10 (June 1895), 2–3

*Satie, Erik: *Oui. Lettres d'Erik Satie adressées à Pierre de Massot [1922–4]* (Alès, Editions Pab, 1960)

   (ed. Henri Borgeaud): 'Trois lettres d'Erik Satie à Claude Debussy (1903)', *Revue de Musicologie*, 48 (1962), 71–4

   (ed. Ornella Volta, trans. Frieda van Tijn-Zwart): *Texten* (Amsterdam, Em. Querido, 1976)

   *(ed. Ornella Volta): *Ecrits* (Paris, Editions Champ Libre, 1977; rev. ed. 1981) (Ve in text)

   For other letters by Satie, see Volta, Ornella; Wilkins, Nigel

   *(ed. Ornella Volta): *Le Piège de Méduse, comédie lyrique en un acte de M. Erik Satie, avec musique de dance du même Monsieur* (with cassette recording) (Paris, Le Castor Astral, 1988)

   *(ed. Ornella Volta): *Correspondance* (Paris, Editions du Placard; complete annotated ed. in 3 vols., in preparation) (Vc in text)

Sauguet, Henri: 'Vive Satie!', *La Bataille* (5 July 1945), 4

   **'Souvenirs et réflexions autour d'Erik Satie', *Revue musicale*, 214 (June 1952), 95–9; repr. in *Revue musicale*, 386–7 (1985), 106–10

   'Erik Satie', *Le Courrier musical de France*, 52 (1975), 129

   *(ed. Pierre Ancelin): 'Henri Sauguet. L'Homme et l'œuvre', *Revue musicale*, 361–3 (1983), see 237–49

Saunders, William: 'Erik Satie', *Musical News*, 53 (1 Sept 1917), 131–3

   'Erik Satie's Forms and Harmonies', *Musical News*, 53 (8 Sept 1917), 147–8

Schloezer, Boris de: 'Réflexions sur la musique: Le cas Satie', *Revue musicale*, 5 (Aug 1924), 173–6; repr. in *Revue musicale*, 386–7 (1985), 44–7

*Schmitt, Florent: 'Erik Satie', *Montjoie!*, 1/11–12 (Nov–Dec 1913), 11–12

Schwarz, Arturo: *Almanacco Dada* (Milan, Feltrinelli, 1976)

Sens, Suzanne: *Découverte d'Erik Satie* (Manlévrier, A.-H. Hérault, 1984)

*Shattuck, Roger: 'Satie et la musique de placard', *Revue musicale*, 214 (June 1952), 47–54

   **'Erik Satie. Composer to the School of Paris', *Art News Annual*, 27 (1958), 64–8, 186–91

   The Banquet Years (London, 1955; rev. ed., New York, Vintage Books, 1968), see 88–145

Skulsky, Abraham: 'Erik Satie', *Musical America*, 70 (15 Nov 1950), 5, 32, 36
  'Satie Controversy?', *Musical America*, 70 (15 Dec 1950), 12 (see Cage, John for the other part
    of this public argument)
Steegmuller, Francis: *Cocteau: A Biography* (Boston, Little, Brown and Co., 1970)
Storm, John: *The Valadon Drama: The Life of Suzanne Valadon* (London, Longmans, Green and
    Co., 1959)
Stravinsky, Igor (with Robert Craft): *Conversations with Igor Stravinsky* (London, Faber, 1959;
    repr. 1979)
Sypher, Wylie: *Rococo to Cubism in Art and Literature* (New York, Vintage Books, 1960)
*Templier, Pierre-Daniel: *Erik Satie* (Paris, Editions Rieder, 1932); trans. Elena and David
    French (Cambridge, Massachusetts, MIT Press, 1969)
Thomson, Virgil: *The Musical Scene* (New York, Knopf, 1945; repr. 1947)
  Music Right and Left (New York, Henry Holt, 1951)
  'La place de Satie dans la musique du XXe siècle', *Revue musicale*, 214 (June 1952), 13–15
    (trans. by Marcelle Jossua from *The Musical Scene*, 118–20)
Tinan, Mme Gaston de: 'Memories of Debussy and his circle', *Recorded Sound*, 50–1 (April–July
    1973), 158–63
Tomasi, Gioacchino: 'Erik Satie e la musica del surrealismo', in *Studi sul Surrealismo* (Rome,
    Officinia Edizioni, 1976)
Valotaire, Marcel: *Charles Martin* (Paris, Les Artistes du Livre, 1928)
Varèse, Louise: *Varèse: A Looking-Glass Diary. Vol. 1: 1883–1928* (New York, Norton, 1972)
Veen, J. van der: 'Erik Satie', *Mens en melodie*, 8 (1953), 389–94
Verkauf, Willy (ed.): *Dada: Monograph of a Movement* (London, Alec Tiranti, 1957; repr. 1961)
Viñes, Ricardo: 'Tres aristocratas del sonido: semblanzas de Claude Debussy, Erik Satie y
    Maurice Ravel', *La Nacion* (suplemento literario) (11 Feb 1934), also pubd as booklet in
    Buenos Aires, 1934 (16pp.)
Volta, Ornella: *Erik Satie: Ecrits*, see Satie, Erik
  Erik Satie: D'Esoterik Satie à Satierik (Paris, Editions Seghers-Humour, 1979)
  L'Ymagier d'Erik Satie (Paris, Editions Van de Velde, 1979; repr. 1990) (Vy in text)
  *(ed.): *Erik Satie à Montmartre* (Catalogue of the exhibition held at the Musée de Mont-
    martre between Dec 1982 and April 1983) (Paris, Musée de Montmartre, 1982). In this
    Volta contributes the articles: 'Satie sur la butte' (5–9) and 'L'itinéraire d'Erik Satie à
    Montmartre' (21–30)
  *(ed.): *Satie dans les salons* (Catalogue of the exhibition held at the Centre Culturel Arturo
    Lopez, 12 rue du Centre, Neuilly-sur-Seine between 12 March and 23 April 1985)
    (Neuilly, Imprimérie Schnieder, 1985)
  *'Dossier Erik Satie: L'os à moelle', *Revue Internationale de Musique Française*, 8/23 (June
    1987), 5–98. Contains the following articles by Ornella Volta: 'Le rideau se lève sur un os:
    quelques investigations autour de Satie' (7–10); 'Cinéma' (11–15); 'Geneviève de Brabant'
    (16–32); 'Gnossiennes' (33–6); 'La Belle Excentrique' (37–40); 'Sports et divertissements'
    (41–53); 'Uspud' (54–79); 'Editions et manuscrits' (81–92); 'Travaux universitaires autour
    d'Erik Satie' (93–4); 'Avis de recherche' (95–8)
  *(ed.): *Erik Satie & la Tradition Populaire* (Catalogue of the exhibition held at the Musée des
    Arts et des Traditions Populaires between 10 and 30 May 1988) (Paris, Fondation Erik
    Satie, 1988)

*(trans. Michael Bullock): *Satie Seen Through His Letters* (London, New York, Marion Boyars, 1989) (Vl in text)

*'A la recherche d'un fantôme: *Paul & Virginie* d'Erik Satie', *Revue Internationale de Musique Française*, 10/29 (June 1989), 47–70

Catalogue général de l'œuvre d'Erik Satie (Paris, Editions Salabert, in preparation, 1990)

*(trans. Andrew Thomson and Elizabeth Carroll): *Satie and the Dance* (Layton, Utah, Gibbs M. Smith (Peregrine Smith Books), in preparation, 1990)

Vuillermoz, Emile: 'La Musique: Les Ballets Suédois', *Excelsior* (29 Oct 1923), 3

'Ballets Suédois: *Relâche*', *Excelsior* (6 Dec 1924), 5

Weber, Eugene: *France. Fin de Siècle* (London/Cambridge, Mass., Bellknap Press of Harvard University Press, 1986)

Wehmeyer, Grete: 'Saties Instanteismus' in *Musicae scientiae collectanea: Festschrift Karl Gustav Fellerer* (Cologne, 1973), 626–39

Erik Satie (Regensburg, Gustav Bosse, 1974)

*Whiting, Steven Moore: *Erik Satie and Parisian Musical Entertainment, 1888 to 1909* (Master's diss., University of Illinois, 1984)

Wiener, Jean: 'Un grand musicien', *Arts*, 1/25 (13 July 1945), 4; (20 July 1945), 4

'Aimer Erik Satie', *L'Humanité*, 43/645 (4 Sept 1946), 3

Allegro appassionato (Paris, Belfond, 1978)

*Wilkins, Nigel: 'The Writings of Erik Satie: Miscellaneous Fragments', *Music and Letters*, 56/3 (July–Oct 1975), 288–307

*'Erik Satie's Letters to Milhaud and Others', *Musical Quarterly*, 66/3 (July 1980), 404–28

*(ed. and trans.): *The Writings of Erik Satie* (London, Eulenburg, 1980) (W in text)

*'Erik Satie's Letters', *Canadian University Music Review*, 2 (1981), 207–27

Index of Satie's works

General index

Académie des Beaux-Arts, xxii–xxiv, 50, 274, 278, 342 n. 33
Albert-Birot, Germaine, 362 n. 56
Allais, Alphonse, xxi, 210, **359 n. 12**
Allan, Maud, 45, 121
Almanach de Cocagne, L', 10, 327
Andersen, Hans Christian, 219
Anderson, Margaret, 221
Annunzio, Gabriele d', 59
Ansermet, Ernest, 314, 338 n. 9
Antheil, George, **221**, 250
Antwerp, *see* Satie, Erik: Belgium
Apollinaire, Guillaume (Guglielmo Alberto Wladimiro Alessandro Apollinaire de Kostrowitzki), 17, 205–6, 217, 219, 224, 230, 257, 360 n. 35, 362 n. 56
Aragon, Louis, 234
Arcueil-Cachan, xxiv, xxviii, 3–10, **15–16**, 18–19, 113, 212–13, 223, **263**, 293–5, **360 nn. 28–9**
Astruc, Gabriel, xxxi
Auberge du Clou, L', xxi, xxii, 6, 40, 41, 49, 108, 208
Audran, Edmond, 33, 200, 204
Auric, Georges, xiv, xxix, xxxii, xxxviii, xxxix, 2, 19, 234–5, **248**, 249, 250, 255, 256, 260, 299, 314, 327, 347 n. 3, 361 n. 39
Auriol, Georges, 16
Avril, Jane, 212

Bach, Johann Sebastian, 26, 69, **87–8**, 95, 103, **246**, 258
Bailly, Edmond, xxi, 40, 336 n. 4
Balguerie, Suzanne, 220, 317, 362 n. 56
Balla, Giacomo, 224
Ballets Russes, 8, 65, 106, 178, 223, 282, 312, 314, 325, 328, 329
Ballets Suédois, 178, 223, 236, 248, 325, 333, 354 n. 44
Barbier, Jules, 328
Barnetche (Caroline Joséphine Elisabeth) Eugénie (stepmother), xix, 3, **11**

Baron, Emile, 41
Bartók, Béla, 120, 194, 248, 250
Bathori, Jane (Jeanne-Marie Berthier), xxxiv, 22, 24, 52, 311, 312, 317, 322, 327
Baudoux, E., 51
Beach, Sylvia, 220, 221
Beaumont, Comtesse Edith (de Taisne) de, 223, 227, 229, 318, 325, 326, 366 n. 4, 367 n. 20
Beaumont, Comte Etienne (Bonnin de la Bonnetière) de, xxxviii, xxxix, 19, 226–32 *passim*, 284, 326–30
Beethoven, Ludwig van, xx, 4, 42, 95, 161, **246**, 258; 8th Symphony, 33, 201
Bellon, Jean, 51, 52
Benois, Alexandre, 328
Bénoist-Méchin, Baron Jacques, xxxviii, 365 n. 18
Berg, Alban, 142
Berlin, Irving, 203, 313, 356 n. 15
Berlioz, Hector, 57
Bernardin de Saint-Pierre, Jacques-Henri, 322, 363 n. 70
Berners, Lord (Sir Gerald Tyrwhitt-Wilson), 245, **247**, 365 n. 9
Bertin, Pierre, xxxvi, 56, 120, 248, 298, 320, 322, 349 n. 22
Bertrand, Eugène, xxii, 9, 275
Bibi-la-Purée (André Salis), xxiv, 15, 16, 337 n. 12
Biqui, *see* Valadon, Suzanne
Birtwistle, Harrison, 261–2, 330
Bizet, Georges, 34, 253, 335
Blès, Numa, 209, 287, 347 n. 10
Blom, Eric, 255–6
Boileau (or Boileau-Despréaux), Nicolas, 20
Bois, Jules, 9, **44–5**; *Noces de Sathan, Les*, 45; *Porte héroïque du ciel, La*, xxiii, **45**, 211, 278, 341 n. 25
Boîte à Fursy, La, xxiv, 6
Bongard, Germaine (*née* Germaine Poiret), xxxii, 222, 311, 312, 361 n. 45
Bonnaud, Dominique, xxvii, 209, 264, 287, 347 n. 10
Bonsdorff, Edith, 179, 333